India-Australia Relations

INDIA-AUSTRALIA RELATIONS

CONVERGENCES AND DIVERGENCES

Edited by

D. GOPAL

SHIPRA

ISBN: 978-81-7541-411-2

First Published in India in 2008

India-Australia Relations: *Convergences and Divergences*

Published by:
SHIPRA PUBLICATIONS
115-A, Vikas Marg, Shakarpur, Delhi-110092, INDIA
Phone: 91-11-65277210, 91-11-22500954
Fax: 91-11-22458662
E-mail: info@shiprapublications.com
www.shiprapublications.com

Preface

In the past too often both Australia and India have been seeing each other through the prisms of outdated perceptions and stereotypes. In the fast changing global order of today neither of them can afford to let such myopic views determine any more their policy decisions because without doubt they belie the depth and complexity of the mutuality of the evolving relations between the two countries.

One of the basic objectives of the Indian Association for the Study of Australia (IASA) is to encourage scholars from both sides of the Indian Ocean to engage in meaningful and sustained dialogue on issues of mutual concern. At its biennial conference held in Pune in 2006, IASA invited scholars from both India and Australia to exchange ideas on the general theme of convergence and divergences between India and Australia. The scholarly exercise spread over three days was quite rewarding as it offered the right ambience to discuss at length a variety of themes ranging from political-economic relations to security-related matters.

A select number of papers presented by leading scholars from both India and Australia in the IASA Conference is published in this compendium.

The Editor of this compendium takes this opportunity to thank all the contributors who, on request, readily revised their scholarly papers for publication and record his gratitude to the Australia-India Council (AIC) for extending funding support for its publication.

New Delhi
1 December, 2007

D. Gopal
School of Social Sciences
Indira Gandhi National Open University
New Delhi

[illegible] Jawaharlal Nehru University
New Delhi

Contents

1

Introduction

D. GOPAL

Currently witnessed developments in India-Australia relations are admittedly engaging the attention of scholars on both sides of the Indian Ocean and concerted efforts are afoot to examine in depth the different dimensions and the direction of the evolving bilateral linkages.

Keeping in view the critical contemporary relevance and interest on the subject, the Indian Association for the Study of Australia (IASA) invited papers at its 3rd International Conference on the general theme: *Australia and India: Convergence and Divergences.* No less than two hundred scholars and specialists drawn from different disciplines had gathered at Pune to discuss a variety of issues and aspects of Australia-India relations. There were too many formal presentations. The Executive Committee of IASA decided, therefore, to publish in the form of a compendium in two volumes a select number of papers having bearing on the general focus of the Conference. As many as twenty-five papers presented at the different sessions of the Conference by scholars in Social Science and Humanities were edited and are published in this volume.

Editing a volume such as this is by no means an easy task. For one, the themes dealt with in these papers are varied. For another, a few of them may not have a direct bearing on the general theme of the Conference. Yet they are welcome additions to an understanding of the larger questions of relevance in the evolving bilateral relations between India and Australia.

No less daunting was the task of arranging these papers in a sequential order keeping in view the range of issues raised therein. Readers may find that some of the papers included in the present volume are beyond the purview of the overarching focus of the Pune Conference. Yet, the editor is of the view that the inclusion of these papers would only enhance the merit of this compendium enriching further our understanding of the dynamics of the evolving bilateral relations.

At the dawn of the 21st Century, both Australia and India are admittedly coming to terms with the stark realities of the emerging global order and the attendant imperatives against which they perforce need to calibrate their policy posturing and approaches. For Australia such a task calls for overcoming its past anxieties and apprehensions—however "imagined" or "cultivated" they were—towards India and its Asian neighbours.

Keeping this in perspective, it is perhaps best to commence the editorial commentary with the first three presentations in a sequence dealing specifically with issues relating to racial discrimination in Australia in the years since it became a federation. Cultural historian David Walker in his paper "Conspicuous Hospitality: Cultivating a New Racial Etiquette in Australia, 1930-1960" examines the period of transition from the 1930s to the early 1960s when old certitudes about "White Australia" came under increasing scrutiny. There were substantial changes over the following decades, including the formal abandonment of the "White Australia" policy and the growth of multiculturalism. Yet another critical issue having bearing on the "White Australia" policy relates to the question of identity and representation of the Aboriginal peoples of Australia. Priti Singh examines critically the federal policy on Native Title—a scheme that is purported to provide redressal to the dispossessed aboriginals of Australia. In doing so, she examines at length the government structures and management of these structures as given in the Native Title Act and see whether these structures facilitate the goals envisaged in the framing of Native Title. For, in the final analysis, recognition of Native Title does not have any meaning unless the legal bodies approved by the enabling legislation are adequately armed to meet the challenges posed to them. Notwithstanding the significant initiatives intended to redeem racial inequality in Australia, the culture of "benign whiteness" is still hesitant to a proactive dedication to evolve an egalitarian society. Explicating this undercurrent of Australian culture, Auriol Weigold in his presentation dwells at length on Australia's colonial settlement and goes to the roots of the White settler ambivalence towards non-whites including the aboriginals and relates its contemporary expression in shifts of meaning ascribed to race, racism and "whiteness".

The following four papers are set in a sequence for the insights they offer in respect of Australia's world view both during the colonial and post-colonial phase of its history. Peter Putnis' paper is essentially a study on the communication experience of the Indian indentured labour that had emigrated to Fiji. What, however, is of interest in his presentation is the role Australia had played in the life of Indians in Fiji and their communication links with home, and sees in the process something of the specific conditions of their lives of separation. Varalaxmi Naik draws attention to the concerns and contradictions that have arisen as a result of movement of people into new cultures such as Australia and how these issues are addressed by two nations in the Asia-Pacific—Australia and Japan—with regard to the discrimination made towards the immigrants; policies of the state, prevalent notions on immigrants and of their rights and domestic compulsions are the specific subject matter of the paper. Ruchira Ganguly-Scrase and Roberta Julian offer a comparative perspective on women migrants in India and Australia drawing critical attention to the weakness of the concept of refugee in contemporary post-colonial contexts by highlighting its gendered complexities. Analysing clinically the 2005 Cronulla Beach incident, Greg Battye in his paper suggests that true security is not provided by technology—military or otherwise, but by building and investing in cultural understanding with outside world, particularly Asia.

Peter Gale offers an interesting backdrop to the current Australia-India "convergence and divergence" discourse. Though his study is focussed on the differing stance that the present Australian government took on two Asia-related issues—Tsunami victims and the Asian "boat people", the conclusions he draws are admittedly appealing. He says: "For a convergence between...India and Australia there needs to be a greater level of acknowledgment that there is a close relationship between domestic politics and foreign policy. There also needs to be an increased recognition of the ongoing effects of the discourse on a war on terror with the heightened level of division within an imagined national identity." Upon this he suggests that the challenge for Australia is to address the perceived binary of "us and them", and notions of a clash of cultures through closer relations between Asia and Australia. Susan Cowan's *Glimpses of India: A Military Dekko* is an exploratory study of three Australian travellers with a focus on India from a military angle. Interspersed with amusing accounts of the encounters of Australian military officers, Cowan's analysis nevertheless underlines the lack of genuine interest of Australia on India and of its cultural moorings.

Any academic exercise purported to explore the evolving convergence between any two nation-states need to begin with historical antecedents and identify the existing commonalities between them. In that respect, Swaraj Basu's *Understanding Nationalism in India and Australia* offers a good starter for the rest of the papers in this volume. By looking at the differing approaches with which independent India and Commonwealth Australia dealt with the issues of the underprivileged segments in the two societies—the *Dalits* and the Aboriginals, Basu points out that though India and Australia were British colonies, nevertheless their journey towards formation of national identity were different.

Focussing on the series of structural economic reforms unleashed by both India and Australia in recent decades both countries are poised to dovetail their economies provided the policy makers on both sides take cognizance of the strengths and weaknesses of each other's economic strategies. Here, D. Gopal pleads that the prospects for the future convergence between the two economies are encouraging if efforts are made to focus now on IT-enabled service exchanges between India and Australia. As he rightly points out: "Mere merchandise trade alone cannot sustain the economic linkages. It is here, it needs to be underlined about the importance of trade in services as it has immense potential" because India is already beginning to play an increasingly important role as a consumer of Australian education services which is one of Australia's fastest growing sectors. No less important is the role of small scale industries in both countries is the suggestion of Sailaja Gullapalli. She is of the view that collaboration with the international network of small scale industries and mutual cooperation offer prospects for strengthening economic linkages between India and Australia. Yagama Reddy, Rupakjyoti Bora and Jasbir Singh in their presentations offer useful insights into the evolving India-Australia relations and highlight the issues of concern—political, economic and security. Amita Singh's paper underlines the need for diversification of India-Australia linkages and shows that ICT could be a useful vehicle to forge closer relations between the two countries. Comparing the emerging middle class in both India and Australia following the economic restructuring process, Timothy Scrase and John Robinson show the complexities and contradictions of the reform process and substantiate their findings on the basis of random sample of the middle class in both countries.

Security is an important element in the ongoing bilateral relations between Australia and India as security issues have become even more complex since 9/11. Dwelling at length on the currently witnessed geopolitical transformations together with recurrent incidence of international terrorism, Chintamani Mahapatra calls for a strategic triangular arrangement between Australia, India and US which can work as a bulwark against security threats that are yet to incubate and may surface in future. Rajesh Kapur in his paper traces the responses of Australia, India and Japan to international terrorism following the 9/11 attacks and argues that the resultant, largely unanticipated change in policymaking that has occurred in these countries is actually more robust than many analysts have thus far been prepared to acknowledge. Tej Pratap Singh's paper is focused on the current security challenges that confront both countries and examines at length the efficacy of Indo-Australian strategic convergence.

Dennis Rumley and Sanjay Chaturvedi not only go beyond the conventional concerns of security but perceive it fundamentally as "human security". They argue in favour of an increase in the "democratisation of security" around the Indian Ocean region in order to maximise "real" security. Yet another element in the realm of security is energy. How countries such as India and Australia are dealing with issues relating to energy security is dealt at length by Nabeel Ajmal Mancheri. According to Mancheri there exists considerable scope for India to learn from the experience of Australia.

Vanlaltluangi Aruna Ruth's presentation focuses on the need for India-Australia cooperation on specific issues such as maritime security, sharing of intelligence, joint actions against terrorism, proactive role in flushing out the terrorist bases in the Indian Ocean region. Uttam Kumar Jamadhagni and Humayun carry further Ruth's analysis and argue that the Indian Ocean region offers tremendous potential for joint India-Australia initiatives to deal not only with maritime security but also with the developmental issues of the region as a whole. The last paper in the volume of Yeshi Choedon gives a graphic account of the peacekeeping operations of both India and Australia under the aegis of the United Nations and notes the positive contribution they have made for the maintenance of international peace and security. Building their image as a responsible power and enlarging their influence in international relations are admittedly the major objectives of India and Australia.

Scholarship on both sides—Indian and Australian—it is hoped would welcome this compendium purported not only to sustain meaningful scholarly exchanges but also to provide the much-needed useful insights to the policy makers of both countries.

2

Conspicuous Hospitality: Cultivating a New Racial Etiquette in Australia, 1930-1960

DAVID WALKER

In Australia there are opposing tendencies at work… . There are certain qualities—virtues, they may be called—that come of repeating themselves, to form some integral part of the life of the community. The foremost of these good qualities is hospitality. And here a singular anomaly presents itself. Politically the Australians are the most exclusive and the most inhospitable race on earth.[1]

From the 1930s the need for Australia to cultivate closer ties with Asia attracted increasing support among intellectuals and within government. In 1934 the federal government dispatched a "Goodwill Mission" to the "East"—the Netherlands East Indies, China and Japan. Led by the Attorney-General, John Latham, this was the first mission of its kind by an Australian government to Asia. Trade and security were the dominant concerns, but the cultivation of "goodwill" and the development of a new racial etiquette among Australians were also important considerations. If events in Asia were to play an increasingly important role in Australia's future, as seemed apparent, knowing the countries and cultures of the region was vital. This paper examines a period of transition from the 1930s to the early 1960s when old certitudes about "White Australia" came under increasing scrutiny. There were substantial changes over the following decades, including the formal abandonment of the White Australia policy and the growth of multiculturalism, which, although vital to an understanding of modern Australia, fall outside the particular historical focus of this chapter.[2]

Goodwill, friendship and hospitality are hardly precise categories and for that reason may not have attracted historical scrutiny or analysis from students of International Relations. Yet, one of the consequences of a shrinking and more internationalised world is the breakdown of insularity and, with it, increasing cross-cultural contact. In the space of a generation, from the late

1930s to the early 1960s, Australia changed from being a nation largely apart from Asia to one increasingly involved with Asia and, according to some, part of Asia. In this period it was no longer sufficient to express goodwill, it was increasingly necessary to find ways of representing goodwill as an Australian attribute. In more recent years, as tourism has assumed a larger role in the economy, service and hospitality have come to the fore. There is now an established hospitality industry, replete with diplomas and a literature of its own. In the 1950s and 1960s it was not tourism but the need for an improved image in Asia that fuelled the drive to have Australia represented as an hospitable nation whose people were largely free of racial superiority. To do this, a case emerged that the practices associated with hospitality in outback Australia might also inspire a new and more racially inclusive spirit of regional engagement. The belief that it might prove possible for the nation to change from an often narrowly conceived "bush" hospitality to something much broader required a considerable leap of faith and imagination.

The hospitality owed to strangers is deeply embedded in the teachings of all the major religions. Classical societies ritualised the relations between host and stranger; so too in Christianity, Islam, Buddhism and Hinduism hospitality assumes powerful moral dimensions. Hospitality, like other values, is also historical in that its meaning and conduct vary over time and place. For a wide variety of cultures, hospitality has provided a moral pillar around which social order can be maintained. Private hospitality was integrated into a "matrix of beliefs that were shared and articulated publicly", and so regulated social behaviour.[3] The host-guest relationship, then, had religious and social implications that regulated and reinforced social relationships between different groups. It consolidated a moral universe in which the host-guest relationship helped define the culture. Tom Selwyn observes that where host and guest formulate a new relationship, acts of hospitality can be structurally transformative. "Hospitality converts", Selwyn argues, "strangers into familiars, enemies into friends…outsiders into insiders".[4] "Hospitality" was commonly invoked through the 1950s as an Australian attribute. How much transformation occurred within that culture as a result of contact with non-white guests is a question deserving fuller scrutiny than it has so far received.

In some of the more popular accounts of Australia in the 1930s there was a considerable emphasis on the hospitable nature of the Australian people. William Hatfield travelled extensively throughout Australia and was the author of some of the best-selling accounts of Australian life, including *Australia through the Windscreen* (1936) and *I Find Australia* (1937). He experienced this hospitable friendliness on his first journey inland, and noted: "I struck the same thing wherever I went in the back country, right through the years".[5] Hospitality, he insisted, was a particular Australian gift, explaining it: "No matter where you chose to stop and yarn, you could help yourself from the billy of hot tea standing near the fire, or roll a cigarette from the owner's pouch...The poorest wayfarer's table is yours if you'll share it, the length and breadth of the great wide Bush".[6]

Such an "atmosphere of easygoing friendliness", Hatfield assures us, "is no mere superficiality", associating it with "the man on the land...the pioneer spirit, a legacy from the times when to every colonist another colonist was a possible friend and ally in case of emergency".[7] Hatfield's explanation for this phenomenon of hospitality was a familiar one: the hardships of Australian settlement, the floods, droughts and bushfires, and particularly the isolation, had fostered a spirit of co-operation. Settlers had to help each other out. It was also assumed that Australians had lost or discarded much of the stiffness and formality attributed to the class-conscious English. Egalitarian Australians, such observers maintained, were not like that, nor could they afford to be in a demanding continent where survival dictated collectivist approaches to settlement. "Australian society is built up on the principle that a man is as good as the next", the English traveller Thomas Wood commented. "Titles and decorations", he continued, "which carry some weight in other countries carry none here; unless—very important—the holder is considered a good fellow on his own account....At the same time no distinction is considered high enough to justify aloofness on the one hand or servility on the other."[8]

Wood had come to Australia in connexion with his work in 1931 and was so taken by the experience that he stayed on for another year. Arnold Haskell, the ballet critic, was another English visitor who saw this spirit of egalitarianism as a key element in Australian hospitality. Haskell also came out for reasons connected with his work, but unexpectedly fell in love with the place and wrote his book, *Waltzing Matilda*, in celebration of the fact.[9] Haskell relates how, as a guest of the government, he was assigned an official driver for a four-day trip through the country and describes trying to engage in conversation with his driver, who was at first somewhat stand-offish and monosyllabic, a bit suspicious of this visiting English dignitary. The driver thawed only when Haskell got them to stop at a pub and bought drinks, whereupon he "brightened up and began to talk", a change brought about, Haskell explains, not by the drink itself (which was non-alcoholic), but by "the offer". From that point on, the driver became his "delightful companion", Haskell says; "He treated me as an equal and I was pleased, he treated me as his friend and I was delighted. Australia is like that; a country entirely free from servility." Owing to the country's isolation, "The Australian is immensely interested in the stranger and eager to hear what he has to say", much more interested, Haskell observes, than an Englishman would be and "also far more familiar". Accordingly, a visiting stranger "interests him but in no sense overawes him": that is the character of the exchange. "And so, whoever he is, he treats you as his equal, and if you behave normally...then you are accepted as a friend from the word go; if not, there will be very little pretence....It is this...that makes the quality of the hospitality."[10]

Unlike Wood and Haskell, Hatfield had a special status as something of an insider-outsider from having spent more than twenty years living and working in the bush, but it was because he later toured Australia as an outsider, an Englishman, that his observations gained the authority of independent testimony. Such views could not be dismissed as the special pleading of the locals. Indeed, even if the locals did recognize their talent for friendliness—like Malcolm Uren avowing to Thomas Wood, in *Cobbers*, "we're a hospitable race"[11] —it bestowed a particular cachet to have that pointed out to them by an outside observer. Wood relates how he had been told, before even reaching Australia that its people "are the most hospitable" his well-travelled English informant had "ever come across in the whole of my life".[12] Thomas Wood's account of Australian society, *Cobbers*, first published in 1934 and reprinted many times thereafter, was written from the outside, but it reinforced Hatfield's message. Wood's own observation was that Australia had a "national genius for hospitality"[13] and, as if in recognition of this, in his book the terms "friendliness" and "hospitality" are simply indexed "*passim*".[14] Hatfield and Wood did not create the idea of "hospitable Australia", but they certainly popularised it in the 1930s and 1940s.[15] Australians were growing accustomed to hearing themselves described as a uniquely hospitable race.

These English writers no doubt told Australians what they wanted to hear and they evidently wanted to hear that, unlike the English, they were a friendly, out-going people. In reality, while the strangers in question may have been outsiders, they were not so dissimilar culturally from their Australian hosts. As Wood himself conceded, "the Empire itself, so far as the white races are concerned, is, in my experience, nothing less than a chain of affiliated clubs, which never fail to give the right kind of welcome to the right kind of new-comer".[16] The White Australia policy not only reinforced the view that there was a wrong kind of new-comer, it also ensured that there were relatively few opportunities to test the extent of Australian hospitality in circumstances where the strangers were either racially different or unused to British practices. While hospitality was widely regarded, even celebrated, as an Australian attribute, it had hardly been tested in the demanding world of inter-cultural and inter-racial exchange. These challenges lay just over the horizon.

The scale of the challenge soon became apparent. In the late 1940s, Arthur Calwell, as Minister for Immigration in the Chifley Labor government, aroused enmity throughout the region for his aggressive and inflexible administration of the White Australia policy. Calwell deported non-Europeans from Australia with such zeal that it appeared that only the removal of the last drop of non-European blood would satisfy him. It was a sign of the times that the second "Goodwill Mission" to Asia in 1948 attracted bitter criticism from journalists in the region. It was clear that a newly independent Asia was not willing to accept racial humiliation in silence. The leader of the mission, academic and occasional diplomat, William Macmahon Ball, returned to Australia in 1948 with a warning that Australians had a lot to learn about good manners and racial etiquette. He made it clear that there was no time to lose: "Goodwill towards these people must become a national habit, built on respect for the racial sensibilities and national aims of our neighbours."[17] This was a call for a new code of racial conduct.

From the late 1940s, there was an increasing acceptance among political leaders of the need to broaden Australian sympathies and reduce the open expression of racial prejudice. For one of the most trenchant critics of the White Australia policy, Rev. Alan Walker, the policy was radically flawed on at least two counts. It offended Christian principles of brotherhood and it aggravated Australia's crippling isolation: "The soul of Australia is parochial. Visitors to our shores tell of many an incident which reveals a narrowness of outlook and limitations in understanding."[18] The Reverend Walker believed that adherence to the White Australia policy virtually ensured that Australians would fail to meet their international obligations and in so doing remain a socially backward people forever at odds with the coloured world. The test of hospitality was changing from a self-congratulatory celebration of how the "white club" treated its own to a more critical scrutiny of whom it snubbed and excluded.

The urgent call for a new spirit of conciliation is evident in the proliferation of neighbourly references in accounts of Australia's place in the region. A display of welcoming friendliness seemed a feasible way of addressing Australia's newly discovered proximity to Asia. R.G. Casey, Australia's Minister for External Affairs through the 1950s, helped set the tone by calling his account of Australia in the world, *Friends and Neighbours* (1954).[19] The language is painfully bland and evasive, but its purpose was clear: to promote an image of a youthful and innocent people whose only desire was to live on friendly terms with others. If their neighbours needed help, Australians would be happy to provide it; after all, wasn't helping others the Australian way? This comforting portrait of a warm-hearted if not particularly sophisticated people was designed to alert the locals to a new standard of racial etiquette while also sending a reassuring message of friendliness to the region.

Through the 1950s "Good Neighbour Councils" were formed across Australia with the express purpose of extending a helping hand to newcomers from European countries.[20] In retrospect, the language of "neighbourliness" may appear glib, patronising and barely worth examining. But the attempt to broaden the meaning of hospitality and extend its applications to people who, in the 1930s and earlier, would not normally have been included does merit analysis. The term had also found its way into the preamble of the United

Nations Charter, a reliable guide to the new vocabularies of post-war international etiquette. The preamble invited the nations of the world "to practice tolerance and live together in peace with one another as good neighbours". The attempt to create a culture of tolerance and neighbourliness had emerged as an important internationalising project. Percy Spender reflected this in Australia's parliament in March 1950, as he acknowledged the difficulty of reconciling Australia's history and its geography. "We live side by side with the countries of South and South-East Asia", he proclaimed, "and we desire to be on good-neighbour terms with them."[21] In the Australian case, it was an attempt to equip an insular culture with the means to acknowledge difference, but it was also designed to educate the nation to the need for an image more suited to the post-war world. Critics would have seen this as an attempt to conceal a complex and compromising history of racial exclusion behind some opportunistic image making.

Extending the boundaries of hospitality and improving Australia's reputation as an hospitable nation was far from straightforward. At a time when the White Australia policy was still in force, the hospitality extended to people of Asian background was highly qualified. Every effort might be made to make such visitors feel at home, but they always had to be reminded that immigration was quite out of the question. They were encouraged to feel at home within Australia, but not to call Australia home. Accordingly, every effort was made in the 1950s and 1960s to establish the absence of a "colour bar" in Australia as the key indicator of a friendly and receptive culture rather than have immigration itself as the measure of Australian hospitality. In fact, the refusal to allow Asian immigration intensified both the affirmations of friendliness and avuncular denials of prejudice. Convincing people of Asian background that Australians were well-disposed towards them, but did not want them as immigrants, was no easy task, but it would be a mistake to imagine that the Menzies government believed it to be an impossible one. On the contrary, if Asian visitors to Australia were lavished with hospitality while also being insulated as far as possible from racial insults, it seemed possible to hope that Australia might yet manage to remain white, while also escaping criticism for wanting to do so. If "superior" white was the wrong way to go, "hospitable" white was likely to prove both more effective in the region and better suited to Australian self-representations.

Australia's relationship with India proved to be a vital test of the possibilities and limits of hospitality and particularly so during the period from 1953 to 1956 when General Cariappa served as India's High Commissioner to Australia and New Zealand. It is hard to imagine a figure better-placed than General Cariappa to expose the limits of Australian hospitality and the racial basis of the immigration programme. Cariappa had served the Empire well as a soldier and in doing so helped make Australia more secure. He spoke the beautifully rounded English of well-educated officers and was thoroughly attuned to British customs and practices. He smoked, as a gentleman should, personally initialed Sobranie cigarettes, enjoyed a drink and observed no dietary restrictions. We glimpse him addressing a crowd in V.S. Naipaul's, *An Area of Darkness*: "On a high floodlit platform...General Cariappa, the former commander-in-chief, erect, dark-suited, was addressing a small, relaxed crowd in Sandhurst-accented Hindustani".[22] Cariappa was undoubtedly a man's man, but he had an extensive record collection, danced divinely and enjoyed playing cards in mixed company. He was everything an English gentleman should be, everything except white.

As India's pre-eminent soldier after Independence, General Cariappa was appointed by Prime Minister Nehru to head the Indian army. His role as Commander-in-Chief is not the subject of this chapter, although Cariappa is credited with keeping the Indian army out of politics. At the time of his appointment as High Commissioner, Cariappa was a household name in India and remains so today. Very few Australians now know of General Cariappa, but in the 1950s no diplomat serving in Canberra had a higher profile or travelled more widely than the General.

Nehru's reasons for appointing Cariappa as High Commissioner are not altogether clear, a subject that Indian historians are better placed to explain than students of Australian history. The Cariappa family speculate that having such a popular General a long way from home may have removed a potential political rival. This may be so, although Nehru's place was secure in 1952/53 whereas Cariappa had not paid his dues as an aspirant to political office. It seems more likely that Nehru may have dispatched Cariappa to Australia because he was a person of real standing and one whose very "British" presence challenged the racial exclusivity that underpinned the White Australia policy. While he was in Australia, Cariappa drew upon two interrelated claims in pressing the case for closer ties between India and Australia. He insisted that the Commonwealth was a family of nations and that "family" members had special reasons to look after each other. This was certainly a test of hospitality. Cariappa also stressed that as an ex-serviceman he had much in common with his Australian counterparts.

It is apparent from his private papers that the General was quite a favourite among the upper echelons of Australian society and particularly, it would appear, among titled ladies. His marriage had ended a number of years earlier and this, no doubt, made him an object of interest and concern. Cariappa had persuaded a niece, Sagarie Chengappa to accompany him and his ten-year-old daughter, Nalini, to Canberra. Sagarie was just twenty and the responsibility of acting as a hostess in a strange culture was a considerable burden made heavier by her strong preference to pursue her legal studies in India. Cariappa was clearly an attractive and charming man, but he was also a strict disciplinarian. Shoes had to be polished to within an inch of their lives, clothes had to be just so, dinners were exactingly formal, not an easy household for a twenty-year-old to preside over as hostess. Moreover, she was not allowed to forget that India's reputation appeared to rest on the conduct of the household.

It was natural enough for Cariappa to be welcomed into the best homes, where a strong British ethos, reinforced by the honours system, set the tone. Although there were exceptions, there was a considerable British patriotism in this class and, in the manner suggested by David Cannadine's *Ornamentalism*, a more worldly and accepting response to racial difference.[23] As a "Sandhurst man" who had stood by the Empire in its hour of need, Cariappa could be accepted on equal terms as a gentleman. Among ordinary Australians and particularly so in the labour movement, the titled classes were suspect when it came to White Australia and racial purity. They appeared to fraternise with non-Europeans all too readily and some made it known that while Australians may have prided themselves on being racially pure they were often inferior types. The more General Cariappa was courted by the wealthy elite, the more suspicion his presence aroused among those who feared that he was plotting to flood Australia with coloured labour.

Cariappa was certainly critical of the White Australia policy and was offended by it. He also pressed the case for Indian and Pakistani ex-servicemen to settle in Australia. He believed they had demonstrated their loyalty during the war and would fit in well, given their British training and good character as soldiers. In Cariappa's eyes, these men were worthy members of the Commonwealth family, making it all the more appropriate to treat them with consideration. It galled Cariappa that citizens from former enemy countries, particularly Germany and Italy, were welcomed into Australia, while the door remained firmly shut against his countrymen. Protestations that Australians were an open and friendly people without racial prejudice rang hollow to Cariappa. Cariappa's compatriot, Sripati Chandrasekhar also felt inclined to criticise: his 1954 *Hungry people and empty lands* detected among Australians some recognition of the racial problems caused by white prejudice. More hopeful than analytical, he also thought Australians might be recognising that "no country is entitled to hold or control a vast territory and vast resources simply to protect its cultural heritage, in a world too where large areas are suffering from intense over-population and land hunger".[24] For his part, Cariappa was in no doubt that colour prejudice determined who was allowed into Australia and who was not.

These tensions erupted into open controversy in June 1954, when a reporter from the Brisbane *Courier-Mail* interviewed Cariappa. He was reported to have said that Australia's immigration policy had more to do with skin colour than character and might result in turning millions in India and

Pakistan away from the Commonwealth and towards communism.[25] Cariappa believed that a country that made frequent references to the Commonwealth as a family while also turning away family members as potential immigrants on the grounds of their race endangered the Commonwealth ideal and emboldened its critics. Cariappa's remarks generated a great deal of comment in the media, irritable responses from the federal government and bellicose denunciations of Cariappa's undiplomatic conduct from Calwell and the Labor opposition. Some media reports of the incident noted that Cariappa had merely raised in public an issue that had previously been addressed in private discussions. He had done little more than state the obvious. However, the bulk of media commentary persisted with the view that Cariappa and other like-minded critics of Australian immigration policies were mistaken in seeing race and colour prejudice as important factors in either policy formation or the population at large.[26]

Writing to the *Courier-Mail*, a "Gallipoli veteran" claimed it was possible to take "the offence out of our immigration laws" without significant change to the policy itself. He claimed that Australians had no racial animosity: "we do not consider that colour of skin is any indication of character". However, he still wanted white settlers: "we do have a prejudice in favour of white skins and consider that any wholesale mixing of the races would ultimately result in the disappearance of the whites".[27]

General Cariappa was routinely criticised for his failure to understand that racial prejudice was virtually unknown in Australia. Indeed, raising the issue at all could be interpreted as a sign of immaturity. Walter Crocker, Australia's leading diplomat in the 1950s and High Commissioner in New Delhi in June 1954 when the Cariappa controversy first emerged, was particularly critical of what he considered Cariappa's ignorance and ineptitude. From Crocker's perspective, raising the issue of racial prejudice at all was a sign of instability. He reported from Delhi that he thought Cariappa was mentally unstable.[28] Cariappa had not identified a weakness in Australian policy or Australian attitudes on race but, according to Crocker, had revealed a disabling weakness in his own character.

Crocker was closely associated with Australian diplomatic initiatives in Asia. Through the 1930s he had accumulated considerable diplomatic experience in Africa and had worked with the League of Nations in Geneva. At the outbreak of the Second World War, Crocker enlisted in the British Army, spending much of his time in Africa. After demobilisation he was appointed chief of the Africa Section of the United Nations Secretariat in New York, a position he held until 1949. By the time he left the UN to become foundation Professor of International Relations at the newly established Australian National University in Canberra in 1950, Crocker was a seasoned internationalist and a respected author on international issues, including *The*

Japanese Population Problem: The Coming Crisis (1931).[29] He was then entering his fifties and it appeared that Crocker would see out his working life as an academic. However, in 1951 Casey lured Crocker back to the diplomatic service, where he remained for the next eighteen years. He served in two of the most important of Australia's Asian postings, India (1952-55 and 1958-61) and Indonesia (1955-56). Crocker brought a lifetime of experience and sustained reflection to the theory and practice of diplomacy and to the need for Australia to understand Asia in particular and the non-European world in general.

In 1956 Crocker's *The Racial Factor in International Affairs* was published by the Australian National University in Canberra.[30] It was the single most important statement by a senior Australian figure on the question of race in the post-war world. It was an acknowledgement that racial etiquette was a vital consideration in the conduct of international affairs. The sensitivities aroused during the Cariappa controversy had certainly brought the issue to public notice and may well have been a factor in the decision to publish Crocker's lecture. It provided a means of addressing a profoundly important issue, but without the federal government being identified with the views expressed.

On three occasions within the first two pages of his published lecture Crocker identified accusations of racial prejudice with "emotionalism". Crocker makes no reference to General Cariappa, but it can be inferred that in raising the issue of race Cariappa had also succumbed to emotionalism. Crocker did not acknowledge and perhaps did not recognise that attributing poor emotional control to people who felt discriminated against on the grounds of race was in itself racist. There appeared to be no way, in his terms, that an aggrieved Indian, or the racially aggrieved more generally, could raise their grievance without appearing immature in doing so. Such people were readily dismissed as exceptionally thin-skinned.[31]

A logic of self-preservation was fundamental to Crocker's argument. He maintained that European power and prestige had been in decline since the beginning of the twentieth century as Asian and African peoples mastered Western technology. The gap was closing, but the Second World War accelerated the pace of change so dramatically that in a matter of a few years, so Crocker argued, Asia and Africa achieved levels of equality that may have taken half a century or more had there been no war. In a world in which Europeans represented a minority whose influence and prestige was in decline, Crocker maintained that claims to superiority and displays of racial prejudice were dangerous folly. There was no change more urgent than a comprehensive disavowal of "white" superiority. Crocker insisted that Australians may have been white but they did not consider themselves superior on that account. He repeated the post-war mantra that Australians were among the least prejudiced people in the world.[32]

Crocker was drawn to the psychology of race and to the view that apparently small slights could develop into enduring grievances. Since the race problem was located in the mind of both the perpetrators of racial prejudice and their victims, the key to solving racial tensions lay, so it appeared, in a change of attitude. Crocker cited Gandhi's experience in South Africa to show the repeated insults to which coloured people were subjected, and while he did not make light of these systematic acts of discrimination, he also referred to circumstances in which apparently minor or distant insults had produced what seemed to him a wildly disproportionate response. It followed that the white world, which had been the cause of so much "wounded self-esteem", had to learn the error of its ways. It had to learn that the open expression of racial prejudice might well produce a deadly and destructive backlash from the coloured world.[33] A decade earlier Pearl Buck, perhaps the most influential writer on matters oriental, had issued a similar warning, which was repeated by Rev. Alan Walker: "The white people are a minority in the world. They had better learn to get along with coloured peoples. What are the white peoples going to do with this embarrassing world where God in His inscrutable wisdom made us a minority people and Satan in his malicious mischief gave us a majority complex?"[34]

The psychological view of race presumed that the coloured world did not understand the rules and disciplines of civilised discourse. Logic and rationality were, according to this view, primarily European attributes. They made diplomacy possible. Crocker left no doubt that many of those who claimed to be the victims of racial prejudice were emotionally unbalanced, hence the unpredictable excesses grouped under the catch-all of "emotionalism". This style of analysis was apparent in some of the reporting of the famous gathering of Asian and African nations in Bandung in 1955, an event that Crocker had attended as an observer. For some, the long, florid speeches and passionate rhetoric pointed unequivocally to childishness and instability. These were people who lacked self-control. Then again, too much self-control in an Asian leader could appear sinister. It was a very fine line.[35]

If racial grievances could be traced to "emotionalism" and psychological causes, it followed that the best way of dealing with the problem was to employ psychological strategies in return. Europeans had to learn that coloured people were extremely sensitive about real and perceived racial slights, so much so that it was better to run the risk of being too polite and courteous than not courteous enough. If the disadvantage of race being "in the mind" was the emotional volatility that surrounded the issue, the benefit was that such a grievance could be addressed without the need to sacrifice European living standards; it was not resources that needed redistribution but "esteem" in the hope that this might result in fewer bruised egos among non-Europeans. Crocker concluded his address with a plea for behavioural change: "it is common sense and a matter of self-interest to be scrupulously courteous, always avoiding the provocative and always cultivating the conciliatory approach on both sides".[36] The message for white Australia was clear: Australians would have to show that they did not consider themselves superior to coloured people. If Australians could establish their reputation for friendliness, it was just possible that they might also be accepted as a people free of racial prejudice and therefore entitled to be left to develop and populate the country as they saw fit. In short, a change of manners accompanied by a firm repudiation of racial superiority might well avoid the need to change the immigration policy itself.

This reform strategy was at its height in the 1950s and its purpose was not to dilute immigration restrictions and weaken the White Australia policy, but to maintain it. Crocker recognised that it was not easy to sustain the argument that a people without racial prejudice might still claim the right to exclude non-Europeans. Australians were not discriminating on the grounds of race, Crocker maintained, but were seeking to avoid "communal problems" of a kind that had caused so much tension and bloodshed, not least in India following partition. To accommodate those who argued that it was not necessary to impose an absolute exclusion on non-European immigration in order to avoid a communal problem, Crocker conceded that small numbers of non-Europeans might be allowed to settle in Australia. It was Crocker's hope that Australia could present itself to the world, and more particularly Asia, as an hospitable neighbour with no racial prejudices and no history of discrimination: "The good nature and friendliness of the average Australian fortunately predisposes him to being a good neighbour, as Asian students coming to Australia are discovering".[37]

The Australian Prime Minister, Robert Menzies, followed a line very similar to Crocker's, with the important exception that he did not believe in a quota system for non-European immigrants. In April 1958 Denis Warner, one of Australia's leading journalists specialising in Asia, interviewed the Prime Minister on "Meet the Press", a leading current affairs television programme.[38] The topic was "migration questions". Warner was consistently anti-communist in his views and was far from being a political radical, but his travels through Asia and his contacts with people high and low had convinced him that the White Australia policy was an acute liability and a barrier to Australia's acceptance in the region. While showing his Prime Minister the respect common to the press corps of the day, Warner nonetheless probed what he saw as the contradictions in the government's position on race and immigration.

It was Menzies' gift to appear at once imperturbable and the voice of sweet reason. Cricket analogies appealed to him. Menzies showed no sign that Warner was sending down some curly deliveries. He began by acknowledging that the post-war immigration programme had been vital in building Australia's population and was adamant that the programme had to continue. In rejecting the idea of a quota for non-European immigrants, Menzies insisted that his position had nothing to do with feelings of superiority. He did not have the "faintest idea that we are superior to the people of Asia. Of course we are not." It is not so much the literal meaning of the words themselves that matters here, but the air of bewildered astonishment that a proposition so ludicrous could be expressed at all. In Menzies' view, racial superiority and colour prejudice were largely absent from Australia and, that being the case, it was his intention not to "reproduce in Australia a state of affairs in which prejudices existed and social divisions and dislikes existed on the basis of colour." These were represented as disorders that afflicted other societies.

White Australia had long held the view that it was an island of good health in a sea of disease. In the nineteenth century these were typically infectious diseases like smallpox, cholera and the plague. In arguing as he did, Menzies extended this understanding of Australia's freedom from disease to include healthy attitudes towards others. It followed that, as a psychologically healthy people, Australians enjoyed social harmony and a pleasing absence of colour prejudice. Just as smallpox had been represented as something imported into the continent from Asia in the late nineteenth century, so too was colour prejudice represented as foreign to Australia: Australians did not think that way and to imagine they did was taken as a sign of ignorance.

Warner was not convinced and asked: "Are you aware, Sir, that this total exclusion of Asians is regarded as an unwarranted insult by us to most of our Asian neighbours?" Menzies admitted that he had heard something to that effect, "but I am bound to say it has never been said to me". We may never know what General Cariappa said to Menzies in private, but his niece Sagarie noted that he once emerged from a discussion with Menzies saying, in a conspiratorial whisper, that he had raised the subject of White Australia.[39] He may not have called it an "unwarranted insult", but nor could he have expressed satisfaction with a policy that offended him deeply. Warner countered Menzies' denial by saying he could find "many students now in Melbourne who would be delighted to come and tell you just what I have said".

There was a familiar answer to Warner's allegation. Crocker had used it in his 1956 lecture when he stated that Asian students had discovered the "good nature and friendliness of the average Australian". Menzies said that he had been informed that when Asian students went home they "tell their friends and relatives that they have never been in a place where they have found less colour consciousness than in Australia". It was the standard official response to allegations of the kind raised by Warner and others like him who had travelled widely through Asia and kept in regular contact with Asian people living in Australia. Asian student opinion was appropriated to support the view that Australia was the least colour conscious nation in the world. It was a finding that Menzies was happy to repeat.

There was, nonetheless, an element of truth in this claim. Asian visitors to Australia in the era of the White Australia policy often expressed some anxiety at visiting a country that set such store on remaining white. There was a common expectation that they might experience racial insults and "colour bar" restrictions in their access to restaurants, theatres and public transport. When Laksiri Jayasuriya arrived at Sydney University as a private student from Ceylon in the early 1950s, he was showered with hospitality, invited into people's homes and given every encouragement to join in.[40] In retrospect, it appeared to be a community determined to show that its racist reputation was undeserved. By the late 1950s, Richard Casey presided over an Asian Visitors Programme, funded by Colombo Plan money and designed to show Asian leaders of opinion, particularly journalists, that Australians were not a colour conscious people. Casey also saw to it that all Australian cities had formed Australia-Asia Associations to ensure that Asian visitors were looked after. Hospitality was encouraged and supported in the knowledge that Australia's reputation was at stake. The objective was to disentangle the White Australia policy from allegations of racial superiority. In the aftermath of the Second World War, the elimination of feelings of racial superiority was considered a national priority and not, as it might seem, in order to relax and modify the White Australia policy but to maintain it. In a similar manner the term "White Australia" was never used in official documents and Casey repeatedly discouraged its use among journalists.[41]

While Menzies steadfastly denied that there was any element of racial discrimination in Australia's immigration policy, the Cariappa controversy made the pretence that much harder to sustain. Cariappa may have behaved indiscreetly and undiplomatically, but he could not be dismissed as ignorant or out of touch with Asian opinion. Veteran journalists like Warner knew the policy was widely regarded in the region as an insult, just as they knew that it was a question constantly under review in the Department of External Affairs. At the height of the Cariappa controversy in July 1954 one of the senior figures in the Press Gallery, Douglas Wilkie, pointed to the widening gap between what Australians wanted to believe about their immigration policy and how it was perceived in the region: "The plea that our White Australia policy is purely economic, and not based on racial prejudice, may satisfy us. But to most Asians it sounds like poppycock." Wilkie had no faith in the official strategy of maintaining that "informed Asians" understood and accepted the White Australia policy. However, as skeptical as he was, even Wilkie clung to the hope that Asian opinion could be effectively placated and conciliated by the introduction of a quota system. This, he believed, would help "preserve the White Australia doctrine" while also purging it "of its offensiveness to Asians".[42] Preserving the doctrine remained the focus of attention.

Through the 1950s the Australian government placed enormous faith in winning acceptance in Asia, if not support, by declaring Australians to be an hospitable people free from colour consciousness. This strategy was prompted by the belief that the Second World War had accelerated the pace of change in the non-European world, while simultaneously reducing European power and influence. In a world growing increasingly "coloured", the white races would have to not only shed pretensions to superiority but adopt a new and more conciliatory racial etiquette. In Australia, which had been so explicit about the preservation of a "white nation", the denial of racial superiority was considered particularly critical as was the need to cultivate a reputation for hospitality. These strategies were not designed to reform Australian immigration laws, but to prolong White Australia. This is not to deny that an increased exposure to Asia through the 1950s also created genuine interest and deeper cross-cultural awareness.

The ambiguities in this process are apparent in one of the final acts of the Cariappa drama. In 1960 Prime Minister Menzies floated the idea that Governors-General should be drawn from Commonwealth countries. He made it known that General Cariappa might well be a suitable Governor-General for Australia. It seems an unlikely proposition; but, for all his criticisms of the White Australia policy, Cariappa liked Australia and, though still a comparatively young man, had found no fulfilling role in India. Moreover, it appeared that he and Menzies got on rather well. The advantages for Menzies are also apparent. It would surely demonstrate that Australia was a country without colour consciousness if it was prepared to welcome General Cariappa as Governor-General. Unhappily for historians, this was not to be.

End Notes

1. Alfred Buchanan, *The Real Australia* (London: T. Fisher Unwin, 1907), pp. 2-3.
2. For an overview of White Australia and its aftermath, see Laksiri Jayasuriya, David Walker, Jan Gothard (eds.), *Legacies of White Australia* (Perth: UWA Press, 2003); see also Gwenda Tavan, *The Long, Slow Death of White Australia* (Melbourne: Scribe Publications, 2005).
3. Felicity Heal, *Hospitality in Early Modern England* (Oxford: Clarendon Press, 1990) p. 2.
4. Tom Selwyn, *An Anthropology of Hospitality*, in Conrad Lashley and Alison Morrison (eds.), *In Search of Hospitality: Theoretical Perspectives and Debates* (Oxford: Butterworth Heinemann, 2000), p. 19.
5. W. Hatfield, *I Find Australia* [London: OUP, 4th imp., 1940 (1937)], p. 44.
6. Hatfield, *I Find Australia*, p. 78.

7. W. Hatfield, *Australia through the Windscreen* (Sydney: A&R, 1936), p. 19.
8. Wood, *Cobbers* [London: OUP, 3rd edn., 1961 (1934)], p. 179.
9. Arnold L. Haskell, *Waltzing Matilda: A Background to Australia* [London: Adam & Charles Black, 1943 (1940)]. Haskell devotes his final chapter, which he subtitles *On Falling in Love With a Continent*, to discussing these feelings: see chapter xvii, pp. 283-87.
10. Arnold L. Haskell, *Waltzing Matilda: A Background to Australia* [London: Adam & Charles Black, 5th edn., 1943 (1940)], pp. 252-55.
11. Thomas Wood, *Cobbers*, p. 10.
12. Wood, *Cobbers*, p. 4.
13. Wood, *Cobbers*, p. 132.
14. See pp. 251-52 of the index to the Oxford edition cited.
15. Evidence that this theme was established well before that can be seen, for example, in Captain W.K. Harris's 1913 "*Account of the Longest Overlanding Journey Ever Attempted in Australia with a Single Horse*", in which the first chapter, entitled "The Hospitality of Outback Australia", extols "The exceeding great kindness and hospitality which are such innate features in the make-up of the Australian": Captain W.K. Harris, *Outback in Australia* [Letchworth: Garden City Press, & Newcastle, New South Wales: Harris & Son, 3rd edn, 1919 (1913)] chapter 1, pp. 1-6.
16. Wood, *Cobbers*, p. 58.
17. Chris Waters, The Macmahon Ball Mission to East Asia 1948, *Australian Journal of Politics and History,* 40 (1994), pp. 351-63; Gary Woodard, "Macmahon Ball's Goodwill Mission to Asia 1948", *Australian Journal of International Affairs*, 49 (1995), pp. 129-34. For the Macmahon Ball quotation, see W. Macmahon Ball, "*Report on a Mission to East Asia: May 27-July 6, 1948*", National Archives of Australia (NAA): CRS A1838/2, 381/1/3/1.
18. Rev. Alan Walker, *White Australia?* (Glebe, NSW: Christian Distributors' *Association*, [1946]), unpaged.
19. R.G. Casey, *Friends and Neighbours: Australia and the World*, (Melbourne: F.W. Cheshire, 1954).
20. See Gwenda Tavan, "Good Neighbours: Community Organisations, Migrant Assimilation and Australian Society and Culture, 1950-61", *Australian Historical Studies,* No. 109, Oct. 1997, pp. 77-90.
21. From Statement on Foreign Policy by the Minister for External Affairs (The Hon. P.C. Spender, K.C., M.P.) in the House of Representatives 9th March 1950; reproduced in Percy Spender, *Politics and a Man* (Sydney: Collins, 1972) p. 315.
22. V.S. Naipaul, *An Area of Darkness* (London: The Reprint Society, 1966) p. 263.
23. David Cannadine, *Ornamentalism: How the British Saw Their Empire* (Oxford: Oxford University Press, 2001).
24. Sripati Chandrasekhar, *Hungry People and Empty Lands: An Essay on Population Problems and International Tensions* (London: Allen & Unwin, 1954), p. 81.
25. *Courier-Mail*, 22 June, 1954, For an examination of this controversy, see David Walker, "General Cariappa Encounters White Australia': Australia, India and the Commonwealth, *Journal of Imperial and Commonwealth History*, in press.

26. *Age*, 23 June, 1954.
27. A.E. Rayment, *Courier-Mail*, 23 June, 1954, p. 2.
28. Crocker to Secretary, Dept. *External Affairs*, Canberra, 2 Sept 1954, Crocker papers, Series 10, V2.2, University of Adelaide Archives.
29. W.R. Crocker, *The Japanese Population Problem: The Coming Crisis* (London: George Allen & Unwin, 1931). For Crocker's diplomatic background, see Walter Crocker, *Travelling Back: The Memoirs of Sir Walter Crocker* (Bangalore: Macmillan, 1981).
30. W.R. Crocker, *The Racial Factor in International Relations* (Canberra: Australian National University, 1956).
31. *Ibid.*, pp. 11-12.
32. *ibid.*, p. 15.
33. *ibid.*, p. 12.
34. Alan Walker, *White Australia?*, [1946], unpaged.
35. See David Walker, Nervous Outsiders: Australia and the 1955 Asia-Africa Conference in Bandung, *Australian Historical Studies*, 37 (125), April 2005.
36. Crocker, *The Racial Factor in International Relations,* p. 34.
37. *Ibid.*, p. 32.
38. Transcript from the tape-recording of the prime minister's comments on migration questions at the "Meet the Press" interview on TV station HSV 7, Melbourne, 27/4/1958. NAA: A446/182, 1961/65971.
39. Personal communication, Sagarie Muthanna to David Walker, January 2006, Bangalore.
40. Laksiri Jayasuriya, interviewed by David Walker for the Oral History Collection, National Library of Australia, TRC 4904/1, 12 November, 2002.
41. Casey to Counsellor Solly, 3 June, 1954. NAA: A1838, 581/1 part 2.
42. Douglas Wilkie, Snub for our Allies, Melbourne *Sun*, 13 July, 1954, p. 6.

3

The Process of Positive 'Native Title' Determination in Australia: Leading to a 'Negative Title'?[1]

PRITI SINGH

One of the main issues of concern for the indigenous peoples in Australia pertains to 'Native Title'. Although Native Title has been recognised by other countries with legal systems similar to Australia, such as the United States of America, Canada and New Zealand, it was recognised in Australia only in 1992. The judgement passed by the High Court of Australia in the Mabo case in 1992 recognising Native Title, was the highpoint for indigenous rights in Australia because it acknowledged that land at the time of colonisation in Australia was not *terra nullius* (no one's land).[2] In other words, the judgement took away the very argument for colonisation of Australia. Ever since, it has been argued that there have been a number of disappointments regarding judgements on Native Title.[3] Why have subsequent judgments on indigenous land rights been considered disappointing and how do they impact on Native Title? What is Native Title and what does it mean to the Aboriginal peoples?[4] How does one prove that it exists, and what is the relationship between Native Title in customary law and Native Titles defined and legislated by the government? When and how can Aboriginal customary rights and interests in land be lawfully extinguished or suspended? In seeking answers to this host of questions, some more questions surface, which elude definitive answers.

The process of determining Native Title is long-winding and expensive involving huge annual costs for research, information, legal and other expertise, and connection reports. In spite of these legalities, the process itself does not seem to have made a very deep impact on the aborigines. Even if a land claim made by an aboriginal claimant is successful, it is difficult for aboriginal communities or groups to manage the land acquired through Native Title because not all communities possess the required skills. Is Native Title an alien system thrust upon the aborigines? In this paper an attempt is made to address this question.

Available data suggests 80 Native Title determinations have been passed so far, out of which 55 have been positive or in favour of the Aboriginal peoples, giving recognition to Native Title be it through unopposed determination, consent determination or through litigation. *(Data provided by the NNTT, 23 December 2005).*[5] Most of the cases resulting in 'negative' determinations (which do not recognise Native Title) have been the subject of open debate and criticism.[6] But even among the positive determinations, Native Title is recognised not necessarily in the entire area that has been claimed. Recognition has been given only to parts of the area. And what happens after the determination? While the process of claiming rights to Native Title itself is long and cumbersome, the process of actually exercising rights to Native Title after the determination is no less complicated.

The main objective of this paper is to examine the government structures and management of these structures as given in the Native Title Act, to see whether these structures (especially after a positive determination has been made) help facilitate the goals envisaged in the framing of Native Title. Recognition to Native Title does not have any meaning unless the legal bodies approved by the Act are adequately armed to meet the challenges posed to them. This paper seeks to show the gap between what apparently emerges from a positive determination and what actually does. Does the Native Title Act really achieve what it purportedly sets out to in its preamble?[7]

Keeping these in focus, this paper is divided into three sections. The first section gives a brief account of what is understood by the term Native Title and explains the process of Native Title determination; the second attempts to discuss and analyse the end result or outcome of this entire process; and the third concluding section offers some critical comments.

Understanding Native Title

Native Title is a concept in the law of Australia that recognises the continued ownership of land by local Indigenous/Aboriginal Australians. Native Title is derived from land/water, which is key to Aboriginal development. It may be defined as the communal, group or individual rights over land or water held under traditional law by Aboriginal people or Torres Strait Islander people. Native Title can only be claimed in places where it has not been extinguished—in vacant Crown land; state forests, parks and reserves; oceans, seas, lakes; in areas of non-exclusive pastoral and agricultural leases. In places where successfully claimed, the area will be shared with other people with rights and interests in that area. In other words, Native Title can co-exist with non-indigenous proprietary rights. It is also possible that different indigenous groups can exercise their Native Title over the same land. In this way, it represents a local example of the fragmentation of proprietary interests. More particularly, it is also an example of two distinct systems of law operating within the same geographic, national and jurisdictional space. It is not simply a question of land rights, but something more than that—territory. But in Australia, focus has been more on land and less on the concept of territory. Under the Australian legal system the differentiation between land rights and Native Title is that while both are based on traditional rights, land rights are granted by the Australian legal system whereas Native Title cannot be granted because these are rights and interests preceding the British colonisation of Australia or have been in existence prior to the advent of the nation-state. These rights can at best be recognised by the state. Therein lies the problem. How does the modern independent Australian State (formed as a federation of six former separate colonies) recognise Native Title?

The Australian government has set up a legal process which determines Native Title claims. But the problems encountered while mediating or negotiating and reaching Native Title agreements further highlights the differences in the perception of law and customs of the Western world as against those of the Aboriginal peoples.

Thus the content and meaning of Native Title is ambivalent and is interpreted variously by the courts in Australia case by case. So much so, what constitutes Native Title has been called into question time and again. It is recognised by Common Law in Australia (a system of justice based on the British legal traditions introduced in Australia in 1788) but neither is it defined by it nor a part of it. Native Title describes the rights and interests of indigenous inhabitants in relation to particular land or waters possessed under traditional laws and customs observed by the Aboriginal peoples and originates from it. The nature of Native Titles dependent on these laws and customs and thus is unique. It does not constitute State/property and can be extinguished by a valid exercise of Legislative or Executive power. The NTAA 1998 in Section 4 (1) recognises and protects Native Title. It provides that Native Title cannot be "extinguished contrary to the Act". Yet, it also confirms that enactments made before the Mabo decision that are either valid or have been validated could extinguish Native Title. *Once extinguished, Native Title does not revive.*[8] Native Title cannot be held on freehold property or in the case of Torres Strait Islanders on Deed of Grant in Trust (DOGIT) land held by the island council that coexists with Native Title. So, while Native Title seems to arise out of customary laws and traditions, it is given legality through the Common Law. And while Common Law does not give birth to Native Title it certainly validates its survival or extinguishment or even partial extinguishment.

It is here that the argument being made by Michael Williams becomes pertinent. Even when Native Title is recognised, the legal formalities are such that an aboriginal community finds it extremely difficult to manage this title.

The Australian Government has devised an exhaustive managerial system to get the Aboriginal peoples their rights to 'Native Title'. The main actors in this task are the Federal Court, the National Native Title Tribunal (NNTT), the Native Title Representative Bodies (NTRBs), the Prescribed Body Corporates (PBCs) and a number of others like the Federal Minister for Reconciliation, Federal Attorney General's office, Indigenous working groups as well as anthropologists, historians and linguists.

The Institutional Arrangements for Process of Determining Native Title

Federal Court

A host of institutions and federal/provincial agencies act and function as wheels-within-wheels. Under the amendments made in 1998 to the Native Title Act (1993), a Native Title claim or application (claimant, non-claimant, or compensation) is now lodged with the Federal Court or the High Court of Australia. The Court then advises the National Native Title Tribunal (NNTT) which registers the claim. Again, it is the Court which makes a Native Title determination and not the NNTT. Once the determination is made, the Court notifies the NNTT and the determination is registered in the Native Title Register.

National Native Title Tribunal

The Native Title Amendment Act, 1998 gives the National Native Title Tribunal power to provide assistance or undertake mediation in other matters relating to Native Title.[9]

1. The 1998 amendments set out a *registration test*, which the applicants have to fulfill to remain on the register of Native Title claims. Inclusion in the register allows access to certain rights like the right to negotiate, or to be consulted over future acts—in other words, whether the application meets certain threshold requirements to have access to rights provided in the NTA to undetermined applications.[10] The test requires detailed information: identification of the area claimed; identification of the people claiming the area[11] ; and identification of the Native Title rights being claimed. This should be accompanied by a description of any activities in exercise of those rights which are being claimed. But as has been argued by a lawyer, "the groups should describe the rights and interests claimed as broadly as possible, as the very purpose of negotiation towards a determination of Native Title—or litigation, if that path is chosen—is to clarify and refine the relationship between the stakeholders concerned".[12]

Applications lodged in the Federal Court must contain a general description of the factual basis on which it is asserted that Native Title and rights exist or should be able to prove an association with the area, that there exist traditional laws and customs observed by the group and that the group has continued to hold the Native Title in accordance with those traditional laws and customs.

But in assessing some applications, petitioners are required to submit evidence proving the actual exercise of each right and interest asserted, by at least some of the group members. This reflects the ongoing debate since the Mabo decision about Native Title rights and interests—whether it is a usage right, a 'bundle of rights' or rights to land.[13]

The most basic problem in most of these criteria for a registration test or negotiation/mediation process is the stress on 'traditional'. While it seems perfectly logical to do so, the problem begins with the lack of understanding. While the rights and interests of indigenous groups arise from their primordial customs and practices, the "expression of these rights and interests change over time to take advantage of changes in technology, economy and society." As is further explained by a writer, "they [Australian legal system] are happy to recognise our rights to hunt and gather, as long as we use spears and boomerangs. We would not be allowed to use dogs, not allowed to use cars, and not allowed to use guns.... A frozen in time argument such as this must be quickly responded to by saying, 'Okay, if you want to put us in that position, you dig your gold out with a pick and shovel.'"[14] Also, Native Title as it exists is unique to the circumstances of the group asserting it, reflecting their laws and customs.

The provision for the *Right to Negotiate* which is feasible after undergoing the registration test also does not amount to much. While the NTA gave Native Title holders opportunity to negotiate, states could develop their own right to negotiate regimes but within the framework of Commonwealth standards. The NTAA's alternative right to negotiate allowing states and territories to wipe out the right to negotiate by setting up alternative regimes with minimum standards, thus providing the means to wipe out the right to negotiate of all past and present pastoral leases.

2. The second new function of the NNTT is the development and registration of Indigenous Land Use Agreements (ILUAs). This is a part of the function of the NNTT as a mediator. The legitimacy of mediation as a tool for conflict resolution is the saving in cost and time to the justice system. ILUAs are a kind of outcome of mediation and are contractually binding on people entering them. They take a number of forms and deal with any issue affecting land use including future acts, exercise of access for traditional purposes and can even involve recognition or surrender of Native Title. The parties can seek to have the agreement entered in the register maintained by the NNTT registrar.

Native Title Representative Bodies (NTRBs)

The Native Title Act empowers Representative Bodies to assist Aboriginal people to make and present claims to the Federal Court. What is important is that these representative bodies are expected to perform some tasks like synchronising the requirements of indigenous and non-indigenous law in relation to Native Title applications as well as juggle the different social, cultural, political and legal traditions of the range of communities which are constituents of the NTRB or which the NTRB represents. The NTRB represents indigenous interests in negotiations and proceedings in relation to acts affecting Native Title and for compensation claims.

The functions that an NTRB is expected to perform includes (i) facilitation and assistance; (ii) certification; (iii) dispute resolution; (iv) notification; (v) agreement making; and (vi) internal review.

Again, it is the Court, which makes a Native Title determination, and not the NNTT. Once the determination is made, the Court notifies the NNTT and the determination is incorporated in the Native Title Register.

Prescribed Bodies Corporate

Once a determination is passed recognising the Native Title rights of the claimant groups, the NTA 1993 provides for management of the Native Title through corporations that act as trustees or agents of the Native Title holders. These corporations are called Prescribed Bodies Corporate (PBCs) and establish the way in which future dealings affecting Native Title may proceed. The choice of a PBC has to be made at the time of or just before a determination is made. If the Native Title claimant group is unsuccessful in picking out its PBC, then one will be chosen for the group by the Court. Thus the PBC is set up in order to fulfill the criteria set out by the Act.

The reasons for having a PBC are also understood in terms of the Australian common law. Firstly, a PBC acts as a legal entity which can be identified by law as the holder of the Native Title. It is an administrative mechanism to manage and hold the rights and interests conferred by the Native Title. Secondly, it is easier for an outsider to deal with a corporate body instead of groups whose membership may keep changing. Thirdly, a PBC acts for the Native Title holders thus protecting their interests and also regulates rights between the members of the Native Title group.

The crucial question that needs to be asked is in what way are the PBCs addressing Native Title issues. The PBCs seem to be constructed on the basis of common law to address what should be purely a customary and traditional system of land tenure.

David Martin and Christos Mantziaris talk in terms of Native Title being a product and part of the "recognition space" between the traditional customs of the Aborigines and the Australian legal system.[15] However, Native Title according to them is a legal construct in this area of interaction between the two societies. This idea had originated from an aboriginal lawyer who had pointed out:

> The High Court tells us in Mabo that Native Title is not a common law title but is instead a title recognised by the common law. What they failed to tell us, and something which we have failed to appreciate, is that neither is Native Title an Aboriginal law title. Because patently Aboriginal law will recognise title where the common law will not. Native Title is therefore the space between the two systems, where there is recognition. Native Title is want of a better formulation of the recognition for space between the common law and the Aboriginal law which afforded recognition in particular circumstances.[16]

The function of a Prescribed Body Corporate in this vast area of interaction can perhaps be limited to the management of Native Title and not to manage the system of relations between the law and custom of the group and the country. Needless to say then, they cannot be seen as leading to a wider goal such as self-determination. A PBC is by its very name a corporation with limitations and governed by a statute and is limited by restrictions and regulations as well as in its design to take into account the various aspirations of the Native Title group/groups.

In that sense, as has been argued by critics, the Native Title at best is a mere translation of the Aboriginal customs and practices into the Australian legal system. So this system may not actually operate in terms of the interpreted rights and interests of the Aborigines. It could therefore operate on a fundamentally different set of properties.

Australian route to self-determination has been through establishment of various types of corporations rather than through treaties between peoples. The fact is that the corporation is the vehicle by which service delivery occurs, by which Aboriginal groups of various kinds—all the way from smaller family groupings to very large conglomerations, groupings of people—seek to achieve various ends including political, economic and social. So the corporation in a sense is a 'given' of the landscape. Prescribed bodies corporate are not there to manage the ways Aboriginal people relate to themselves, amongst themselves, in their own systems as well as relate themselves to the larger Australian society. Being a creation of the Australian legal system which caters principally to the interests of the larger society at best makes a meek effort to incorporate the rights and interests of the Aboriginal people into it.

The above prescriptions require that the Native Title claimant groups should be able to nominate a PBC as soon as the determination is passed so that the Court can select one. This has been also called the "simultaneous determination problem".[17] This problem poses a number of riders. One, it is not possible for the claimants to decide on a body corporate representing their interests unless it is clear which of the many claimants are going to be recognised by the Court's determination. Two, even once the participating claimants are confirmed, it may take quite some time to sort out internal disagreements of representation before a viable option is finalised. The varying functional duties and participation of different groups or individuals make it difficult to have a defined boundary or category, labelling them as Native Title holders.

How can one identify the group with the corporation? It is next to impossible to get a complete congruence between the members of the group and the members of the corporation. Secondly, the general meeting procedures in most corporations are run on a majoritarian principle, so there can be a decision of the corporation which does not reflect the wishes of the individual Native Title holder. Moreover, corporate power can be delegated to the board of the corporation, so there can be a divergence between the will of the people and the board of the corporation.

As is argued by a scholar, it is in the interests of the development agencies such as the representative bodies, ATSIC and the National Native Title Tribunal to "achieve economies of scale by dealing with the largest group possible" when dealing with a claim. This may result in the rights of a smaller group being "submerged" in the interests of a larger one leading to a dispute. [18] In the event of the claimant groups choosing an agency model for its PBC, the PBC would comprise either the entire Native Title group or a subset of the group acting on its instructions. Then, questions arise as to the liability of the PBC to the third party creditors in case of any. It would take time to sort out and mould the corporate structure in accordance with the requirements of the various groups involved. A Native Title claimant group cannot prepare in advance of a determination, so there is always a time gap between the determination and the setting up of the PBC. This time lag is disadvantageous to the claimants as it means that any "grant of NT [Native Title] by the courts is technically in 'limbo' either temporarily or permanently depending on the circumstances of the group. Cash strapped NT groups will be seriously disadvantaged."[19] Moreover, in the event of the failure of the successful Native Title claimants nominating any PBC at all, "short of the court procuring the incorporation of a PBC itself, it cannot determine '*which*' PBC is to fulfil the necessary functions as there is no such body."[20]

The practical reality is that most prescribed bodies corporate will lack the resources and expertise to properly perform their functions. In particular these bodies will not possess the legal and 'anthropologist expertise', and may not have sufficient impartiality, to recognise the succession of traditional Interests over time. Some developers will take advantage of this situation to the detriment of traditional interests. Resultant litigation will create uncertainty for industry.[21]

These apart, the funding of the PBC is to be borne by the claimant group besides seeking a large input of professional expertise which only adds to the financial burden of the claimants. How can the legislative framework that Australia has in place decide the scale of the PBC and also provide the resources for setting it up? At the moment, the setting up of a PBC is a cumbersome legal process which the successful Native Title group will have to fund. In addition to that once the Native Title holders have demonstrated their traditional laws and customs to the satisfaction of a Court, they should be able to rely upon that system. Yet are they really able to do that? Given these limitations, the Native Title recognition is more an ideal than a reality at least from the point of view of the claimants.

Concluding Observations

There is therefore a fundamental contradiction in the functioning of this system. On the one hand you have this huge edifice of amendments, which make the representative body virtually like a statutory authority. On the other hand, the statutory authority structure is imposed on community based groups.

Under these circumstances, does self-determination mean anything at all for Aboriginal people? Is it realistic to think of the Native Title Representative Bodies or PBCs as vehicles for Aboriginal self-determination? Or are they simply service delivery bodies, for instance like a legal service, seeking to advance the interests of its clients? These being the questions do these bodies provide or offer an opportunity for the Aboriginal people to attain their primordial interests and objectives? In effect, Native Title has not radically changed lives. The practical reality is that most prescribed bodies corporate perhaps lack the resources and expertise to properly perform their functions. Organisations, including Native Title representative bodies and communities themselves, who have had the responsibility of managing benefits associated with Native Title simply haven't had the capacity to do it effectively for the benefit of the people. A large chunk of the aboriginal population is still dependent on government support.[22]

In turn, this raises a few more questions such as: is the march towards this regimentation of traditional practices inevitable? Is it essential? Are Native Title holders really going to need trust deeds or agency agreements in addition to their formal determination, regulations requiring consultation and the rules of their association?

The Australian route to self-determination has been through establishment of various types of corporations rather than through treaties or any other similar political instruments. The corporation is the vehicle by which service delivery occurs, by which Aboriginal groups of various kinds—all the way from smaller family groupings to very large conglomerations—seek to achieve various ends including political, economic and social. So at the moment the corporation in a sense is a 'given' in the landscape. All statutes are based on values and practices that have their origin in the dominant legal, political and economic system. The more one attempts to understand better the indigenous systems through formal corporate structures, the more the risk of the informal indigenous forms being supplanted by these formal structures. Therefore there is a strong argument for not codifying the informal indigenous realm within government mechanisms and instead establishing corporations that fall within the indigenous informal realm.

Be that as it may, the innovative approach to the legal recognition of Native Title certainly is a step forward. According to an Aboriginal scholar: "We need to be prepared to recognise where Native Title fits in the jigsaw of reconciliation and Indigenous affairs." Nevertheless, she justifiably points out that Australia has "not lived up to the promise of the Act.... We need to face up to a failure of imagination and competence" and adds "It is not yet a lost opportunity but it's an opportunity in the process of being lost".[23] To redeem the anomaly most critics are of the view that "Native Title must be liberated from the constraints imposed by legal technicalities so that we can take advantage of the culture of negotiation it created."[24]

End Notes

1. I have borrowed the use of the term "negative title" from Prof. Michael Williams, the Director of the Aboriginal and Torres Strait Islander Studies Unit at the University of Queensland. According to him, Native Title is an alien system thrust upon the aborigines and that is what I seek to explore in this paper. I would also like to put on record my sincere thanks to Dr. David Martin, associated with the Centre for Aboriginal and Economic Policy Research, Australian National University, Canberra and Ms. Jackie Huggins, Deputy Director of the Aboriginal and Torres Strait Islander Studies Unit at the University of Queensland and Co-chair of Reconciliation Australia.
2. *Mabo and Another V. The State of Queensland and Another* [1988] *High Court of Australia* 69; (1989) 166 Commonwealth Law Reports 186 F.C. 88/062 (8 December, 1988)
3. Examples of well-known cases may be cited like the *Wik Peoples V. The State of Queensland & Ors; The Thayorre People V. The State of Queensland & Ors [1996] Hca 40* (*23 December, 1996*) or Yorta-Yorta.
4. The indigenes or the indigenous peoples of Australia comprise 'Aboriginal' and 'Torres Strait Islander' people. The former occupy the mainland and tend to have a common ethnology. Those of the Torres Strait islands have vastly different ethnographic origins. In the context of human rights and equal opportunity, it is correct to refer to these people as either 'indigenous Australians' or as 'Aboriginal and Torres Strait Islander Australians'. However, this paper also refers to them as Aboriginals.

5. For details see http://www.nntt.gov.au/applications/determinations.html Accessed on 2 January 2006.
6. Recent examples judgements on Native Title cases can be cited like the Yorta Yorta *Members of the Yorta Yorta Aboriginal Community v. The State of Victoria* [2002] HCA 58, 96 (Gleeson C.J., Gummow and Hayne J.J.).
7. The preamble states: The people of Australia intend: (a) to rectify the consequences of past injustices by the special measures contained in this Act, announced at the time of introduction of this Act into the Parliament, or agreed on by the Parliament from time to time, for securing the adequate advancement and protection of Aboriginal peoples and Torres Strait Islanders; and (b) to ensure that Aboriginal peoples and Torres Strait Islanders receive the full recognition and status within the Australian nation to which history, their prior rights and interests, and their rich and diverse culture, fully entitle them to aspire.
8. As listed by Alex Rorrison, in Native Title: 'Bundle of Rights' or Interest in Land? *Native Title News*, Vol. 4, No. 3, June 1999, pp. 49-50. The NTAA 1998 in Section 4 (1), Overview of Act, *Recognition and Protection of Native Title,* states: "This Act recognises and protects Native Title. It provides that Native Title cannot be extinguished contrary to the Act". Yet, it goes on to state in Section 4 (6): "This Act also confirms that many acts done before the High Court's judgment, that were either valid, or have been validated under the past act or intermediate period act provisions, will have extinguished Native Title. If the acts are *previous exclusive possession acts* (see section 23B), the extinguishment is complete; if the acts are *previous non-exclusive possession acts* (see section 23F), the extinguishment is to the extent of any inconsistency."
9. Schedule 1, Amendments relating to acts affecting Native Title, *Native Title Amendment Act 1998,* No. 97, 1998.
10. Anne De Soyza, Claimant Applications: Merit and the Registration Test, *Native Title News*, Vol. 4, No. 2, April 1999, p. 22.
11. In the process of identification, all peoples with common group rights or interests in accordance with traditional laws and customs would ideally be involved leading to several overlapping applications. Also, naming all people in a group is impractical especially if the group is large.
12. *Anne De Soyza*, No. 10, p. 24.
13. Kado Muir, Registration, Negotiation and Arbitration: 'Statutory' Native Title Rights and Interests, in Lisa Strelein and Kado Muir (eds.), *Native Title in Perspective: Selected Papers from the Native Title Research Unit 1998-2000* (Canberra: Native Title Research Unit, Australian Institute of Aboriginal and Torres Strait Islander Studies, 2000), p. 101. Also see Ward v. Western Australia (2000) 170 ALR 159 at 178.
14. Kado Muir, *Ibid.*, p. 102.
15. Christos Mantziaris and David Martin, *Native Title Corporations: A Legal and Anthropological Analysis* (Sydney: Federation Press, 2000).
16. Noel Pearson, The Concept of Native Title at Common Law, *Australian Humanities Review*, March 1997. Christos Mantziaris and David Martin use the term 'recognition space' in a way different to Noel Pearson's original use of the term. It should also be understood that their model is just that: a device for explaining a complex reality.

17. *Muir*, No. 14, p. 97.
18. Patrick Sullivan, A Sacred Land, A Sovereign People, An Aboriginal Corporation: Prescribed Bodies and the Native Title Act, *North Australia Research Unit (NARU) Report Series No. 3*, 1997, p. 6.
19. Dave R. Tewhatu, Native Title Corporations and Prescribed Bodies Corporate: How They Will, Or Won't, Work For You, *Land Rights Queensland Newspaper (LRQ)*, February 2000, pp. 2-3.
20. Mantziaris and Martin, No. 15, p. 96.
21. Ron Levy, Twenty Years of Land Rights: Lessons for the Native Title Act, *Indigenous Law Bulletin*, Vol. 3, No. 76, October 1995.
22. David F. Martin, Rethinking the Design of Indigenous Organisations: The Need for Strategic Engagement, Technical Report Discussion Paper No. 248, 2003, Centre for Aboriginal Economic Policy Research, Australian National University.
23. Jackie Huggins, Indigenous Good Governance Begins with Communities and Institutions, Speech given to the 10th Annual Cultural Heritage and Native Title Conference, held in Brisbane on 30 September, 2003. Accessed on 30 June, 2006 from http://www.onlineopinion.com.au/view.asp?article=784
24. *Ibid.*

4

Benign Whiteness in Australian Race Relations

AURIOL WEIGOLD

Benign whiteness is best described in an Australian context as a symbolic regard for Indigenous issues. This was well illustrated in the Sorry Day marches across Australia in May 2000. The marches were a demonstration of support and good will for reconciliation and a symbolic gesture of solidarity with indigenous Australians by white Australians, but not a commitment to change. If a conscious or unconscious choice was made it was to continue in the accustomed way.

Benign whiteness as evidenced in the Sorry Day marches is about being tolerant, respectful, non-racist but not at the vanguard of change. It is not about a pro-active dedication to achieving equality between settler Australia and the indigenous population.

The marches, part of the 1991 to 2001 reconciliation process, was a government supported project to heal rifts and build bridges between Indigenous and non-Indigenous Australians. It took on the status of any anti-racist movement, reflected in an outpouring of goodwill towards Indigenous Australians.

Whiteness studies more generally, however, emerged from the premise that "all whites benefit from their racial identity", bringing to the foreground the "structure and dynamics of race".[1] Thus within a dominant white culture a space has been created where the notion of benign whiteness may be discussed.

This paper therefore will address the benchmarks and utility of benign whiteness with reference to issues such as the 1967 Referendum on Citizenship for Aboriginal people, land rights and Australia's history wars. The paper will then focus on Aboriginal Senator Aden Ridgeway's understanding of reconciliation, and Pauline Hanson, leader of the One Nation Party's unintended identification and allocation of space and a place for benign whiteness in the debate about national identity.

Finally the paper will refer the reconciliation process under Prime Minister John Howard and conclude that reconciliation has switched tracks from reconciliation as previously understood by Australians, to a practical reconciliation based on what has been called mutual responsibility. By way of illustration, this mirrors loosely the Howard Government's shift from regional race-based wars about who could be 'Asian', to a practical economic, security and aid-based engagement between Australia and the Asia-Pacific where racial difference is seldom an issue.

As preface, this paper is not derived from Whiteness Studies, but a political-historical tracking of a story. Briefly, however, and to paraphrase Fiona Probyn, University of Sydney, Whiteness Studies has been important in the United States for some twenty years, but it wasn't until Ghassan Hage's *White Nation* and Jon Stratton's *Race Daze* were published in Australia in 1998, that "'whiteness' became a focus of mainstream academic critique" here. [2]

Major areas of research in the field include the historical process by which a white racial identity was created by a white power structure to justify discrimination against non-whites, and sustainable arguments that whites see race as the property of 'the other', that whites do not see whiteness racially.

Delving into historical murkiness for a lateral Australian 'take' on whiteness, the paper looks first to Australia's colonial settlement for the roots of white Australia's unease or ambivalence towards what D'Cruz and Steele describe as "people of colour". [3] Based in settler insecurities, white Australia looked at the Australian Indigenous people "as inferior…for it has felt itself inferior". [4] Inferior on account of its convict origins and social exclusion during the formative years of the colony, settler Australia needed to identify a group less privileged than itself to express its ambivalent feelings.

Ashis Nandy argued that it did not have to be so, there could have been a different Australia, not obsessed by its self-imposed inferiority in the face of the superior British colonial power. Australia's first identity could have been one of dissent, as many "exiled" to the penal colony were dissenters. Dissenters from the relentless industrialisation of Britain, the new work culture that went with it, or victims on the enclosure movement, or deported Irish nationalists, always recalcitrant, always "fit candidates for exile". [5]

Instead of a national identity based on dissent, however, Australians clung to their safe if not comforting 'Anglo' or western heritage for identity and esteem, to mark them as different, anchored as they were in what appeared to be a geographically alien place.

D'Cruz and Steele see that the present Government's re-asserting of 'Anglo' values and reconstruction of an 'Anglo' identity for Australia as a reaction to the threatening world "out there". But also threatening is the world, "in here", where Anglo notions of Australian identity are being subverted by the fact of cultural diversity. [6]

Here the government in its push for a national identity that has no relevance for much of multicultural Australia, including the indigenous population, has reawakened in the Australian community, ideas of Australia-under-siege.

(This is not a new political device. Indeed it has surfaced in India, notably when first Indira Gandhi and then Rajiv Gandhi mobilised an idea that Hindu India was under threat, whether real or imagined, from minority communities, and communicated this to the majority community).[7]

Such tension with Australia's multicultural community was envisaged some twenty years ago when Australian historian, Geoffrey Blainey, said "should a time come when ordinary Australians began to feel crowded or pressured by new arrivals, resentment might soon end the ready acceptance upon which migrants hitherto knew they could rely on".[8]

Blainey's perception of a loss of privilege for settler Australians rather horrifyingly raises the spectre of the "injured" nature of whiteness in the southern United States' white supremacist identity, injured by "the perceived loss of all-white social spaces, by the re-formation of a national imaginary" there.[9]

The extent to which European migrants post World War II, felt they were readily accepted is not an issue for this paper, however, we may ask whether indigenous Australians could ever rely on ready acceptance in the white community?

There have been such moments that demonstrated tolerance, or benign acceptance in the white Australian community for the Indigenous people. In 1967, for example, in an overwhelmingly positive referendum vote, Indigenous people gained the right to vote but this act of acceptance, of tolerance, did not mean that they were recognised as equal citizens.

An article in a recent issue of *The National Indigenous Times*, while acknowledging white enthusiasm for the reconciliation process, explored this inequality in the context of white Australia's failure to understand the indigenous other:

The abuse and mistreatment of a traditionally unique and spiritual people continues today, often hidden from sight, because the injustices lay in the minds of people who simply do not understand the complexities of the after-effects of colonisation. [10]

Reiterating D'Cruz and Steele's hypothesis, Ghassan Hage elaborated on the idea of the threatening world. He argued that the culture of worrying, most obvious in movements such as Pauline Hanson's One Nation Party, primarily a European Australian phenomenon, has become the "dominant cultural form of expressing one's belonging to the nation".[11]

Worrying indicates the primacy of fear about the fate of the nation, and arguably the present government has promoted fear, most notably the fear of asylum seekers, migrants more generally, terrorism and, in another example, welfare benefits given to indigenous people that are perceived to advantage them and disadvantage the majority culture. In this way, tides of racism can rise and fall, and in partnership with worrying about the nation, reflect the relationship between the state and it population.

Camilleri, in his article 'The Howard Years: Cultural Ambivalence and Political Dogma', argues that a deeply ingrained racism continues to hamper reconciliation with Indigenous Australia. Camilleri, like D'Cruz and Steele and Hage, also identifies the threatening world out there, positing that "Australian society preferred to close in on itself, and return to the language and symbolism of an earlier period"[12] represented by a resurgence of Anglo culture.

To understand the role of whiteness and the commitment to an idealised national identity in Australia's political priorities under the Howard government, is to appreciate that a shift has been registered in the meanings attached to the words 'whiteness', 'race' and 'racism'. So that despite the possibility of a deeply ingrained racism in Australia, as suggested by Camilleri, and shared by other settler nations as "a collective and active cultural inheritance", racism has been reconstructed in Australia as 'an individual moral aberration'.[13]

This reconstruction of racism has set in place a broad consensus expressed in claims of moving beyond racism, to a tolerant acceptance of diversity, creating another space for recognition of a 'benign' white population.

Thus the 1967 Referendum on Aboriginal citizenship is remembered as a signal of the end of racism in Australia and a symbol of goodwill expressed in their vote for the referendum by white Australians. Similarly benign whiteness was perceived to be in action when the Mabo decision on Indigenous land rights appeared to overturn the long relied-on certainty of *terra nullius* and established a national native title regime. Despite this popular assumption across the community, the High Court's case was not a finding on *terra nullius* but on whether the common law recognised native title.

Australia's history wars, however, have inserted a revisionist view of Indigenous-European relations, designed to make the Australian population worry less, to use Ghasson Hage's term, about the limits of reconciliation and other issues between the settler and indigenous populations. Settler Australian treatment of the native population in the revisionist view has been justified to debunk any historical evidence for their early, often violent dispossession.

The so-called 'black armband' version of history that has held sway in recent decades, so uncomfortable for many Australians, was given expression by historian Henry Reynolds in his 1998 book *This Whispering in Our Hearts:*

Australians of today who find comfort in the history of the [19th century] humanitarian crusades should reflect that the protesters had little influence on events. Their assertions, however cogent, their moral appeal however persuasive, were largely ignored... What the humanitarian story shows is that an alternative agenda was aired, a more humane course projected, was listened to, understood and then comprehensively rejected... . The colonists were offered a choice and chose to continue in accustomed ways, preferring violent dispossession to purchase, treaty and negotiation....[14]

Such an alternative agenda was "aired" as Reynolds said, in the 1967 Referendum, in the land rights awards and the reconciliation movement but, as mentioned earlier, the choice to move actively towards equality in Australian society was again and again not taken.

A generally benign, tolerant white community, however, as recognised by the *National Indigenous Times*, shows support for Aboriginal rights and recognises the importance of reconciliation, but does not have the desire to take it into the realm of the Australian Prime Minister's oft-stated maxim, a fair go for all.

Why is this? Mackie in 'Reconciliation, racial prejudice and 'soft Hansonism' in Australia's future', suggests that community support for Aborigines was often tentative, perplexed and rather confused, but open to the possibility of inspired leadership. [15] That leadership, today, has only embraced what is termed practical reconciliation, linked with policies of mutual obligation.

Perhaps some light on this ambivalence or confusion by the white Australian community referred to above may be shed by D'Cruz and Steele who have identified what they call a paradox of postcolonial racism.

A paradox because in the middle of resentment (or confusion), there can also be sympathy and, at the same time a recognition that while some 'others', indigenous peoples (or migrants or refugees) do not have enough, they may end up having too much. Too much, that is, from the Australian welfare or social security system.

Thus Anglo Australians are capable of seeing 'the other' as lacking which produces sympathy and guilt, and as gaining, which produces anxiety and resentment, both at the same time.

Is Australia caught in this paradox that is arguably embedded in its institutions and built on individual prejudices, but disguised in the 'outpouring of goodwill' during the reconciliation decade?

Arguably a way around the white Australian resentment of Indigenous people having too much, was the introduction of 'practical reconciliation' and 'mutual obligation', under which a remote Aboriginal community, for example, might request some capital expenditure to benefit their community, in return for which they undertook to a institute change or end a practice which the government found unpalatable.

Seen as constructive by some sectors of Aboriginal representation, Whiteness Studies theorists have embraced assumptions of a "re-ignition of assimilation", and describe mutual obligation as "a neat solution to an array of issues facing remote communities".[16] The argument continues that for such solutions to be effective, "amnesia on the part of colonialism's victims as well as its beneficiaries", is required.[17]

To return to reconciliation and benign whiteness in action: Senator Aden

Ridgeway, an Aboriginal elected to the Senate in 2000, who lost his seat in the subsequent election, also saw the reconciliation process as largely symbolic, an issue he raised in a speech to the United Nations Human rights Commission on 26 March 2001.

His speech on the theme tolerance and respect acknowledged the goodwill amongst the Australian population for reconciliation, the "majority" of whom were willing to "start afresh in their relationship with Indigenous Australians". Yet even as he acknowledged this "goodwill" he made the point that in Australian race-relations, "goodwill and good intentions do not require concessions from white Australians".[18]

Senator Ridgeway said in conclusion

Non-indigenous Australians are keen to embrace the rhetoric of reconciliation, so long as it does not require them to take effective action to share the country's abundant resources and political power. Most are not prepared to make any significant adjustments to how they live their lives, or how they see their future.[19]

It has been argued that Senator Ridgeway's comments were significant because criticism of the reconciliation process was rare, envisaged as it was as an anti-racist movement, but also because he was an Aboriginal member of Federal Parliament, cautioned by the Prime Minister not to be critical of Australia when overseas. His remarks to the United Nations about Australia's *terra nullius* of the mind brought strong criticism in Australia.

The idea of a *terra nullius* of the mind was recalled in the *National Indigenous Times*, mentioned earlier, when it referred to the minds "of people who simply do not understand the complexities of the after-effects of colonisation", and that "The abuse and mistreatment of a traditionally unique and spiritual people continues today, often hidden from sight, *because* the injustices lay in the mind".[20]

Prime Minister Howard stated in reaction that "overwhelmingly Australians are quite open and tolerant and we have absorbed races in this country, more successfully than any country in the world".[21] Senator Bob McMullen, then Opposition Spokesperson for Aboriginal Affairs, said that Senator Ridgeway "had misread the community, and the level of support for reconciliation".[22] Other critical comment also positioned Australian whiteness as essentially benign, identifying "the position of whites as a group, and placing white Australians at the centre of an imagined nation" where it "absorbed" other nations, as the Prime Minister said, yet formed the backbone of support for the Indigenous people.[23]

Positioning Australian whiteness as essentially benign was of great importance to opponents of Pauline Hanson's reassertion of whiteness. Hanson, first elected to the Federal Parliament as in Independent, in March 1996 found popularity in her identification of a racist problem in Australia. By this she meant her perception of racism against the white population, driven by excessive funding of Indigenous (and multicultural bodies) by the Australian Government. She thus also positioned the majority white community as "perpetual victims" of Indigenous advantage.[24]

Her views were the subject of much analysis and denial. Such an explicit reassertion of whiteness moved it from the margins to the centre of political debate, where the benign whiteness at the centre of Australian society had long been assumed, and racism was deemed to be an aberration, as mentioned earlier.

The book *Two Nations: The Causes and Effects of the Rise of the One Nation Party in Australia*, published in 1998 with chapters by eighteen writers, saw Australia as being divided by Pauline Hanson. This divide operated in a number of ways. It was described by the then Federal Minister for Health, Michael Woodridge as a divide into two separate cultures, the "policy culture" and the "community culture".[25]

This divide made space to bring forward John Howard's remarks made in 1988 that indigenous rights and Asian immigration were divisive, and were extrapolated to set him apart from the majority of Australians who were part of "a remarkably tolerant nation".[26] John Howard had notably taken some days before condemning Pauline Hanson's views.

The mechanism of a divide caused by Pauline Hanson allowed both the "policy culture" and the "community culture" cited above to foster the divide between themselves, tolerant and non-racist, and the "racists", by declaring that she was wrong in her views. Ghasson Hage, in an article written during Pauline Hanson's election campaign, noted this as the establishment of "impeccable anti-racist credentials" rather than as trying "to understand and explain the phenomenon".[27]

This establishment of a place and a space for a benign and tolerant white Australia, has also been described as "soft Hansonism", where "the largely unconscious, thinly-veiled racist prejudices wrapped up in statements of good intentions that find expression throughout our society in varying degrees, is widespread".[28]

So what are we to understand about benign whiteness during the Howard years? That it is, on the one hand, a comfortable response to the threatening and worrying world out there and in here, as identified by D'Cruz and Steele and Hage above and, on the other, an uncertainty about the resurgence of an Anglo identity for Australia? That it is a continuing response to the reconciliation project that caught the hearts and minds of the white community; that Australian Whiteness Studies have allowed the tolerance implicit in benign whiteness to have a credible history, back to the 90 per cent support for the 1967 referendum on Aboriginal citizenship?

It may be all of those—and the process from Henry Reynolds' accounts of late 20th century attempted humanitarianism towards Indigenous people, to today when racism and racial prejudice are far less prevalent in white Australian society than they were a hundred years ago.

But Whiteness Studies, *ipso facto*, is about race and that conversation has not yet ended. Whiteness studies is precisely to create awareness of the relationship between whiteness and its racialised others. The question "why whiteness studies?" contains within it "why does it exist and who does it benefit"? "Why study it" and "whose ends does it serve and whose voice does it privilege"? Thus "how can we challenge it and explore it without reinforcing it?" [29] points to the further need to examine how it is understood.[30]

In an historical search, this leaves us with a divide between the questions raised in Whiteness Studies and the pragmatic policy position that a shift has been registered in the meanings attached to the words "whiteness", "race" and "racism". So that despite the possibility of a deeply ingrained racism in Australia, racism has been reconstructed in Australia as 'an individual moral aberration'.[31]

Thus the general practice of benign whiteness within or alongside understandings of Whiteness Studies, and under the shifting purview of present and past governments, has allowed the undemanding habit of tolerance to become comfortable, less worrying than facing a history of racialism.

End Notes

1. Rachael Standfield, "A remarkably tolerant nation? Constructions of benign whiteness in Australian political discourse", in *Borderlands e-journal,* http://www.borderlandsejournal.adelaide.edu.au, Vol. 3, No. 2, 2004, pp. 1-2.
2. Fiona Probyn, "Review" in Aileen Moreton-Robinson, ed., *Whitening Race*, Australian Humanities Review, Issue 35, June 2005, p. 1.
3. V.D.'Cruz & W. Steele, *Australia's Ambivalence Towards Asia* (Melbourne, Monash University Press, 2004) p. 55.
4. D'Cruz & Steele, p. 3.
5. D'Cruz & Steele, p. 4.
6. D'Cruz & Steele, p. 55.
7. R. Manchanda, "Militarised Hindu Nationalism and the Mass Media: Shaping a Hindutva Public Discourse', *South Asia*, Special Issue, The BJP and Governance in India, vol, XXV, no. 3, December 2002, p. 305.
8. *The Australian*, 15 December 2005, p. 10.
9. Robyn Wiegman, "Whiteness Studies and the Paradox of Particularity", *Boundary*, Vol. 2, No. 26 (3), 1999
10. *National Indigenous Times*, 23 June 2005, p. 19.
11. Ghasson Hage, "On Worrying: The Lost Art of the Well-administered National Cuddle", *Borderlands e-journal*, Vol. 2, No. 1, 2003, p. 1.

12. Jospeh Camilleri, "The Howard Years, Cultural Ambivalence and Political Dogma", *Borderlands e-journal*, Vol. 3, No. 3, 2004, pp. 1-2.
13. Fiona Nicoll, Editorial, *Australian Critical Race and Whiteness Studies Association Journal*, Vol. 1, 2005, p. 1.
14. Henry Reynolds DATE, *This Whispering in Our Hearts*, (Sydney: Allen & Unwin, 1998), p. 249
15. Jamie Mackie, "Reconciliation, Racial Prejudice and 'Soft Hansonism' in Australia's, future", in *Dissent*, No. 3, Spring 2000, p. 14
16. Irene Watson, 'Settled and unsettled spaces'. Paper presented at *Placing Race/ Locating Whitenes Conference*, Flinders University, South Australia, 2003,
17. Irene Watson, *Placing Race/Locating Whiteness.*
18. Rachael Standfield, 2004
19. Senator Aden Ridgeway, "Address to the UN Human rights Commission", 26 March, 2001, in Rachael Standfield, 2004.
20. *National Indigenous Times,* 23 June, 2005, p. 19 (Emphasis added).
21. *The Australian*, 27 March, 2001, p. 7.
22. *Herald Sun*, 27 March, 2001, p. 10.
23. Rachael Standfield, 2004.
24. A. Markus, 2001, *John Howard and the Remaking of Australia*, (Sydney, Allen & Unwin), pp. 151-52, 156
25. R. Manne *et al.*, 1998, *Two Nations: The Causes and Effects of the Rise of the One Party in Australia*, (Melbourne, Brookman Press, pp. 179-82.
26. Rachael Standfield, 2004
27. G. Hage, "The Limits of Anti-Racist Sociology", *The UTS Review*, 1995, Vol. 1, No. 1, p. 73.
28. *J. Mackie,* "Reconcilation, Racial Practice", p. 14.
29. Damien Riggs, "We don't Talk About Race Anymore': Power, Privilege and Critical Whiteness Studies", *Borderlands e-jounral*, Vol. 3, No. 2, 2004, p. 6.
30. Damien Riggs.
31. Fiona Nicoll, Editorial, *Australian Critical Race and Whiteness Studies Association Journal*, Vol. 1, 2005.

5

Indians in Fiji in the Nineteenth Century: An International Communication Perspective

PETER PUTNIS

The diasporic experience involves a consciousness of separation from a homeland. The intensity and salience of this experience of separation varies greatly according to the circumstances of the journey afar. Was the journey voluntary economic migration in search of a better life? Was it a flight from repression? Was it part of a colonising or imperial governance enterprise? Was it, as in the case of Indian emigration to Fiji, part of an indentured labour programme? The experience of separation following the journey abroad would also change as time passed and between generations as the immediate anguish of family separations gave way to recollection of a more distant past homeland—as first hand memory gave way, in a later generation, to emotional links with a more evidently textually constructed and imagined land of origin.

A further factor, the one which is the prime subject of this paper, relates to the conditions of communication between the diasporic community and the homeland-communication both at the level of personal and family links and at the more general level of shared information and experience via news media and the flow of cultural products between the homeland and the diasporic community. At one extreme we might think of the experience of separation as an "excommunication"—a complete break of communicative links; at the other (at least in our own time) we might think of physical separation as greatly mitigated by the opportunities provided by new technologies, in particular their capacity to create networked communities with a global reach. How did the Indians in Fiji in the nineteenth century fare in this respect? Were they totally cut off or could retain reasonably regular communicative links and hence a sense of connectedness with India could be maintained? Expressed in more abstract terms, what was the structural relationship between the transoceanic communication systems of the day and the new long-distance communication needs generated by the organised transportation of labour from India to a group of islands in the Pacific?

The nineteenth century was an age of great advances in communication across the globe, particularly through the establishment of regular steamship mail services and, in the second half of the century, a global telegraphic network. These new communication links both followed and further embedded the geo-political structures of empire and the emerging communication/ transport priorities of global capitalism. However, the extent and accessibility of communication links between newly created diasporas and homelands varied enormously from situation to situation. British migrants moving to the "neo-Britains" of nineteenth century Australia and New Zealand could, despite vast distances, see these far away places as, nevertheless, part of an expanded "British world" in which maintenance of links with home was a major priority of governments. The communication history of Australia in the nineteenth century involved transition from an initial state of "ex-communication" to a "re-bonding" as government-subsidised mail services and passenger and telegraphic links were established and routinised and the flow of news media and other cultural products from Britain to Australia facilitated. It is a history of isolation being slowly but surely overcome as relatively direct, purpose-built centre-periphery links were established between Britain and Australia which could sustain, even in distant Australia, a sense of imperial belonging. By contrast, communication links between India and the Indian community in Fiji were indirect, ill-suited to needs and, from the perspective of the imperial centre, entirely peripheral.

This paper explores the "communication experience with home" of the more than seventeen thousand Indians who emigrated to Fiji between 1879 and 1897 and of their almost three thousand ship-board born or Fijian-born children. It locates this experience in the communication network history of the Asia-Pacific region. The emigration of indentured labourers to Fiji continued till the 1920s but the focus of this paper is on the early period. The years 1879 to 1897 represent a kind of "first generation", covering as they do the time from the arrival of the first group from Calcutta in the cholera and small pox infected *Leonidas* on the 15 May 1879 till the single child, born during that first journey would, if she or he survived, have turned eighteen.

One should at the outset acknowledge that little is known of a direct nature about the desires, expectations and actual experiences of the "communication with home" of these indentured labourers. There appear to be no first-hand accounts from this early period.[1] But perhaps we can catch some glimpses of this experience, or at least gain some aid in imagining it, via a discussion of the general international communication conditions of the day and by seeing what can be gleaned from extant official sources such as the Annual Reports on Immigration tabled each year in Fiji's Legislative Council. This paper attempts at once to see something of the global forces that shaped the story of Indians in Fiji and their links with home, and yet also see, albeit fleetingly, something of the specific conditions of their "lives of separation."

Globalisation and Communication Links in the Asia-Pacific

By the late 1870s, when the first indentured labourers from India came to Fiji, the world was already functioning, to a significant degree, as a globalised economy wherein events in one part of the world had major consequences for people in countries far away. The American Civil War, it might be recalled, had led to a global cotton drought which had had a devastating effect on the Lancashire cotton industry. It was this cotton drought that had led to the expansion of European settler cotton plantations in Fiji and, subsequently, to the demand for Polynesian and later (though by this time largely to meet the needs of the sugar plantations) Indian labour. Global trade in goods and trade in labour went hand in hand. The indentured labour trade in areas like Fiji, which had not previously had slave-based economies, was intimately linked with a new phase of nineteenth century imperialism. Lands made available through imperial expansion were converted by entrepreneurial white settlers to sugar plantations dependent for their operations on cheap labour.[2] India was seen as an unlimited resource for such labour and was hence a key element in achieving the conjunction of capital, natural resources, and labour deemed necessary for a successful plantation economy. It was touted as such at the 1879 International Exhibition in Sydney, where the colonial Fijian authorities mounted a major display and extolled the virtues of investment in Fiji by claiming, amongst other things, that, "it is...satisfactory to know that should the supply of labour from Western Polynesia fail, there is India with its inexhaustible supply of coolies to fall back upon."[3] As Sarva Daman Singh has put it, "Indian indentured labour was the human subsidy paid, for the pecuniary profitability of Britain's colonies".[4]

Imperial expansion and economic globalisation went hand in hand with the development of communication networks of linked shipping and telegraphic routes. The distribution of these routes reflected the priorities of commerce and imperial ambition. The later nineteenth century communication history of the Asia-Pacific region is an inextricable aspect of the history of the expansion of the British Empire. As Daniel Headrick put it, "information was the lifeblood of European imperialism: business deals, administrative reports, news dispatches, and personal messages sustained the colonizers and assured them the support of their own people."[5] The tendrils of communication reached out eastwards from London, encouraged and usually subsidised by the distant colonists. Headrick notes that as early as 1825 the British community of Calcutta, "which felt isolated from its homeland—a round trip took a year or more—saw in steam a means of accelerating communications" and "offered a prize to the first steamer to make the trip in seventy days or less".[6] While this initiative failed, further efforts by the steam lobby in India led to the establishment of regular steamship mail services to and from London by the 1840s. A telegraphic link between England and India was established in the mid 1860s. Australia's steam lobby succeeded in having a mostly steamship mail service with England from the mid 1850s while a telegraph link with Europe was established in 1872. These developments also resulted in improved communication links between India and Australia.[7]

Fiji was an important communication link between Australia and America. Indeed Britain's annexation of Fiji in 1874 was in large part prompted by Fiji's strategic importance as a coaling port and its position in the direct marine line between Sydney and San Francisco. Fiji's white settlers, many with established links to Australia, saw the annexation of Fiji by Britain as an extension of Australian interests with one prominent campaigner for annexation even asserting that, "the opinion of myself and the majority of settlers is that Fiji is a necessity to, almost a birthright of, the Australian colonies."[8] For the colonists of Fiji the priority was the establishment of regular communication links between Fiji and Sydney between which a regular mail service was established in 1873.[9] Fiji was linked by telegraph to Sydney (and thence via existing telegraphic links to India) in 1902 when the Pacific cable between Australia and Canada was completed.

Such communication as there was between India and Fiji around 1880 was via Australia or, in the case of shipping which did not call at an Australian port, via southern Australian waters. There were no established passenger-or merchant-shipping routes between India and Fiji linking the Indian and the Pacific oceans across the north of Australia. There was at the time a monthly mail service between Europe and Australia conducted by the Peninsular and Oriental Steamship Company (P & O). This service had, as one of its hubs, Point de Galle in Ceylon. Here mail could be transferred from steamers which had travelled from Bombay and Calcutta to Galle, to steamers travelling to Melbourne and Sydney via King George's Sound on the south-west tip of Australia. The journey from India to Australia took approximately four weeks. In 1873, a monthly mail service was established between Sydney and San Francisco via Fiji by the American-owned Pacific Mail Steamship Company. The journey from Sydney to Fiji took about six days. Hence the postal route between India and Fiji and vice-versa was via Australia. The post between Fiji and Sydney was subsidised by Fiji's colonial government. However, mail going on to India was charged at a much higher relative rate. In 1879, the postal rate for an ordinary letter between Fiji and Sydney was two pence while the rate between Fiji and India was one shilling. It is significant to note that it was more than the rate from Fiji to England via San Francisco which was eight pence.[10]

As noted earlier, imperial expansion and the globalisation of agricultural production and trade were linked to large population movements and to the development of communication networks based on the technologies of the steamship and telegraph. However, the resultant global order could involve deeply disjunctive relationships between the flow of people and the global configuration of communication systems.[11]

Conditions of Separation

Fiji's indentured labour programme was made possible by legal and logistical connections between India and Fiji arising from the administration of the British Empire. Northrup has noted, with respect to Indian indentured labour as a whole, that "most of the 1.3 million Indian migrants who ventured overseas were processed through British depots, travelled on British ships, and worked in British colonies, with the whole operation co-ordinated and regulated by British officials in Westminster and New Delhi."[12] While indentured labour schemes have regularly been portrayed as a disguised continuation of slavery, recent scholarship on the Indian portion of the trade has emphasised the voluntary nature of most indentured migration and the "push" factors such as poverty and food shortages which motivated Indians to emigrate. Northrup argues that "in comparison to the China labor trade, Indian migration was effectively regulated from an earlier stage" and "had fewer lapses and abuses."[13] While there were many instances of misrepresentation and coercion in the recruitment process, "the Indian trade was constructed and run to maximize consent and understanding."[14]

It is also noteworthy that the migrants did not solely derive from the lower stratas of society. Brij Lal's analysis of the caste composition of immigrants to Fiji in the first phase of immigration suggests that Fiji Indians comprised a normal cross section of the North Indian population. Brahmins and other high castes constituted about twelve per cent of immigrants.[15] This is important from a communication perspective. Shiu Prasad has noted that, "since Brahmins in India belonged to the literate class, many of them brought their own holy books to Labasa and continued occasional religious discussions with other castes. Because they were more conversant with the principles of Hinduism, could speak fluently in what seemed to be correct Hindustani to other castes, and wrote letters to relatives in India for illiterate people, many of them commanded respect".[16]

Many indentured labourers were doubtless victims of deception. Others are likely to have made a considered decision that circumstances abroad would be better than those at home. Few, however, embarking for Fiji would have had sufficient knowledge of geography to understand just how isolated a place their destination was and how distant they would be from home and kin. The sailing ships specially chartered to transport Indian indentured labourers to

Fiji travelled far south, all the way around Australia, and then north to Fiji. This gives one pause for thought. Let us consider for a moment the journey of the *Poonah*, which left Calcutta on the 28 June 1882 with 491 immigrants (311 men, 133 women, thirty-one children and sixteen infants) on board, and arrived in Fiji, after an eighty-one day non-stop voyage, on 17 September. Fourteen persons died on that voyage. The Acting Agent General of Immigration noted that sickness and deaths were more frequent during the latter than the earlier months of the voyage and speculated that "this may possibly be accounted for by the southerly course which has been observed by sailing vessels making the voyage…and the cold weather encountered in consequence."[17] Little wonder there was cold weather, given that the *Poonah* would have been in the Southern ocean in winter when temperatures could fall below freezing. Or consider the voyage of the *Ganges* which left Calcutta on the 14 April 1885 with 544 immigrants on board, twenty-one of them infants, and arrived in Fiji seventy-two days later on the 27 June. There were eighteen deaths, nine of them of infants. In this case the deaths were thought by the Agent General not to be attributable to the weather since the period of the journey covered a "healthy period in most parts of the southern hemisphere" and that the *Ganges* reached its highest latitude of the voyage (i.e. its furthest point south) of 40 degrees south as it passed through Bass Strait between Tasmania and mainland Australia. Here it also encountered the minimum temperature reached during the voyage of fifty-one degrees Fahrenheit.[18]

Knowing that the journey that these people made was via a southern route around the continent of Australia through Bass Strait, a route notorious for its gales and inclement weather, suggests to us that for these immigrants the journey was not only a great ordeal but truly a journey afar. It was a journey across climatic zones and hemispheres. Fiji to them must have seemed a world away from India. Were they, one can't help wondering, prepared for a voyage of this nature? One can, with Satendra Nandan, only imagine "the sense of geography" these Indian villagers brought to this journey. These villagers had, till this journey, "scarcely ventured outside their ancestral *habitus*—that amalgam of practices linking habit with inhabitance"—that shaped their lives and constituted their "structured world".[19]

The lack of any direct shipping route between Fiji and India also meant that there was no easy way back home. The Government ordinance covering the conditions of indentured labourers in Fiji guaranteed a free return passage to India after ten years. However, there was some uncertainty, with respect to the first groups of immigrants, whether this right could be claimed after an initial five years of indenture. In 1885 two immigrants and their families claimed the right to return to India because they had terminated their indentures after five years. This presented a problem for the Government because of the uncertainty of the legal situation and "in consequence of the absence of any means of direct transit from the Colony to India, passengers having to change steamers at least twice via Australia and Ceylon." In the upshot, it was decided to send these families, as well as three chronic invalids, back to India via this steamship passenger route "as an experiment" under the supervision of an "English-speaking sardar [foreman] who was an old West Indian coolie and his wife". The Agent General of Immigration reported that "they eventually reached Calcutta, though at a very considerable cost, and after undergoing various delays and difficulties; and on the whole the experiment cannot be viewed with sufficient favour to warrant its repetition."[20] The practice was not repeated. The first realistic opportunity the remainder of the immigrants had to return to India was in 1889, ten years after the arrival of that first immigrant ship, the *Leonidas*, when the government, according to its obligation, chartered a vessel for this purpose. Of the 480 Indians who had arrived on that first ship 148 took the opportunity to return, together with sixty-nine of their children who had been born in Fiji. Many would have decided to stay on but many others would have died in that decade given that mortality rates amongst the Indians were about four times those of European settlers.[21] Between 1879 and 1889 the total number of Indians introduced to Fiji and their Fiji-born children was 7,161. But in the same period 1,612 Indians, or well over twenty percent of the population, had died.

In the period 1879 to 1897 over 17,000 Indians were transported to Fiji in thirty separate shippings. Most migrants were aged between eleven and eighteen.[22] All over ten were classified under the special "Indian classification" as adults. After the first arrival in 1879 no further immigrants came for almost three years but there were two shiploads in 1882. In 1884 there were four shiploads but the usual pattern became two shiploads per year.

Reports on Indian immigration tabled annually in Fiji's Legislative Council provide a chillingly depersonalised record of this traffic in labour. Statistical tables about arrivals cover numbers of embarkations, deaths at sea, number hospitalised on arrival, and numbers allotted to various plantations. Overall population statistics record births, mortality rates and causes of death. Then there are the extensive tables on labour disputes and court appearances, measurement of work, and records of wages, which averaged less than 1 shilling per day. In this bureaucratic discourse, the Indians of Fiji are represented as anonymous but highly regulated units of labour. Concern may be expressed in these Reports about mortality rates, but it is the detached concern of officials faced with negative statistics rather than any concern which springs from an engagement with individual cases. Needless to say, in these texts the Indians of Fiji have no voice.

We as readers are left to wonder at the nature of the actual experiences of the people of whom these reports are such a partial, de-personalised representation. What, for instance, did it mean for the evolving Indian community that, amongst immigrants, the male population was two and a half times that of the female population? What can be inferred about living conditions and emotional states from the long lists of causes of death including the suicides attributed to "melancholia" and "nostalgia"? The immigration authorities acknowledged that the immigrants would experience what the authorities called "nostalgia" for their homeland and families, but this was something that they expected immigrants to soon overcome.[23] But this was not always the case as we can judge by the comment of the Agent-General for Immigration on the eight suicides that took place in 1900: "The suicides were of the usual character in cases among indentured people. They were new immigrants. One of them walked into the bush and was found hanging there a week afterwards. No other cause than depression of spirits or nostalgia can be assigned for these acts. In one case a woman drowned herself after a quarrel with her husband."[24]

What suffering and injustice must have lain behind the Agent-General of Immigration's detached, perhaps plaintive, observation of the "task work" system that

> [m]anual labour cannot be regulated or assessed with that preciseness which is possible in the case of machinery; and, whether carelessness or indifference be the cause, the fact remains that cases were brought to notice, and more possibly escaped notice, in which immigrants were committed to prison for the non-performance of acts that they were not capable of performing, and in one or more instances the condition of immigrants was found to be such, on entering gaol, as to necessitate their speedy relegation to hospital.[25]

On a more positive note, the Reports also record efforts by the Indian immigrants to build community resources including schools. While there was no Government provision for the education of the Indian children, the establishment of plantation based schooling is recorded as early as 1882 with the Agent-General for Immigration reporting that on an official visit to the estate of Rabi he "had the gratification of witnessing the highly creditable progress made by a number of adults and children in reading, writing and arithmetic."[26]

Provisions for Communication

The nature and length of the journey from India to Fiji would, one imagines, have suggested to Indian immigrants that Fiji was a world away from India and that this journey did indeed mean total separation despite assurances they probably were given by recruiters. But it was clearly not the intention of immigrants to completely sever links with their homeland. Indeed, the length of separation involved in indenture was an important issue for them. In the negotiations in 1877/78 between Fiji and India, the Indian authorities warned that Fiji's proposal that immigrants be only entitled to a free passage home after ten years, rather than the five that pertained in some other colonies, was likely to make recruitment difficult.[27] The Agent-General for Immigration for Fiji replied that the anticipated costs of the programme, whereby every adult would "cost about twenty-seven pounds sterling by the time he is allotted", meant that he could not see "how it would pay the colony to import them for a shorter period." He added: "From enquiries made I have ascertained that though at times difficulty is found in obtaining the number of immigrants indentured by some of the colonies yet, when there is a scarcity of food in some parts of India much greater numbers than those indentured can be found" and that, "the Colony of Fiji must therefore in this respect…be permitted to take its chance along with the other colonies."[28] Food shortages in India, it appears, were a necessary "stimulus" to indentured emigration under the Fijian conditions and, arguably, the existence of such shortages was necessary for the recruitment system to work. Certainly, acceptance of the conditions was not an indication that communication with home was unimportant.

The issue of communication was raised in the 1877/78 negotiations regarding immigration between the Colonial Governments of India and Fiji. The Indian Government asked, amongst other things, "what facilities exist for communication with India, and for the transmission thither of savings which the immigrants may make?"[29] Fiji's Agent-General for Immigration replied that there was a monthly steamer to Sydney subsidised by the Government of Fiji and regular steamers from Sydney to India.[30] This cursory answer appears to have satisfied the bureaucratic needs of the Indian authorities. They made no further comment. The very fact that the issue of communication was formally raised is important since it underlines the point that, in theory at least, schemes of indentured labour brought with them communication responsibilities. For example, the ability to repatriate money was an essential element of such schemes.

The specially chartered ships which conveyed Indians to Fiji from 1879 and provided return journeys from 1889 were a channel of communication as well as the vehicle for transport. However, while new arrivals would have been a major source of news from India, these ships were too infrequent and irregular to function effectively as a communication link. Indians in Fiji who wanted to maintain regular links with home needed to fall back on the postal system. This system was not, of course, designed to meet their needs involving as it did bureaucratic procedures conducted in English which would have been quite alien to most of the immigrants. Despite this, Fiji Indians learnt to successfully use the system. Indeed, it could be argued that, spurred on by their circumstances of separation, Fiji Indians became "early adopters" of western modes of communication and financial transaction.

The history of postal arrangements between Fiji and India in the last two decades of the nineteenth century (and the experience of these arrangements by Fijian Indians) arose from a unique interaction between global developments and local practices and priorities. One of the most important developments in international communication in the late nineteenth century was the establishment of a "penny post" throughout the British Empire in 1898 after a long campaign, particularly in Britain and Canada.[31] At the global (or, at least, Imperial) level great importance was attached to cheap postal communication as a way of unifying the British Empire and, while the focus was on ease of communication between London and major centres in Canada, Australia, India and South Africa, "peripheral communications" such as those between Fiji and India also benefited. In contrast, postal communication between Fiji and India was seen by Fijian postal authorities as a low priority, indeed a nuisance. Given these oppositional forces between the global and the local it is perhaps not surprising that postal arrangements for Fijian Indians writing to India underwent quite dramatic shifts in the last decades of the nineteenth century.

During the initial phase of immigration, a system of free postage for Fijian immigrants writing to and remitting money to India was developed utilising both the post office and the services of immigration agents in India. The arrangement was formalised in 1883 when the Fijian Governor confirmed that he "approves of the transmission of letters and remittances by Indian Immigrants in this Colony to their friends in India under cover to the Agent in Calcutta On Her Majesty's Service."[32] Such postal arrangements were, according to the Governor, "quite customary…in Coolie Colonies as a matter of policy in order to induce recruits to come to Fiji to meet their friends."[33] They grew out of the practices of the global trade in Indian labour and were viewed as an aid to recruitment.

In 1886, one hundred and forty-one immigrants used the free postage service to India leading the Agent-General of Immigration to comment that, "immigrants have not availed themselves as largely of the facilities offered for them for correspondence as might have been expected."[34] However, for whatever reason, there was subsequently a marked increase in usage and in 1887 four hundred and twenty five letters were sent, that is about one letter per fourteen persons in the Indian community, including children and infants.[35]

Opposition to this scheme developed amongst local bureaucrats who saw no special obligation to the indentured labourers as far as communication facilities were concerned. Unfortunately for the Indian community, their increasing use of the free mail service contributed to a decision to discontinue it from 31 March 1888. Their entitlement, once it became popular, was re-construed as a "loss of revenue" which leads one to suspect that the free service was really only acceptable to the bureaucracy if little used. Post office officials had always been opposed to the scheme. Indian mail caused "headaches for the postal authorities."[36] They complained of the cost and the loss of revenue. In 1886, the Colonial Postmaster wrote to the Colonial Secretary complaining that, "not only does the Department lose one shilling postage on every half-ounce letter so sent, but we have to pay Melbourne one shilling and seven pence an ounce for carrying same." He objected that Fiji could not afford to lose this revenue and that "on principle it is an injustice to exempt one portion of the community from paying dues as it imposes a heavier burden of taxation on the remaining portion." He was supported in these views by the Acting Colonial Secretary who opined that, "I believe Indians are all able in most cases to pay the postage of their own letters."[37] The comment is quite remarkable given that, at the time, the average daily wage of Indian labourers was around eight pence a day and that letters to India carried a largely un-subsidised postage rate of one shilling while Europeans sending letters to Sydney or Auckland paid two pence and received proportionately much higher subsidies.

It is also evident that the post office was not well equipped to handle Indian correspondence and saw little responsibility to develop its capacity in this area. Historian of the Fiji post J.G. Rodger noted that by the late 1880s, "increasing numbers of letters from India to Indians in Fiji addressed wholly in Indian languages, created an almost insuperable problem for the postal authorities." In 1889 J.W. Davidson, Clerk and Hindustani Interpreter in the Immigration Department, who assisted in the distribution of letters, told the Agent-General for Immigration that, "Last time I went to the PO to read the addresses on Indian letters I found a heap which I had not the time to go through. Every mail brings letters addressed in hieroglyphics to the coolies here, and it seems these letters accumulate in the PO without the slightest prospect of their ever reaching the hands of the persons to whom they belong…Mr. Walker the Colonial Postmaster is anxious to get rid of these letters as the extent to which they are piling up is getting alarming."[38]

Clearly, the Fijian Post Office regarded correspondence to and from India as a nuisance and would have welcomed the decision of Fiji's Executive Council to cease the free service from the end of March 1888. That decision was made in November 1887 and reported in the *Fiji Royal Gazette* of December 2, 1887. Tellingly, the matter was regarded as being of little importance to the European readers of *The Fiji Times. The Times* noted the publication of the *Gazette* in its edition of December 3, 1887. It recorded various minor appointments that had been announced, provided details of how claims could be made against the Government for outstanding accounts, and noted that "the Bulletin of the Botanical Department, Jamaica, is available at the Colonial Secretary's Office." There was no mention of the radically changed postal arrangements for Fiji's Indians. Indeed, the paper concluded its report with the remark that, "the remaining portion of the *Gazette* refers to matters which have no public importance."[39]

For a number of years the postal rate between Fiji and India remained at one shilling. However, as indicated previously, in the last decade of the nineteenth century Fiji benefited from a concerted move to lower postal rates across the British Empire in the interests of imperial unity. In this dimension of the nineteenth century globalisation of international communication Indian Fijians found themselves to be beneficiaries. In October 1891, after Fiji joined the Universal Postal Union, the rate to India was reduced to 5 pence, but as Rodgers has pointed out the biggest breakthrough was the introduction of "universal penny postage" on Christmas Day 1898 when the cost of letters to India and also to the United Kingdom fell dramatically to one penny. Ironically, for a time postage from Fiji to India was less than postage to Australia which remained at two pence until the "penny post" was extended to Australia in 1905.[40] Doubtless because of the cheapening of postal rates the average number of letters received each month in Fiji from India rose about sixty percent between 1897 and 1902 from 221 to 352.[41]

We can see, then, that by 1897, that is eighteen years since the arrival of the first group of immigrants in 1879, the quantity of postal communication between Fiji and India had increased greatly. Rodgers records that in 1897 around 2,650 letters arrived from India and one assumes that a similar number would have gone to India from Fiji. By this time the Fijian Indian population had grown to around 12,000. Nevertheless, it appears that a significant proportion of Fijian Indians were in some form of correspondence with their homeland thus reflecting a continuing sense of connectedness.[42]

While the Fijian Indian population at the end of 1897 was recorded as being 11,970 there had been, between 1879 and 1897, 17,349 arrivals. In addition, 2,971 births had been recorded. So the total number of Indians who lived in Fiji for some or all of the eighteen years in question was 20,220. Of these, 3,550 had died by the end of 1897. 4810 are recorded as having left the colony.[43] The vast majority of those who had left Fiji had returned to India though a few ended up in Australia. Indian immigrants who had completed their indenture could apply for passports and leave Fiji at their own expense. In 1889, 179 immigrants did this. Of these 136 returned to India; thirty-four stated their destination as Sydney and one, Melbourne. In later years more would probably have chosen Australia as a destination but for the fact that a new restrictive Immigration Ordinance was introduced in 1892 which prevented Indians travelling to Australian Colonies "without the consent of the Governor".[44] The Ordinance was designed to cut off the possibility of emigration to Australia and would have been passed at the behest of the Australian colonies in the context of an emerging "white Australia" policy.

Response to the Indian Famine of 1896/7

As was indicated early in this paper, little is known of a direct nature about the experiences of Indians in Fiji communicating with home and receiving news from home. However, extant records convey something of the "communication conditions" under which Fiji Indians lived. There were many communication barriers. Many attempts at communication were unsuccessful. Rodger tells us that in 1897 there were two hundred and eighty eight letters which reached Fiji which were returned to India, being judged as undeliverable.[45] What important news, one wonders, did they contain?

But in all this one point is clear. Despite all the difficulties of language, literacy, distance, geography, officialdom, and life conditions, it is evident that the sense of connectedness between Indians in Fiji and their homeland remained very strong indeed. Further telling evidence for this claim can be found in the response in Fiji to the Indian famine of 1896/97.

In 1896, India's monsoon arrived late. By August there had still been almost no rain. By November famine conditions were officially recognised with the hardest hit areas being the North-Western provinces, a major source of Indian emigrants. First news of trouble was published in *The Fiji Times* on 25 November, 1896, in the form of a telegram, datelined London, November 9, which would have been copied from an Australian newspaper recently arrived by steamship from Sydney. It read: "News from Bombay states that 5,000 starving people created a riot at Sholapur in the Bombay Presidency today and looted the grain stores. The police were compelled to fire upon the rioters, killing four and wounding six." Hence, news about the famine in India reached Fiji via London and Sydney and was framed by a British perspective on the tragedy. This pattern reflected the international news distribution system of the day whereby London was the hub for receipt and dispersion of global news. News of the famine would have been telegraphed to London by the Indian branch office of Reuters news agency. From there it would have been distributed globally including (ironically via India) to Sydney. The final leg of the journey to Fiji would have been by steamship, until the opening of the Pacific cable in 1902.

First mention of the word "famine" in *The Fiji Times* was in a report, datelined London, January 1, which appeared on 23 January 1897 and stated that the "Lord Mayor of London has declined to open an Indian Famine Relief Fund until he has been requested by the Government to take such steps." A fuller report, noting amongst other things that a relief fund had been established, appeared on 30 January, 1897 under the heading "The Famine in India." It consisted of a series of London telegrams datelined between 12 January and 17 January reporting on relief efforts and noting the extent of the crisis. On the 17 February 1897, *The Fiji Times* announced that an Indian Famine Relief Fund had been established in Fiji, appealed for support for the fund, and indicated that the paper would be acknowledging subscribers through its columns. Over the next few months 1,274 pounds was donated to the fund. Of this, 811 pounds was given by Indian immigrants. The Chairman of the fund noted that, "the subscriptions [of Indian immigrants] ranged from three pence to five pounds...the number who declined to subscribe might be counted on the fingers of one hand." In the same period private remittances to India also increased sharply from 196 remittances, valued at 1022 pounds in 1895 to 590 remittances valued at 2650 pounds in 1897.[46] In all, payments of well over 2000 pounds, that is around two day's wages for every adult and child, can be attributed to famine relief. Even *The Fiji Times*, not known for its sympathy for the plight of Indian immigrants, was moved to comment that, "These figures speak eloquently for the generosity of our fellow subjects from India, and it is worthy of note that a large number of the indentured labourers have given a week's earnings and over."[47] We shouldn't make too much of *The Fiji Times*' expression of fellowship with Indian immigrants. This was surely hypocritical given the paper's usual advocacy of plantation interests against those of indentured labourers. But one cannot deny the point made. The figures do speak eloquently of the strength of the emotional connection Fiji Indians had with their homeland. This connection was maintained despite the physical separation and the tenuousness and unsuitability of the communication links between Fiji and India available to Fiji Indians at that time.

Conclusion

Indians who emigrated as indentured labourers to Fiji in the late nineteenth century maintained strong links with their homeland despite the fact that the available means of communication were ill-suited to their needs and, in certain periods, were very expensive. There was a disjunction between the communication needs generated by this particular movement of people and the configuration and operational priorities of a communication system which had been developed to meet the needs of European settlers. Some effort was made to ameliorate this problem in the early years of the programme via a free postage scheme but this was dropped in 1888. An analysis of the changing "communication circumstances" of Indians in Fiji demonstrates how their situation was determined by an interaction of global developments such as the "penny post" movement and local factors such as an unsympathetic postal bureaucracy. Spurred by the circumstances of separation, Indians in Fiji adapted as best they could to "modern" communication methods, albeit with at best grudging support from colonial authorities.

End Notes

1. Satendra Nandan notes that "out of the deracinating experience of girmit in Fiji only two fragments have emerged, both by a girmit man named Totaram Sanadhya. His *My Twenty-one Years in Fiji* and *The Story of the Haunted Line*, both autobiographical fragments, are now priceless pieces. Both narratives were ghost-written in Hindi with the help of Bonarsidas Chaturvedi, a journalist and friend of Mahatma Gandhi." *Fiji: Paradise in Pieces* (Adelaide: The Centre for Research in the New Literatures in English, 2000), p. 90. There are some first hand accounts from later periods, notably those collected by Shiu Prasad, *Indian Indentured Workers in Fiji* (Suva: South Pacific Social Sciences Association, [1974]).
2. David Northrup, *Indentured Labor in the Age of Imperialism, 1834-1922* (Cambridge: Cambridge University Press, 1995).
3. *Fiji at the International Exhibition 1879* (Sydney: Foster and Fairfax, 1879), p. 11.
4. S.D. Singh, The Indian Diaspora, in Adesh Pal & Tapas Chakrabardi, eds., *Theorizing and Critiquing Indian Diaspora* (New Delhi: Creative Books, 2004), p. 94.
5. Daniel R. Headrick, *The Tools of Empire: Technology and European Imperialism in the Nineteenth Century*, (NewYork: Oxford University Press, 1981), p. 129.
6. Headrick, p. 20.
7. For an analysis of links between the communication histories of India and Australia see Peter Putnis, The Collins connection: Reuters in India and Australia, *Communicator: Quarterly Journal of the Indian Institute of Mass Communication*, Vol. XXXV, No. 4, 2000, pp. 13-21.
8. Mr. Thurston, Prime Minister to Thakombau, in March 1870 quoted in the 1871 petition proposing Britain's annexation of Fiji.
9. J.G. Rodger, *The Postal History of Fiji 1876-1910* (Suva: Philatelic Society of Fiji, 1983), p. 157.
10. Annual Report on Indian Immigration for 1882, in Fiji Dept. of Immigration, *Annual Reports on Indian Immigration to Fiji, 1879-1920* (Suva: Central Archives of Fiji and the Western Pacific High Commission). Microfilm copy held at the National Library of Australia.
11. For a discussion of such disjunctive relationships see Arjun Appadurai, *Modernity at Large: Cultural Dimensions of Globalization.* (Minneapolis: University of Minnesota Press, 1966).
12. Northrup, p. 60.
13. Northrup, p. 60.
14. Northrup, p. 70.
15. Brij V. Lal, Fiji Girmitiyas: the Background to Banishment, in Vijay Mishra ed., *Rama's Banishmen: A Centenary Tribute to the Fiji Indians 1879-1979* (London: Heinemann Educational Books, 1979), pp. 12-39.
16. Prasad, p. 34.
17. Annual Report on Indian Immigration for the Year 1882.
18. Annual Report on Indian Immigration for the year 1885.

19. *Nandan*, p. 102.
20. Annual Report on Indian Immigration for the year 1885.
21. Annual Report on Indian Immigration for 1893, p. 362.
22. Deryck Scarr, *Fiji: A Short History* (Sydney: George Allen & Unwin, 1984), p. 81.
23. For example, in discussing the motivations of Indian emigrants, the Secretary to the Government of India G.H.M. Batten, commented "emigrants, in leaving this country for a distant field of labour, look, not to be gaining of a mere subsistence...but to the prospect of saving money with which either to return home or to establish themselves (when the first effects of nostalgia have passed away) as settlers in the colony." G.H.M. Batten to the Agent-General for Immigration in Fiji, 15 February, 1878. In *Fiji Royal Gazette*, 1May, 1878, p. 83.
24. *Annual Report on Indian Immigration for 1900*, p. 19.
25. *Annual Report on Indian Immigration for 1886*, pp. 462-3.
26. Annual Report on Indian Immigration for 1882. Unfortunately, such developments appear to have had mixed success. Twelve years later, in 1894, the Agent-General reported that "various voluntary efforts have been spasmodically made by free immigrants to start schools and get their children educated in Suva and elsewhere. The want of cohesion amongst them, and of confidence in the teachers available caused these efforts to fail." "Annual Report...1894", p. 477. It is evident that there were still no government provided schools for Indian immigrants.
27. G.H.M. Batten to Agent—General of Immigration for Fiji, 4 December, 1877 in *Fiji Royal Gazette*, 23 March, 1879, p. 69.
28. Charles Mitchell to G.H.M. Batten, 27 December, 1877 in *Fiji Royal Gazette*, 23 March, 1879, p. 73.
29. G.H.M. Batten, Officiating Secretary to the Government of India to C. Mitchell, Agent-General of Immigration in Fiji, 6 November, 1877 in *Fiji Royal Gazette*, 9 February, 1878, p. 29.
30. C. Mitchell to G.H.M. Batten, 13 November, 1877. In *Fiji Royal Gazette*, 9 February, 1878, p. 34.
31. For an outline of this campaign, and notably Canada's role, see Robert Pike, "National Interest and Imperial Yearnings: Empire Communications and Canada's Role in Establishing the Imperial Penny Post", *Journal of Imperial and Commonwealth History*, Vol. 33, No. 3, Fall 1998, pp. 5-30.
32. *Rodger*, pp. 170-171.
33. *Rodger*, p. 171.
34. *Annual Report on Indian Immigration for 1886*, p. 468.
35. *Annual Report on Indian Immigration for 1887*, p. 368.
36. *Rodger*, p. 169.
37. *Rodger*, p. 170.
38. *Rodger*, p. 171.
39. *The Fiji Times*, 3 December, 1887.
40. *Rodger*, pp. 173-4.
41. *Rodger*, p. 172.
42. This number of letters, one should note, sits uneasily with the standard view that the emigrants were nearly all illiterate. It is, however, consistent with Brij

V. Lal's analysis of the caste composition of the North Indian immigrants of this period noted earlier.

43. *Annual Report on Immigration*, 1897, p. 424.
44. *Annual Report on Immigration*, 1893.
45. *Rodger*, p. 172.
46. Annual Report on Indian Immigration, 1887, pp. 435-36.
47. *The Fiji Times*, 27 March, 1897, p. 2.

The author would like to acknowledge the assistance of Ms Christine Wise who undertook substantial primary research for this paper.

6

State and Citizenship in the Asia-Pacific: A Case Study of Japan and Australia

VARALAXMI NAIK

The study of migration and migrant populations has, in recent times, seen a new dynamism as the rate and diversity of communities that have begun to migrate across the world has increased dramatically in the last two decades. Understanding the nature and politics of migration has become important to theorising globalisation. This is in sharp contrast to earlier studies of globalisation that focused on the flow of capital as against labour across national borders. The attention to migration, may in part, be attributed to the increased visibility of Third World communities in the First World and the attendant cultural tensions produced in the mainstream national culture as well as internally within immigrant communities.

The process of globalisation and compression of 'time and space', following the phenomenal advancement in the technologies of transport and communication, has given rise to closer interaction between numbers of a community displaced across the world in different countries. Any process of emigration involves physical movement of people across the boundaries of their nation-states. They invariably carry with them a socio-cultural baggage which consists of, among other things, (i) a predefined social identity, (ii) a set of religious beliefs and practices, (iii) a framework of norms and values governing family and kinship, (iv) food habits and dress and, above all, (v) a language. They settle in the host society as immigrants and strive to maintain their relations with the kith and kin at the place of their origin.

These immigrants become a permanent feature of the host society once they acquire the citizenship and their hopes for returning to their 'motherland' gradually recede. More importantly, the migrants are not inevitably and irrevocably cut off completely from the land of their origin.

While the study of diasporic and transnational cultural flows, with the migrant as the subject of such cultural productions, has provided invaluable insights, the political-economic context and implications of migration have received less attention. Most specifically, the role of the State in producing the migrant as cultural subjects of globalisation is largely unexamined. Some theorists have been far more cautious and have resisted the suggestion that the nation-state is becoming irrelevant. The State influences not only the 'fact' of migration but is also part of constructing the 'mental space' of migrant subjects.

Attempt is made here to draw attention to these concerns and contradictions that crop up as a result of movement of people into new cultures. The dilemmas and the notions while on one side satisfy the nationalist, on the other side generate international pressure for human rights. One such issue is citizenship, which provides legitimacy for people to stay and ask for more benefits from the government concerned. How these issues are addressed by two nations in the Asia-Pacific, i.e., Australia and Japan—the discrimination made towards the immigrants, policies of the state, prevalent notions on immigrants and of their rights and domestic compulsions—are the specific subject matter.

Immigration and growing cultural diversity poses a dual challenge to nation-states. First, admitting the other into the national community through citizenship appears as a threat to national cohesion and identity. The process of immigration has become so rapid that there is no time to obliterate difference, let alone to forget it. Second, sharing a shrinking social cake with new groups appears as a threat to the conditions of local workers. The social polarisation brought about by economic restructuring and policies of privatisation and deregulation leaves little room for minority rights. It is much easier to turn these groups into the scapegoats for the social crisis, by blaming them not only for their own marginality, but also for the decline in general standards. Migration is therefore seen as a central aspect of the North-South conflict, and migrants may be perceived as infiltrators who will drag the rich countries down to Third World poverty.

Immigration and Australia

Australia prides itself on its capacity to integrate immigrants, but many of their aboriginal people are excluded from most of the real benefits of citizenship.[1] Citizenship in nation-states is deeply *differentiated.* Such differentiation has always been a characteristic feature of citizenship.[2] Globalisation means rapidly increasing mobility of people across national borders. The period since 1980 has been marked by migrations of all kinds: temporary and permanent movements; economic migrations and refugee exoduses; individual and family flows; highly skilled specialists and manual workers.

In Australia, where immigrants rapidly became citizens and voters, politicians and officials found they had to take account of the needs and values of ethnic communities. The result was the rise of multiculturalism as a government strategy combining the principles of cultural diversity and social equality.[3] The state recognised the legitimacy of distinct communities with their own languages, religions and cultural practices, while at the same time adopting measures to ensure that members of these communities had equal access to government services and education, and protection against discrimination.

In contrast to the Pacific Island states whose national survival relies on having a substantial number of their citizens living outside the country, Australia is frequently cited as an immigrant country whose national development has been predicated on its openness to migrants for permanent settlement. Certainly, with nearly one quarter of its population born overseas and over 40 per cent either overseas born or having at least one parent who is an immigrant, Australia is far more a 'country of immigration' than the United States of America. As a nation built on extensive immigration, Australia superficially appears as a country where migration without borders has been effectively implemented. In reality this is to misunderstand the highly complex nature of Australia's migration regime and how it has been developed and operates. In particular, it ignores the strategies used to ensure that high levels of immigration and settlement have been achieved with what is, by international standards, a very low level of social conflict. Since the first British settlement, the colonial administrations and then the Australian state have played a major role in promoting and controlling migration entry and settlement.[4] In the first instance, active state intervention was a prerequisite for population growth in a country distant from Europe and proximate to populous Asian countries such as China and India.

The 1970s saw several major shifts in the immigration policy. First, Australia began to experience substantial levels of unemployment with structural change in the economy, the movement of manufacturing jobs away from Australia, and the entry of the baby-boom cohorts into the labour force. Immigration policy shifted from an emphasis on the recruitment of semi-skilled and skilled foreign workers for manufacturing to a more complex programme with four main components: Economic migration: Attraction of people with skills in demand in Australia; Family migration: Relatives of Australian residents (specific regulations of this part of the programme have changed over the subsequent years);

Refugee and humanitarian migration; and Special categories. The largest is New Zealanders who can move more or less freely across the Tasman Sea.

One of the most significant changes in Australian migration policies during the 1990s was the abandonment of the long-standing opposition to temporary labour migration. This opposition was forged in the 19th century with the growth of the trade union movement and its involvement in the campaigns to prevent Asian migration it saw as a potential threat to the hard-earned gains of the Australian working class. As a result, migration to Australia has always been viewed as involving permanent settlement and there were only extremely limited opportunities for entry by those who did not qualify for permanent residence.

The impact of globalisation on international labour markets and businesses, together with the Australian desire to become a major economic force in the Asia Pacific region, meant that, by the 1990s, lobbying by employers to overcome shortages in the Australian professional and technical labour market by the entry of foreign workers on temporary contracts was successful. Arguments favouring this change included the need to fill temporary gaps in the labour market rapidly and without the delays inherent in assessment for permanent residence and, also, the preference of multinational companies to bring in their own high level executives and managers rather than recruit them locally. It was also noted that many of the highly skilled workers were not interested in settlement but preferred to move internationally in the emerging globalised skilled labour markets. The extent of Australian willingness to embrace highly skilled temporary labour was evident by the end of the 1990s when, for the first time, more long-term temporary migrants eligible to live in Australia for periods longer than 12 months arrived than did permanent settlers.[5]

Although a significant change in the openness of Australia's migration regime, it is noteworthy that there has been very little opposition to it by the general public or, indeed, the trade unions. Whether this tolerance would continue if the programme were extended to unskilled labour as is common in many Asian countries is, however, uncertain. To the extent that the Asian region is the most obvious source of such unskilled labour, their arrival could be viewed negatively by the anti-Asian immigration groups, which re-emerged in Australia during the 1990s. Their appearance coincided with the growth in Asian permanent settlers, as highly educated Asians became an important component in the economic migration programme.[6]

Australia has become an attractive haven for migrants because Australia is seen as a welfare state.[7] This is perceived through advertising, television and various multimedia resources. Advertisements often portray and mislead the glamour of the urban life. In this way globalisation and the increasing importance of the corporate dollar is influencing not only the movement from rural to city but also cultural identity and national sovereignty.

Immigration and Japan

Globalisation has brought many foreign workers to Japan. How to guarantee these foreign workers their rights is presently a very important legal issue.[8] The Immigration Control and Refugee Recognition Act (hereafter referred to as the Immigration Control Act) regulates the fair administration of immigration control and the Alien Registration Law regulates the relation of residence and social position of foreigners living in Japan.[9] The Immigration Control Act was enacted in 1951 and the Alien Registration Law was enacted in 1952, but both were revised many times. The American Immigration and Nationality Law was the model for the Immigration Control Act. Japan, however unlike its model, does not have a system to accept immigrants with permanent resident permits at the time of entrance. Some people who have entered the country with limited residence status can become permanent residents after a certain period of residence. In this regard, the Japanese system rather resembles that of the European immigration systems.

The Japanese government's attitude toward foreign workers is basically twofold: foreign workers who are to be employed for their special skills are admitted as much as possible, while various issues concerning the admission of unskilled labours are to be fully studied.[10] The following three fundamental tenets can be identified as the basis for Japan's current immigration policy: (i) Admitting foreign workers, on whatever basis, should be a last resort; (ii) No unskilled workers should be admitted; (iii) All foreigners should be admitted on a temporary basis only. Indeed, Japan is one of few countries, which maintains remarkably strict migration control standards like that of Singapore, and a traditional policy of not opening the labour market to foreign unskilled workers. However, three detours were established in recent years. First, it is said that illegal workers are present in Japan not because they can slip through the government's strict control but because the government turns a blind eye. The Japanese government is trying to satisfy the labour needs of small and medium-size companies by accepting foreign workers through the "back door". Since the 1990s a person who encourages illegal workers to engage in illegal work may be punished with imprisonment for up to 3 years and/or a fine of up to 2 million yen (Article 73-2 of the Immigration Control Act). Second, workers of Japanese origin are allowed to work without restriction of activity through the "front door". Third, trainees are also employed as unskilled workers through the "side door". The formal purpose of trainees is to acquire technology, skills or knowledge at a public or private organisation; however, the trainee system is seen as functioning as an informal measure recruiting cheap unskilled workers.

Historically, Japan experienced a major isolation period (1639-1853). Besides the migration between former Imperial Japan and its colonies, immigrants were small in number but about 777,000 emigrants moved to mainly America and Latin American countries (1853-1945). The Supreme Commander of Allied Powers strictly controlled immigration and emigration

(1945-1951).[11] During the time of advanced economic growth in the 1950s and the 1960s, the Japanese worked long hours and applied the automation system without admitting foreign labourers to the country. Since the 1980s however, Japan has been experiencing an unexpected amount of foreign residents because high economic growth needs 'newcomers' from various countries. Foreigners staying in Japan for 90 days or more are required to register as foreign residents. According to 1998 statistics, there were 1,512,116 registered foreigners in Japan, constituting about 1.20 per cent of Japan's total population. The major foreign legal residents are Koreans (638, 828: 42.2 per cent), Chinese (272,230: 18.0 per cent) and Brazilians (222,217: 14.7 per cent).[12] Additionally, it is estimated that there were an estimated 271,048 over-stay persons at the beginning of 1999. The major irregular foreigners are Koreans 52,387), Filipinos (42,547), Thais (39,513) and Chinese (38,296). It is said that in total, around 1,800,000 foreigners live in Japan.

After Japan ratified the International Covenants on Human Rights in 1979 and the Refugees Convention in 1981, many social security laws were amended and social rights were guaranteed for refugees and aliens who settled in Japan.[13] Both treaties aimed for the equality of social rights between nationals and non-nationals. Indochina refugees, so-called 'boat people', are compared with the American Commodore Perry and his frigates 'Black ships' because both of them influenced to open Japan to foreign intercourse. The Japanese feudal government had to change its isolation policy in 1853, in the same way the recent Japanese immigration policy was altered in 1982. The citizenship requirement clauses were eliminated from the National Pension Law and the National Health Insurance Law, etc. This has not solved the whole situation with foreigners, however. There are often remaining problems such as employment as public servants and voting rights for 'settled aliens'. All of them include the descendants of Korean and Taiwanese (approximately 600,000), who were previously subjects of Japanese colonies and also called '*Zainichi*' (foreign residents in Japan) or 'old comers'. These foreigners are guaranteed stable rights of permanent residence, but also shoulder many disadvantages due to their lack of Japanese citizenship.

Some rights are not accorded to foreigners in Japan.[14] Under the Japanese Constitution, there is no special regulation regarding alien's rights. Therefore, there is a "Word Doctrine", which accepts aliens' rights as long as the titular of human rights clauses is "every person" instead of "national". However, today's dominant theory was established after the *McLean* case (Supreme Court judgement, Oct. 4, 1978), as "Nature Doctrine", which accepts aliens' rights so long as the nature of rights allows it. This is based on the universality of human rights and the constitutional principle of international co-operation. Furthermore, the distinction between permanent or long-term resident and short-term resident is important as well as the distinction between legal resident and illegal resident. Therefore, permanent resident aliens are guaranteed rights as well as citizenship with some small exceptions, but short-term resident aliens are not sufficiently guaranteed their rights, and irregular aliens encounter serious problems living in Japan.

Japan organises its labour markets for foreign workers hierarchically according to "race" or "nationality." *Zainichi* foreigners and *nikkeijin* are at the high end of the racial hierarchy with better jobs, higher pay, and better working conditions than other foreign workers. At the bottom end are South Asians with casual jobs, poor pay, and dangerous working environments. This racialised hierarchy, which produces differentiated wages and other privileges across different groups of foreign workers, is a political construction of Japanese government officials, who form policies that establish both the legal superiority of certain races over others and constrain the operation of each tier of foreign workers. Japanese employers perpetuate this labour market arrangement by cooperating with government bureaus and *yakuza* in maintaining labour disciplines tailored to each racial group.[15] These actions create and sustain a racialised economy in Japan that is characterised by inferior jobs, little security, and few benefits for certain sectors of the labour market.

This hierarchy of foreign workers is a cultural product: Japanese view certain races and nationalities as being uniquely qualified for certain kinds of labour and they grant privileges and legal rights to workers on this basis. Japanese government policies, particularly those of the ministries of Justice and Labour, are primarily shaped by a racial typology that associates specific races with specific kinds of labour in Japan. Officials may have different interpretations of this racialised typology of foreign workers in line with the focus of their particular ministry, but taken together, the policies they enact generate a multiplicity of constraints on the lives and work of foreign labourers.

They result, for example, in silence by welfare officials when foreign workers do not receive medical services and immigration and police officials turn a blind eye to the employment of illegal Asian workers. Integral to Japan's racial typology of foreign workers is a repertoire of disciplinary mechanisms that sustains a semi-underground, semi-public racialised economy—not the celebrated one of life-time employment, but rather one characterised by inferior jobs, little security, and few if any benefits. Jobs are organised hierarchically by race and nationality such that those of "superior" origins (i.e., or foreign-born Japanese) are at the high end, obtain better jobs, enjoy legal rights, and are subjected to less direct surveillance by immigration and police officials. "Inferior" workers, such as "darker" South Asians, are at the low end and have casual jobs, poor pay, and few benefits; they are also subject to more coercion by police and (organized crime). Japanese employers cooperate with government bureaus and *yakuza* to coordinate and maintain labour disciplines that are tailored to each race and nationality. The kind of labour suited to each fits with the Japanese racialist imaginary. Such "coordination" is often implicit (i.e., immigration and police officials stage raids when illegal foreign workers appear in need of intimidation), but no less real. Employers discipline foreign workers by threats of reporting them to authorities or otherwise take advantage of them (i.e., by withholding pay or insurance benefits). Meanwhile, government policies, which are generally geared to employers', are not consistent across all ministries.

Conclusion

Given the diversity characterising Asia-Pacific nations, it is also not surprising to find diversity in their migration regimes and policy objectives. To the extent that there is evidence of convergence towards allowing freer movement across borders it is somewhat contradictory. On the one hand, easier access for tourists, highly skilled workers and business people is evident in a number of regional and domestic initiatives. Except for the case of traditional countries of immigration such as Australia, or countries heavily reliant on emigrant remittances, opportunities for permanent settlement are largely ignored within a framework where the ability to control entry in what are defined as 'national interests' dominates government thinking. Significantly, there is little evidence that permanent immigration and settlement is widely viewed as contributing to the national interest. Even in countries such as Australia with a tradition of accepting refugees and settlers on humanitarian grounds, calls for more open access for asylum seekers on the basis of human rights considerations remain the prerogative of opposition lobby groups. The same also applied in countries with unskilled temporary worker programmes where it is usually left to their home country to call for their better treatment. While it is sometimes suggested that the concept of human rights is essentially a Western, individualistic concept, which has little resonance in Asia with its more communal tradition, this certainly is not applicable to Australia. While on the other hand Japan's economic compulsions force it to loosen the immigration controls, differential treatment among foreigners themselves is the key feature in Japan whose labour market is also based on race and nationality. What is, more, evident is a pervasive ideology of 'management', which characterizes much regional governmental thinking on migration issues. Underlying this focus is a concern for 'legitimacy' to ensure that migration decisions are acceptable to the general population. While commendable in itself, since otherwise migrants can all too easily become the targets for discrimination and hostility, this focus on managing the domestic effects of migration can also be used to justify restrictions on the free movement of people and their integration.

While 'security' threats may be useful as a basis for legitimizing otherwise difficult initiatives, they also can create a climate of personal fear and insecurity, which interferes with efforts to make migration flows more open.

From a governmental perspective, for example, how does one resolve the desirability of making entry easy for tourism and international students who are important potential sources of revenue, without sacrificing the ability to 'protect' the domestic population? As always in policy making there is a need to balance decisions. However, the point of the present argument is that in the Asia-Pacific, despite some evidence of easier access for certain migrant groups with desirable economic attributes, there is currently little evidence that opportunities for permanent migration are improving. And, indeed, that there is evidence of a shift towards limiting freer access and international mobility.

End Notes

1. G.J. Hugo (1999), A New Paradigm of International Migration in Australia, *New Zealand Population Review,* Vol. 25, Nos. 1-2.
2. Stephen Castles (2005), Nations and Empire: Hierarchies of Citizenship in the New Global Order, *International Politics*, Vol. 42, Palgrave Macmillan Ltd.
3. See Goot, M. (1988), *Immigration: A commitment to Australia*, The Book Printer, Victoria, Australia,
4. C.A. Price (1979), *Australian Immigration: A Bibliography and Digest*, No. 4, (Department of Demography), Australian National University, Canberra.
5. OECD 2003 p. 130).
6. Kubat, D. (1993), The Politics of Migration Policies: Settlement and Integration The First World Into the 1990s, Centre for Migration Studies, New York, pp. 17-18.
8. See Helmut Loiskandl (1995), Illegal Migrant Workers in Japan in Robin Cohen (ed.), *The Cambridge Survey of World Migration* (Cambridge: Cambridge University Press.
9. Hiromi Mori (1997), *Immigration Policy and Foreign Workers in Japan* (London: Macmillan, pp. 1, 96).
10. Takamichi Kajita (1995), Characteristics of the Foreign Worker Problem in Japan, *Hitotsubashi Journal of Social Studies*, Vol. 27, No. 1 pp. 10-13.
11. Yoshio Hagino (1983) The Japanese Immigration System—An Introduction, *Nanzan Hôgaku,* Vol. 7, No. 2.
12. Japan Immigration Association, *Statistics on Immigration Control 1998*, (Tokyo: Japan Immigration Association, 1999), pp. 54, 72-76.
13. Yoshio Hagino (1984), New Japanese Immigration—Control and Refugee-Recognition Act of 1981, *Nanzan Hôgaku*, Vol. 8, No. 1.
14. Piper, N. (2004), Rights of Foreign Workers and the Politics of Migration in South-East and East Asia, *International Migration*, 42(5): 71-98.
15. Thomas K. Bauer Astrid Kunze (2004), The Demand for High-Skilled Workers and Immigration Policy, IZA DP No. 999, January.

7

Minority Women and Forced Migrations: A Comparative Study of Flight and Settlement Experiences of Women Refugees in India and Australia

RUCHIRA GANGULY-SCRASE AND ROBERTA JULIAN

This paper draws attention to the factors and experiences of displacement and the ways in which women cope with forced migration and resettlement. Through our comparative analysis of the resettlement experiences of women within the developing countries in the South Asian region and women from the Asian region who have settled in Australia, we challenge and problematise the various bureaucratic categories of 'the displaced' (such as political refugee, economic migrant, asylum seeker, illegal immigrant).

The field of refugee studies has a number of weaknesses and limitations. These include: (1) a predominance of small-scale local studies and an associated lack of longitudinal studies. As Khalid Koser has noted: 'It would be really useful to trace the development of refugee populations or diasporas, or transnational communities...over ten or twenty years'; (2) the lack of a comparative perspective and the need to be grounded in a wider context such as globalisation, transnationalism; (3) the predominance of empirically based and policy-oriented studies and thus the limited attention to building theory in refugee studies; and (4) the need to go beyond a good/bad dichotomy implicit in viewing refugees as 'either vilified or seen as victims'[1].

Further, as Ien Ang states:

> ...we are interested in finding out what it means to be a refugee in this time and age, in all its complexities, in all its ambivalences, and in all its contradictions, looking beyond either a total revulsion or moral outrage[2].

We attempt to embark on the challenge of addressing these limitations. We are working towards a comparative analysis of the resettlement(s) of women who have experienced forced migration and displacement, and one that locates these local studies within an analysis of macro-processes of neo-liberal globalisation. We believe that such an approach will contribute to the building of a theory in refugee studies and offer a greater understanding of the complexities of forced migration and settlement for women.

The complex processes of decolonisation and increased integration of the world economy have set in motion large-scale population movements that render meaningless distinct categories of dislocations. Therefore, we emphasise that the boundaries of various types of gendered forced displacements often intersect and are blurred.

Increasingly, nation states have closed their borders to "alien" outsiders. In relation to forced migrations we are concerned with the particular inflection the dichotomies of "economic migrants" and "refugees" proper manifest in Australia and the Indian sub-continent. This paper is also guided by a concern over the problem that goals of national development in post-colonial states are often at odds with the rights of minority groups.

Feminist scholarship in this field makes the important point that when addressing the situation of minority women gender justice tends to become sidelined due to problems of women being the embodiment of the minority community's identity. Based on comparative research among East Bengali/ Bangladeshi women in West Bengal[3] and Hmong refugee women in Tasmania, we argue that in the global South artificial boundaries constructed in the process of nation making have suddenly rendered the movement of certain groups as illegal despite their long history of migratory journeys and interactions. This has specific gendered consequences. Our argument concerning the global North also refers to another artificial boundary construction, namely the distinctions between economic migrant and political refugee. Through our comparative analysis, this paper draws critical attention to the weakness of the concept of refugee in contemporary post-colonial contexts by highlighting its gendered complexities. Our empirical work on diverse groups of displaced women will show that the conventional demarcations between economic migrant and political refugee are inadequate to explain their experiences. In particular, our analysis of Hmong women's settlement experiences will highlight that gender and generation are more significant axes of contestation in the construction of displaced women's identities.

Forced Migration and Exclusion: Nation States and Border Control Policies

Forced and economic migrations are closely related and often interchangeable expressions of global inequality and societal crisis[4]. It is through the deconstruction of various bureaucratic categories that both the diversity and similarity of people experiences can be exposed. According to Sivanandan the distinction between political refugee and economic migrant is a false one and is vulnerable to differing interpretations depending on the interests of who such categories serve[5]. It is the interests of the powerful that have resulted in the blurring of these categories. Even when experts have examined transnational migration with a gender lens and note the increasing "feminisation"[6] their attention on the productive sphere and the social production of gender have left out the complexities of different and gendered experiences of migration in an overall theoretical frame[7]. Neoliberalism with its focus on structural adjustment programmes resulted in reduced social spending, leading to the impoverishment and eradication of social, welfare and educational provisions to people in developing nations. Resistance to poverty cannot be separated from political resistance and persecution[8], thus turning the political refugee into an economic migrant. In addition, millions of people become displaced each year as a result of development programmes[9]. It is normally difficult to tell the difference between environmental, economic and political factors and therefore the category, environmental refugee, can obscure the very complex reasons underlying environmental disasters. Often the underlying causes of such forced migration might be found in the chosen path of development followed by the state[10].

According to Castles discussions which focus on forced migration are essentially linked to the concerns that nation-states have with their national security and border control[11]. Recent developments in industrialised countries indicate that governments are gradually restricting entry of immigrants and asylum seekers[12]. This is most apparent in the border security planning of Australia and a number of countries in the global North such as England, the nations within the European Union, and the United States. In line with the establishment of border control policies in the North, Australia has developed policies that are increasingly exclusionary. Australian Prime Minister John Howard has developed a very firm connection between sovereignty and exclusion in present asylum policies, emphasising the distinction between "genuine" asylum seekers and economic migrants. Recent changes to the Migration Legislation Amendment Act in 2001 (MLAA) suggest that these policies are particularly discriminatory against women[13]. Australia's current anxiety over asylum seekers is, according to Devtak, consistent with Australia's past fear of otherness[14].

However, the very notion of displaced persons can be called into question by an examination of the diverse forms of displacement in Northeast India. This is outlined by Samaddar's (1999) reconceptualisation of the distinction between "migrant" and "refugee", which posits the nexus between the two terms and the shared common factor of victimisation[15]. Samaddar argues that giving different definitions to displaced populations is a meaningless exercise as "in reality…differences are fruitless"[16].

Historically, the conceptualisation of the displaced person can be traced to the inception of the UN Convention of 1951 within the context of post-war reconstruction. Here, the definition of a refugee was characterised as a person who,

> Owing to a well founded fear of persecution for reasons of race, religion, nationality, membership of a particular group or political opinion, is outside the country of his nationality and is unable, or owing to such fear, is unwillingly to avail himself of the protection of that country[17].

Although this definition may have been adequate in the reconstruction of post WWII Europe, it is arguably both antiquated and insufficient in the 21st century[18]. With its focus on individual persecution and sovereignty, this paradigm is subsequently Eurocentric and reductionist. Indeed, it has been argued that there is a close relationship between the UNHCR and Western nations that donate large amounts of aid and subsequently, the UNHCR is not as independent as it appears to be[19].

Writers such as Hathaway[20] argue that the definition is anachronistic because refugee movements today are different from those which pertained during the Cold War period in which the earlier one was coined. The stereotype of an individual person fleeing from the persecution of a political system is no longer relevant. Today's refugees are more likely to arrive in much larger groups than those of the 1950s and in much poorer condition. They do not have the opportunity or the time to prepare for their flight and present themselves at borders without documents or identification. They are often injured or in poor health. Over eighty per cent of them are women and children, as the biggest reason for flight is civil unrest or war, and men are often killed or imprisoned or hide from the threat of continued persecution.

Arguably, this paradigm also excludes the experiences of women in forced displacement and the experiences of internally displaced persons. Feminist writers also argue that the stereotype of a "refugee" conforms to the Cold War image which is predominantly male. The language of the UN Convention on Refugees is gender blind. That is, it does not refer to females nor does it specifically recognise persecution on the grounds of gender. Although, for example, rape has been recognised as a war crime, the Refugee Convention does not identify rape as sufficient ground for refugee status. However, Haines argues that

> The failure of decision makers to recognise and respond appropriately to the experiences of women stems not from the fact that the 1951 Convention does not refer specifically to persecution on the basis of sex or gender, but rather because it has often been approached from

> a partial perspective and interpreted through a framework of male experience[21].

In 1985 the Executive Committee of the UNHCR (EXCOMM) recognised women refugees and asylum seekers as a "particular social group" under the terms of the Refugee Convention but this is not always followed by either member or non-member countries.

"Economic refugees" are not recognised as bona fide refugees because they do not suffer from "persecution" but are assumed to have an element of choice in their movements. It seems that nation states expect that families will stay in their own countries and starve rather than cross borders to a country where employment opportunities, however limited, are available.

Recent neo-liberal prescriptions in both Australia and India have been often accompanied by aggressive border protection policies, giving rise to growing xenophobia towards asylum seekers. In post-colonial states the resultant impact has affected women even more adversely than men. In the making of post-colonial nation states boundaries were drawn arbitrarily through ethnic, religious cultural and economic communities. Homogenisation underpinning nationalist ideologies also led to the creation of marginalised and displaced "minority" groups who did not belong in the nation state. In the Indian sub-continent, tensions and contestation over artificially constructed boundaries have continued since simple movement of populations in border regions can become an illegal act. However, the pursuit of market liberalisation does not seem to be leading to greater tolerance of ethnic and religious differences[22]. On the contrary, border controls are being vigorously reinforced to keep alien *others* out. Most undocumented forced women migrants we spoke with reiterated their inability to secure asylum as they did not meet the official's notion of who aught to be considered a genuinely persecuted individual.

Borders of nation states are artificial constructs arbitrarily drawn through ethnic, religious, cultural and economic communities. Such borders exist, for example, between Kashmir and Pakistan, China and India, and Israel and Palestine. In India the artificiality is exemplified by the case in Tripura where a border divides a football field[23]. The fluidity of borders that often isolate communities is highlighted, for example, where a river which often changes course is a national border. Political decisions can also produce borders which are moveable, as for example where Australia has excised Ashmore Reef and Christmas Island from Australian territory for the purposes of establishing refugee status. Another recent example is the barrier currently erected between India and Bangladesh.

Gendered Displacement

Women have often been relegated to the periphery in mainstream refugee debates. As noted earlier, women have been excluded from both the internal and external displacement debates due to the very definition of what it means to be a refugee. Recent literature has shown that women are systematically excluded from refugee debate due to the specificity of female experiences, despite the overrepresentation of women in refugee statistics[24]. It has been contended that the UNHCR definition of the "refugee" is simultaneously individualistic and presumptuous in its intimation that violations must be specifically committed by the state. Boyd suggests that this definition privileges the public side of public/private divide by focusing on the actions of the state. This definition "fails to acknowledge forms of persecution that occur in private settings"[25]. As women are more likely to be persecuted in the private sphere, they are less likely to be officially seen as refugees.

It has been argued that refugee law is intrinsically gendered and subsequently, needs to be altered[26]. Boyd posits that female persecution eventuating in displacement can be conceptualised in two ways. Firstly, a woman can be persecuted as a woman, not because she is a woman. This means that the form of persecution is gendered, such as in the case of rape. Similarly, women can be persecuted because of her gender or because she has broken social mores pertaining to her gender[27]. This distinction is made clearly by Haines who describes the former form of persecution as gender-specific and the second as gender-related. Citing Crawley Haines also describes persecution by sexual violence as a weapon of war, when the "...violation of women's bodies acts as a symbol of the violation of the country." [28]

Significantly, gender inequity and stratification can be reproduced in places of relocation, where women generally possess less education and fewer skills than their male counterparts and hence lack bargaining power in the community[29]. Another important aspect of this analysis is the way in which women's bodies often become sites of contestation in relocated communities. The central findings of our comparative research indicate that the degree to which women are controlled is often a symbol of reconstructed patriarchal authority in many displaced communities[30].

Methodology

Our observations are based on ethnographic research carried out in the border regions within South Asia and institutional ethnography. Intensive fieldwork among the displaced enabled us to challenge the conventional epistemic notion of what it means to be a refugee, allowing us to present the life worlds of the researched as active agents within our study rather than passive victims. We followed Sorensen's ethnographic approach to deconstructing pre-existing categories of displacement by showing which aspects are relevant on the ground[31]. Roberta Julian along with her colleagues was commissioned to undertake research on the settlement experiences of recently arrived refugees in Tasmania[32]. The findings on the Hmong for this paper are based on almost ten years of association with Hmong people—mainly in Australia and the United States, but also more recently, in Thailand. We utilised data that has been collected through a methodology known as "institutional ethnography"[33]. In explaining this methodology, Dorothy Smith states:

> Institutional ethnographic research and analysis does not displace or reconstruct the experiences of those implicated in an institutional regime. Rather, by locating people's site of experience in the social relations of the institutional regime and explicating what we can of the relations that enter into that experience, we can create something like a map of the relations in which people's own doings and experiences are situated and by which they are shaped[34].

The institutional ethnographer recognises that people are "expert practitioners of their everyday worlds" and is interested in learning from them[35]. However, institutional ethnography "looks for the ways in which the particularities of people's everyday doings bring into being the distinctively generalised forms of the institutional order"[36]. The aim is

> ...to locate in their accounts the junctures between the everyday worlds as they told them and how they are hooked into relations that connect them beyond scope of experience. [For Smith,] '(t)he project is analogous to cartography. [37]

Importantly, this approach also acknowledges the fact that 'researchers are in the same world that they are investigating'[38].

The findings on East Bengali/Bangladeshi women are derived from fieldwork among forced women migrants in 2004-2005 in Calcutta (now Kolkata) in the Indian state of West Bengal and its border regions. The women were aged between sixteen and seventy-five and included single, widowed, married women and deserted wives. The observations and analysis are also informed by intensive and intermittent fieldwork carried out in this region over a sixteen-year period. The first period of intensive fieldwork was carried out by Ruchira Ganguly-Scrase for eighteen months in Nadia, a district bordering Bangladesh, where the second largest settlement of refugees has taken place.

Close and continuing relationship since 1988 have been maintained with a number of the current key informants. Our earlier work focussed on comparative gendered migratory journeys[39] ; other related research examined the social consequences of economic liberalisation[40]. Throughout this period close links were formed with a number of displaced Bangladeshi women. Such contacts permitted entry into networks of dislocated communities. This access was critical since emerging hostilities towards alien *others* stemming from changes in the political climate in recent years has made refugees and newly arrived undocumented migrants fearful and reluctant to talk to outsiders. Gaining their trust was vital in uncovering the detailed accounts that were presented.

Hmong in Tasmania, Australia

Hmong refugees from Laos had begun to arrive in Tasmania in the mid-late 1970s but it was not until the early 1990s that their presence became visible to "ordinary" Tasmanians at various sites around Hobart, the state's capital city. One such site was Salamanca Market, held every Saturday predominantly for tourists. The Hmong became familiar faces at Salamanca Market where they sold fresh organically grown vegetables of the highest quality. Their "Asian" faces and broad smiles ensured that they stood out from the crowd in a city where the local population was (and still is) overwhelming "white" and Anglo. The members of the extended Hmong families who congregated around the vegetable stalls provided the market with a multicultural presence and their colourful and unique embroidery *paj ntaub*, for sale alongside the fresh vegetables, provided an opportunity for the consumption of cultural artifacts. Locals were quick to buy the *paj ntaub* for their aesthetic value. The majority were unaware that they were contributing to the maintenance of transnational ties, as the proceeds of the sale would be remitted to Hmong relatives residing in Thai refugee camps.

Tasmanians welcomed "the Hmong at Salamanca" as they became known to locals. The Hmong quickly came to symbolise a new openness to Asia, a new Tasmanian identity that was inclusive of people of Asian origin. The Hmong became an icon of multicultural Tasmania; they were seen to have successfully integrated into Tasmanian society while simultaneously maintaining their cultural identity, an ideal expressed in government policy statements on Australian multiculturalism[41]. In this context, however, it can be argued that Hmong identity becomes commodified, trivialised and marginalised. The Hmong are represented as "the exotic Other", as a marketable tourist commodity. This encourages an essentialist notion of Hmong identity which homogenises what is, despite its small size, a heterogeneous "community". The dominant representation of Hmong femininity complies with this. Women become the bearers of cultural tradition—cultural icons whose images are a marketable commodity. The Hmong women and children selling vegetables at the market are popular subjects of the "tourist gaze"[42]. Many visitors to Hobart would have a photograph or two of "the Hmong at Salamanca" in their memoirs. Importantly, however, this image belies the economic hardships and settlement difficulties experienced by almost all the Hmong in Hobart.

Minority Status and Collective Remembering

Just as the history of Partition in India is deeply etched in the resettlement experiences of Bangladeshis in West Bengal, the history of minority persecution and political turmoil in South East Asia, particularly the long and protracted wars in Indo-China marks the flight and memory of resettlement of Hmong communities. This has also shaped the dominant refugee narrative which we return to later.

The Hmong in South East Asia

The experiences of women in this study are part of a larger, on going, cross border fluid movement of populations into North East India. Looking at it historically, it is noted that seeds of dissension along communal lines were sown way back in 1901 when the British ruled India. The province of Bengal was partitioned into East and West with the former being largely predominated by Muslims and the latter by Hindus. Based on this, partition took place in 1947 with two nation states being carved out, viz., India and Pakistan. In 1947, a large majority of Hindu Bengalis arrived as refugees in West Bengal but a significant proportion continued to live in East Pakistan as their identification was along local cultures rather than nationalist identities. Bengali cultural nationalism drawing on secular principles and regional identity intensified in East Pakistan against Punjabi dominated exclusionary politics of Pakistan, culminating in the war of Independence and formation of Bangladesh in 1971. In Bangladesh growing instability, poverty and militarisation has given rise to Islamic fundamentalism[43] progressively pushing out Bangladeshi Hindus[44] as well as the Muslim poor. In the Indian state of West Bengal in the past half century while cultural politics and public culture has been shaped largely by secular and democratic principles, often spearheaded by the post-partition "East Bengali" refugees, fractures are also appearing as a consequence of assaults on two fronts: Islamic fundamentalism of Bangladesh and growing Hindu nationalism of greater India. Since the 1970s West Bengal's ruling Left Front government and especially the Communist Party has consistently maintained an anti-communal stance and enjoyed popular support due to its pro-poor policies. At the same however, its pragmatic approach of expanding its support base by incorporating immigrant Bangladeshis (including Muslims), into the electoral list and thereby indirectly engineering citizenship rights is a source of intense hostility. While discourses of "foreign infiltration", initiated primarily by Hindu nationalists have dominated public debate in West Bengal in recent years, in the surrounding States, the resentment is far more violent[45].

Refugee Narratives of Dislocation

Bangladeshi refugee women narrated their experiences in terms of the factors that forced them and their families to migrate to India. Some were categorical in stating the fact that fear of religious persecution compelled them to leave their homeland and find shelter in another country. Yet, despite their references to communal tensions being a cause for their dislocation, they did not personally experience physical attacks or coercion on them by the Muslim majority. What they did acknowledge was that there had been a constant fear in their minds given that they had young daughters at home. They had heard of incidents whereby Muslims had abducted Hindu girls or even raped them. It is interesting to note that while they recounted such details of Muslim atrocities happening somewhere in their country, in case of their own safety, they were grateful to the Muslim neighbours who had protected them.

Such views are evident in the comments that were repeatedly expressed by a number of women refugees:

> Hindu women and grown up girls had to live with a sense of insecurity. We normally avoided venturing alone in places outside our house. Women and girls from our community were constantly under threat. There were incidents of sexual harassment by Muslim youths… But we were not physically attacked. There was fear of an attack always… (40 year old, deserted woman, from Rajsahi district, Bangladesh).

This was remarkably similar to the sentiments of post-partition refugees:

> About Bangladesh, I can only tell you about riots…. When it started, I must have been about 9-10 years old. Some of it is a blur now. …Oh! It was because of the riots that we had to leave. …We were chased by the Muslims, we ran here & there…We were hearing that this one's daughter was taken and cut up in front of the mother… But as far as we were concerned, we were alive because of the Muslims' help. Yes, the Muslims saved us. There were good and bad among them… (60 + year old, married woman, from Dhaka, Bangladesh)

Few recent (1990s-2001) refugees attributed poverty as well as a reason for migration. Such views were typified by comments such as a woman said:

> …Then after the trouble, we came here because of persecution by the miyas (Muslims)… It is because of poverty that we had to leave…It is because of persecution and poverty that we had to leave, I mean if we could not gather grains, then how can we bring up our children. (40 year old married woman migrant from Khulna district in Bangladesh).

Here, it is important to note the radically differing views of young people. For example a sixteen-year-old girl who worked as a seamstress in Kolkata emphatically noted that she did not really like being in India as she failed to relate to the local Bengalis. She was unlike older women who appeared to be grateful to have a home and livelihood in West Bengal.

Most of the refugees said that they had migrated with their families. Only one mentioned doing so in a group of fifty to sixty people.

From the discussions with the immigrants from Bangladesh, it can be inferred that reasons for migration were not merely political and religious persecution as minorities, but economic as well.

Hardships in Resettlement

Even though there were not many hardships faced by the refugees while crossing the border all of them had to struggle with regard to finding a place to stay and employment. Some of them mentioned being harassed by local hoodlums and some said that there was a constant fear of eviction for which they had to bribe the local police.

While in Bangladesh, most of these women stayed within the confines of their homes, in India, they were compelled to find jobs so as to be able to support themselves as well as their families. Like many Hmong women, Bangladeshi refugee women play an active role in the public sphere since their husbands were out of work and did not support them financially. Subsequently, women had to assume the role of the breadwinners in their families. Curiously however, they seemed to be enjoying more freedom in the place of settlement in terms of movement within the city and feeling safe as well secure. As one woman summarised these sentiments,

> In Bangladesh, we never moved around freely, life was confined within the walls of the house. I could never think of doing a job outside my house in Bangladesh. Besides there was ever present threat of physical (sexual) assault at the hands of local Muslim youth. In West Bengal, there are no such threats. The atmosphere in West Bengal is easier for women. Women can be seen everywhere in the markets, at the workplace and in the fields of West Bengal, which was not the case in Bangladesh. (33 year old, deserted wife, Rajsahi district, Bangladesh)

When in need, almost all the refugees mentioned that neighbours as well as employers helped them but not always financially. If they required food items, neighbours came to their help and in case of illness, employers gave them leave and sometimes money to get themselves treated. Most of them got financial help from their relatives living nearby.

Elaborating on their current financial situation, they mentioned more or less a hand to mouth kind of an existence. This was further reinforced when the participants were asked whether they remitted any money back to their relatives living in their native villages. While some said that they had no relatives back in their natal villages, others were vehement that they hardly earned enough to manage their own households. As one woman remarked bitterly, "No, I can't even manage my own family."(40 year old, widow, migrated from Daulatpur, Bangladesh)

Maintaining Kinship Networks

Most of the women immigrants from Bangladesh reported having a kinship network in West Bengal with some of members of their families living in and around Kolkata as well as in other parts of West Bengal.

As mentioned above, displaced Bangladeshi women have been compelled to take up gainful employment in contrast to what their role had been back in their natal villages. Most women were employed either as domestic help or as seamstress after migrating to Kolkata. Their educational status varied from being illiterate to completion of primary school. Their monthly earnings were quite meager ranging from Rs. 300 to Rs. 1000, with the exception of one woman, who ran a small business. Although in most cases, women were the main breadwinners, they did not attribute their decision-making powers within their households solely to their financial independence. It varied according to the woman's location within the life cycle. Older women with sons exerted greater power. The following comments typify older women's views:

> …Even if I am not earning money, it is my voice that is heard. But if I am earning, my voice is heard loud and clear" (70 year old, married woman, migrated from Narangar, Bangladesh)

and,

> No, in my house, whatever my words, whatever I say, others do the same. I distribute, spend money. I am the one to do it. Everyone brings it to me. (40 year old, married woman, migrated from Raghunathpur, gram, Bangladesh)

Younger women, by comparison, despite being breadwinners had little decision making power.

In terms of freedom and safety/security, these women refugees felt that it was certainly better here than back in their natal villages in Bangladesh.

Our informants suffer from economic deprivation and policies that systematically exclude them from outside assistance. Our findings among displaced women in India also reveal that female labour within impoverished communities is taken for granted and capitalised on. In both situations, female labour doubles, yet labour within the home is taken for granted within the global market system. In the specific case of structural readjustment in India, job loss for men also entails an extra burden for women, who have to provide for their families[46].

While women are exposed to many vulnerabilities, confront threats of violence[47], and reinforced patriarchal authority, our findings also reveal that there are possibilities of empowerment. Most women valued their freedom of mobility and enhanced sense of self-confidence that the new environment presents them. However, women who have arrived as undocumented migrants, their awareness of being non-citizens is acute. They openly speak about their sense of being deprived the rights of citizenship. For example, they find it difficult to obtaining ration cards[48], enrolling their names on electoral lists and even in admitting their children to schools (where they are asked to produce birth certificates). They can never aspire to have a regular job on the basis of their education (they achieved in Bangladesh) because that is not recognised in India. They feel disadvantaged for not being Indian citizens, particularly due to the continual harassment by the local police. They compare their situation with earlier migrants (who are fellow villagers, caste fellows or relatives) who have now established themselves in economic, social and political arenas.

Growing class inequalities and mobilisation by the CPI (M) has facilitated a shared degree of identification between local West Bengali and Bangladeshi displaced women. Both groups provide essential urban services to the middle classes, but are frequently labelled as "undesirables". As Kaviraj's account of India's Toquevillain revolution suggests, elites are compelled to share public spaces with their "habitual inferiors" which often includes crowded and filthy pavements, middle class neighbourhoods being run over by shanties, standing or sitting next to a shirtless fellow citizen on a public bus and so on[49]. Additionally, Bangladeshi women were further demonised as "illegals" and "infiltrators."

Despite their hardships in resettlement women repeatedly emphasised the freedom of mobility in their place of settlement and enhanced feelings of safety and security. However refugee women while emphasising the accommodative atmosphere among the local population, held the police responsible for threatening their security. This is a radical departure from earlier decades. West Bengal government, traditionally supportive of refugees regardless of their legal status, has enacted draconian laws under pressure from both the Central government and localised reactionary forces. The West Bengal police now have a special cell for the detection of illegal migrants. Further, official discourses of producing "documentation" of all kinds amounts to targeting vulnerable immigrants since vast majority of non-literate Indian citizens do not possess many of these documents. Indeed, accusations of illegal infiltration and ill treatment of Bengali rural poor who have travelled to major cities elsewhere in India, in search of work highlight the impossibility of distinguishing between internal labour migrants and cross border refugees[50].

Hmong Women's Active Role in Resettlement

Women's labour has been significant in Hmong settlement strategies. Like many Bengali male refugees there is high levels of unemployment amongst Hmong men; they have also found it difficult to reconstruct meaningful identities in the process of resettlement. By contrast women have made important economic and cultural contributions to their family, clan and community. Yet, despite women's contributions to the household economy, men are more highly valued than women in this social system[51] and women are subject to male authority and decision-making in the household.

Hmong women in Tasmania are subject to the constraints and expectations of a matrilineal kinship structure. A Hmong woman becomes a member of her husband's clan upon marriage and is expected to fulfill the expectations of a daughter-in-law. This includes looking after young children, doing the housework, growing vegetables on the family's land and generally being involved in all household activities under the supervision of her mother-in-law. There are close parallels here with Bengali daughters-in-law.

However, women have been central actors in rebuilding the displaced Hmong community in Hobart. They have played active roles in all spheres of social life namely health, education, work and kinship. The first contacts to be made with the health and education systems are typically made by women in relation to child birth and child care activities. Knowledge of Hmong customs by mainstream service providers thus often develops through their efforts to deal with the needs of Hmong women and children[52]. For example, Hmong women have had to negotiate birthing practices and post-natal care with hospital staff and administrators.

While in Laos the political leaders and representatives of cultural tradition are men, in the context of settlement it is women who play the more public roles. Hmong women have strong relations with the social world outside their minority community; these include younger women helping older women negotiate the school system, women who have resided in Hobart for longer periods of time accompanying new mothers to the hospital to assist in the negotiation of birthing practices and older and younger women together being responsible for selling vegetables at the Saturday market.

Despite this extensive involvement in life outside the Hmong community, it is male leaders who remain as the spokespersons for the Hmong community and who, as powerful gatekeepers, manage the "image" of Hmong culture which is being constructed to fit the context of Australian multiculturalism. High unemployment rates contribute to a pattern in which male social networks are relatively closed and confined predominantly within the Hmong community. It is this image-making that lies at the heart of the problem of resettlement of the minority Hmong community in Hobart and it presents a great challenge for gendered identity formation. Our final section therefore focuses on this issue.

Gendered Implications of Dominant Refugee Narratives

The dominant identity narrative in the global discourse on Hmong identity can be described as the quintessential "refugee story". It is a "heroic" narrative that incorporates a number of themes: the war and the military; exodus and the refugee experience; and continuity with the past through a valuing of clan ties, "traditional" Hmong culture and memories of a "lost" homeland. While this dominant narrative is predominantly articulated by male elites, it is also reproduced by women. This is most apparent in the "storycloth" (*paj ndau*), a form of needlework first made around 1976 in Ban Vinai refugee camp[53]. Commonly, the storycloths chronicle village life in the mountains of Laos, depict religious ceremonies, or illustrate Hmong folktales. The majority created in the "west" or for the western market, however, recount the transition from village life prior to the war, through the escape from Laos after the war, to life in refugee camps in Thailand and often "end" with an image of the plane in Bangkok that was to take them to "freedom" in the United States.

Countering Dominant Narratives

The narratives recounted here support and reinforce an essentialist notion of Hmongness and encourage the maintenance of ideas of "tradition" and "authenticity". However, it is possible to identify resistances and challenges to the global hegemonic discourse identified above. Such resistances arise where the narrative of the "refugee success story" does not resonate with lived experience. These resistant voices arise in local contexts and reflect differences within the Hmong diaspora based on gender, age, class, religion, "migrantness" and place. The voices of resistance are predominantly those of educated Hmong women, primarily located in the United States. Nowadays, they have been joined by the voices of Hmong youth, both male and female. The main topics of contestation and debate include clan structure; youthful marriage; cross-cultural marriage; polygamy and levirate; "kidnap" marriages; women's education; and the significance of Hmong language for Hmong identity. New communications media, such as the Internet, provide a means of reaching a global Hmong audience. There is an on-line Hmong Journal and at least one Hmong home page in both America and Australia. Young Hmong people in the United States and Australia discuss issues surrounding Hmong identity in various chat rooms.

Yet, the repertoire of adaptive strategies (including gender strategies) available to the Hmong in Australia (compared to their US counterparts) is more restricted. As a very small and dispersed population with generally low socio-economic status, the Hmong in Australia have limited resources to draw upon. For Hmong women in Australia, the global narrative provides the dominant "cultural notion of gender at play". At the level of the nation-state, the rhetoric of multicultural policy in Australia "encourages" the presentation of Hmong identity. Typically, however, multicultural spaces in Australia are aimed at the white middle-class or the tourist market—the identities presented are essentialist and "traditional". As Hage has argued, they are limited to representations that sustain "fantasies of white supremacy among the dominant majority. In Australia, multicultural policy thus reinforces the power of the global narrative; it does not offer spaces for translation"[54]. Consequently, while in the United States, resistance takes the form of "translation" and "reinvention in the third space"[55], the lack of such spaces in Australia leads to "a wholesale rejection of, or disinterest in, Hmong cultural traditions"[56].

Given Australia's ambivalent relationship with Asia and "Asians"[57], spaces for the creation of hybridity are limited. They include an emerging media in the field of popular culture[58] but the Hmong have limited access to these. Nevertheless, there are two such spaces available to the Hmong. Significantly, both are grounded in the transnational social space. One is the Internet and the other is the transnational "community" of Hmong women. First, the Internet offers a space within which Hmong in Australia can engage in the translation of Hmong identity. It is used by Hmong youth and is dominated by Hmong in the west[59]. Second, Hmong women who have made their mark as "trailblazers"[60] in the United States have become increasingly aware of the situations of Hmong women in Australia. Through e-mail communication and visits to Australia, they have begun to establish transnational ties. Importantly, these ties are not clan-based: they are *gendered* ties between Hmong women. Educated Hmong women in the US are offering themselves and their experiences as resources for the translation of Hmong femininity in Australia. The ultimate goal, however, is to contribute to the survival of Hmong identity in the diaspora.

Conclusion

In this paper we have highlighted gendered complexities of forced displacements by exploring the resettlement experiences of Hmong and Bangladeshi refugee women. Our findings suggest that women's narratives of displacement can redress the problems of exclusion in forced migration debates. They challenge the normative and functionalist accounts of displacement debates that construct the forced migrants' identities as static. Additionally our comparative methodology demonstrates that ethnographic approaches operate to dispel the precise narratives of citizenship, nationhood and territorial contiguity that the existence of displaced persons threatens to disrupt.

The major difference that underpins in displacement experiences of the two groups of women is in relation to the younger generation. Hmong young women have some opportunities opening up to them, which enables them to challenge the dominant patriarchal norms and traditions, while Bangladeshi young women continue to be subjected to greater vulnerabilities. This is in part due to the absolute poverty of the latter community.

While enduring many difficulties in the settlement process, Hmong women have played a significant role in re-building their communities. However, under current draconian policies in Australia asylum seekers face a grim future. In the present post-Cold War era, the Hmong would not have been considered worthy recipients of refugee status. Similarly hardening attitudes towards Bangladeshis prevail in India. The building of barriers along the Indo-Bangladesh border is an example of this. Despite the fact that a large section of post-partition refugees were turned into veritable beggars, there is equal evidence of the positive role East Bengali refugees played in their self-rehabilitation[61]. Future generations may not be so lucky.

End Notes

1. Khalid Koser, Pnina Werbner and Ien Ang, "Cultural Research and Refugee Studies: New Knowledge, Methodologies, and Practical Implications: A Panel Commentary", *Social Analysis*, Vol. 48, No. 3, 2004, pp. 59-65.
2. Koser, p. 64.
3. This research is supported by URC grant, *Gendered Exclusion: Women and Forced Migration*, University of Wollongong.
4. Stephen Castles, Towards a Sociology of Forced Migration and Social Transformation, *Sociology,* Vol. 37, No. 1, 2003, p. 17.
5. A. Sivanandan, UK: Refugees from Globalism, *Race and Class,* Vol. 42, No. 3, 2001, p. 87.
6. J.A. Tyner, "The Web-based Recruitment of Female Foreign Domestic Workers in Asia," *Singapore Journal of Tropical Geography,* Vol. 20, 1999, pp. 193-209.
7. See for instance, Nina, L. Glick Schiller, Basch and C. Szanton Blanc, "From Immigrant to Transmigrant: Theorizing Transnational Migration," *Anthropological Quarterly*, Vol. 68, 1995, pp. 48-63.
8. Kuntala Lahiri-Dutt and Gopa Samanta, "Fleeting Land, Fleeting People: Bangladeshi Women in a Charland Environment in Lower Bengal, India", *Asian and Pacific Migration Journal,* Vol. 13, No. 4, 2004, pp. 475-497.
9. Smitu Kothari, Whose Nation? The Displaced as Victims of Development, *Economic and Political Weekly,* Special Issue, Vol. 31 No. 24, 1999, pp. 1476-1485. See also G.W. Robinson, *Risks and Rights: The Causes, Consequences and Challenges to Development-Induced Displacement*, (Washington DC: The Brookings Institute-SAIS Project on Internal Displacement, 2003).

10. O. Mishra ed. *Forced Migration in the South Asian Region*, (Washington D.C.: Brooking Institute 2004).
11. Stephen Castles, Towards a Sociology of Forced Migration and Social Transformation, p. 13.
12. See for example Theresa Hayter, "No Borders: The Case Against Immigration Controls," *Feminist Review*, Vol. 73, 2003, pp. 6-18.
13. L. Mckay, Women Asylum seekers in Australia: Discrimination and the Migration Legislation Amendment Act No 6, (Cth). *Melbourne Journal of International Law,* Vol. 4, No. 2, 2003, p. 444.
14. R. Devetak, in Fear of Refugees: The Politics of Border Protection in Australia, *International Journal of Human Rights*, Vol. 8, No. 1, 2004, p. 103.
15. Ranabir Samaddar, *The Marginal Nation: Transborder Migration from Bangladesh to West Bengal,* (New Delhi, Sage, 1999).
16. Ranabir Samaddar ed. *Refugees and the State: Practices of Asylum and Care in India 1947-2000* (Sage, New Delhi, 2003), p. 11.
17. Article 1, United Nations Convention Relating to the Status of the Refugee, 1951.
18. A. Suhrke and K. Newland, "UNHCR: Uphill into the future," *The International Migration Review,* Vol. 35, No. 1, 2001, p. 284.
19. Gil Loescher, The UNHCR and World Politics: State Interests vs. Institutional Autonomy, *International Migration Review,* Vol. 35, No. 1, 2001, p. 64.
20. Cited in Chimni 2000, p. 61.
21. R. Haines, Gender-related Persecution in F. Nicholson, T. Volker and E. Teller ed., *Refugee Protection in International Law: UNHCR's Global Consultations on International Protection* (Cambridge: Cambridge University Press, 2003) p. 327.
22. Chris Hann, Nation-State, Religion and Uncivil Society: Two Perspectives from the Periphery, *Daedalus*, Vol. 26, No. 2, 1997, pp. 27-45.
23. J.M. Acharya, M. Gurung and R. Samaddar, Chronicles of a No-Where People on the Indo-Bangladesh Border, *SAFHR Paper No 14*, (Kathmandu: South Asia Forum for Human Rights, 2003), p. 6.
24. Boyd, M., Gender, Refugee Status and Permanent Settlement, *Gender Issues,* Vol. 17, Issue 1, pp. 5-25; Cohen, R., "What's So Terrible about Rape?" and Other Attitudes at the United Nations," *SAIS Review,* Vol. 20, Issue 2, 2000, pp. 73-7; and A. Macklin, Refugee Women and the Imperative of Categories, *Human Rights Quarterly*, Vol. 17, No. 2, 1995, pp. 213-77.
25. Boyd, *Gender, Refugee Status and Permanent Settlement*, p. 8.
26. Macklin, *Refugee Women and the Imperative of Categories*, p. 218.
27. Boyd, *Gender, Refugee Status and Permanent Settlement*, p. 9.
28. Haines, *Gender-related Persecution*, p. 336.
29. Boyd, *Gender, Refugee Status and Permanent Settlement*, p. 12.
30. Ruchira Ganguly-Scrase and Roberta Julian, The Gendering of Identity: Minority Women in a Comparative Perspective, *Asian and Pacific Migration Journal*, Vol. 6, Nos. 3-4, 1997, p. 435.
31. Birgette Sorensen, Anthropological Contributions to Forced Migration Studies: Critical Analysis and Ethnography, *Conference Paper-Researching Internal displacement*, NTNU Trondheim 7-8 February, 2003, p. 15. and B. Sorensen,

Anthropological Research on Forced Migration: Contributions and Challenges", *Acta Geographica,* Vol. 6, 2003, pp. 65-83.

32. Roberta Julian, Adrian Franklin and Bruce Felmingham, ed., *Home From Home: Refugees in Tasmania*. (Canberra: DIMA, 1997).
33. Dorothy Smith, Institutional Ethnography in Tim May (ed.) *Qualitative Research in Action*. (London: Sage, 2002), pp. 17-52.
34. Smith, *Institutional Ethnography*, p. 40.
35. Smith, *Institutional Ethnography*, p. 21
36. Smith, *Institutional Ethnography*, p. 29
37. Smith, *Institutional Ethnography*, p. 21.
38. Smith, *Institutional Ethnography*, p. 28.
39. See Ruchira Ganguly-Scrase and Roberta Julian, The Gendering of Identity: Minority Women in a Comparative Perspective; Ruchira Ganguly-Scrase and Roberta Julian "Minority Relations and the Experiences of Migration." *Women's Studies International Forum,* Vol. 21, No. 6, 1998, pp. 633-48.
40. Ruchira Ganguly-Scrase and Timothy J. Scrase, "Who Wins? Who Loses? And Who Even Knows?—Responses to Economic Liberalisation and Cultural Globalisation" *South Asia*, vol. 2, no. 10, 2001, pp. 141-158; Ruchira Ganguly-Scrase "Paradoxes of Globalization, Liberalization and Gender Equality: The Worldviews of the Lower Middle Classes in West Bengal" in *Gender and Society*, vol. 17, no. 4, 2003, pp. 544-566.
41. Office of Multicultural Affairs (OMA) *National Agenda for a Multicultural Australia: Sharing Our Future*, (Canberra: AGPS, 1989).
42. John Urry, *The Tourist Gaze*, (London: Sage, 2002).
43. Bertil Linter, Bangladesh A Cocoon of Terror, *Far Eastern Economic Review*, April 4, 2002.
44. Amnesty International Report, 2001, *Communalism Combat*, vol. 8, no. 74, pp. 10-17.
45. The Bharatiya Janata Party (the BJP) pro-Hindu nationalist party and the Hindu Right in general speak in terms of Muslim Bangladeshi immigrants as 'infiltrators' who must be driven out from India, while Hindu cross-border migrants are regarded as bona-fide refugees. These claims are more pronounced outside of the state of West Bengal. See Michael Gillan "Refugees or Infiltrators? The Bharatiya Janata Party and 'Illegal' Migration from Bangladesh", *Asian Studies Review*, vol. 26, no. 1, pp. 2002, pp. 73-95; also S. Ramachandran "Operation Pushback: State, Slums and Surreptitious Bangladeshis in New Delhi", *Singapore Journal of Tropical Geography*, vol. 23, 2002) pp. 311-332.
46. Dolly Arora, "Structural adjustment programme and gender concerns in India," *Journal of Contemporary Asia,* Vol. 29, Issue 3, 1999, pp. 328-361; S.M. Okin "Poverty, Well-Being and Gender: Who Counts? Who's Heard?" *Philosophy and Public Affairs,* Vol. 31, Issue 3, 2003, pp. 280-316.
47. This is particularly so in the case of increased sexual violence, where female refugees lack male figureheads; see Anonymous, "Protecting Refugee Women: From policy to programme implementation," *Migrant World Magazine,* Vol. 23, Issue 5, 1995, p. 30.
48. The significance of the ration card is that the government provides subsidised food and fuel to all citizens. Therefore anyone holding a ration card is always

synonymous with being a citizen. However, it is also important to note that under neo-liberal adjustment policies these subsidies are under threat. While the Indian middle classes with education and skills to access high paying jobs in the new economy (i.e. not needing a ration card), the poor are under even greater threat of marginalisation.

49. Sudipto Kaviraj in N. Gopal Jayal, ed., *Democracy in India*, (New Delhi: Oxford University Press, 2000), p. 241
50. see Digital Installation: *Border Crossings: Rethinking Women and Forced Migration in Post-colonial States of Asia* by Ruchira Ganguly-Scrase and Tamara Gulic, 2003.
51. Nancy D. Donnelly, *The Changing Lives of Refugee Hmong Women*. (Seattle: University of Washington Press, 1994)
52. For details of such interaction see Pranee Liamputtong Rice, When I had my baby here! in Pranee Liamputtong Rice (ed.) *Asian Mothers, Australian Birth*, (Melbourne, Ausmed Publications, 1994) pp. 117-132.
53. June Anderson, *Mayko's Story: A Hmong Textile Artist in California*, (San Francisco: California Academy of Sciences, 1996) p. 30.
54. Ghassan Hage, *White Nation: Fantasies of White Supremacy in a Multicultural Society*. (Sydney, Pluto Press, 1998).
55. Bhabha, (1990)
56. Nicholas Tapp, Hmong Diaspora in Australia in Nicholas Tapp and Gary Lee, ed., *The Hmong of Australia: Culture and Diaspora,* Canberra: Pandanus Books, 2004).
57. Ien Ang, "Asians in Australia: A Contradiction in Terms?" in John Docker and Gerhard Fischer, ed., *Race, Colour and Identity in Australia and New Zealand* (Sydney: UNSW Press, 2000) pp. 115-130.
58. See Ien Ang, Sharon Chalmers, Lisa Law and Mandy Thomas, ed., *Alter/Asians: Asian-Australian Identities in Art, Media and Popular Culture*. (Sydney: Pluto Press, 2000).
59. Tapp, 2004
60. Bays, 1996
61. Jasodahra Bagchi and Subhoranjan Dasgupta, ed., *The Trauma and the Triumph: Gender and Partition in Eastern India* (Street: Kolkata, 2003); Pradip K. Bose, *Refugees in West Bengal: Institutional Processes and Contested Identities*. (Calcutta: Mahanirban Calcutta Research Group, 2000).

8

Culture and Security: A Lost Opportunity?

GREG BATTYE

What constitutes security from mob violence and its possible further consequences, and how is that security to be generated and maintained? Is it reasonable to assert that a hardening in attitudes to migration and cultural diversity in Australia over the last decade has led to an increased risk of such violence? These are some of the questions pondered, in particular relation to contemporary Australia, in this paper.

The paper was commenced before the events of late 2005 at Cronulla Beach in southern Sydney.[1] While the Cronulla episode served to make concrete some possibilities about which many people in Australia had been worried for some time, it had been my intention to discuss the reasons for the existence of those possibilities rather than any actual event. Cronulla is important however, both because it represents an escalation of the theoretical into the actual, validating earlier warnings that something of this sort might happen—and, more ominously, because such events have the potential to become by themselves causes for worse things. This paper therefore attempts to contextualise Cronulla in the framework of my original goal. It discusses the changed attitudes to migration and multiculturalism, and the corresponding encouragement of a vaguely defined but strongly jingoistic version of Australian 'culture,' which have been pervasive in Australia since the election of the Howard Liberal government in 1996. It further proposes that these attitudinal changes are likely to encourage, if not actually produce, the very instability that their proponents claim to be seeking to avoid.

There is a long history of resistance to social difference in the Sutherland Shire, which contains Cronulla Beach and which is now very distinctive among Sydney suburbs for the low percentage of people born in non-English-speaking countries. Only 18 per cent of Shire residents were born overseas, as compared to 22 per cent for the rest of Australia; of those overseas-born, roughly half were born in the U.K. or New Zealand.[2] The Shire is thus "frighteningly white."[3] Sutherland residents have always been highly protective of their precious beaches, even from other Anglo-Australian outsiders; violent confrontations between local surfers and surfers visiting from the western suburbs have occurred repeatedly over the last 40 years. These days, while the social and ethnic profile of Sutherland locals has remained relatively static for decades, visitors are likely to be young Muslims from those same western suburbs where now nearly 50 per cent of residents were born in non-English-speaking countries—and most of the other residents are their children[4]. Young women bear the brunt of many disputes, and various myths, of which some variant was once possibly true, are repeatedly quoted as encapsulating what is wrong: "a young Muslim woman has her *hijab* torn from her head and is chased down a sand dune by a pack of braying men. A young Anglo woman runs from a pack of braying men who are threatening her because she wears a bikini. Eventually, she runs into the sea and swims off."[5]

Aggressive gang behaviour on the beaches of the Shire by groups of young Lebanese-Australian men had already been identified as a problem prior to the 2005 Cronulla riot, even within the Lebanese-Australian communities in Lakemba and other western Sydney suburbs from whence the young men emanated. It had also, for some time, been a problem which combined badly with the fierce defense of 'their' beaches by Anglo-Australian local Sutherland youths. Early in December, two Anglo-Australian lifesavers were attacked, apparently by 'young men of middle-eastern appearance,' and in response, a series of inflammatory text messages urging "Aussies" to gather at North Cronulla beach for violent gang action against "lebs" and "wogs" was widely distributed by mobile telephone. Implicit support, at the very least, for the actions of the Anglo-Australian youths was provided by the broadcast of anti-Lebanese sentiments on Sydney talkback radio. On Sunday 11 December, a large group of aggressive and very drunk youths, some carrying or wrapped in Australian flags, some wearing offensive T-shirts, many of them chanting confused slogans about Anzacs or singing altered versions of 'Waltzing Matilda,' converged on Cronulla beach and began a running series of cowardly mob attacks on anyone of middle-eastern appearance. Over the early part of the following week, major retribution attacks by mobile convoys in the Cronulla shopping centre left a trail of severely damaged cars and shop windows, with several personal injuries from assaults.

While the Australian Prime Minister, John Howard, has denied that racism was the basis of the disturbance, the clear consensus among observers both in Australia and overseas has been that this represents the tip of a large iceberg of racially-based fear and suspicion. However one might rate the dangers of home-grown terrorism in Australia—and there seems little reason to rate such dangers as significantly different from those other countries which have already suffered such attacks—it should take little insight to understand that events such as the Cronulla dispute can become a trigger for far worse violence along related ethnic and racial lines, and for violence with a far more explicitly political motivation. Such insight can be readily gained from understanding a little of the world view of contemporary disaffected young men in a globalised Australia.

The global political situation forms an important part of the background to the mind-set of anyone with a propensity to graduate from racially based mob violence to actual terrorism. Relative to many countries, Australia is an outward-looking country with a good exposure to global news. Many global events which do not directly involve Australia are nevertheless ingredients in the world view of Australians, and some events stand out as likely to particularly bear on the world of disaffected young men, whatever their background—that is, on those most prone to causing certain serious breaches of security.

First among these is the attack on New York on 11September 2001. As Mark Danner has pointed out in the *New York Times*,[6] the key weapon for this attack was not the aeroplane, but the television set. All day for weeks, and frequently over all the subsequent years, every television set in every corner of the globe, in every language and in images which spoke clearly above and beyond language, demonstrated as incontrovertible fact that the United States was vulnerable; that 19 fanatics armed with office supplies could successfully attack the world's richest nation, supposedly protected by the world's most powerful military force, and turn notification of their victory into the world's most extensively televised media spectacle, all without paying a cent in advertising. Do we know if this recruiting drive for short but spectacular careers in terror worked? We have Bali, London, Madrid and the whole tragic Iraq insurgency to suggest that it did, but even more tellingly we have Osama bin Laden's claim, probably true, that in one city in Holland alone, "the number of people who accepted Islam in the days following the operations [September 11 2001] were more than the people who accepted Islam in the last 11 years."[7] The September 2001 attack was an event described by the German avant-garde composer Karlheinz Stockhausen as "the greatest work of art imaginable for the whole cosmos,"[8] and by Italian playwright and Nobel laureate Dario Fo in the following terms:

> Big speculators joyfully splash about in an economy that lets millions of people die every year in misery. What are 20,000 dead in New York by comparison?... Regardless of who carried out the massacre, this violence is the legitimate daughter of the culture of violence, hunger and inhumane exploitation.[9]

Are there likely to be Australians who similarly felt inspired rather than merely horrified? Surely we would need far more evidence to confidently answer 'no' than to confidently answer 'yes.'

Secondly, we can point to the split brought about within Australia by its unquestioning alignment, at country-to-country level, with the United States in military action in Afghanistan and Iraq. Australian views of the US have always been characterised by great cognitive dissonance. We have deeply absorbed American culture; we respect American freedom, erudition and capacity for dissent in the best of its press and academia; we largely, if selectively, welcome American investment; we express gratitude, albeit sometimes grudgingly, for the US role in the Pacific in World War II. On the other hand, we now frequently denigrate both the US role in the Vietnam War, and our own participation in that war at the behest of the US. Polled support for the Howard Government's involvement in Iraq has never risen even to a marginal majority, but in a poll by the *Weekend Australian* on 31 December, 2005, support for the war stood at 27 per cent and opposition at 66 per cent, with only 43 per cent support even among Coalition voters. In the light of the US Government's increasingly desperate, and increasingly unsuccessful, attempts to paint the war in Iraq as a rational response to the 11 September attack, Australian association with this American enterprise is arousing more and more resentment. The split is along several lines: those who continue to support the American and Australian involvement are forced into a sequence of continuously changing, and increasingly irrational, modes of defence, while those who originally opposed both US action and Australian involvement feel increasingly justified in their stance. Australian Muslims, for whom the US-Australian alliance over Afghanistan and Iraq has always seemed largely to be about persecution of their faith, feel themselves to be living with the enemy.

On the domestic front, issues relating to illegal immigration and border security have, over roughly the same period, exacerbated divisions within the country along similar lines, and with even greater practical effect because of their deployment in election campaigns. Politically, the Howard Government has juggled border security issues with a cynical cunning, managing to keep the day-to-day conduct of legal immigration largely untainted by these more contentious matters, and broadly maintaining the formal immigration policy framework inherited from their predecessors — all while simultaneously harvesting the votes of those who, for various reasons, resent or oppose all or some migrant groups. This two-faced approach is unsustainable, and is ultimately a dangerous one for community stability.

Of the various policy frameworks within which migration has taken place in Australia, multiculturalism has been by far the most successful. The term was imported from Canada, during the Whitlam era (1972-75), where it had been used to encapsulate the arrangements struck between descendants of English-and French-speaking settlers as to language use and preservation of their respective cultural traditions. In Australia, the policy was undertaken to avoid the danger of non-English speaking migrants becoming 'non-people' who would play no economic (or other) role in society. It was also intended to reduce general awareness of ethnic group differences as a basis for possible discrimination, while preserving a space for the positive celebration of such differences as a source of enjoyment for all. Rather than identifying known or possible target groups and legislating to protect them, the Australian approach sought to ensure that individual rights would not be infringed on the basis of ethnicity, culture, religion or similar factors. The policy continued to evolve, and probably reached its most thoroughly enunciated form in 1989 when the Commonwealth Government endorsed the principles of the National Agenda for a Multicultural Australia,[10] with three key points:

- Cultural identity—the right of all Australians, within carefully defined limits, to express and share their individual cultural heritage, including their language and religion;
- Social justice—the right of all Australians to equality of treatment and opportunity, and the removal of barriers of race, ethnicity, culture, religion, language, disability, gender or place of birth; and
- Economic efficiency—the need to maintain, develop and use effectively the skills and talents of all Australians, regardless of background.

What is Australia's current official approach to Multiculturalism? It is important to emphasise that the policy had bipartisan support from the time of its introduction, and still has, at least nominally. However, where, for a long time, Multiculturalism and the importance of its position as the binding overall perspective on the nation's view of immigrants, featured prominently in governmental responses to any situation involving immigration or relations between ethnic communities, any such response now from the Howard Government will rather involve vague affirmations about the importance of 'Australian values.'[11]

This change is not along party-political lines: possibly the most active support for Multiculturalism came from the Fraser Liberal Government, in the form of very clear advocacy from Prime Minister Fraser himself. Fraser was a particularly strong supporter of black African struggles for freedom and democracy against Apartheid in South Africa and against the former Ian Smith regime in Rhodesia, and his commitments to democracy and racial equality have been unwavering both while in government, and since leaving it. The Fraser Government endured the most difficult period in the process of settling the Vietnamese migrants who arrived in significant (in Australian terms) numbers either as refugee 'boat people,' or later as 'legitimate' migrants when the post-1975 Vietnamese Government decided to allow selected former political opponents to leave the country rather than supporting them in 're-education' camps. Fraser certainly saw a political opportunity in using Multiculturalism to attract significant parts of the migrant vote from Labor, and succeeded in that goal partly by playing on residual Eastern European and Vietnamese migrant fears of Communism. Nevertheless, his commitment to the substantive principles of Multiculturalism was genuine and consistent. John Menadue, Head of the Department of Immigration and Ethnic Affairs under the Fraser Government and working to then-Minister for Immigration and Ethnic Affairs Ian Macphee in the early 1980s, describes that position as "the most meaningful job of [his] life"[12] and makes the following comparison between the Fraser years and the more recent handling of 'boat people' under John Howard:

> ...the handling of the Indo-Chinese outflow by the Fraser Government in the late 1970s and early 1980s, demonstrated that it is possible to conduct a humanitarian policy while maintaining the integrity of our borders. At that time, more than 4,000 came by boat but were managed carefully and firmly. The major difference between Malcolm Fraser and John Howard is that Malcolm Fraser did not attempt to exploit the problem for party-political purposes, although he did come under quite severe criticism by some unscrupulous people on the left in Australia.

The refugee numbers that Malcolm Fraser dealt with were vastly more than the 'threat' that John Howard faced. At the peak in the late 1970s, there were about 400,000 Indo-Chinese in the refugee camps in Thailand, Malaysia and Indonesia. In one year, we took 15,000 refugees from Indo China alone. Instead of demonising refugees, we acknowledged their plight and heroism. Bogus refugees were quickly processed and deported. The rhetoric was intense at times but humanity was served. We are now proud of what we did.[13]

Multiculturalism continued to attract firm support through the Hawke and Keating Governments to 1996, and was formally reaffirmed via a Parliamentary Statement on Racial Tolerance moved by Prime Minister Howard on 30 October 1996. At about the same time however, Howard also disbanded the Office of Multicultural Affairs and the Bureau of Immigration, Multiculturalism and Population Research, and commissioned an inquiry which debated the complete dropping of the word 'Multiculturalism' before finally changing it to 'Australian Multiculturalism.' We continue to have a Minister for Citizenship and Multicultural Affairs (John Cobb, at the time of writing this paper), but it is unlikely that even a politically aware Australian could name him if asked to do so.

In the spirit of that weak reaffirmation, the formal policy of Multiculturalism has in practice been supplanted in the public mind by Howard's repeated affirmations of the importance of 'Australian values,' implicitly denigrating that positive sense of the value of cultural difference and variety which Multiculturalism had set up over a long period, with a generally remarkable degree of success. For the person in the street who takes little note of official documents or policy statements, a very different perception of immigration and the government's role in it has been constructed. This clearly serves the current government politically, but it also sows the seed of future instability of which the Cronulla episode is likely to be but a mild example.

It should be emphasised here that the perceptual and attitudinal change to which I am pointing has taken place in parallel not just with a maintenance of a similar immigration profile by the Howard Government, but with a clear increase in numbers of the very categories of people about whom the immigration debate has been conducted. In 1994-95, the financial year immediately preceding the election of the Howard government, "Australia accepted 87,000 immigrants." In the financial year 2004-05, "Australia accepted 123,000 new settlers" — a 40 per cent increase, with a 10 per cent increase in the past year alone.[14] The Howard government "has admitted more Asian immigrants than any previous government, more Muslim immigrants than any previous government, and more Muslim refugees"[15] than any previous government. At any time, the integration of such numbers of culturally different people into a relatively small country—and, in most cases, into one city, Sydney—would seem to require great care. In the context of both genuinely substantiated concerns about terrorism, and unfortunate suspicions in the popular mind about inherent links between terrorism and certain ethnic groups, there is clearly a need for a policy framework that allays unwarranted fears and suspicions, and facilitates a unified community response to any genuine internal security threats.

The changed perceptions have been brought about by several distinct incidents and even more by the Howard Government's responses to them. The first was Pauline Hanson, whose inept and naïve efforts together with One Nation, the reactionary party which she began but which eventually sidelined her, prompted Howard's sharp move to the right prior to the 1998 election with a populist policy of turning away boatloads of asylum seekers before they could reach the Australian mainland. Howard had reacted belatedly to Hanson's comments on race and immigration in the 1996 federal election, made at first as a Liberal Party candidate; the Liberal Party subsequently expelled her. He eventually reacted only by saying, in essence, that Ms Hanson was entitled to her opinions. He thus began to cultivate his singular skill at "dog-whistle politics" —Australian journalist Laurie Oakes' term for Howard's ability to allow certain parts of his constituency to receive a message that had not actually been enunciated. By this means Howard signalled to One Nation's constituency that he was, at some essential level, in agreement with their concerns about race and immigration, without ever actually saying so. By the time of the 1998 federal election the One Nation vote had indeed more or less disappeared, soaked up by the Coalition side.

Far more shameful and far more influential in polarizing community attitudes on immigration, were the Tampa and SIEV-X incidents in 2001, leading up to the election of 10 November the same year. On August 27 2001, the Howard government refused docking rights at Christmas Island for 433 rescued Afghani refugees aboard the Norwegian freighter Tampa, thus breaching international conventions for the treatment of asylum seekers. The refugees were later forcibly transferred to the Australian troop carrier, HMAS Manoora, and removed under conditions of great discomfort to hurriedly-erected detention centres on the Pacific island of Nauru, despite the refugees having formally applied, in writing, for protection visas under the International Convention on Refugees.

Such brutal treatment of people who were, prima facie, genuine and deserving refugees, who had already suffered appallingly even prior to their rescue by the Tampa, was a watershed in Prime Minister Howard's manipulation of populist opinion. In the words of Robert Manne:

> Tampa not only assured the government of victory in the November election. It also altered the balance of forces in Australia in a fundamental way. After Tampa, John Howard realised that he could appeal directly to popular instinct and bypass the kind of fussy moral arguments advanced by the educated, left-leaning section of society his government called the 'elites.'[16]

On 19 October 2001 the SIEV-X, an overloaded refugee boat traveling from Indonesia, sank in international waters, drowning 353 people. The sinking took place "well inside the Operation Relex zone where the Prime Minister and [then Minister for Immigration] Mr. Ruddock had proudly boasted a few weeks earlier that Australia would be conducting saturation surveillance."[17] Under the clear leadership of the Prime Minister, a cover-up of Australia's possible responsibility for the drowning was turned into a disgraceful character assassination, by key members of the Government front bench, of the refugees—already routinely characterised by the Government since 1996 as 'queue-jumpers' and 'illegals'—as people who might (but were later proven not to) have thrown their own children overboard to save themselves as the boat sank.

By the time of the federal election in November 2001, John Howard had successfully conflated the events of September 11 with a carefully orchestrated fear and loathing of the refugee groups—most of whom, at that time, were from Afghanistan or Iraq. Dog-whistle politics, and the fears it successfully created within the electorate, returned the Government in that election, against some expectations, and with an increased majority. Subsequent major disturbances in the detention centres for illegal immigrants, set up in remote and inhospitable areas and run essentially as prisons, were used by the Government to cast further slurs on potential refugees awaiting assessment, even though by far the majority of these people have subsequently been accepted as legitimate refugees and admitted to Australia.

The Cornelia Rau and Vivian Alvarez Solon cases served to show how far the Government's perspective on immigrants had penetrated the culture of the Immigration Department itself. Cornelia Rau, an Australian citizen of German origin who suffered from a mental disorder, was summarily classified as an illegal immigrant after spending six months in a Queensland jail and then incarcerated in a detention centre for three months without investigation of her case; despite being, for this whole time, on the missing persons list. Vivian Alvarez Solon, an Australian citizen of Philippine origin, had her passport seized and was wrongly deported to the Philippines, despite having been badly injured in an as-yet-unexplained accident shortly prior to her deportation. An internal cover-up in the Department further delayed remedial action when the mistake was first discovered. In both these incidents, and in many other matters concerning the detention centres, it became clear that the Immigration Department had been empowered by the Howard Government to act as a law unto itself. It could, for instance, successfully (if illegally) deport an Australian citizen—so long as they were clearly of non-Anglo-Australian Heritage—without any independent monitoring by a court of law.

In the press, post-Cronulla observers pointed to these and other events as having created "a declining level of tolerance and a rising sense of prejudice."[18] Even those who also pointed to local tribalism and the exacerbating effects of alcohol as causes have admitted to the evidence of "a resurgence of nationalist, racist politics."[19] It is becoming hard to avoid the conclusion that the stage has been set, albeit unintentionally, for severe and possibly continuing social dislocation along the same racial, ethnic and religious lines as have characterised the unfortunate 'War on Terror.' Multiculturalism has either failed or, more likely, has simply broken down from lack of real support and maintenance for a decade. To a population already far too attuned to Mr. Howard's dog whistle, the Prime Minister's denial that racism is involved, even while he condemns the violence itself, simply appears to confer an obscure form of approval on the attitudes underlying the Anglo-Australian side of the thuggery observed at Cronulla.

The situation in Sydney is fresh, fluid and still the subject of ongoing analysis. It is salutary therefore to look outside Australia to find situations in which ethnic tensions have similarly erupted into violence—or not—and to try to determine the causes in each case. Is the key to harmonious relations, as the Prime Minister suggests, adherence to some single set of shared national values, or are other things more important? Looking to Europe, we can see that a comparison of France and Germany, apropos the November 2005 ethnic tensions in France, indicates some factors that may be truly key to whether violence breaks out or not.

France has been a multiethnic society for decades, and apart from the gruesome historical exception of the Vichy regime's dispatch of some 75,000 Jews to the Nazi death camps, has generally managed integration effectively. The model of integration, however, bears some likeness to what John Howard appears to be expressing as desirable for Australia: resolute opposition to any show of loyalty to any entity (whether an ethnic group, a religion, or anything else) other than the nation itself. The continuing fierce French debate over the wearing of Muslim headscarves in schools has its origins in the perception that some dissolution of civic unity would follow from any dilution of national loyalty.

The French model of widespread acceptance of immigrants, as long as they wanted ultimately to be French, began to break down with large-scale immigration from its mainly-Muslim former colonies in the 1960s. The fact that these people were Muslim, however, "was not the cause of this collapse"[20] of integration; rather, the cause was precisely their post-colonial status. These were colonies which had shocked France by rejecting French authority and French culture; there was strong prejudice against them, and little energy or motivation left in the old model of integration to bring them into the national fold. They were "shunted into bleak suburban housing projects,"[21] where their descendants remain—separated from French society, unemployed, aware of the racist attitudes directed at them from the rest of France should they seek employment, and deeply angry. The children of the original immigrants are citizens by virtue of being born in France—the same situation as holds in Australia—but their citizenship has been of no help to them. The French riots in November 2005 were not examples of Islamist militancy as broadly construed elsewhere—or at least, not yet. But any such incident generates a rich compost of resentment in which to plant the seeds of far worse trouble; and the seeds, of course, are blowing everywhere in the wind.

France thus failed to meet an expectation, on the part of immigrants, of certain rights and fruits of citizenship. Germany, with a large immigrant population which includes many Muslim guest workers from Turkey, has had a very different experience.

German citizenship is based on 'blood'—on German parentage, wherever one is born. Descendants of the guest-worker programmes of the 50s and 60s—Italians, Spaniards and Turks who came for work in a rapidly-expanding economy—could not become citizens, but could also not legally be deported when the guest-worker programmes ended, and many of them brought their families to Germany to settle down. Even without citizenship, and without being subject to any all-encompassing policy initiatives such as Multiculturalism, they were granted some of the very things which a policy like Multiculturalism might have been expected to provide for them: the right to participate in some political processes, membership of unions and labour councils, and freedom of speech and movement.[22] Most significantly, "they settled not in separate housing projects, but in war-damaged inner city neighbourhoods"[23] where their integration through immediate participation in the economy and in urban renewal was a plainly observed fact, growing organically from everyday life. As France burned for two weeks in November 2005, there were no riots in Germany.

The original policy of Multiculturalism in Australia had sought to allow a space for cultural difference by explicitly, and simultaneously, recognising cultural differences and bringing those differences under the umbrella of an inclusive understanding of common social and political institutions, and values. But conservative forces in Australia, aided if not actually led by Prime Minister Howard, have perverted Multiculturalism by picturing it as something which, by celebrating other cultures, denigrates 'Australian values.' This has led in turn to a new and ugly form of nationalism which is preoccupied with identifying who does, and who does not, belong to the Australian nation. By extension, those who are deemed not to belong become targets for processes of further exclusion—or worse. Cronulla showed what might only be the beginning of this process. Again, an eye cast towards Europe over the last 60 years will provide several models for where such a process may easily lead if not stopped early.

Perhaps it is indeed time to review Multiculturalism, and to provide a better and tighter framework for similar ideas now that the original need has been significantly intensified, and the original meaning so corrupted. Even if there is just great uncertainty about what Multiculturalism means—and it seems that there is—then ultimately it means nothing, since its real value is as a symbol which inspires allegiance to the policies and procedures it spawns. Certainly, multiculturalism must be a means to an end, and perhaps after thirty years it has become a hollow ideal for too many people; a mere end in itself which now lacks rhetorical or motivational strength.

All the more urgent, therefore, is the need for a replacement policy, a rejuvenated mechanism for "recognis[ing] difference within a common and shared set of constitutional and political institutions and values."[24] The real requirement for unity is "that we identify with the political nation, conceived of as a self-governing, political and moral community and not a cultural nation derived from some set of mythical core cultural values signifying unifying cultural values of the dominant group in society."[25] What Cronulla demonstrated with singular and alarming clarity is the logical result of the Howard Government's insistence on pulling back from the "excesses" of multiculturalism and attempting to replace it with a confected and poorly conceptualised set of symbolic loyalties: to the Australian flag, the Anzac legend, the national anthem, and even to a crudely reworked version of Australian history. These were precisely the symbols on show at Cronulla—in the hands of Anglo-Australian thugs.

Cronulla was a market week, and a recruiting drive, for the very worst elements in Australian society—and not, of course, just for Anglo-Australian elements. For those against whom the forces of exclusion have been directed, not just at Cronulla in December 2005, but over the decade since 1996, other possible allegiances wait in the wings. These allegiances are most attractive precisely to those who feel most alienated, and to those who feel a need to strike out against a society that seems to have turned against them. Conservatives who point to ethnic and racial tensions as a possible source of much worse violence than Cronulla are absolutely correct—but at the moment, it is they who are most actively pushing us towards a situation which makes such further violence all the more likely.

End Notes

1. A summary description of the Cronulla riots themselves, including some background and analysis, can be found in the Wikipedia at: <http://en.wikipedia.org/w index.php?title=2005_Sydney_race_riots&oldid=42243744>.
2. Figures from 2001 Australian Census. Qtd. in Jenna Price, "Tribal war a repeat of history," *Canberra Times*, 13 December, 2005, p. 4.
3. Jennifer Cornwall, co-author of a history of Sutherland Shire, qtd. in Price, "Tribal Ear A Repeat of History," p. 4.
4. Information from Centre for Population and Urban Research, Monash University. Qtd. In Lee Glendinning, "A Tale of Two Sydneys: Affluent Versus Aspiring," *Sydney Morning Herald* Weekend Edition 17-18 December, 2005: News p. 7.
5. Jenna Price, An ugly face erupts, *Canberra Times* 17 December, 2005: p. B1.
6. Mark Danner, Taking Stock of the Forever War, *New York Times Magazine* 11 September, 2005, cover story. This article may also be seen on Mark Danner's own web site at: http://www.markdanner.com/nyt/091105_taking.htm
7. Mark Danner, Taking Stock of the Forever War.
8. Mark Danner, Taking Stock of the Forever War.
9. William Osborne, quoted on his web site: http://www.osborne-conant.org/documentation_stockhausen.htm
   The original source was an email newsletter sent out by Dario Fo himself, and subsequently quoted in Steven Erlanger, "In Europe, Some Say the Attacks Stemmed from American Failings," *New York Times* 22 Sept. 2001, online edition.
10. See: http://www.immi.gov.au/multicultural/_inc/publications/agenda/agenda89/toc.htm
11. John Howard has made particular use of the publicity surrounding his 10th anniversary as Prime Minister to promote his views on the adoption of 'Australian values' by migrants. See for example "Howard marks his 10 years as PM by

telling migrants...Live here, be Australian," *Sydney Morning Herald Weekend Edition* 25-26 February, 2006: p. 1.

12. John Menadue, "Australian Multiculturalism: successes, problems and risks," *ON LINE OPINION: Australia's e-journal of social and political debate* 27 Nov. 2002. http://www.onlineopinion.com.au/view.asp?article=523
13. John Menadue, Australian Multiculturalism: Successes, Problems and Risks.
14. Paul Sheehan, Little squares that define a nation, *Sydney Morning Herald,* 2 January, 2006: Comment p. 11.
15. Paul Sheehan, Little squares that define a nation.
16. Robert Manne, How Tampa sailed into 2002, *Age* 30 Dec. 2002 online ed.: http://www.theage.com.au/articles/2002/12/29/1040511254630.html
17. Marg Hutton, "SIEVX & The DFAT Cable: The Conspiracy Of Silence," downloadable from the SIEVX.com site at: http://sievx.com/archives/2003_05-06/20030520.shtml
18. Hugh Mackay, qtd in Jenna Price, A Tale of two Sydneys, *Canberra Times,* 13 December, 2005: News p. 4.
19. Fear and suspicion after 9/11 have been fuel on the fire, *Canberra Times,* 13 December, 2005: News p. 4.
20. David, A. Bell, Why the French Forgot How to Assimilate, *New Republic*, 17 November, 2005 online edition.
21. *Ibid.*
22. Andrew Curry, Why There were No Riots in Germany, *New Republic* 16 November, 2005 online edition.
23. *Ibid.*
24. Laksiri Jaysuriya, Our Shared, Core Values are But a Myth Underpinning this New Racism, *Sydney Morning Herald*, 21 December, 2005: Comment p. 11.
25. *Ibid.*

9

Compassion and Fear—Convergence and Divergence: Politics and the Media

PETER GALE

The public response in Australia to the Asian Tsunami was seen by many as unprecedented. The reaction by the Howard Government with pledges of aid, military resources and ministerial visits to the region was also seen as significant in contrast with the treatment of asylum seekers arriving by boat from Asia over the past decade.[1] The effects of the tsunami along with the Australian aid effort were widely reported in the Australian media. For example, *The Australian* under the headline, "PM's $500m Aid Package" features a picture of un-named children in a refugee camp in Banda Aceh.[2] The Reverend Tim Costello, the chief executive of World Vision Australia, commented on this unprecedented aid response by Australians claiming this as his proudest moment when Australians donated record sums to the tsunami appeal—noting that this was the "...moral moment that really, that really extended the sense that we're a global village".[3]

The moral moment appeared to be oppositional to what was seen as the emergence of anti-Asian racism in Australia through the late 1990s associated with Hansonism. Pauline Hanson, elected in 1996, attracted unprecedented media attention in the first years of the Howard Government following her inflammatory comments on Australia being "swamped by Asians". Hansonism became synonymous with both xenophobia and a politics of division and discontent.[4] With much of the support for Pauline Hanson coming from the traditional conservative National and Liberal Party coalition it was not surprising that a politics of fear became a feature of the three subsequent federal election campaigns. For example, during the 2001 federal election campaign the fear of terrorism featured prominently, as 11 September was coupled with the fear of a flood of asylum seekers following the events surrounding the asylum seekers aboard the Tampa.[5] The appearance of a refugee crisis leading up to the 2001 election and the subsequent re-election of the Howard Government were significant inclusions in this new era in contemporary Australian political life, including what is seen as dog whistling, or wedge politics. Dog whistle politics is seen to target a particular constituency with a message that engenders political support from an attuned electorate, often in the form of a populist national appeal.[6]

Since 11 September and following the deaths of Australian citizens in Bali in October 2002, there has been a heightened level of debate over issues of national security and policies on border protection as a discourse associated with the war on terror. Such debates have centred on Australia's relationship with both the US and our closest neighbours in East Asia. Debates on national security have also renewed the focus on Australia's relationship with nations in the Asia Pacific region. The response to terrorism among many western nation states has reproduced what is seen as the binary between the west and the rest, or more commonly identified as the west and Islam.[7]

Similarly, media reporting in Australia on both criminal activity and terrorism often draws links between Islam and violence, particularly in some sections of the media, contributing to an increased level of anti-Muslim sentiment.[8] Since 7/11 fear has become a central feature of contemporary politics in countries such as Australia.[9] However, the present-day politics of fear in Australia draws on a long history of fear and hatred.[10] Frank Furendi highlights the significance of fear under both the Bush administration and the Blair Government, but makes the point that the current discourse is not isolated to post 9/11. However, Furendi argues that the contemporary manifestations of such a politics of fear, heightens the risk of the electorate becoming dis-engaged on issues of substance and bypassing democracy.[11]

At the end of a decade under a Howard Government in Australia, there has been significant debate on both economic and social policy.[12] For example, the former Prime Minister, Malcolm Fraser argues that the Howard Government has been driven by a politics of fear.[13] Others have argued that there has been an ideological crisis in Australian politics with very little difference between the major political parties, with a significant focus on social issues such as the policy and treatment of asylum seekers.[14] As political journalist Nicholas Rothwell highlights, Howard's populist politics with the Australian flag as a backdrop for press conferences and speeches. He also argues that John Howard has courted the Hansonite constituency as a nationalist leader during the war on terror, and being seen as the patron of the troops in Afghanistan and Iraq.[15] This is explored further in the following section that focuses on the contrasting discourse of the war on terror and the political response to the tsunami.

The War on Terror and the Tsunami

The reporting on the Tsunami and the political response that followed can be seen to stand in blunt contrast to the media reporting on the Bali bombing and war on terror. The overwhelming response to the Asian Tsunami by the Australian public can be identified as either a substantive shift towards a shared sense of global responsibility as a universal imagined community, or alternatively, as a brief symbolic moment of generosity on the part of western nation states fuelled by an unprecedented level of media coverage of a disaster in the light of more recent hard line policies on asylum seekers.[16]

Either way, the Tsunami can be seen as a significant moment in foreign policy following the military interventions in Afghanistan and Iraq. The Howard Government entered the forefront of international media attention in East Asia in 1996 as the media gaze was drawn to issues of racism in Australia, followed by Australia's intervention in East Timor. The Government's response to the Tampa in 2001, and the subsequent policies on border protection, continued a sustained focus on Australia in the East Asian media. Some have argued that this media reporting has damaged Australian relations with East Asian nations over the past decade.[17] For example, Broinowski highlights the significant level of coverage surrounding the conflict in East Timor and the media coverage of the crisis between 1998 and 2000. Broinowski also includes some discussion on the media reporting in East Asia on the bombings in Bali on 12 October 2002 and how such reporting closely replicated the representations of Australia during the East Timor crisis.[18]

During the years following the terrorist attacks in the US and the participation of Australia among the coalition of the willing in the war in Afghanistan and Iraq there has been renewed media attention on the relationship between white Australia and people of middle-eastern appearance.[19] Anti-Muslim sentiment has been heightened through such media reporting in Australia, fuelled by the connections made between asylum seekers and terrorism in debates on both immigration and border security.[20] Correspondingly, debates over issues such as border protection and security in Australia have taken place at a time when the world appears to be divided between the West and Islam. While many people around Australia viewing images of the "race riots" in Cronulla, Sydney, in December 2005 were shocked and disturbed, perceiving such events as being un-Australian, some commentary on Cronulla concluded that such racial conflict was the result of the heightened politics of fear and anxiety over the past decade, associated more recently with the war on terror.

While neither the West nor Islam are homogenous entities media reporting on issues of terrorism or the war in Iraq continues to represent a binary between the West and Islam. The war on terrorism is often identified as being associated with fundamentalism, and in media reporting this is commonly represented as a war on Islam.[21] For a Muslim minority in a western nation, people of middle-eastern appearance have experienced an intensification of anti-Muslim sentiment since 11 September 2001.[22] While Pauline Hanson may have faded from the media spotlight, nevertheless, Hansonism as a politics of fear, and in particular, 'anti-Asian' or 'anti-Muslim' sentiment remains an ever-present feature of contemporary Australian politics and media attention. Racism, both in Australia through the recent event at Cronulla, and in many other western nation states, is then seen as the inevitable outcome of the clash of cultures. Few question the political discourse surrounding foreign policy and the war on terror, or debate on policies on border protection and security, as contributing to racial violence.

Analysis of the relationship between debate on domestic policy issues and foreign policy, and political discourse on nationalism and symbolic markers on inclusion and exclusion, is central to exploring the underlying issues related to racism as experienced at Cronulla. One critical question centres on the role of the media in the democratic process in western nation states such as Australia. Central to such debates is the relationship between media discourse and contemporary politics in an era where political ideology is often supplanted by populist and nationalist politics. For example, the analysis of media discourse on social policies such as immigration or national security should also include an exploration of the role of the media in producing and reproducing public opinion.

Similarly, in his analysis of Australian prime ministers, James Curran argues that the central aspect of political leadership since federation has been the relationship between political policy and national identity.[23] For example, the concept of white Australia can be seen as a defining feature of Australian politics since federation and whiteness remains central to contemporary discourse on Australia as a nation, and what is seen as the mainstream, or middle Australia. Whiteness has been synonymous with the cultural heritage and core values of the nation. However, whiteness has also been a position of privilege, while also being unseen, as the taken for granted mainstream.[24] This is demonstrated by Ghassan Hage who highlights the perceived threat to mainstream Australia in his analysis of paranoid nationalism.[25] However, within the context of the politics of fear associated with the war on terror, there appears to be a contradiction between such a politics of fear and the Australian response in aid to the tsunami. This is explored further through the paper based on analysis of media and political discourse on the tsunami in national and regional newspapers.

Methodology

Analysis of the discourses on the tsunami and the war on terror was founded on the *Newsbank* newspaper data base using key words associated with the reporting on both the war on terror and the tsunami. The sample period for the reporting on the tsunami is taken from newspapers between the 27 December, 2004 and the 16 January, 2005 with an emphasis on *The*

Australian and *The Weekend Australian*, as a newspaper with a national daily circulation, along with other major regional newspapers such as *The Age* and the *Sydney Morning Herald*. Articles that made reference to the tsunami were included in the analysis. This included a sample of 200 articles reporting on the Tsunami taken from over 2000 articles published during the three weeks. A comparative data base on the war on terror was taken from the media reporting during the initial three week period following the events of 11 September 2001.

The research employed critical discourse analysis, placing an emphasis on particular metaphors that form the basis of contrasting ideological perspectives. While texts do not have a fixed meaning the analysis sought to identify the contrasting themes based on the structure of an article, consisting of the headline, lead, the main body of the text and the concluding comments. For example, Fairclough argues that the generic structure illustrates the way a newspaper seeks to present a particular perspective or persuade the reader as well as the provision of information. While the genre of news reporting often presents what is perceived as two sides to a debate, the way in which this debate is framed with headlines, lead sentences and concluding comments suggests there is often a clearly preferred position of the writer on the issue under discussion.[26]

Within media discourse there are often apparent disparities even within an article or newspaper. Inflammatory headlines can conflict significantly with editorials. For example, headlines are often based on a perceived audience demand for stimulating and exciting news, as well as being a form of entertainment, therefore often creating the image of a crisis.[27] Similarly, conflict and controversy are also seen as newsworthy, while news reporting can also reproduce ideological or cultural consensus through what is included or omitted. There are also divergent methodological approaches to media studies. For example, in his analysis of news reporting, Teun van Dijk places an emphasis on the ways in which racism is reproduced in news-making within western societies and concludes that white people are the beneficiaries of discriminatory practices in education and employment as well as health and housing. Correspondingly, most white people are not confronted daily by a public discourse, such as the media, challenging their material goals and interests.[28] News reporting in the media can be seen to reproduce normative principles that construct symbolic national and cultural boundaries of inclusion and exclusion.

Media Discourse and the War on Terror

Based on the level of media coverage for a news event, it could be argued that 11 September 2001 was one of the most significant events in the modern era.

The political response and media commentary in western nation states such as Australia formed the basis of what became identified as the war on terror. However, unlike other conflicts this was one that had few tangible boundaries, geographic or otherwise, apart from that which was defined within the discourse on the war on terror. The fear of terror and national security has significantly shaped a perceived binary between the imagined national community and the other. For the Muslim and people of middle-eastern appearance this imagined binary has very tangible outcomes in Australia. As described by Ghassan Hage in terms of paranoid nationalism, since 11 September, the Muslim has become the un-questioned other and a "...community of people always predisposed towards crime, rape, illegal entry to Australia and terrorism."[29]

Much of the reporting on 11 September featured the clash of civilisations.[30] Fear became synonymous with the New World Order following the terrorist attacks, as the war on terror was seen as a struggle of "good versus evil".[31] A significant feature of the discourse on the war on terror, are what is seen as the shared values of "freedom and democracy" in the west and being tough on issues relative to national security.[32]

The hard line approach to the threat of terrorism has mirrored the common political stance of being seen to be tough on crime in relation to law and order policies. State governments of both major parties around Australia have sought to maintain electoral advantage by being seen to take a hard line approach to crime. Similarly, the Howard Government has adopted a hard line approach to immigration, particularly in relation to asylum seekers arriving by boat. Following 11 September, this approach has broadened from border security to what are seen as issues of national security. Fear, threat, and crisis were three of the dominant metaphors in the reporting on 11 September and following the deaths of over one hundred Australians in Bali in October 2002, with newspaper headlines such as "fear in our time".[33] Some media commentators focussed more on the threat within Australia following 11 September with arguments that radical Islam was a threat to Australia and that there was a "culture of hate".[34] The war on terror was identified as a time of crisis that justified at times extraordinary actions such as the inclusion of Australian troops in the war in Iraq. Similarly, within such a time of crisis changes in Government policy that would have normally been seen to encroach upon civil liberties prior to 11 September, have been accepted and embraced as necessary in the name of the war on terror. One such example can be seen in the debate on the mandatory detention of the children, and asylum seekers more generally. While there was widespread community support for such policies, and arguable significant electoral support leading up to the 2001 election, there was some opposition to such actions. For example, some political leaders, even within the Liberal Party, as part of the coalition

Government in Australia, have argued that the mandatory detention of asylum seekers, and in particular, the detention of children, is un-Australian. However, others such as the social commentator Hugh Mackay argue that

> …it's actually not un-Australian at all. It might be unjust, unkind, unfair, unreasonable and inhumane but, unhappily, it's not un-Australian.
>
> The melancholy truth is that it has, indeed, been Australian to persist with a policy of indefinite and even brutal mandatory detention of asylum seekers. Our Government has been doing it for years with broad community support, so we might as well accept that it is a characteristically Australian act. In fact, it's so characteristic of us that some other countries, including Britain, are now examining ways of adopting the 'Australian' model of mandatory detention.[35]

Similarly, a focus on Indigenous health, education, and criminal justice in Australia also reflects what is Australian and the boundaries of compassion in Australia. Life expectancy of Indigenous Australians remains more than twenty years less than for non-Indigenous Australians, infant mortality is three times that of mainstream Australia, and unemployment rates of over four times the national average at over twenty percent, with mean income for Indigenous Australians at only 65 percent that of non-Indigenous Australia.[36] Correspondingly, the number of deaths in custody and substance abuse among Indigenous young people, including petrol sniffing in remote communities, is reflective not only Indigenous disadvantage but also level of hope in a future among Indigenous young people.

This is echoed in the comments of Justice Marcus Einfeld who questions:

> What jurisdiction in Australia, indeed what country in the world would jail petrol sniffers? Where in the world is there such inhumanity?[37]

Justice Einfeld is even more strident in his comments on the detention of asylum seekers in Australia, noting that:

> To detain such people without justifiable cause is bad enough in itself, especially as we do so quite indiscriminately of how young or old, sick or in need of special concern they are. But to detain for more than a few hours or days people who flee impossible persecution and unimaginable horrors, have risked their lives and perhaps paid all the money they had and more, to reach Australia in leaky river craft over thousands of kilometres of dangerous and unfriendly seas, is completely inhumane and without justification.
>
> To detain children who may have lost their parents in the course of their journey is even worse. Yet we are doing it on this very day. And we are now the only developed country in the world which practices

> indiscriminate, indeterminate, incommunicado detention of asylum seekers. Alone of all the countries in the world, including Canada, the United States and the various nations of Europe, we have indiscriminately detained all of them, the elderly, the children, the sick and the pregnant…how can detention possibly be just?[38]

The comments of Justice Einfeld appear to highlight the apparent contradiction between what is seen as an unjust and inhumane policy of mandatory detention and the perceived compassion surrounding the Australian public response to the tsunami. The following section explores further the discourse surrounding the tsunami and reflects upon the parallels between the reporting on the war on terror and the tsunami.

Mission Discourse and the Tsunami

The media response to the tsunami was overwhelming with continuous extensive coverage through the new-year period, and throughout January 2005. For example, the major national and regional newspapers in Australia included daily front page coverage and up to 16 page sections on the tsunami during the post-tsunami period. Similarly, television coverage included repeated visual footage of the tsunami taken by many holiday makers who captured images of the effects of the tsunami as they found themselves part of the devastation during the New Year holiday period in Asia. A significant feature of this news reporting were the innocent victims of the tsunami, represented as deserving the compassion, and aid, from western counties with the capacity to provide health care and expertise required in response to the tsunami.

This is illustrated in the ongoing newspaper coverage of the tsunami. For example, the Adelaide based *Sunday Mail* on the 9 January 2005, under the headline of "let us help" and featuring full front page pictorial coverage of Fitri Indriani, a nine year old orphan girl whose family and village was reported as being wiped out by the tsunami.[39] Children feature prominently in such media reporting, along with images of the relief and aid from the west. However, such images stand in stark contrast to one of the major themes in media coverage of asylum seekers and representations of the other. In particular, the reporting on the "flood" of arrivals by boat from East Asia is represented as a threat to national sovereignty and border security. This theme featured prominently leading up to the claims that children were thrown overboard from asylum seeker vessels and the arrival of the Tampa in 2001. Such coverage highlights a binary between the deserving and the undeserving.

As noted above, an example of the public response to the tsunami is reflected in the comments of Tim Costello, brother of the Federal Treasurer, noting that this was a "…time when the global reserves of compassion filled noticeably." Australians contributed over three hundred million Australian dollars to relief appeals. Tim Costello highlights the plight of innocent children, also noting that even with the generous response of so many Australians to the relief effort, "…it takes less than four days for the same number of children who died in the tsunami to die of poverty. Every day twenty nine thousand under-fives die from largely preventable diseases, resulting in 10.6 million deaths a year."[40]

Within what can be identified as a mission discourse related to aid from Australia, there is a binary between the deserving and the undeserving, and boundaries of compassion. This binary is explored further in the following section, focusing on the apparent contradiction between the harsh treatment of asylum seekers and Australia's more recent record on human rights, and the compassion in response to the tsunami.

Analysis of the discourse surrounding the tsunami highlights how such divergent responses are indeed encompassed within, and consistent with, what can be seen as a Christian colonising mission discourse. Such a discourse embraces both fear and compassion. The features of such a discourse can be illustrated in the media coverage of the tsunami and the visit of Peter Costello with his brother Tim Costello to the devastation in Asia and the Australian aid effort in Banda Aceh in Indonesia. For example, the national daily newspaper, *The Australian* featured front page illustrated coverage of Australian surgeon Dr. Peter Sharwood operating on 13-year-old tsunami survivor Syahrul. The article concludes that "through grateful tears", the teenage boy's brother is reported as saying "…thank you, thank you so much" to the Australian doctors.[41] Front page coverage of the tsunami was dominated by headlines and pictures of the suffering of innocent victims, and the aid effort from Australia. This is reflective of a mission discourse of the deserving poor and the capacity of advanced western nations to help through aid, and in particular, through advanced medical technology. The following section explores the relationship between aid from Australia to the Asia Pacific region, and domestic politics in Australia.

Foreign Policy and Domestic Politics

Since 11 September 2001, and following the killing of innocent Australian citizens in Bali in October 2002, there has been a heightened level of debate over issues of personal and national security and policies of border protection. Such debates have centred on Australia's relationship with both the US and our closest national neighbours in East Asia. Debates on national security and the "war on terror" have also renewed focus on Australia's role in the region, in what is commonly identified as a western nation in Asia. The response to terrorism among western nation states such as Australia has also often reproduced what is seen as the binary between the west and Islamic nations.[42] Similarly as noted above, media reporting in Australia on terrorism often draws links between Islam and violence, particularly in some sections of the media, contributing to an increased level of anti-Muslim sentiment.[43]

The Howard Government entered the forefront of media attention in East Asia during the late 1990s with the exceptional level of media coverage on issues of racism in Australia, followed by Australia's intervention in East Timor and US and Australian military intervention in Afghanistan in 2001 and Iraq in 2004.[44] Similarly, the Howard Government's response to the Tampa and the subsequent policies on border protection has continued a sustained focus on Australia in the East Asian media. Many would argue that this media reporting has strained relations between Australia and East Asian nations during the first decade of the Howard Government.[45]

A major focus of attention in foreign policy during the Keating Government during the early 1990s was on developing a closer relationship between Australia and Asia. Economic and trade relations had been a common focus of attention among researchers and commentators. For example, Stephen FitzGerald explored the interrelated questions and issues surrounding the relationship between Australian identity and relations between Australia and the Asia Pacific region.[46] Correspondingly, as noted above, Alison Broinowski examined the relationship between East Asia and Australia but did so through a review of the way in which the Howard Government has been perceived in Asia.[47] Broinowski focuses on representations of Australia as a colonising western nation and the Howard Government as behaving like colonisers. While there is analysis on what was identified as the xenophobia associated with opposition to Asian migration between 1996 and 1998.[48]

What is clear from the analysis of media reporting on Australia in Asia is that domestic politics is closely related to foreign policy. For example, the Tampa incident and Australia's policy on asylum seekers and border protection leading up to and following the 2001 election has refocused the Asian gaze on Australia. Similarly, Australian intervention in East Timor has maintained a heightened level of scrutiny and attention of Australian relations in the region. While the perceptions of Australia as tolerating anti-Asian sentiment dominated media reporting during the late 1990s, the shift in the focus towards questions over what is perceived as a growing anti-Arab or anti-Islamic sentiment has centred renewed attention on the Howard Government.[49]

The political significance and influence of conservative Christianity over the first ten years of the Howard Government is also seen as an important aspect in the analysis of contemporary Australian politics. This is explored by Marion Maddox in her analysis of the relationship between religion and politics in contemporary Australia. One of the central pillars of the rise of the religious right in Australia is founded on a discourse of us and them. While the binary of us and them may be in a constant process of change and may not be fixed, Maddox highlights that the mainstream part of us stands in contrast with, and in opposition to, the imagined threat of them, the other. For example, following the last federal election John Howard proclaimed that he seeks to focus on the things that unite us. However in terms of the political aspirations of particular groups this discourse excludes Aborigines, Muslims, and same-sex couples.[50] As discussed above, such a binary between us and them is a feature of mission discourse in relation to both foreign policy and national security.

The discourse of us and them in debates on both immigration and foreign policy is founded on a binary of the deserving, and the un-deserving. The deserving refugee stands as oppositional to those categorised as "illegal" arrivals. Similarly, the law abiding migrant, who contributes to national wealth, is seen as oppositional to descriptors of people of middle-eastern appearance. In relation to foreign aid, the deserving victims of the tsunami are seen as distinct from the threat of the Islamic other.

Maddox and others also highlight the significance of the conservative Christian movement on the outcome of the recent federal election in 2004 and it is clear that one of the major factors in the Liberal Party success was the electoral support for the Liberal and National Parties through the flow of preferences from the newly formed conservative Family First Party. As a new party, it has a support base clearly located in the traditional mortgage belts of the major cities made up of traditional Liberal and Labour party voters—the ordinary mainstream Australian with concerns over interest rates and what are seen as family values. Family First was founded on what is identified as family values. The values have often been the focus of John Howard, so called traditional values that the Howard Government and the Family First Party share in common.

The Howard Government has placed an emphasis on what is commonly referred to as traditional values and has carefully targeted the traditional family through tax and welfare packages. This is a constituency that John Howard is attuned to, and appeals to, and in many ways is part of what he seeks to uphold as being the traditional values of ordinary Australians. In electoral terms John Howard has been able to build upon his primary electoral support through preferences flowing from the Christian values based Family First Party. This was a partnership of shared values, the values that John Howard has sought to place at the forefront of Australian politics over the past decade. Such values are seen as the symbolic markers of Australia as a nation during a time when personal and national security remain issues at the forefront of media attention.

The 2004 election campaign was significant as much for the absences and silences in debates than what became the central issues during the campaign. One difference that marked the 2004 election from that of previous elections was the focus on what is identified as mainstream Australia-policies that targeted the ordinary Australian. There were no images of refugees, limited debate on the detention of asylum seekers. There was no debate on native title, or very little attention accorded to Indigenous health and more broadly Indigenous issues. Contemporary Australian politics has been mainstreamed. With the focus on the war on terror there has been very little attention on the level of funding to address Indigenous health or housing.[51] In relation to foreign policy, domestic political concerns have outweighed the engagement with Asia that was a feature of foreign policy during the Hawke and Keating governments. Following 11 September 2001 the alliance with the coalition of the willing, through military intervention in Afghanistan and Iraq, have overshadowed the engagement in Asia. In the aftermath of the tsunami there maybe a renewed focus on relations in the region as there is a convergence of interests in reconstruction and aid, however what is more likely is the continued divergence between Australia and Asia as the discourse of us and them predominates with the emphasis in foreign policy being limited to aid and trade.

The Deserving and the Undeserving: Convergence and Divergence

The Howard Government has targeted mainstream Australia through populist and nationalist appeal associated with what is seen as traditional values and national identity, particularly since 11 September. This is reflective of a clear political strategy that John Howard and the Liberal Party have taken from the popular appeal of Pauline Hanson among middle Australia. John Howard has consolidated his leadership of a party through his appeal to the mainstream, while also seeking to cover a broad political spectrum, from the political centre through to the conservative political right. During the 2001 election John Howard took up the populist position on asylum seekers while during the 2004 election Howard reaffirmed his concern for the things that unite us. This sought to engage with and confirm his close relationship with the political agenda of the newly emerging conservative Christian based Family First party. In this context, the reference to the things that unite us within mainstream politics is clearly defined along what is seen as Christian and western democratic traditions with a renewed focus more broadly on historical ties with the ANZAC tradition and western alliances.

The Howard Government has been successful in maintaining an emphasis on the concerns and fears of ordinary Australians, not only fears and anxieties associated with the war on terror, but also fears coupled with interest rates and the Australian dream of owning the family home, and family values. However, the question remains as to why the extraordinary levels of inequality between Indigenous and non-Indigenous health, or the mandatory detention of asylum seekers are not a political concern for ordinary Australians, many of whom responded generously to the recent tsunami appeal. While it can be argued that there was a brief convergence of identity as neighbours in the region, this explanation is outweighed by the ongoing binary discourse between western nations and what is commonly seen as the rest of the world, during a time of war on terror.

This is a discourse founded on a belief in the fundamental differences between us, represented as Christian and western nations, and them, seen as non-western and non-Christian cultures. It is often reported in the media as the clash of cultures in what is identified as the new world order. This is reinforced by the fear of terrorism associated with the war on terror. Within such a narrative there is nothing new in the colonising mission of bringing democracy to the non-western world, or giving charity to the innocent non-western other who may be suffering through natural disasters.

However the divergence between Australia and Asia remains a dominant feature of the discourse founded on what is seen as a clash of cultures, reinforced by domestic policy debates over immigration from Asia, and the treatment of asylum seekers and incidents such as the Tampa. What is clear is that the war on terror has also included an imagined binary between us and them within Australia, and some would argue that the race riots in Cronulla in December 2005 reflect not only this but also an end to multiculturalism in Australia.

For a convergence between nation states such as India and Australia there needs to be a greater level of acknowledgment that there is a close relationship between domestic politics and foreign policy. There also needs to be an increased recognition that the ongoing effects of the discourse on a war on terror with the heightened level of division within an imagined national identity. It will be the task of future governments to address the perceived binary of us and them, and notions of a clash of cultures, through closer relations between Asia and Australia that is moving beyond an emphasis on aid and trade. It is clear that after a decade of the Howard Government, issues that are seen to be a divergence between Australia and Asia will need to be the focus of future governments as the discourse of fear associated with the war on terror, and domestic political interests, continue to be a symbolic barrier between Asia and Australia. However, through moving beyond a discourse of fear there can be a convergence of interests between Australia and Asia.

End Notes

1. Peter Gale, *The Politics of Fear: Lighting the Wik*, (Sydney: Pearson Education, 2005).
2. Patrick Walters and Roy Eccelston, PM's $500m aid package, in *The Australian*, (Sydney), 4th January 2005, p. 1; see also Stephen Fitzpatrick, 2005, Survivors too scared to return, in *The Australian*, (Sydney), 4 January, 2005, pp. 1, 6.

3. *ABC News Online*, Monday, June 13, 2005, http://www.abc.net.au/news/newsitems/200506/s1390472.htm 15 June 2005.
4. Helen Dodd, *Pauline: The Hanson Phenomenon*. (Brisbane: Boolarong Press, 1998).
5. Gale, *The Politics of Fear*.
6. Peter Manning, 2004. *Dog Whistle Politics and Journalism: Reporting Arabic and Muslim People in Sydney Newspapers*. (Sydney: University of Technology Sydney, 2004); See also Marcia Langton, "Pauline as the Thin End of the Wedge", in *The Retreat From Tolerance: A Snapshot of Australian Society*, ed., Philip Adams. (Sydney: ABC Books, 1997).
7. Bobby S. Sayyid, *A Fundamental Fear: Eurocentrism and the Emergence of Islamism*. (London: Zed Books, 2003).
8. Scott Poynting, "'Street Arabs' and 'Mug Lairs': Racism, Class Relations and Moral Panic About Lebanese-Australian Youth", in *Arab Australians Today: Citizenship and Belonging*, ed., Ghassan Hage (Melbourne: Melbourne University Press, 2002).
9. Gale, *The Politics of Fear*.
10. Andrew Markus, *Fear and Hatred: Purifying Australia and California 1850-1901*. Neutral Bay (NSW: Hale & Iremonger, 1979); see also Geoffrey Gray and Christine Winter, eds. *The Resurgence of Racism: Howard, Hanson and the Race Debate*, Clayton, (Victoria: Monash Publications in History, 1997).
11. Frank Furedi, *Politics of Fear: Beyond Left and Right*, (London: Continuum, 1995), p. 99.
12. Nick Cater, ed. *The Howard Factor: A Decade that Changed the Nation*, (Carlton, Victoria, Melbourne University Press, 2006).
13. Michael Gordon, Fraser Ponders Quitting 'Party of Fear', in *The Age*, November 30th (Melbourne, 2005), p. 2; see also Gale, *The Politics of Fear.*
14. Michelle Grattan, The Politics of Fear, in *The Age*, November 5th, (Melbourne, 2005).
15. Nicolas Rothwell, Please Explain, in *The Howard Factor: A Decade that Changed the Nation*, ed. Nick Cater, (Melbourne University Press, Carlton, Victoria, 2006), pp. 107-122.
16. Benedict Anderson, *Imagined Communities: Reflections on the Origin and Spread of Nationalism*, Revised Edition, (London: Verso, 1991).
17. Tony Kevin, Foreign Policy, in *The Howard Years*, edited by Robert Manne, (Melbourne: Black Inc. Agenda, 2004).
18. Alison Broinowski, *About Face: Asian Accounts of Australia*, (Melbourne: Scribe Publications, 2003).
19. Poynting, "'Street Arabs' and 'Mug Lairs'".
20. Ghassan Hage, Postscript: Arab-Australians Belonging After 'Sepember 11', in *Arab Australians Today: Citizenship and Belonging*, edited by Ghassan Hage, (Melbourne: Melbourne University Press, 2002).
21. Sayyid, *A Fundamental Fear.*
22. Hage, Postscript: Arab-Australians Belonging After 'September 11'.
23. James Curran, *The Power of Speech: Australian Prime Ministers Defining the National Image*, (Carlton, Victoria: Melbourne University Press, 2004).

24. Richard Dyer, *White*, (London and New York: Routledge, 1997), p. 44.
25. Ghassan Hage, *Against Paranoid Nationalism: Searching for Hope in a Shrinking Society*, (Pluto Press, Annandale NSW, 2003).
26. Norman Fairclough, Media Discourse, (London and New York: Edward Arnold, 1995), pp. 68-72; 85-6.
27. Stuart Hall, Chas Critcher, Tony Jefferson, John Clarke, and Brian Roberts, *Policing the Crisis*, (London: Macmillan, 1978).
28. Teun van Dijk, *Racism and the Press*, (London and New York: Routledge, 1991), p. 39.
29. Hage, *Against Paranoid Nationalism*, pp. 67-8.
30. Tony Parkinson, The Clash of Civilisations, in *The Age*, (Melbourne), September 15th 2001, p. 1.
31. Gay Alcorn, Bush picks up father's quest for New World Order, in the *Sydney Morning Herald*, (Sydney), September 15th 2001, p. 10.
32. Dennis Shanahan, Touched Howard embraces moment, in the *Weekend Australian*, (Sydney), September 15th, 2001, p. 33; see also Darrly Jarvis, "US declares war of Western democracies against terrorism", in the *Sydney Morning Herald*, (Sydney), September 14th 2001, p. 10.
33. Stephen Romei, "Fear in Our Time", in *The Weekend Australian*, (Sydney), October 13-14th, 2001, pp. 19, 22; see also Martin, Roger, Howard Weeps at 'Cruel View of Humanity', in *The Weekend Australian*, (Sydney), October 19-20th, 2002, p. 1.
34. Andrew Bolt, Culture of Hate, in the *Herald Sun*, (Melbourne), 17th 2001, Melbourne, p. 27.
35. Mackay, Hugh, Just who is un-Australian?, in *The Age*, June 20th 2005, http://www.theage.com.au/news/Hugh-Mackay/Just-who-is-unAustralian/2005/06/19/1119119722702.html?oneclick=true 21 June, 2005
36. Larissa Behrendt, *Achieving Social Justice: Indigenous Rights and Australia's Future*, (Annandale, NSW, The Federation Press, 2003).
37. Justice Marcus Einfeld, 2001, ABC Radio National, Sunday 3 June, Produced by Kirsten Garrett, http://www.abc.net.au/rn/talks/bbing/stories/s307878.htm, 15 June, 2005.
38. Justice Marcus Einfeld, ABC Radio National.
39. LET US HELP, in the *Sunday Mail*, Sunday, (Adelaide), January 9th, 2005, p. 1.
40. *ABC News Online*, Monday, June 13, 2005. 9:06am (AEST) http://www.abc.net.au/news/newsitems/200506/s1390472.htm,15 June 2005.
41. Stephen Fitzpatrick, 2005, Cutting corners to produce miracles, in *The Australian*, Monday January 3rd, pp. 1, 6., and Patrick Walters and Stephen Fitzpatrick, 2005, "Global aid effort kicks", in *The Australian*, (Sydney), Monday January 3rd, p. 1.
42. Sayyid, *Fundamental Fear*.
43. Poynting, 'Street Arabs' and 'Mug Lairs'.
44. Gale, *The Politics of Fear.*
45. Tony Kevin, Tony, Foreign Policy, in *The Howard Years*, ed. Robert Manne. (Melbourne, Black Inc. Agenda, 2004), pp. 291-313.

46. Stephen, FitzGerald, Stephen. 1997. *Is Australia an Asian Country?* (St Leonards, NSW: Allen & Unwin, 1997).
47. Alison Broinowski, *About Face: Asian Accounts of Australia*, (Melbourne: Scribe Publications, 2003).
48. Broinowski, *About Face*.
49. Gale, *The Politics of Fear*.
50. Marion Maddox, 2005, *God Under Howard: the Rise of the Religious Right in Australian Politics*, (Crows Nest NSW, Allen & Unwin, 2005), p. 78.
51. Larissa Behrendt, "Indigenous Policy: No Quick Fix", *Australian Policy Online*, http://www.apo.org.au/webboard/results.chtml?filename_num=80532, 5 June, 2006.

10

Glimpses of India: A Military *Dekko*[1]

SUSAN COWAN

Australia's response to military action abroad has perhaps been typical of a country geographically isolated from the rest of the world. The urge to leap to the breach has been prompted not only by feelings of goodwill and loyalty to the (then) mother country, but in the wider context as an opportunity to plant Australia's name abroad and, perhaps more importantly for some who are driven by the touristic impulse, to explore the world and to experience different cultures. A.B. Facey, the Western Australian author of *A Fortunate Life* (1981), for example, joined up in 1914 and recalls the excitement and allure of travel: "We all felt that we should go, we were fit, and another thing that appealed to us was that we should be travelling overseas, and would be able to see what the other part of the world was like".[2] But it was a grim adventure from which he was medi-vaced home, sick and dispirited from losing his brother and many mates. Patrick White used his spare time while serving in Egypt to write part of *The Aunt's Story*. In contrast, the reluctant Jim in David Malouf's *Fly Away Peter*, (1982) notes that immediately after Gallipoli, people were suddenly "fiercely patriotic and keen for battle". He muses that "if he didn't go…he would never understand, when it was over, why his life and everything he had known were so changed, and nobody would be able to tell him".[3] A fear of facing possible death is suppressed by feelings of curiosity and nationalism and he signs up and travels across the world to his own death. Malouf comments that WW I in particular, bridged the distance between Australia and the great world; the celebrated volunteer forces of 1914-18 made "a leap beyond the limitations of pure geography into an experience that would amount to a remapping of their world". This attitude to war has woven itself into Australia's heritage. As Robin Gerster observes "it is a truism of Australian history that the fighting of foreign wars has been crucial to the development of a national identity".[4]

This paper looks at the work of three Australian writers who converged on India where they lived and wrote, long before the hippy trail of the 1970s, focusing on perspectives and commentaries on India from a military angle. It examines Ethel Anderson's Indian oeuvre, how her work portrays India and is influenced by military connections and compares these views with those of Mollie Skinner in *Tucker Sees India*[5] and John Lang in *The Wetherbys*.[6] These texts have been largely and to my mind unjustly neglected and my interest in reviving them stems from personal exposure to the military environment, and a desire to explore Anderson's work, which has been described as "in some respects near being a masterpiece".[7]

The earliest of these writers, John Lang was born in 1816 and has the distinction of being not only the first Australian-born novelist, with his authorship of *Legends of Australia*[8] but, according to C.D. Narasimhaiah, the first Australian-born novelist on Indian soil.[9] Lang lived for many years in India, where he regularly wrote for the Moffusilite, died in 1864, and is buried in Mussoorie.

Lang's tale of *The Wetherbys—Father and Son* shows a dissolute, but ultimately redeemable side to military life in India. Published in 1853, it takes more of a racy approach as the novel is filled with the escapades of the heavy drinking and gambling which seem to have been *de rigueur* in regimental life. One way out of this round of dissipation is to qualify for a staff appointment which entails learning at least Hindi or Urdu and Persian. As Robert Wetherby observes "in this country—it is every man for himself" (p. 54).

Lang's Robert Wetherby was born in India and lived there until he was twelve while his father served in the Bengal Light Cavalry. He is taken back to Britain to be educated and falls in love with Sophy whose father is *persona non grata* in the eyes of Mr. Wetherby. Wetherby senior lives his life retrospectively, and finds that everything in England is inferior to that which he was used to in India—the food particularly, the horses and indeed 'there was no playhouse in London that could hold a candle to the Station Theatre of Meerut". The irony, Robert observes, is that the grumbling comes "after upwards of thirty years' service in a country which, when in it, he was perpetually abusing" (p. 26).

Robert is dismayed that his mother "approved of my being transported at once to India for, perhaps, the term of my natural life" (p. 33). This remark harks back to Lang's origins as he was the grandson of a Jewish convict transported to Australia. Wetherby sails to India with a commission in the Honourable East India Company's cavalry. He lives the high life in Calcutta, drinking and gambling and getting heavily into debt before being posted to his father's old Regiment. Wetherby observes, "It is extraordinary how intimate and familiar people become in the East, even on the shortest acquaintance" (p. 43). The irony is perhaps lost on him that through his accelerated relationship with Ellen Fletcher, whom he met on board ship, and her "petticoat influence", he later secures a staff appointment (p. 59). Stationed at Cawnpore, Wetherby is received with great warmth by many Subahdars and Havildars (native officers), as well as many of his family's servants. He reacquaints himself with Hindustanee and settles into his new military life. Wetherby's new staff appointment is short-lived after he is provoked into a fight at the racecourse. Robert later marries Sophy who is an excellent household and financial manager and imagines that she is able to "check the frauds for which all Indian servants are notorious" (p. 85).

Lang's background and long association with India gives him little sympathy for the efforts of his countrymen. His military wives are strong and powerful, and consequently show up their weak, self-indulgent husbands. The satirical Mrs. Brill, who reminds us that she is the grand-daughter of Major General Sir Bunbetine Mactaren KCB, no less, (p. 99) garnishees Brill's pay and bullies him into studying hard, which pays off, as he subsequently becomes "certainly one of the best Oriental scholars in the service"(p. 52). Surprisingly, Brill was "not only grateful to her for having reformed him, but actually fond of his hideous jailor". This was not unusual as "[a] couple like Lieutenant and Mrs. Brill were to be found in every station and perhaps in every regiment throughout the service" (p. 53). Mrs. Brill in pursuit of wealth, urges her husband to carry out a spot of looting: "if you should happen to kill any Seiks (sic), search 'em, and pull down their back hair: that's where they carry their money and jewels and valuable things".

As Wetherby's character develops and matures, Lang diverges from chronicling the dissipated life of his young officers in India. He now attempts to expose the weaknesses of the military and question the usefulness of its presence. Robert Wetherby becomes progressively disgusted with the officers further up the chain of command as his ambitions deepen. He remarks that his senior officer Colonel Baxter, while a kindly old gentleman, was "totally unfit to command a regiment on active service having neither the bodily strength, the mental vigour, or the clearness of head to inspire confidence" (p. 145). Wetherby goes on to note that "but infirm and unfit as was Colonel Baxter, there were officers commanding Brigades who were even more decrepit and confused. There were more than one who required the assistance of a chair and a couple of troopers to get them into their saddles!" (146). The shambles of the battles of Ferozeshah and Moodkee resulted in the erroneous report of Wetherby's death of whom it was reported "unfortunately, getting amongst some stragglers of the Seik cavalry, he was cut to pieces" (p. 155).

In his examination of the novel Rick Hosking observes that In the Wetherbys there is no fine and solemn writing about Empire. Instead, Lang describes the sordid experience of cantonment life whose rakish subalterns and ancient, incapable colonels are supposedly in charge of disorderly regiments, there the 'Titans of the Punjab' are seen as barely able to cope with disorderly marital situations and brittle domestic arrangements.[10] (p. 49)

Born 60 years later, Mollie Skinner, a writer with a more direct link to the military, and a qualified nurse and midwife, went to India in 1913 at the age of thirty-seven. Four years later she joined the Australian Imperial Force, remaining at the base hospital at Jardee.[11] The roguish hero of her 1937 novel *Tucker Sees India*, Richard Smith (Tucker) sees India from a variety of angles within and outwith the military from which he has absconded. A reluctant enlistee into the Australian Light Horse, Tucker is a self-confessed waster who "may have an objection to killing people" (13), and joins up "for dear mother's sake". After a big drinking session, the hungover Tucker misses the boat to the Great War and remains in Bombay, before taking off on a series of adventures around India in many different, but ostensibly military, guises. Sent on his way by his cousin Reggie who happens to be serving in Bombay, he meets up with a British woman and her daughter "the Cornwalls", both of whom at various stages imagine that they are in love with him.

Any preconceived ideas of the stereotypical Australian encountering India for the first time are swept away as Tucker ad libs outrageously and becomes variously a food tester, a nurse—and even a midwife—rescues a woman hostage and halts a train with some wirecutters which leads to the capture of some "evil-faced ruffians" (p. 67) who are holding up the engine driver. Tucker behaves like a tourist and in his egalitarian style pumps everyone he meets for information. Unlike some of his compatriots, Tucker moves among the throngs and he feels uplifted by the "stream of dark life" (p. 22). He quickly masters some Urdu and Hindi, which he perfects by quizzing the locals for the correct pronunciation (p. 17). He travels all over India, connecting at times with military personnel whom he treats with a marked lack of deference, and with the locals whom he sees as equals, carrying out assigned military tasks and, chameleon-like, rearranging his credentials to suit the occasion. He is fascinated by the military presence in India:

> Military police and doctors, so many little white threads holding back the huge dark mass of Indian humanity—how do they do it? Because of the divisions below, Hindu against Mussulman, caste against caste. Or because of the fear inspired by the great white powers over the seas. Was it out of fear they bowed down to the officials in their uniforms, representatives of the British Empire and the princes? Or from indifference? A great mystery it was… (p. 181)

For one who is so ready to learn about local customs, language and history, imperialism is an imponderable for Tucker. Distinguished towards the end of the novel as a "gallant hero" for his efforts with the train raid, Tucker is modest, refusing to accept a bravery award from the very imperialists that he questions.

The larrikin Tucker faints at the sight of blood which gives rise to the suggestion that Skinner may also have wished to "minimize, even eradicate the ubiquitous notion that all Anzacs were bloodthirsty sharp-shooters or vicious sabre-wielding killers".[12] Skinner, by linking her "hero" with two female characters, humanises Tucker and gives a different perspective to his war effort. Tucker the rascally antihero, the street-wise traveller, avoids the fighting and fulfils his desire to "see" India and to find out about its people. In *Tucker Sees India*, Skinner speaks with authority of her wide experiences in that country and depicts Tucker, with the quintessential characteristics of the laid-back Australian, a larrikin, filled with curiosity, challenging authority. She softens the image of the bronze Anzac and questions the motives of the military presence and its effect on the local people.

Turning now to a contemporary of the Australian artists Thea Proctor and Grace Cossington-Smith, and a fifth-generation Australian, Ethel Anderson lived for ten (1904-1914) years with her British military husband in several parts of India. Despite her "intimate connection with…top military circles"[13] Anderson sought to escape the boredom and loneliness of being a military wife, by honing her accomplishments in writing, painting and music and became a lively chronicler of events in India, writing for the Indian Pioneer (as did Kipling in 1887 as a sixteen-year-old). Unfortunately few of these writings are extant, but those that have survived are well informed, colourful and sprinkled with Hindustani words,[14] giving a further edge of credibility to her work. Anderson's lively *Indian Tales* (1948)[15] and *Little Ghosts* (1959)[16] were written after she had left India but time and distance have not blunted her keen eye nor her interest in the lives of the people, particularly the women, around her. While her social life was restricted to the higher echelons of Indian society (p. 64), she also managed to move easily alongside the local people in the many parts of India in which she lived.

While Anderson's husband Austin, a British gunner, served with his battery in Campbellpore, Dinapore, Lucknow and finally at Nainital, Anderson put her mind to learning about India and its history.[17] She learned to ride side-saddle (p. 65) and caused quite a stir by winning the army sports day event with the four-in-hand (p. 68). Possibly these vigorous activities were an antidote to her disappointment in her husband's patriarchal and jealous attitude, which was so different from the attitude of Robert Wetherby who was delighted that his wife was "a great favourite with the Regiment" (p. 83). Anderson therefore chose to appear in a subservient role to keep the peace while quietly gathering material from life around her (p. 64).

Ethel Anderson's best-known story "Mrs. James Greene" (1959)[18] arose out of a request by Lord Kitchener to Austin Anderson to look into the rumour that there was an English woman who had survived the Indian Mutiny and had been taken into protection by Mirza Khan, an Indian *sowar* or cavalryman in James Greene's regiment (p. 77). In Lucknow there is a memorial to the many who died at that time and Mrs. James Greene's name quite erroneously appears on it. The romantic side of this story would seem to have appealed to

Anderson and she wove into her story earlier favours to Mirza Khan's family resulting in a *quid pro quo* and the heroine being saved when her husband was bludgeoned to death. The theme of mixed liaisons fascinated Anderson and it is this aspect around which she bases this richly textured novella.

Mrs. James Greene—spelt with an "E" as is pointed out in any discussion of the story—escapes with her baby daughter from the murdering mutineers and ends up in Mirza Khan's household, ostensibly until it was safe for her to rejoin her own people. Anderson romanticizes the actions of her heroine who earns the respect and love of the *sowar*'s womenfolk for teaching them "the simple arts, she had learnt in her English country home: tatting, knitting, the making of peculiarly good cheeses, and of various preserves, comfits, jams, pickles and sauces...which they sold with profit in the bazaar in Sitapur" (p. 77). I would venture that these "simple arts" would be exceedingly unusual talents for a 16 year old Englishwoman of her class.

Observed admiring Mirza Khan as he bathes in the courtyard, Mrs. James Greene tries to make plans to return to her friends in Lucknow. Not in a hurry to despatch his houseguest, Mirza Khan deems it unsafe for her to do so. She is saved again, and is dressed in Indian clothing, when her enemy visits the household and catches sight of her blue eyes shining out of her dyed brown face. Mirza Khan has no option but to kill the marauder and it is at this moment, dressed as she is in his wife's clothing from her wedding-night, that romance sparks and the dynamics of the household change. In the spring Mrs. Greene follows tradition, lays out her love mat—a quilt of neem-flowers and jasmines, and waits for Mirza Khan to visit her (p. 86).

The story jumps some forty years when Mrs. James Greene, having chosen to relinquish her British origins and remain with her lover, is observed by "a famous traveller" dressed in the tattered rags of extreme poverty, with her Indian protector. Her loyalty to the now blind Mirza Khan is evident in her tender solicitude towards him and she ensures that he at least is wearing "garments of a much better quality, clean and neatly darned" (p. 86).

This female conventionality redeems her, and allows her as Paul Sharrad observes: "to appear as the titular heroine of a tale whose historical context might otherwise erase her, safely leaving her marked only by an official monument as a racially/culturally pure and dead victim of perfidious native violence".[19] The young widow, who appears to have grieved only briefly for her slaughtered husband, is highly regarded in the household of Mirza Khan, and as the mutual respect and admiration eventually turns into love, Mrs. James Greene is prepared to sever connections with her own people to live like a pauper with her Indian lover.

Ethel Anderson gently mocks Eurasians in her story "The Eurasian"[20] by overdoing the "chee-chee" speech of her characters and giving them outlandish names with a Spanish/Portuguese flavour. Don Manoel Jeronimo Henriques

William de Azevdeo, who is the head of the household, had been a lieutenant in the Goanese army. One of his daughters, Khujasta, is saved from drowning on the night of the Festival of the Lamps by the typically dashing hero, Major Hew Adam, who is later accused by the jealous colonel of trying to defraud her. Both men are subsequently killed on a night march. A colleague of Adam's, Major Wylde, investigates the story and finds the true culprit. Yet again, the ending redeems Anderson, as she marries off the sole remaining daughter to Major Wylde who adores her, although she has inherited a plantation and great wealth. Anderson clearly understands the male fascination with Eurasian women. In contrast to Mrs. James Greene who accepts the poverty that goes with her love for Mirza Khan, this story gives the impecunious English officer his heart's desire and the wealth that goes with it. For the romantic Anderson, both women get their men.

Anderson successfully draws on her observations of military life as a basis for her stories. Her spirited, autobiographical short story "Bombardier Gwyllam's Night Out"[21] relives an astonishing feat while she and her husband were stationed in Lucknow. Anderson's ambition to learn to drive a four-in-hand was realised through the expertise of the eponymous Welshman. The story describes her initiation into handling the four-horsed battery "brake" by Gwyllam, her challenge to his instructions, his revenge, and her ultimate triumph.

Pulling together the strands and attitudes of Anderson's life in India, the reader can see that while she abhors the poverty, she delights in deftly drawing out personal achievements in close observation of the lives of the local and military women. From her privileged position, the romantic Anderson does not question the military presence—and the issues that concern Lang and Skinner.

From this small sample of writers who distinguished themselves, in different ways, in their writings from India, Lang's perspective in 1853 exposes the amoral, dissolute life led by the forces serving there. He creates an ambitious character, who, over time, pulls himself together and takes responsibility for the fiasco he sees around him. It is interesting to speculate that the entrepreneurial Lang's unsympathetic view of Empire may well have been influenced by his own situation in which he, in his legal practice, acted for an Indian firm of army contractors and the Ranee of Jhansi. "In both cases", a biographer observes, "he received large fees and rich presents",[22] making it easier for him to see things from an insider's perspective. Skinner's Tucker on the other hand, exploits his position by turning his so-called tour of duty into a touristic journey, evading the military, seeking cultural opportunities and trying to fathom the mystery of India and its people. Described as a "unique figure in Australian letters"[23]

Ethel Anderson's position of privilege, security and scholarship permits her to explore and profit from her experiences with the people whom she has grown to love in India.[24] The long periods of enforced loneliness as a military "grass widow" do little to dampen her high spirits, but fuel her curiosity particularly about women and their relationships. Although she enjoyed interacting socially with upper-class Indian women, she did not concern herself with the lot of the oppressed and underprivileged. In no way did she seek to be a radical reformer or challenge the conventions of the status of women. That was not her brief. Anderson died in 1958, a formidable and feisty seventy-five year old who sported a silver ear-trumpet. Her lively voice, which is little heard today, nevertheless makes a rich and important contribution to literary studies.

End Notes

1. The Hindi word *dekho* has been absorbed into Australian and British English with the spelling slightly modified, but still retaining the same meaning, i.e. look.
2. A.B. Facey, *A Fortunate Life* (Fremantle, WA: Fremantle Arts Centre Press, 1981), p. 234.
3. David Malouf, *Fly Away Peter* (London, Chatto & Windus, 1982), p. 55.
4. Robin Gerster and Peter Pierce (eds.) *On The Warpath: An Anthology of Australian Military Travel* (Carlton, Vic: Melbourne University Press, 2004), p. 6.
5. Mollie Skinner, *Tucker Sees India* (London, Martin Secker & Warburg Ltd., 1937).
6. John Lang, *The Wetherbys* (London, Chapman and Hall, 1853).
7. HM Green, *A History of Australian Literature*, Vol. II 1923-1950 (Sydney, Angus & Robertson, 1961).
8. John Earnshaw, John Lang, in Douglas Pike (Gen. Ed.), *Australian Dictionary of Biography*, Vol. 5, (Carlton, Vic: Melbourne University Press, 1974), pp. 58-9.
9. C.D. Narasimhaiah, Introduction, *The Literary Criterion*, XV, Nos. 3 & 4, 1980, pp. xxi.
10. Rick Hosking, "Realms of Possibility: Australia, Britain and India in John Lang's *The Wetherbys*", in Nena Bierbaum, Syd Harrex and Sue Hosking (eds), *The Regenerative Spirit* vol. 1. (Adelaide: Lythrum Press, 2003).
11. William H. Wilde, Joy Hooton and Barry Andrews, *Oxford Companion to Literary History* (Melbourne: Oxford University Press), p. 699.
12. Donna Coates, Guns 'n' Roses: Mollie Skinner's Intrepid Great War Fictions, *Southerly*, vol. 59, no. 1, Autumn 1999, pp. 119.
13. John Thompson, Obituary, *Southerly*, vol. 3, 1958, pp. 177-78.
14. Bethia Foott, *Ethel and the Governors' General* (Paddington, NSW, Rainforest Publishing, 1992), p. 74.
15. Ethel Anderson, *Indian Tales* (Sydney: Australasian Publishing Co., 1948).
16. Ethel Anderson, *The Little Ghosts*, (Sydney: Angus and Robertson, 1959).

17. Foott, 65.
18. Ethel Anderson, Mrs. James Greene, *The Little Ghosts* (Sydney, Angus and Robertson, 1959), pp. 57-87.
19. Paul Sharrad, Trading Yarns: India, Australia, and Ethel Anderson, *New Literatures Review*, vol. 41, April 2004, pp. 85-103.
20. The Eurasian, *The Little Ghosts*, pp. 171-191.
21. Bombardier Gwyllam's Night Out, *Indian Tales*, pp. 139-157.
22. Earnshaw, pp. 58-59.
23. Thompson, 178.
24. Foott, 63.

11

Whose Nation? Understanding Nationalism in India and Australia

SWARAJ BASU

Problems arising out of cultural and ethnic diversities have no longer remained an internal issue within a nation-state; rather this has become internationalised. Nation and national identity are contested concepts. Indigenous as well as disadvantaged social groups very often found themselves marginalised or at the periphery in the given structure of the nation-state. That is why it is not uncommon to notice in different states that more than one version of nationalism either proclaimed or at sub-conscious level exist besides the one promoted and projected by the state. In his book on Indian nationalism G. Aloysius has observed:

> Nationalism, instead of giving birth to one national society, seems to have delivered a whole litter of communities divided from one another in terms of language, religion, region or caste... It is a communal nationalism in a double sense; it is communal not only *vis-à-vis* other religious communities but equally so *vis-à-vis* the large mass of lower castes within the Hindu fold. It is therefore more appropriately termed uppercaste Brahminic nationalism.[1]

This reflects the thinking of certain social groups within India who feel that Indian nationalism that emerged during India's freedom struggle as a kind of national consensus failed to provide equal space to various disadvantaged social groups.

Sue Boland states: "The Australian nation-state was founded on the basis of racism towards both Aborigines and Asians".[2] This observation is reflective of the ongoing debates in Australia on the issue of Australian national identity and within this, the place of the Aborigines. In recent times both India and Australia have seen the growing assertion by certain social as well as political groups to question the legitimacy of the given definition of national identity and nationalism by the respective state authority. India and Australia were once part of the British colonial empire and the rise of nationalism in both the countries is traced from the second half of the nineteenth century. In terms of history and cultural tradition India and Australia may not be comparable not even in terms of the course of nationalist movement that both the countries experienced. However, when one looks at the challenges that both the nation-states are facing today from within, one finds possibilities of making a comparative study of issues arising out of national identity and the dynamics of its formation. Why is the ideological bond of nationalism failing to take care of cleavages within the nation? The central question that needs to be looked into, why is it that the ideology of nationalism externally liberationist but internally hegemonic and dominational? This paper seeks to explore and understand the concerns and anxieties that the *Dalits* in India and the Aborigines in Australia have within their respective nation-state.

India: *Dalits* and National Identity

In course of the Indian nationalist movement under the leadership of Indian National Congress we find that a large section of the *Dalit*s questioned the legitimacy of the Indian National Congress to represent the interests of the *Dalit*s. The *Dalit* leadership did not subscribe to the views and agenda for freedom struggle preached and promoted by the Indian National Congress. Actually there were many voices within the Indian nation and all were having different perspectives in interpreting the concerns and anxiety of the Indian nation. In this context it may not be out of place to quote Amartya Sen on Indian identity. He writes: "It would be hard to claim that there is some exact, homogeneous concept of Indian identity that emerged during the independence movement as a kind of national consensus, or that there were no differences between the way Indianness was seen by, say, Mahatma Gandhi or Rabindranath Tagore (to consider two leading and somewhat dissimilar voices that helped to teach us what we are)".[3] Definition of nationalism given by the Congress may or may not be the dominant one, but the more important point is that the perception of the Congress leadership on nationalism was not shared by large section of the *Dalit*s. Reason for the different perceptions on nationalism basically lies on the hierarchical nature of Indian society based on the ideology of inequality. Jotiba Phule in the nineteenth century opposed the nationalist movement on the ground that a society divided by caste cannot constitute a genuine nation. In this context *Dalit* writer Baburao Bagul's observation may be relevant:

> The national movement was turned into a form of historical, mythological movement and ancestor worship.... Those who propounded inequality and did not wish society to be democratic, started eulogizing history, mythology and ages gone by because, in

> those mythological and historical ages, they were the supreme victors and leaders. The intelligentsia now harked back to and worshipped the past because of this. People such as Phule, Agarkar, Gokhale and Ranade who talked about misery and servitude of the Shudras and Atishudras, who criticized the Varna system, and demanded social, economic and political reconstructions, were declared enemies and attacked from all sides. The intelligentsia won; they succeeded in turning the Indian liberation struggle into a lop-sided fight, and in reducing the other movements to a secondary status. [4]

In spite of various reformative initiatives taken from above by some elites of Indian society the tradition bound Indian society at large was very much tied to the *varna* and caste system. Day to day sufferings of the *Dalit*s in the name of tradition and culture by the upper castes naturally shook their faith even in the reformative initiatives taken from above by the upper caste Hindus. Without addressing the issues pertaining to their age long sufferings and discrimination any short of political liberation appeared to be a myth to majority of the *Dalit*s. It is this social reality which moved Munshi Premchand to question his nationalist friends regarding the utility of talking about nation while the shadow of caste distinctions is looming large over the society. 'Who does not know that caste distinctions [*jati-bhed*] and nationhood [*rashtriyata*] are opposed to each other like nectar and poison?'[5] This makes it relevant to look into the question of nationalism from the *Dalit*'s perspective.

History of Indian nationalism is traced from the beginning of 1850s and with the foundation of Indian National Congress in 1885 Indian national movement was carried forward under its leadership. In its initial phase the Congress leadership was careful not to include the social issues in its agenda of reforms and the congress led nationalist movement was very much confined among the higher strata in Indian society. The colonial rule had a direct bearing in shaping and consolidating the nationalist consciousness in India. But from the very beginning Indian nationalism was being questioned from within by a section from the Muslim community and also from the *Dalit*s. Primarily with the coming of the Census enumeration from 1872 and the recognition of caste category in official discourse we find the growing assertion by various *Dalit* groups against social discrimination and for equal rights. This is well reflected in the various caste literature and a large number of caste associations that were formed to fight for the legitimate rights of various caste groups. Studies that have been done in the recent times on mobilisation of *Dalit*s and assertion for their equal rights clearly indicate the *Dalit*s' concern for an independent political space.[6] This concern is clearly visible from the formation of various *Dalit* associations from the late nineteenth and early twentieth centuries to register their claims for social and political recognition. In a memorial submitted to the Secretary of State for India in November, 1910 the Mahars of the Bombay presidency wrote, "We have long submitted to the *Jagannath* of caste; we have for ages been crushed under its ponderous wheels. But we can no longer submit to the tyranny. We must emancipate our manhood. We may be poor, feeble, ignorant, but we are still human beings; we are besides British subjects, and we seek our inalienable rights as British subjects from the British Government".[7] Being born in the *Dalit* families and because of caste hierarchy prevalent in India the *Dalit*s all over India with little variation in the nature of discrimination never got equal rights and social justice over the years. Till the *Dalit*s were able to mobilise themselves there was no commitment from the leaders of mainstream Indian polity for the liberation of the *Dalit*s. As a result of changes that came in with the colonial rule and the changing economic relationship due to urbanisation and modernisation the elites within the *Dalit*s started questioning the age old predominance of the upper caste Hindus and became vocal for their independent political rights. The social composition of the Congress leadership further strengthened doubts in their minds regarding the justification of the nationalist movement in a country where the upper castes would continue to dominate over them.

> But mere empty promises, with social relations remaining unchanged, coupled with the absence of any concrete socio-economic programme, made the lower caste masses suspicious about the real intentions and motives of the nationalists. The movement, therefore, was identified with the high caste Hindus, being organised for furtherance of their own group interests and thus against the interest of the lower castes.[8]

In his memoir Upendranath Barman (a *Dalit* leader belonging to the Rajbansi community in Bengal who was also a minister in pre-partition Bengal government) wrote that in 1938 Gandhi came to Calcutta and asked the Scheduled caste members of the Bengal Assembly to join the Congress which according to Gandhi was the only national organisation. Jogen Mandal, a dalit leader from the Namasudra community, then said that the Congress was an organisation of the upper caste Hindus, and hence they could not rely on it.[9] This attitude of the *Dalit* leader towards the Congress led nationalist movement was reflective of a general impression all over India among the *Dalit*s regarding the nationalist movement. It cannot be denied that the colonial government through its policy of protective discrimination and other official measures tried to make use of the existing cleavages within Indian society. Nonetheless the overwhelming majority of the upper castes at the helm of the Congress power and the various policies and programmes of the Congress failed to impress upon the *Dalit*s that the Congress was really working in the direction to improve the oppressive socio-economic condition of the *Dalit*s. As a corollary to this the *Dalit*s in general were apprehensive of the outcome of the nationalist movement and did not consider them as part of this movement which was not basically focusing on the *dalits*' socio-economic equality and right. In the given scenario therefore the question which preoccupies minds of many *Dalit* leaders is that the nation envisaged by the nationalists did not take care of social and economic rights of the *Dalit*s. This perhaps was the concern of Jotiba Phule when he challenged the 'nationalness' of the Congress by making the following observation:

> There cannot be a nation worth the name until and unless all the people of the land of King Bali-such as shudras and Ati-shudras, bhils and fishermen etc., become truly educated and are able to think independently for themselves and are uniformly unified and emotionally integrated. If a tiny section of the population like the upstart Aryan Brahmins alone were to found the "national congress" who will take any notice of it?[10]

This dilemma is very well reflected in the writings of various *Dalit* groups and particularly of Dr. Ambedkar. In written evidence before the Southborough Franchise Committee, dated 27 January 1919 B.R. Ambedkar expressed his apprehension that the growing nationalism instead of liberating the downtrodden would justify the domination of the upper castes. Because of this apprehension Ambedkar along with other *Dalit*s were demanding separate electorate for the *Dalit*s.[11] During the course of the Non-co-operation Movement a number of lower caste associations distanced themselves from the appeal of Gandhi. When Gandhi was visiting Bengal in 1925 a *Dalit* giving reference to great nationalist leader like Chittaranjan Das told Gandhi, "we trust you, how we may trust others? They talk of untouchability today, because we are useful pawns in their political game, but the moment their political ends are achieved, they will leave us in the lurch. They do not think in their heart of hearts that it is a question of purifying themselves nor that *Swaraj* is useless without the removal of untouchability".[12] In order to strengthen their voice through collective effort attempt was made to form all India organization of various *Dalit* groups and this resulted in formation of the Depressed Classes Mission Society of India and some other all India bodies of *Dalit*s like All India Depressed Classes Association, All India *Adi* Hindu Mahasabha, All India Scheduled Caste Federation, etc. Through petitions and organising conferences all over India the *Dalit* leaders tried to draw the attention of the British government to the state of discrimination and their deprivation in private and public life. At the same time they tried to prove their disassociation from the Congress led nationalist movement. The considered opinion of the *Dalit* leadership was that without political power the *Dalit*s would not be able to achieve social recognition. As opposed to the *Dalit*'s perception of their problems the nationalists were of the opinion that the problems of the *Dalit*s were basically social in nature and these could be solved through improvement in their social and economic position. Vijay Prasad has observed: "A disturbing element in the character of the initiatives from above was the paternalism of Hindus as well as their inability to analyse the causes of untouchability beyond an inversion of culpability (by attributing to *dalit* habits and customs the cause of their oppression)".[13]

Trilok Nath has shown that how the '*Adi*' myth was created in the early 20th century and the *Dalit*s in different regions started movements claiming themselves as the aboriginal inhabitants of the land. In the south as well as in the north the ideology of "*Adi*" developed to explain that the *Dalit*s are the original people of this country and their religion is *Adi*-dharm and at later stage the Aryans came and suppressed these people by force. 'The *Adi* Hindu leaders projected the past not only as a period when the forbearers of the untouchables were rulers but also as a golden age of social equality…Through their newly constructed history of the original inhabitants of India, the *Adi* Hindu leaders outlined an idealised vision of social equality, and of the past power and glory that the untouchables had lost and were to claim.'[14] V. Prasad has argued that the *Adi* movements tried to "elaborate their own institutions and ideologies, and to ensure that the *dalits* do not get absorbed into the Hindu movement in a subordinate position".[15] According to Prasad because of antipathy to Brahmans and tracing of a glorious aboriginal past the *Adi* movements "provided the political ground for a *national dalit* community…The ground for the claim to nationhood was made through history, and here a history of independent creation provided the elements for a *dalit nationalism*".[16] Dr. Ambedkar's emphatic statement that nobody would remove the grievances of the *Dalit*s unless the *Dalit*s themselves do it which is not possible without getting political power in their own hands makes the perception of the *Dalit*s clear about the upper caste domination in politics of power. Based on this rational Dr. Ambedkar pressed for the separate electorate for the *Dalit*s like the provision for the Muslims and after much heart burning and strong protest from Gandhi he ultimately succumbed to the pressure of the Congress led nationalists and agreed to the Poona Pact which made the reservation of seats in legislatures for the *Dalit*s compulsory.

In his *Thoughts on Pakistan* (1940) Dr. Ambedkar supported the idea of autonomous national states within India and there was a demand from some *Dalit*s for Achhutistan, a separate nation for untouchables following the demand for Pakistan by some sections from the Muslim community. (Swami Achchutanand, Ram Charan and Mangooram advocated the idea of Achchutistan).[17] There was lack of unanimity among the *Dalit*s on the issue of territorial secessionism but their demand for separate nation primarily grew out of apprehension of monopolisation of power in the hands of upper castes in the absence of the British rule over India. Thus nationalism as advocated by the Congress led nationalists failed to impress upon the *Dalits* because of contradictions from within. This might have prompted Aloysius in interpreting nationalism as a Brahmanic and to observe: "With the rise, consolidation and political success of the communities whose interests lay in the perpetuation of caste-varna the process of its identification with the emergent state and nation had also been guaranteed."[18] Gail Omvedt is of the opinion that "...the *Dalit* movement and the overall radical anti-caste movements were a crucial expression of the democratic revolution in India, more consistently democratic—and in the end more "nationalistic"—than the elite-controlled Indian National congress."[19] This observation of Omvedt is made because of anti-feudal and democratic character of the *Dalit* movements.

Australia: Aborigines and National Identity

Walter Baldwin Spencer, one of the first Australian anthropologists, wrote in 1927:

> Australia is the present home and refuge of creatures, often crude and quaint, that elsewhere have passed away and given place to higher forms. This applies equally to the Aboriginal as to the platypus and the kangaroo. Just as the platypus, laying its eggs and feebly suckling its young, reveals a mammal in the making, so does the aboriginal show us, at least in broad outline, what every man must have been like before he learned to read and write, domesticate animals, cultivate crops and use a metal tool. It has been possible to study in Australia human beings that still remain on the cultural level of men of the Stone Age.[20]

This observation of Spencer speaks of the mindset of the colonizers towards the aboriginal people. Here, let me refer to a pamphlet written after the publication of the report by the Human Rights and Equal Opportunities Commission, Australia in 1997:

> To read *Bringing them home*, the report from the National Inquiry into the separation of Aboriginal and Torres Strait Islander Children from Their families (otherwise known as the *Stolen Generations* Inquiry), is to be overwhelmed with rage and horror. Your mind reels before the record of cruelty and misery it records, the kind of reaction you feel when you read about the Holocaust or the killing fields of Cambodia. The only thing that makes reading the report bearable is the knowledge that this attempt at genocide, while causing terrible suffering, could not stamp out the human spirit and could not prevent Indigenous people asserting their identity and demanding the sympathy of masses of ordinary people.[21]

Though this report has come out in 1997 opening before the public gaze the trauma that the Aborigines suffered in the process of colonization but historians have shown that the Aborigines never accepted the colonial domination without protest. In spite of the efforts made by the ruling authority to put the Aborigines in the margin the voice of the Aborigines could not be silenced. In the 1968 Boyer lecture series W.H. Stanner in his lecture titled as 'The Great Australian Silence' has observed that for 150 years Australian history and literature was silent about Aborigines except for some marginal references. Stanner described this silence as 'a cult of forgetfulness' or 'disremembering' that has been 'practised on a national scale'.[22] In the official history of Australia there was no Australian nation before 1788. Mainstream history of Australia starts with the settlements of the Britishers. The entire story of Australia's national identity grew out of the struggles of bush workers and the labour movement without the presence of the Aborigines in the process.

Indigenous people of Australia categorized as Aborigines were pushed into the margin as uncivilised. Initial settlers in Australia, both convicts and free migrants, came overwhelmingly from Great Britain and Ireland. Spread over six colonies for the settlers in Australia links with London were more important than with other cities within Australia. However, over a period of time, particularly from the second half of the nineteenth century, there was a growing sense of identification with the land where they settled for a long time. From the 1850s with the arrival of gold miners in Victoria and the great event of the Eureka Stockade a new spirit to think in terms of an independent Australian identity began to take shape. Peter Lalor, the rebel leader of the Eureka Stockade and the flag of the Eureka rebellion became the symbols of new Australian identity. The *Bulletin* published from Sydney since 1880 became the chief organ of expressing the spirit of emerging Australian identity. Henry Lawson, Banjo Paterson, A.G. Stephens and others contributed to the growth of Australian literature being rooted in the culture and tradition of the new land. Establishment of trade unions and the rising voices of workers against their exploitation further strengthened the sentiments for a new nation. In the backdrop of this growing urge for an identity different from the identity as Britishers as well as the growing need of the Australian colonies for a common government brought the six colonies of Australia together without any bloodshed and gave birth to the Australian nation in 1901. Step by step Australia was transformed into the Commonwealth of Nations and got political independence from Great Britain with the accepted symbolic authority of the British Crown.

In the narrative of making of Australian national identity the major omission is the complete absence of the Aborigines. Question needs to be answered is that where one should situate the Aborigines within Australian national identity? This question has become more relevant in the 1990s with the High Court of Australia's decisions in the Mabo and Wik cases recognising the indigenous claims to ownership of land. With the establishment of a penal colony at Sydney Cove on 26th January 1788 the British settlers declared the land as desert without settled inhabitants or any sovereign authority. As the process of colonisation began in Australia very soon the Britishers realised the need to adjust with the indigenous people as there was no land without owners.[23] Gatjil Djerrkura has observed: "The writings of early ethnographers, explorers and missionaries suggest that knowledge about Aboriginal land use and tenure was widespread well before the middle of nineteenth century. By the end of the nineteenth century, enough was known of the law and governance of Aboriginal tribes to suggest a society that had exercised sovereignty prior to the arrival of Europeans."[24] Studies have shown that the indigenous peoples had their own laws and usages and they never surrendered without fight for their right. This position is further vindicated by the Australian High Court's recognition in the case of Mabo the indigenous peoples pre-existing rights. The High court decisions have brought to the forefront the simmering discontent that the Aborigines had over the denial of their rightful place in the land of their forefathers. In spite of the strong reactions from sections of politicians and historians strong voices are raised against past injustices to indigenous Australians. In spite of the presence of a sizeable indigenous population in Australia at the time of colonisation the country was declared *terra nullius* by the British meaning by the complete non-recognition of the existence of the Aborigines in their own land. There is great ambivalence in the attitude of the white majority population towards Aborigines in Australia. As a result of long colonial dominations a number of stereotypes were constructed to refer to the Aborigines and they are represented as hunters and gathers, trackers and they live in a very traditional way.

Since the 1970s Australian historians like C.D. Rowley, Sharon Morgan, Henry Reynolds, Lloyd Robson, etc. have produced number of studies, which challenge the idea of Aboriginal passivity and project the Aboriginal people as active agents in shaping the history of Australia. There is growing assertion by the Aborigines to voice for their legitimate rights and place in the making of Australia. Important developments in the Aborigine's struggle for rights are narrated in the study done by B.A. Twood and A. Markus in their book, *The Struggle for Aboriginal Right: A Documentary History* (1999). Commenting on the process of introducing non-indigenous law in Australia it has been observed that instead of negotiating in a systemic manner the pre-existing system of law and regulation has been devalued and destroyed:

> As the fulcrum and the map of indigenous law and power, indigenous kinship systems were destined to be the target of a policy aiming to establish a new, absolute and unique sovereignty. The attack on the indigenous family was waged at every level. Uprooting peoples from

> their traditional lands, separating peoples within a kinship group, eliminating traditional means of survival and sources of food, forcing adult men and women to other parts of the country to work within the colonial system, and removing children from their families are but the most obvious forms...The common law of Australia now acknowledges that we, the indigenous peoples have always known: that we have our own laws and systems which are not merely historical or cultural curiosities; that colonization did not eradicate all of those laws; and that in some instances we have the legal right to apply those laws in our lives today.[25]

Henry Reynolds argued that although there was no central coordination and many tribes had very little sense of a common Aboriginal identity, Aboriginal resistance was on a substantial, even massive, scale.[26] Ann Mcgrath does not agree with Reynolds' observation that violent conflict was of overwhelming importance in overall relations between Aborigines and colonists.[27] Reviewing Keith Windschuttle's book *The Fabrication of Aboriginal History: Volume One, Vand Diemen's Land 1803-1847*, the reviewer has observed that "Windshuttle...wishes to portray Australia as a virtuous, moral, and heroic nation. He does this by denying the existence of Aboriginal massacres, and by implication, that Aborigines had any reason to resist...The fabrication of Aboriginal History, then, is a therapeutic history for white (Anglo-Saxon) Australians that distorts and distracts."[28] Before moving further we can say that by categorising the indigenous people of Australia as Aborigines and inferior compared to the Europeans in terms of culture and by reinforcing this stereotype based on scientific theories of nineteenth century anthropology the Europeans were able to construct an Aboriginal identity. This rationalised the authority of white domination. Challenging this stereotype the Aboriginal activists through protests and petitions have tried to put forward their own political ideas.[29] Lynette Russell has written: "The commonality of experience that aboriginal Australians share—dispossession, deaths in custody, stolen generations, economic, social and physical disadvantage—has tended to ensure that Aboriginal people have not and do not identify with the state, but with their own community. Similarly for much of the last century Australian national identity owed little to the presence of Aboriginal people."[30] Russel has shown how through various acts the colonial government tried to assimilate and absorb the Aboriginal people into the wider community and "citizenship was to be contingent on no longer being Aboriginal". While it became clear not to completely wipe out the Aborigines then the Australian government felt the need of enfranchising the Aborigines and recognising them as citizens. Earlier they were not even counted in the Australian census. But things began to change with the growing assertion of the Aborigines for their legitimate right of citizenship. For the first time in 1967 Referendum the Aboriginal flag was flown. During 1988 at the time of the European bicentenary celebration the Aborigines questioned the legitimacy of this celebration and a most visible sticker displayed was 'White Australia has a Black History'. The report entitled as *Bringing Them Home* revealed that at least "1 in 10 Aboriginal children had been removed from their mothers in the period from the late-nineteenth century to the 1970s. While many children were removed from non-Aboriginal families for neglect, abandonment, cruelty and abuse, ONLY Aboriginal children could be removed simply because their parents were aboriginal."[31] This group is popularly called as 'Stolen Generation'. It is said that more girls compared to boys were removed with the idea to make them domestics for white Australia and to assimilate them gradually. With the assertion of the Aborigines there is a definite shift in national consciousness on the issue of the Aborigines since 1980s. At present the government is for reconciliation and there are public postures to apologise for the past misdeeds towards the Aborigines. But the question still dominates the thinking of the Aborigines is how to reconcile the suffering of the past and the present. Till a mutually agreed answer is found to the concerns expressed by the Aborigines defining Australian national identity remains problematic and partisan. In this context I would like to remind Bain Atwood's suggestion that "…historians and other such scholars must refuse the claim of some Aborigines that there is only one story to be told and the demand that only they should narrate this, or that we should tell it as they do. If we fail to do so, our chances of learning through history will be severely eroded, as will our own sense of self and culture, while the pluralism which lies at the heart of an authentically democratic society and polity will be undermined".[32]

Understanding the Dilemma

As I have stated in the introduction that the journey towards formation of national identity in India and Australia has different trajectory but the concerns of the *Dalit*s in India and the concerns of the Aborigines in Australia towards the question of national identity have many commonalities. In the process of formation of national identity in both the countries the voices of the marginalised failed to make a dent because of the typical mindset of the dominant social groups. In the case of India the agenda before the leadership of the nationalist movement was to mobilise and create public opinion against the colonial domination. The British Raj was projected as the cause for the sufferings of the Indians and a picture of 'we' versus 'they' was created to ignite the imagination of the countrymen. This broad categorisation in spite of its own rationale failed to take note of the concerns of the marginalised within the society or intentionally the dominant leadership tried to avoid the social reality. Naturally to the *Dalit*s the appeal of the nationalists without addressing the *Dalit*s' concerns did not have much consequence. It is true that the *Dalit*s are not a homogenous group and there are divisions within the *Dalit*s along class lines, ethnic, linguistic, regional and other identities. This is also true that during the course of the freedom struggle and even after that many *Dalit*s share the ideology of the Congress party and other nationalist leaders. Still the point remains that the social oppression the *Dalit*s faced over the years and the subordination of their cultural ethos to the upper caste culture in the name of national culture definitely causes resentment among the *Dalit*s. Dr. Ambedkar's observation in his book, *What congress and Gandhi Have Done to the Untouchables*, published in 1945 and his conversion to Buddhism in post-Independent India as well as the assertion of *Dalit* activists even today for social justice and political rights reflect the mental agony that the *Dalit*s have against the nation state dominated by upper echelons of the society. The different brands of nationalism whether secular or *Hindutva* have failed to take note of the concerns of the *Dalit*s. This might be one of the reasons for the emergence of various political parties in different parts of India to voice the grievances of this socially oppressed group. Marika Vicziany and Oliver Mendelsohn observe:" The great change in the politics of the Untouchables is that over large parts of India they can no longer be taken for granted as a dumb vote bank. To a much greater extent than even a decade ago they have begun to shape their own politics".[33] In post-Independent India major political parties in their own ways have tried to accommodate the representatives of the *Dalit*s in their organisations to garner the support of the *Dalit*s in electoral politics. This tokenism unfortunately fails to address the woes of the majority *Dalit*s nor even has it succeeded to save the *Dalit*s from social oppression and economic deprivation. That is why in pre-Independent and even in post-Independent India the *Dalit*s have questioned the legitimacy of the nationalism, which is dominated by the upper castes. In spite of left movement and mobilisation of workers and peasants along class lines in India this social dichotomy is still persisting. Because of the continued social oppression and the marginalisation of the *Dalit*s in the domain of mainstream national politics the *Dalit*s have adopted a different strategy to make their voices heard and to add to their collective power.

In the case of Australia the situation is little different. The colonisation of Australia in the late eighteenth century began with the declaration of Australia as *'terra nullius'*, meaning that Australia had been a legal desert and the British Crown as its first sovereign. The Aboriginal people from different parts of Australia with their complex oral culture and spiritual values and having their own customs to govern themselves faced major threat to their life and culture from the European settlers. Despite the fact that the aboriginal people ruled themselves according to their own laws they became subject to the sovereign authority of the British Crown. There is serious debate among historians and politicians on the nature of violence and the number of violent deaths in the process of colonisation in Australia. The Australian national identity in its formative phase as well as even later kept the Aborigines outside the orbit of the nation state and it was predominantly white centric. Even the trade union movement in its formative stage drew a line against the inclusion of non-whites within its umbrella. Till 1967 when a referendum was held to include the Aborigines in the census and to allow the Federal Government to make laws for their benefit the Australian Constitution did not allow the Aborigines to be included in the census. Their growing assertion and organised efforts to question the authority of the state to whitewash their past in the name of Australian national identity has posed a major challenge before the government how to re-write the Australian history accepting the Aborigines as equal partners in the making of Australian nation. It is a dilemma before the government how to negotiate with the past.

In the light of this comparative study of the question of national identity and the voices of the *Dalit*s and the Aborigines I would like to drive home the point that in the process of construction and projection of national identity unless the marginalised groups are not given their due rights and recognition it becomes difficult for them to identify with the 'nation' as projected by the dominant groups. The *Dalit*s and the Aborigines are not homogenous groups and around different identities, ideologies and interest differences within them are quite apparent. But that should not come in the way of respecting their social equality and political rights. It is not through paternalistic approach but as an equal stakeholder in the making of nation their contribution needs to be reflected in the national agenda then only the marginalised would be able to identify themselves with the 'nation' or else very rightly they would pose the question, 'whose nation'?

End Notes

1. G. Aloysius, *Nationalism Without a Nation in India*, 1997, pp. 1-2.
2. Sue Boland, 'Can Australian Nationalism be Progressive', in *Green Left Weekly*, www.greenleft.org.au/back/1998).
3. A. Sen, *The Argumentative Indian: Writings on Indian History, Culture and Identity,* 2005, p. 349.
4. Baburao Bagul, *Dalit* Literature is But Human Literature, in Arjun Dangle (ed.) *Posioned Bread: Translations from Modern Marathi Dalit Literature*, 1992, N. Delhi, cited in G. Omvedt, *Dalits and the Democratic Revolution—Dr. Ambedkar and the Dalit Movement in Colonial India,* 1994, p. 15).
5. Amrit Rai, (Ed.) *Premchand, Vividh Prasang*, Vol. 2, 1962, p. 471.)
6. (Robert, L. Hardgrave, *The Nadars of Tamilnadu: the Political Culture of a Community in Change*, 1969; Rosalind, O'Hanlon, *Cate, Conflict and Ideology:*

Mahatma Jotirao Phule and Low Caste Protest in Nineteenth Century Western India, 1985; Gail Omvedt, *Dalits and the Democratic Revolution: Dr. Ambedkar and the Dalit Movement in Colonial India*, 1994; Sekhar Bandyopadhyay, *Caste, Protest and Identity in Colonial India: The Namasudras of Bengal, 1872-1947*, 1997; Oliver Mendelsohn and Marika Vicziany, *The Untouchables: Subordination, Poverty and the State in Modern India,* 1998; Vijay Prashad, *Untouchable Freedom; a Social History of a Dalit Community,* 2000; Swaraj Basu, *Dynamics of a Caste Movement: The Rajbansis of North Bengal, 1910-1947*, 2003; etc.

7. The memorial of the conference of the Deccan Mahars, held in Poona in November 1910, cited in A.C. Pradhan, *The Emergence of the Depressed Classes,* 1986, p. 85.
8. S. Bandyopadhyay, *Caste, Politics and the Raj, Bengal 1872-1937*, 1990, p. 159.
9. U.N. Barman, *Uttar Banglar Sekal o Amar Jiban Smriti*, 1987, pp. 73-75.
10. Phule, J., *Collected Works of Mahatma Jotirao Phule, Vol. II*, Govt. of Maharashtra, p. 29.
11. Report of Southborough Franchise Committee, dated 27, January 1919.
12. M.K. Gandhi, Talks with Untouchables, *Young India*, 14 May, 1925.
13. Vijay Prashad, *Untouchable Freedom: A Social History of a Dalit Community,* p. 83.
14. N. Gooptu, Caste and Labour: Untouchable Social Movements in Urban Uttar Pradesh in the Early Twentieth Century, in P. Robb (ed.) *Dalit Movements and the Meanings of Labour in India,* 1993, pp. 290-94.
15. Vijay Prashad, *Untouchable Freedom: A Social History of a Dalit Community,* p. 84.
16. *Ibid,* pp. 84-85.
17. Reference to this is cited in V. Prasad, *Ibid.*, pp. 150-151.
18. G. Aloysius, Caste in and above History in S.L. Sharma and T.K. Oommen (eds.), *Nation and National Identity in South Asia*, 2000, p. 168.
19. G. Omvedt, *op. cit.*, p. 16.
20. Cited in Bain Attwood, The Past as Future: Aborigines, Australia and the (dis)course of History, *Australian Humanities Review*, April-1996.
21. '*Genocide: The Australian Way—The Truth about the Stolen Generations*', A Pamphlet, by Tess Lee Ack and Sandra Bloodworth, 1998.
22. (www.abc.net.au/rn/boyers/stories).
23. H. Reynolds, *Aboriginal Sovereignty: Reflections on State, Race and Nation,* 1996.
24. G. Djerrkura, 'Indigenous Peoples, Constitutions and Treaties,' paper presented at Institute of Commonwealth Studies, London, July 1999.
25. Mick Dodson, The Rights of Indigenous Peoples in the International Year of the Family, in *Family Matters*, No. 37, April 1994, pp. 34-41, published by Australian Institute of family Studies.
26. H. Reynolds, *The Other Side of the Frontier*, 1981, p. 140.
27. A. Mcgrath, *Born in the Cattle*: *Aborigines in Cattle Country*, 1987.
28. Reassuring 'White Australia': A Review of the Fabrication of Aboriginal History, Book Review, *Journal of Social History*, Winter, 2003).
29. For details on this see Geoffrey Stokes, 'Citizenship and Aboriginality: Two

Conceptions of Identity in Aboriginal Political Thought' in G. Stokes (ed.), *The Politics of Identity in Australia,* 1997, pp. 158-170.
30. L. Russell, 'Public Records, Private Life: The Story of One Aboriginal Woman and her Journey from Non-citizen to Citizen', www.arts.monash.edu.au.
31. *Ibid.*
32. Bain Attwood, The Past as Future: Aborigines, Australia and the (dis)course of History, *Australian Humanities Review*, April-1996.
33. M. Vicziany and Oliver Mendelsohn, the Untouchables: Subordination, poverty and the state in modern India, p. 236, 1998.

12

Structural Economic Reforms of Australia and India: Prospects for Bilateral Linkages

D. GOPAL

Hobart's leading marine heritage expert, Michael Nash recently revealed the details about the sinking of the government store ship named *Sydney Cove* that was sent to Calcutta as far back as 1791 for additional food supply from India. According to Nash's account, while the vessel was returning from India loaded with rice, sugar, tobacco, salted meat, soap, candles, textiles, leather wear, livestock and an assortment of sundry effects sank off the coast of Tasmania in 1797. That was quite an ominous beginning in Australia's trade with India. And ever since the two-way trade relations between India and Australia has by and large remained modest notwithstanding periodic efforts on both sides to accelerate the pace and quantum of trade exchanges.

So much so, just about the time when India unleashed its economic liberalisation initiative for the first time in 1991, it ranked as twenty-fourth trading partner of Australia. Between then and now, India's status has improved no doubt but to a point that today it ranks only as fifteenth largest trade partner of Australia. Even a cursory glance at the commodity composition would underline that bilateral trade exchanges are concentrated mainly in traditional goods and merchandise as against non-traditional such as trade in services. In value terms, total two-way flows in 2003 amounted to A$ 4.3 billion. Trade in services between the two countries accounted for just about A$ 0.7 billion in the same year. Of this, Australian exports in service to India was a meagre A$ 0.5 billion which in overall Australian exports in service amounted to no more than 1.5 per cent.

Keeping these in focus, here an attempt is made to look at the prospects of India-Australia economic linkages in the near and the long term and raise a few issues surrounding the convergence of economic interests between the two countries. Towards this objective, the analysis is divided into three parts:

first, delineate Australia's economic reform process towards liberalisation; second, comment on the evolving profile of India following its liberalisation policy; and finally, highlight areas and sectors that lend themselves for the future convergence of India and Australia economic linkages.

Economic Restructuring Initiatives of Australia

In early 1980s, just over a decade ahead of India, Australia officially recognised the need to diversify its economy. Until then Australia remained largely an inward looking economy with tight controls on foreign exchange and trade and in that sense shared the policy objectives of most other developing countries including India.

By all accounts Australia has undergone a remarkable degree of opening up in the late 20th century. The fact that it was accompanied by many domestic economic reforms, and coincided with a long period of rapid global economic growth that was stimulated by the information technology revolution, added to the scope for boosting gains from trade.

The long history of industrial protectionism has its roots in the formation of the Australian Federation in 1901. Tariffs and other import controls were used increasingly through to the early 1970s to protect a wide range on manufacturing industries. That ensured a bigger manufacturing sector than would have emerged under free trade, but it stifled the growth of other sectors, particularly those natural resource-based ones in which the country enjoyed its strongest comparative advantage.[1]

Disenchantment with the interventionist trade and related economic policies gradually spread in the 1960s, but it was not until the 1970s that major tariff reductions began and was accelerated in the 1980s and continued through the 1990s. As a result, the average effective rate of assistance to Australian manufacturing fell from 36 per cent to about 5 per cent over those three decades. In the 1990s alone, both the mean and the standard deviation of Australia's import tariffs on goods halved. This brought the average tariff for manufactures down to 4.2 per cent in 1999. The only manufacturers with significant tariff protection now are motor vehicles and parts, textiles, clothing and footwear. Excluding them, the average effective rate of assistance to Australian manufacturing is just 3 per cent.[2] Agricultural subsidies and regulatory interventions also have been reduced. The average effective rate of assistance to the farm sector has fallen from above 25 per cent in the early 1970s to well below 10 per cent today. Thus discretionary government assistance to both manufacturing and agriculture has now all but disappeared. Service sectors too have not been spared reform. Banking, post and telecommunications, ports, higher education, health, and rail, air, and to some extent sea transport have been opened up; there has been progressive outsourcing of many government services; and substantial reforms to competition policy and practice, including divestment of numerous government enterprises, are well advanced. In addition, a comprehensive programme of review of government regulations at all levels has been under way since the mid-1990s, with the aim of reducing/removing regulations that unjustifiably impede economic activities.[3]

Moreover, by 1983 the Australian dollar was floating and foreign investment flows began to be freed up. That has complemented financial sector reform and has contributed to foreign direct investment (FDI), equity and foreign currency transactions growing at more than three times the pace of Australia's GDP during the past 15 years.[4] Besides, the previously highly unionised labour market too has undergone considerable reform which with higher education reforms has encouraged growth in human capital.[5]

Economic growth of advanced economies typically is accompanied by declines in the primary and manufacturing sectors relative importance and relatively rapid growth in the services sectors. That has certainly been the pattern in Australia too. However, the reduction in manufacturing protection enabled the GDP shares of the primary sectors to increase slightly in the 1990s as resources were freed up to allow those more internationally competitive sectors to expand faster.

Manufacturing now accounts for just one-eighth of Australia's GDP and employment, compared with services' shares of around four-fifths. Australia's trade and other economic policy reforms, together with the slow growth in world agricultural trade, have contributed to a much more dramatic transformation of the structure of its exports. Australia is very abundantly endowed with natural resources per worker relative to the rest of the world, so it is not surprising that it has always been a net exporter of primary products and a net importer of manufactures. The contribution of various sectors to exports has changed considerably during the post-war period though. The growth in the share of manufactures in exports may seem ironic, given that the past two decades has been a period of cuts in government assistance to manufacturers. Its explanation in large part is that the cutting of tariffs that protect Australia's least competitive manufacturers has allowed resources to move to other activities—including other industrial sub-sectors—that can compete better in international markets. For example, not all vehicle parts manufacturing firms have survived, but many of those that have now adopt a global rather than national market perspective and have thereby achieved economies of scale through specialising in producing and now also exporting what they do best. Technological changes in the late 20th century have aided that process, increasing the scope to subdivide the processes of production and distribution into parts that can be relocated anywhere in the world according to changes in comparative advantages over time.[6]

The direction of Australia's trade continues to trend away from traditional markets in Europe and North America and even Japan, as developing East Asian economies expand. Notwithstanding the latter region's financial crisis in the past three years, their share of Australia's trade in 1999 was still well above that of the early 1990s. Europe including Britain buys only one-eighth of Australia's merchandise exports now compared with more than twice that share in the early 1970s. But it still supplies nearly one-quarter of Australia's imports of both goods and services, and is a market for one-fifth of Australia's services exports. North America has a similarly large share of Australia's imports and exports of services, and imports of goods, but only half as large a share of our merchandise exports (11 per cent).

The direction of Australia's foreign investment is somewhat different from the direction of its trade. The United Kingdom and the United States together account for slightly over half of Australia's inflow and outflow of foreign investment, which is more than twice their importance in Australia's trade. Continental Europe's share of Australia's investment, by contrast, is just one-twelfth, the same as its share of Australia's exports and well below its share of imports. The Western Pacific, too, accounts for a much smaller share of Australia's investment than its trade: only one-sixth, compared with about three-fifths of trade.

The composition of Australia's trade is likely to see the mining export share continue to fluctuate with the global business cycle around a long-run trend, which is slightly downwards. Conversely, the manufacturing and services export shares continue to trend slightly upwards. Since the Sydney 2000 Olympic Games tourism services in particular have expanded considerably. As for direction, assuming recovery from the crisis in developing East Asia returns that region to rapid economic growth and further industrialisation in the next few years, its shares of Australia's exports and (especially) investment funds will grow further yet.

Despite the dramatic changes in the composition of Australia's trade, the majority of its exports are still natural resource-based, at a time when those products account for barely one-sixth of global trade in goods and services. Not surprisingly, then, Australia's economy is still perceived as being commodity-based and so its currency still follows the international price of primary products.[7]

A further contribution to Australia's economic growth from abroad has been the opening up of overseas markets. That has boosted the demand for Australia's exports both directly and indirectly. The Closer Economic Relations (CER) agreement with New Zealand, the opening of China and other former socialist economies, the broader Asia Pacific Economic Co-operation (APEC) process, and especially the GATT/World Trade Organisation (WTO) agreements have all been significant.[8] Meanwhile, Australia is also beginning to benefit from the opening up of services markets abroad, following the

Uruguay Round's General Agreement on Trade in Services (although much scope remains for further services trade liberalisation).

India's Economic Reform Initiatives

The impact of the liberalisation policies that India has unleashed since early 1990s is already evident. One positive result has been a significant boost to the economy's overall potential growth rate. Another has been India's re-engagement with the global economy, which in turn has transformed the prospects of key sectors of the Indian economy. This transformation has been most visible in the case of information technology-related services exports, where India has already become an important global player. No less evident are the positive signs in the areas of merchandise trade and international capital flows.

It is true that the economic reform process has been partial. Yet, even if India's progress remains more gradual than that demonstrated by China, it will still be sufficient to see India assume a progressively more important role in the international economy. Interestingly India's progress is most visible in the services sector, where India is combining technological progress in the telecommunications sector with a large supply of well-educated, English-speaking and relatively cheap labour to achieve a growing share of the international outsourcing market. Indeed, this development could be said to be leading to the emergence of a truly global labour market, with all the opportunities, and adjustment strains. Although India's participation in international merchandise trade and capital flows has been much less prominent, yet there are clear signs that India will become a more substantial presence in coming years.

These trends will also have significant implications for Australia. A more open and economically successful Indian economy will become a more important bilateral trading partner. Before the onset of reform in the early 1990s, India was Australia's 24th largest trading partner. By 2003 it had risen to 15th place, and had entered the top ten in terms of Australian export markets following several consecutive years of double-digit export growth. India's relative importance is set to continue to rise, bringing new opportunities for Australian exporters but also challenges for those sectors of the economy that will face increased competition from Indian suppliers of goods and especially services. There will also be consequences for Australia's international economic diplomacy as the emergence of a new economic power helps reshape the region.

Needed Bilateral Policy Initiative

Australia, being geographically on the periphery, has a strong interest in open trade in skill-intensive products whose production location need not matter, such as products related to the digital and bio-technology revolutions and electronic commerce. And being in the East Asian time zone gives Australia a potential comparative advantage in financial services. Hence keeping trade in services open and liberalising such markets more in the next WTO round will help to further the transformation of the Australian economy into more of a high-tech service provider.

The relatively limited nature of India-Australia bilateral relationship before 1990 was partly a function of the Cold War and partly the outcome of India's inward-looking development strategy that limited the possibilities for any deepening of the commercial relationship. In addition, reasons of geography and economic significance meant that for Australia, South Asia had remained a "poor cousin". Despite these untoward developments there is growing recognition of the increasingly important trading partnership between the two. However, what is called for is that both India and Australia need to make concerted moves and initiatives based on mutual consultation.

India's economic reform in the 1990s has helped reinvigorate trade flows and has led to a marked increase in the relative importance of bilateral trade. Major Australian exports to India include non-monetary gold, coal, copper ores, and wool. India is Australia's third largest market for coking coal and its fifth largest wool export market. Recent years have also seen substantial increases in Australian exports of so-called elaborately transformed manufactures including mining equipment and electrical machinery. Australian merchandise imports from India include pearls and gems and textiles. Potential exists for Australian exports in thermal coal, coking coal and possibly for gas along with agricultural exports of fruit and vegetables and wheat.

Mere merchandise trade alone cannot sustain the economic linkages. It is here that it needs to be underlined about the importance of trade in services as it has immense potential. India is already beginning to play an increasingly important role as a consumer of Australian education services (education services are now Australia's sixth largest export and one of the fastest growing sectors). Indian student enrolments in Australian tertiary education have nearly tripled in the past. In recent years Australia has become the third most popular overseas destination for Indian students.

Tourism remains Australia's largest service export and the tourism sector is also set to benefit from rising Indian incomes. Other service sectors such as finance, telecommunications, health, environmental services and the media could also seek a share of the Indian market. On the import side of the equation, Australia is likely to see increased penetration by services imports—particularly IT-Enabled services (IT-ES) and Business process outsourcing (BPO)-related services—as India's international market presence in this sector continues to rise.

To date, India's major export markets for these types of services have been the US and the UK (between them the destination of around three-quarters of all Indian IT service exports). In contrast, Australia's participation in the international outsourcing phenomenon has so far been relatively minor: available estimates show that in 2002 Indian companies' share of Australian spending on application development and systems integration was less than 3 per cent of the total. However, as an important English-speaking economy, Australia is clearly an obvious market for India, and most of the major Indian IT companies (including HCL, Infosys, Pentasoft, Satyam and Tata) now have representation in Australia. Moreover, if Australia is hoping for an increase in the bilateral trading relationship, it is unrealistic to expect greater access for Australian merchandise and service exporters without a corresponding rise in imports from areas of India's comparative advantage.

Any reluctance to allow Indian service providers to compete in the Australian market would clearly represent an obstacle to any future deepening of the Australia-India economic relationship. Australia could hardly expect to benefit from greater access to a growing Indian market while freezing out competition at home. But if India's expansion into the global service marketplace turns out to be as substantial then over time the adjustment strains could potentially be large. This issue could therefore come to represent a significant challenge to policymakers in managing the future bilateral relationship.

Finally, the economic rise of India is also likely to have significant implications for Australian international economic policy. This trend is already apparent in terms of international trade policy. India—along with several other major developing countries—has played an important role in the Doha Round. Australian trade negotiators will increasingly have to factor in the views of India and other major emerging markets in multilateral trade negotiations. This will also have implications for strategy, including the future role of the Cairns Group. For, there is a fair degree of overlap between the group of developing countries in the Doha Round and that of the Cairns Group. Current willingness of both Australia and India to engage in bilateral preferential trade arrangements, can pave the way for a preferential arrangement focusing on the service sector which overtime can be enlarged to include other sectors. The economic resurgence of India since the 1990s without doubt is a positive asset for Australia's future economic well being. Certainly, there could well be some sensitivities and transition strains associated with India's services oriented development path as compared to the merchandise trade driven models followed in the past by the East Asian economies. They are however not insurmountable especially at a time when the logic of economic globalisation is overwhelming.

End Notes

1. K. Anderson and R. Garnaut, Australian *Protectionism* (Sydney: Allen and Unwin, 1986).
2. Productivity Commission, *Review of Australia's General Tariff Arrangements*, Canberra, July 2000); Productivity Commission *Regulation and its Review 1999-00*, Canberra, November 2000b); and Productivity Commission *Trade and Assistance Review 1999-2000*, Canberra, December 2000).
3. *Ibid.*
4. UNCTAD *World Investment Report 2000,* Geneva: United Nations 2000)
5. M. Wooten, "Efficiency in Markets: Labour and Industrial Relations", and B. Chapman, and G. Withers (2001), Human Resource Development, in P.J. Lloyd, J. Nieuwenhuysen and M. Mead, (ed.) *Creating an Environment for Australia's Growth* (Sydney: Cambridge University Press 2001).
6. Jones, R.W. and H. Kierzkowski, "Globalization and the Consequences of International Fragmentation" in R. Dornbusch, G. Calvo and M. Obstfeld (ed.), *Money, Factor Mobility and Trade: Essays in Honour of Robert A. Mundell*, (Cambridge: MIT Press, 1997). See also J. Markusen, The Boundaries of Multinational Enterprises and the Theory of International Trade, *Journal of Economic Perspectives* 9(2): Spring 1995) pp. 169-89.
7. Shields, B. (2001), Efficiency in Markets: Capital, in P.J. Lloyd, *et al.*, No. 5.
8. K. Anderson, Australia's Changing Trade Pattern and Growth Performance, in R. Pomfret (ed.), *Australia's Trade Policies*, (London and Melbourne: Oxford University Press (1995). See also his Agriculture, Developing Countries, and the WTO Millennium Round, in M.D. Ingco and L.A. Winters (ed.) *Agriculture and the New Trade Agenda from a Development Perspective*, (Cambridge and New York: Cambridge University Press (2001) and K. Anderson, and C.Y. Peng "Feeding and Fueling China in the 21st Century", *World Development* 26(8): 1413-29, (August 1998).

13

Small Business Enterprises: A Comparative Overview of India and Australia

SAILAJA GULLAPALLI

The small scale business or small business is a vital component of a vibrant economy. Their importance lies in their small but firm contribution to the macro economic growth of an economy. They provide an opportunity to experiment, innovate and transform the ideas into practice through small entities. They are crucial for socio-economic development of an economy.

A small business may be defined as a business with a small number of employees. The definition of "small" often varies by country and industry, but is generally under 100 employees. These businesses are normally privately owned corporations, partnerships, or sole proprietorships. According to a World Bank report, small business is defined in more than 50 ways. The Small and medium enterprises, in terms of size and shape, are uneven across the globe. They are defined according to different norms such as size of employment, quantum of capital investments or assets.

In India, there are many small scale industries or businesses that have played a significant role in the economic arena. The development of the small business has always found a place in the agenda of different political parties, business houses and often in the budget presentations. They have a remarkable share in the development of the industrial development of the country. This sector employs around 14 million people in India, thus making it a viable option for entrepreneurial undertakings. Also, it provides nearly 80 per cent of manufacturing employment, producing around 7,500 items and contributes almost 35 per cent of national exports.

In Australia, small business sector is vital to its economy, accounting for 58 per cent of employment growth over the past six years and generating about 30 per cent of Australia's economic production. There are around 1.2 million small business enterprises in Australia employing around 3.3 million people. The growth of this sector was reported to be 3.5 per cent every year.[1]

Growth of Small Business in India and Australia

Cottage and small-scale industries have played an important role in the economic growth of India. The objective of these industries was to offer a range of options for individuals in village or cooperative societies/enterprises as a means of employment or as a means of rehabilitating the displaced persons. These industries not only use the local resources for manufacturing products but also help in achieving self-sufficiency in basic consumer goods like food, cloth and agricultural implements. Some of the prime ingredients of the small scale industries are the provision of raw materials, cheap power, technical advice, organised marking of their produce, and where necessary, safeguards against intensive competition by large scale manufacture. Most of these come under the purview of state governments. Moreover, the introduction of micro-credit especially for women to earn their income through self-help groups has given major impetus to small scale industries of late. Since the number of employees and the establishment is smaller in size, its management became much effective and profitable. Efforts are on to integrate these small units with larger establishments and industries. It will be examined, for example, how the textile mill industry can be made complementary to rather than competitive with the handloom industry, which is the country's largest and best-organised cottage industry. The possibilities of further decentralisation are being looked into that would make it viable for the local population to participate on a larger scale. For these industries play a major role in the generation of employment among both urban as well as rural population. In India, the handloom products, bamboo/cane items, spices and other food products are a major source of income for the rural and women population.

In Australia too, small business is a diverse sector and has a higher representation in retail trade, manufacturing, property and construction sectors. Realising the importance of encouraging entrepreneurship in individuals as an innovative way of providing high quality products and goods and services, the Australian government has provided high incentives to this sector. For the last 15 years, the Australian economic growth has been on a higher side, proving that its reforms had paid off well for the good health of the economy. So much so that the economy could successfully generate an estimated 1.8 million new jobs, with a record low level interest rates, which can be hailed as a high achievement. As on today, Australia is considered as the best place to start off a small entrepreneurial venture. Its efforts have been lauded even by the World Bank, terming it as the second easiest economy to start a business and third easiest to procure credit for business. Exemptions from unfair dismissal laws and restoration of flexibility and certainty have contributed to the growth of this sector. This sector accounts for around 30 per cent of the economic production and technology and services and also the tourism industry. It is important to note that over 67 per cent of this business is home-based.

Incentives and Thrust Areas

The incentives and schemes that are extended to the small and medium enterprises range from the process of their registration to the updated technical assistance. In India, the obtaining of the small enterprise certificate is necessary for availing tax benefits and exemption of customs duties on raw materials. They are also extended to the export assistance, for the expansion of the existing enterprises, assistance in the form of information through periodicals and reports, facilitating the networking of the stakeholders including the producers and customers, human resources and strategic management, counseling via workshops, conferences and short and long term training programmes, participation of the enterprise managers in business forums, participation in international fairs, credit guarantee scheme, financial assistance through micro-finance programmes and technical management and giving them awards for innovatory practices in management. Information and communication technology methods are extended for a better productive output of these enterprises. One of the pioneering schemes includes Prime Minister's Rozgar Yojana (PMRY) for encouraging such ventures.[2]

In Australia too similar assistance is extended by the government in the form of facilitating these enterprises with novel schemes such as export market development programme, infrastructure funding schemes, apprenticeship incentives, and indigenous small business funds. Further incentives include changes in superannuation, capital gains tax, simplified tax system, personal income tax cuts for better spending on small business and still better returns, abolition of 3 per cent tariff on business inputs, encouraging investments in innovation, equipment and plant etc.[3] The thrust areas include food processing and water grant schemes, agriculture, timber, textiles and clothing, fisheries, forest and food processing sectors, grain research, rural industries research and development, horticulture, grape and wine research and development. Special use can be made of incentives in ICT and renewable energy development schemes for these small enterprises.[4] Similar steps have been taken in India through the awards of star performance, outstanding entrepreneurs and for quality control.

Technology, Credit and Marketing

Small enterprises are usually endowed with local resources with a negligible account of technological help. Moreover, they are also labour intensive and many times lacking capital to meet the necessary technical facilities and upgradation. This often makes them lag behind their counterparts that get technological patronage from business or corporate houses. This results in the inferior packing and sub-standard appearances of the final products, thus leading to enormous losses. The information, procurement and application of new technologies go a long way in elevating the standard of these products.

Credit remains the most vital component of the small enterprises. Adequate credit facilities not only help in managing the enterprise and related requirements but also for procurement and modernisation. In India the small enterprises usually run on a stringent budget, and the financial requirements are met through the proprietor's self finances, or credit from nationalised or cooperative banks. In Australia, unlike in India, the credit poses no problem with full-fledged support from the governmental support extended to set up the small ventures. Being technologically superior and much more organised than their Indian counterparts, Australian small business is comparatively successful.

While credit and technology pose internal problems, marketing the final product is a daunting task in India. Lack of marketing skills coupled with the volatility in price fixing, the producers often run the risk of selling their products at a marginal profit levels. Devoid of information about the market prices, the producers end up selling their products to the retail management groups at staggeringly lower prices. Steps are now being taken to liaise with the sub-contracting groups to ensure profits to the owners of these ventures.

Certification

Certification with ISO 9000 ensures quality management of the products. This not only assures the consumers of the products they buy but also develops confidence in the consumers about the product. It is a stepping stone to the business venture's future sales of products and creating a niche for their brands. The total quality management, as it is referred to, plays a vital role in the Australian small business. An increasing number of small enterprises are now adopting the ISO 9000 quality management mark as a precondition to managing the quality of their products. Though perplexed by the insistence on certification initially, many of the enterprises have accepted this standard format for enhancing their professional and service-oriented approach. Rather the adherence to these standards is widely being perceived as an adherence to quality, risk management and meeting the needs of consumer satisfaction.

Even the Indian enterprises are widely being encouraged to adhere to the International standard of quality management to enhance the sale value of their products. This not only enables them to face global competition but also helps in their technological upgradation. Moreover, once these enterprises come under the ambit of ISO certification, they are reimbursed almost 75 per cent of the amount spent for acquiring the certification. These measures encourage not only the setting up of the enterprises for employment purposes but also for making a place for themselves in the highly competitive business world.

IPRs, WTO and SMEs

Time and again Australia has been lauded by the World Trade Organisation for its constructive role in managing sound macro economic policies, its structural reforms and adherence to the norms set by the WTO. Realising the need to protect the intellectual property rights (IPRs) in small enterprises, Australia along with other members of the Asia-Pacific Economic Cooperation resolved to "create and use the intellectual property rights of its enterprises; ensure marketing and branding strategies; protecting inventions and utility models; licensing of IP assets; integrating IP in the business and planning strategies".[5]

In India, though the IPRs have been ensured to the small ventures, these enterprises, mostly rural based suffer from a lack of knowledge of the IPs. Many a time, they end up not patenting their products, thus incurring the financial losses as well as fighting prolonged legal issues. As per the norms set by the World Intellectual Property Organisation, the small enterprises are recognised as the most vulnerable sectors of unprotected innovative works and products; some of its programmes are designed in such a way as "to assist the entrepreneurs, SME support institutions and national governments in increasing the awareness and use of the IP systems among the SMEs across the globe"[6].

Institutional Support

Much of the support for the small business ventures in Australia can be attributed to the initiatives by the government. The credit for the economic success of Australia is given to the small enterprises 'the heavy lifters'. The Austrade (The Australia Trade Commission) is contemplating a coordinated approach between the Federal and State governments to increase the number of SME exporters for further productive results. Inspite of the success, the SMEs are still perceived as not so techno savvy, and not open to innovative approaches. An integrated approach of innovation, research, business know-how in the SMEs is being called for that would ensure better results. Policy support for innovation among SMEs is yet to emerge for the Australian SMEs.

In the Indian economy, next to the agricultural sector, it is the small and village industries that hold much of the opportunity to millions of people. Handlooms, handicrafts, coir, sericulture, *khadi*, village and small scale industries comprise the volume of these sectors.[7] Preference to the heavy industries in the earlier Five-year plans has greatly undermined the potential growth of the SMEs. Some of the key support systems that were inadequately given over the years include necessary capital, assistance in market expansion strategies, supply of raw materials, and provision of technical assistance and granting of loans in time. The lengthy and tiresome paper work at the banks and other governmental financial agencies has left no options for those initiating the ventures except to rely on private loans.

While the governmental support is more or less moderate, private investment in the SMEs has been rather negligible. The percentage of returns has been least attractive, thus holding back further potential growth of and prospects in the sector. An integrated approach of state financial corporations, industrial bodies, corporate sector and financial institutions, especially the cooperative banks would go along way in ensuring their success.

SME Institutions in India and Australia

Some of the key partners of small business in India include Ministry of Small Scale Industries, Khadi and Village Industries Commission, Coir Board, National Small Industries Corporation, Small Industries Development Organisation, Small Industries Development Board of India, National Institute of Entrepreneurship and Small Business Development, etc. In India the Ministry of Small Scale Industries, and Agro and Rural Industries is the main body for the policy formulation, promotion and functioning of the small and medium enterprises. The Parliament's approval of 'The Micro, Small and Medium Enterprises Development Act 2006 further facilitates the promotion, development and enhancement of these small business units so that they can contribute better to the national economy.

In Australia, the small business institutions include Small Business Development Corporation, Council of Small Business Organisations of Australia Limited, Small Business Association of Australia, etc. The Department of Industry, Tourism and Resources is the prime organ pertaining to small business in Australia. Small business, notably, has been exempted from Unfair Dismissal Laws in 2006. The Regulation Taskforce in 2005 has extended many a benefit to encourage the small business environment to be expedited. The regulation, simplification and lessening of red-tapism have been aimed for better results and returns in the concerned sector.

SMEs and Sustainable Development/Environment

While the small business enterprises may be lauded for their entrepreneurial skills and generating massive employment opportunities, they face the demerits like paucity of funds, provision of power and infrastructure facilities, poor managerial and organisational skills. One such serious concern emerges in the context of the physical environment facing major pollution challenges. Strict compliance to the environmental norms and assessments need to be maintained to avoid any disasters that may severely affect these enterprises. For example, if the small business pertains to construction and building material, enough care should be ensured against any kind of hazardous material, waste management, soil and water management and pollution due to dust and other waste materials. Similarly, in the fabric units which provide better employment opportunities, the discharge of harmful artificial and chemical-induced materials pollutes the water sources in the concerned area. In the food processing sector that accounts for major employment gains to women in particular, it should be mandatory for precautions in case of not only the quality of food but also in packing, including the quality of cooking oils, containers or aluminum packs and sheets.

It is estimated that the small enterprises are major source of water pollution and that the total waste waters they generate amount to nearly 3900 million litres per day. The units of fabric dyes are ill-reputed for causing groundwater and surface water pollution.[8] Nearly 40 per cent of the total industrial wastewater is emanated from these units in India. While political will to get away with the problem is rather bleak, the response of the civil society too has not been very encouraging. The need of the hour is to enforce "low cost pollution abatement technologies, and move from pollution control to pollution prevention".[9]

Conclusion

The performance rate of the small business units in the growth of national economy has been encouraging and productive especially in the post liberalisation era in India. So is the case with Australia, where the successive governments have been taking path-breaking initiatives to ensure the success of these units so as to make it a vibrant economy. The economic reforms in both the countries have changed the profile of the small business units thus reducing the risks of unemployment, contributing positively to the overall growth of the economies, providing better income opportunities to millions including the physically challenged and women. Another positive feature has been the lessening dependency on the government jobs, thus increasing the self-employment opportunities with a string of benefits like personal income tax cuts and prospects of better living standards. While the restrictions are many and reforms are slow to come by the setting up of the small business units is still a challenging task in India. Excessive red-tapism and stringent rules still exist that act as deterrents to set up these units, thus minimising the prospects of self-employment facilities to millions of people. While the governments in Australia have been quick to make amends, the potentials of the units in India await positive results and further protection with the enactment of the Small Scale Industries Act 2006. Collaboration with the International Network of SMEs and mutual cooperation offer the prospects for development, wider information networks, data banks and technological cooperation for both India and Australia.

End Notes

1. *A Competitive Economy,* Report of the Department of Foreign Affairs and Trade, Canberra, Australia, 2005.
2. Trade Reports of Small Industries Development Organisation. See URL: http://www.laghu-udyog.com/publications/traderep/treport.html
3. Report on Small Business 2005-06, '*Encouraging Enterprise*', Canberra: Commonwealth of Australia 2006, pp. 17-22.
4. Small Business Development Corporations, Australia http://www.sbdc.com.au/drilldown/drilldown.asp?refid=2.20
5. 23rd APEC Intellectual Property Experts Group Meeting 15-16 August 2006, Guadalajara, Mexico. See URL Source: http://www.apec.org/content/apec/documents_reports/intellectual_property_rights_experts_group/2006.html
6. See the World Intellectual Property Rights Organisation Report Guidelines on Small Business. http://www.smallindustryindia.com/emerge/smebrofv.pdf.
7. K.P. Parameshwaran, Institutional Support for small-scale rural processing enterprises: The Case of India. (http://www.fao.org/docrep/s8380e/s8380e0d.htm).
8. Anil Agarwal, *Small Scale Industries Derive India's Economy but Pollute Heavily. What can be done?* Stockholm International Water Institute Publication. (www.siwi.org/downloads/WF20% Articles WF%20small%20scale%20industry.pdf).
9. *Ibid.*

14

India-Australia Relations: Pattern of Alternation between Convergences and Divergences

Y. YAGAMA REDDY

The two Indian Ocean littoral states had for long remained part of the same landmass, known as Gondwana super-continent encompassing Australia, India, Africa and Antarctica, until 160 million years ago. These components got separated from each other, and later, Australia and India drifted away to their present geometrical locations.[1] Their similarities in geological formations and hence in mining conditions, are also at the base of identical mining techniques best suited to both India and Australia. Yet, another geological event of glaciations around 20,000 years ago, resulted in the fall of sea level by 100 meters. As a consequence, the vast stretch of exposed seabed served as a land bridge that facilitated the migration of ancient (primitive) man along with plant and animal species as far east as Australia. Despite lack of evidence of blood group compatibility between the indigenous people in southern India and those in Australia, certain ethno-linguistic evidences and the microliths pointing to the prehistoric links between these indigenous people, can not be discarded altogether.[2] Rise of sea level made these two land bodies endure physical separation. Still, there is a degree of semblance in the climatic pattern. India and Australia do experience tropical, subtropical and temperate climatic conditions, the pattern of which is found in the form of a mirror image, with reference to the equator. The orographic influence on the rainfall pattern, manifest rain-shadow conditions in the form of aridity and droughts have become incidental to both the countries. Thus, the description of Australia as 'the land of droughts and floods', presents a parallel in the occurrence of droughts in India as a result of *El Nino* effect which was recognised by the meteorologists of the two countries during their first ever interaction in 1879.[3] For all the variations in the agricultural typology, the mechanised farming techniques developed by Australia, are found best adaptable to the Indian agriculture, inasmuch as there is broad similarity in the crop structure comprising wheat, sugarcane, banana, fruit crops and livestock rearing.

Lack of human contacts for over several thousands of years, eclipsed the commonalties based on geology and climate until and after the colonisation of these two territories by the British, in 18th and 19th centuries. This facet of history made India and Australia emerge "with shared and fundamental commitment to freedom and democracy and with shared membership of Commonwealth," besides commonalty in the jurisprudence, based on Anglo-American systems and the widespread use of English language. Geography and history have also bestowed on these nations many complementary features of mutual advantage. These commonalties and complementarities have been conducive to promoting the bilateral relations, particularly the trade, from the beginning of 19th century. These prospects would have impressed the Australian renowned historian, Geoffrey Blainey and inspired him to point out that "Australia seemed to be a satellite of India as well as a colony of England".[4]

But the historiography provides ample evidences to the issue of apathy on the part of Australian colonial administration. There were restrictions imposed on the Indian immigration into Australia all through 19th century. Even as Indians were affected by discrimination, Alfred Deakin, much before becoming the Prime Minister of Australia, had reportedly observed as early as in 1893 in his *Irrigated India*, that "the future relations of India and Australia possess immeasurable potencies", which he ascribed to their geographical proximity. But the White Australia Policy (1901) which gave credence to the purity of the race, had sustained discrimination against Indians in Australia. Though the Reciprocity Act officially removed the disabilities afflicting the Indian immigration, Indians seeking residential status in Australia, could not comply with the provisions of Australian laws. As a consequence, the Indian population of 8162 in 1947 was noted to be marginally larger than that of 7760 in 1901. Furthermore, this situation led the Indians to entertain certain misgivings about Australia's commitment to mete out fair treatment to Indians who were also declared as British subjects.

Good Beginnings of Reciprocity

Despite inconsistencies in Australia's policy towards India, certain instances of events need to be appreciated. Dr. Evatt in 1942, was really enthusiastic about India's independence; and his Labor Party government which was extending "moral and often practical support to the measures leading the Asians towards independence" had warmly greeted the Indian Constituent Assembly in 1946.[5] It was at about this time, that there were commendable propositions for strengthening future relations between India and Australia by accommodating each other's attitudes. On the eve of the inauguration of

Australia's diplomatic mission in New Delhi in 1944, Betram Stevens, the Premier of New South Wales, favoured close commercial links with India in view of implicit benefits of trade (for Australia) and of employment opportunities that would improve the living standards in India.[6] Few months before India became independent, while extending a warm welcome to the Australian observers attending the Asian Relations Conference at New Delhi in March-April 1947, Jawaharlal Nehru felt the need for mutual cooperation to find solutions to many problems in common in the Asia-Pacific region. Contrary to the expectations of many people, the Asian Relations Conference regarded White Australia Policy (restrictions on immigration) as essentially "a matter for decision by the Australian society over its own population composition and therefore immigration into Australia."[7] There were also points of agreement between these two nations. Dr. Evatt's staunch support extended to the United Nations was akin to that of Nehru's. In return, Dr. Evatt had won India's approval for his campaign in favour of the 'application of principles of trusteeship and accountability to non-trust colonial areas'. This principle of accommodating attitudes of each other was furthermore strengthened and the gesture was often reciprocated. Australia's Labor government, which ideologically was committed to its policy of extending support to the independence of Asian colonies, collaborated with India in drawing the UN attention to the Indonesian nationalist cause and even participated in the Asian Conference on Indonesia in New Delhi in July.[8]

Brief Phase of *Entente Cordiale*

The spirit of cooperation between India and Australia was sustained in the form of a broad identity of concerns and interests over the issues of regional and international importance. The relations between them were 'close and sympathetic' during the formative years of India's independence, when Australia was under the Labor government of Joseph Benedict Chifley (1947-1949). Chifley's admiration for Nehru was reinforced by mutual reverence and hence, a sound perception of India's non-aligned foreign policy. Besides this, Chifley and Dr. Evatt were credited with playing a prominent role at the London Commonwealth Conferences in 1948 and 1949 so as to facilitate India's admission into the Commonwealth as a republic by fulfilling the stipulation of accepting "the king as the symbol of the free association of its independent member nations and as such the head of the Commonwealth". This evoked serious criticism against the Labor government of having reduced the "Commonwealth into a mere alliance"; and Menzies and his Liberal Party even accused Chifley of "having voted to put the British Commonwealth into liquidation" in his (Chifley) attempt to accommodate India. It was also regretted that admission of India was an "intolerable degradation" of the Commonwealth, and the Labor Party was even attacked as having conspired "to turn Australia into an Asian nation". [9]

Ideological Drift far Greater than Geographical Distance

All that augured well for strengthening the bilateral partnership during the Nehru-Chifley era, did not prove to be of any significance after 1950, when Australia came under the rule of Liberal Party-coalition, particularly with Robert G. Menzies as Prime Minister (until 1965) who had set out with a prejudice against the British announcement of power transfer to India. The Cold War situation made these two Indian Ocean littoral states drift along their respective political ideologies—Australia's alignment with the Western bloc being committed to the policy of containing communism vis-à-vis India's opposition to the very concept of the world being divided between two great power blocs. Their disagreement basically stemmed from their divergent assessments of the international issues. India had cherished for its part, a strong conviction that "Asian affairs were to be solved by Asians by Asian methods in accordance with Asian interests". Australia was, on the other hand, preoccupied with the fact of the US-led pacts and alliances like SEATO, ANZUS and ANZAM and Australia's military involvement in the conflicts in Korea, Vietnam and Malaysia. A divergence of the kind erupted on the West Irian when India, in deference to its age-old commitment to anti-colonialism, supported the Indonesia's claim of West Irian, and Australia was in favour of the exercise of the human rights to self-determination of the inhabitants of West Irian.

However, another source of ill-feeling between them was the racial policies in South Africa. India, having raised the issue of the racial discrimination against people of Indian origin, mustered the support from the newly emancipated states, and accused Australia of having supported the *apartheid* regime in South Africa. Curiously enough, both Australia and India were primarily opposed to the proposals of Western intervention in Indochina. But, the Geneva Settlement of July 1954 became 'the greatest single cause of disagreement' as it testified to their diametrically opposite perception of the potential risks to peace and of the methods for ensuring security in Southeast Asia. Their variable assessments of the impact of communism on the newly emancipated nations of Asia forced them to discard the views of each other. As a sequel to the Geneva Agreements, Australia came to be convinced about the need for the creation of a regional Southeast Asian alliance, to ensure security in the Asia-Pacific region. For all its efforts to persuade India to participate in the regional pacts, Australia could only convince India on one aspect that the pacts were purely defensive in character. Yet, the individual attitudes of two countries to SEATO, was irreconcilable. To India, SEATO was nothing more than "the antithesis of...*Panch Shila*. Through building of

US bases in Pakistan, it has brought the Cold War to the very borders of India. It is the expression of power politics at its worst".[10] On the contrary, Australia was firm about projecting SEATO as "a collective concept" and as an effective method of securing the safety of Australia and other countries of (South Asia), which were susceptible to the communist aggression, perceived as a formidable menace to peace in general and to Australia security in particular.[11] India became critical of Australia's participation in the Western sponsored alliance, while Australia termed India's stand as unrealistic. Resultant substantial divergence impacted negatively on the goodwill generated by the Colombo Plan under which, Australia had contributed to India's economic development. Though the aid under Colombo Plan was too inadequate to serve India's economic development, it had won India's "frank appreciation of the spirit and the humanitarian element of the aid". Even Nehru who was skeptical of Australia's alliance with the Western bloc, described the Plan as "remarkable and significant".

If Nehru was interested in the "changing face of Asia", Menzies dismissed Asia as "irrelevant" and as being "too difficult for any occidental to understand".[12] Their irreconcilable attitudes towards issues other than those concerning their bilateral relationship, made them differ practically on every issue since 1949 and thus impeded their working together.[13] Nehru and Menzies, by virtue of being two towering personalities as well as their commanding positions in policy formulations, chose to assume a key role in foreign affairs. Their deep-felt convictions had prevented them from transcending the diplomatic gap as well as the cultural and psychological distance between the two nations.[14] Despite plenty of opportunities, they were unable to achieve a mutually beneficial relationship between their two countries. Consequently, they had differed in their perceptions of international affairs. Menzies' initiatives on Kashmir issue, for instance, had only won Nehru's displeasure. Similarly, their divergence was explicit in issues concerning British action in Suez crisis, Soviet action in Hungary and the withdrawal of South Africa from the Commonwealth. The resolution, sponsored by Nehru, on the need for negotiations between the nuclear powers, particularly the two super-powers, was countered by Menzies through an amendment which Nehru had vehemently opposed.

Australia's Gesture Manifesting Sobriety of Leadership

Nonetheless, both the leaders exhibited genuine respect and goodwill towards each other which sustained the basic friendly relations between these two countries. Menzies accepted the notion that the policy of the *apartheid* is an international issue and also favoured self-government in Papua-New Guinea. In turn, Nehru acquired a fairly thorough grasp of the circumstances that forced Australia to become part of ANZUS and SEATO, though he became critical of Australia's alliance with the US as a whole. Nehru also regarded the White Australia Policy and restrictions thereof, as a matter of the latter's domestic policy. Menzies too appreciated India's non-aligned policy as one pregnant with merits, in the context of the dividing global situation.

The Chinese armed aggression on India's northern borders in 1962 brought about the much-needed rapprochement between India and Australia. Menzies assured India of his country's "full sympathy and support," as sought by Nehru in his letter addressed to Menzies.[15] Close on the heels of Menzies assurance to Nehru, Foreign Minister Garfield Barwick had announced the offer of military assistance. During the four month period, commencing in November 1962, Australia supplied military clothing, arms and ammunition worth £ A2.0 million (about Rs. 21.0 crores), later announced as a good-will gift.[16] India-Australia engagement witnessed a series of bilateral visits both at the political and the official levels. Barwick offered 'air umbrella' that envisaged the joint training exercises by US, UK and India. Accordingly, later in November 1963, RAAF also participated in the air defence training exercises on the Indian soil. Though Australia's quantum of military assistance to India was modest, it nevertheless helped pave the way for both the nations to come out of the rut of ideological dogmatism. Having identified itself with India against China's expansionism, Australia affirmed its preparedness to meet the Indian military requirements, while India too shed its traditional indifference towards regional security alliances as well as its unduly exuberant enthusiasm for its much professed non-aligned policy. Australia and India tended to develop an identity of outlook towards a number of issues which had earlier betrayed an absence of correspondence of attitudes. Thus, the controversy between them began to be on the wane, in matters concerning South Africa, New Guinea, ANZUS, Commonwealth Secretariat and Indonesian confrontation of Malaysia, although the divergence over the US intervention in Vietnam persisted. Yet the India-Australia relationship continued to be marked by ambiguity and proved to be nebulous and symbolic, rather than being distinct, until Nehru's death in May 1964, and Menzies' retirement in 1965. The post-Nehru era witnessed Australia's tolerance of India's obsession with Asian balance of power and India's recognition of Australia's alliance with the US. Australia consciously did not interfere in the Indo-Pak war of September 1965 and this coincided with Pakistan's gradual estrangement with SEATO, of which Australia was a founder member.

Differential Concerns Over Regional Security Issues

The formation of ASEAN in 1967 during the height of Indochina war assumed significance in the bilateral relationship of India and Australia. A wide range of issues concerning regional security figured prominently in the discussions of Australian Prime Minister John Gordon and his Indian counterpart Indira

Gandhi during her visit to Australia, the first-ever visit of an Indian prime minister, though nothing had emerged substantially out of their talks. Indira Gandhi's professed hopes about Australia's capabilities and her assertion of India's position, sounded logically incoherent, rather obtuse. She fervently expected Australia to act as a proper bridge between the East and the West. At the same time, she drove home the point that India was not a 'sickman' of Asia. On the other hand, Gordon put forth Australia's desire that India ought to evince real interest in playing a major role in the Southeast Asian affairs. Gordon was in the affirmative about Australia's well-conceived policy of enlisting India's candid support to the newly-formed ASEAN, besides being cognizant of India's pivotal position in Asian balance of power.[17] In view of its obsession with Asian politics, India was not at all inclined towards the Australian-proposed regional defence arrangements even though the US participation was ruled out by Australia. Thoroughly disillusioned Australia, later in April 1971, concluded Five Power Defence Arrangements with other Commonwealth nations of UK, like New Zealand, Malaysia and Singapore. In tune with the earlier signs of India's tilt towards the Soviet Union, the Indo-Soviet Treaty of Friendship and Cooperation was concluded in August 1971, much to the chagrin of Australia. Though committed to the pursuit of maintaining equally good relations with both India and Pakistan, Australia in January 1972, glaringly made an invidious choice of recognising Bangladesh, knowing fully well that the liberation of the latter from the clutches of Pakistan, was the outcome of Indo-Pak war of December 1971.[18] Thus, Australia's response was a clear testimony to its acknowledgement of India's pivotal position and potentialities, to exert a salutary influence on the regional security issues.

Gough Whitlam, whose Labor party was voted to power after a lapse of twenty-three years, was also the first Prime Minister to visit India in fourteen years, in June 1973. His Asian-orientation was fully vindicated by his opposition to military alliances including SEATO and White Australia Policy restriction on Asian immigration. Besides endorsing the concept of Indian Ocean Zone of Peace (IOZOP), Whitlam, along with Indira Gandhi, subscribed to the 1971 Kuala Lumpur Declaration that called for ZOPFAN in Southeast Asia.[19] The consensus over the issue of IOZOP, was fortified by Australia's diplomatic persuasion against the naval build-up in the Indian Ocean by the super powers. But there was persistent resistance to the Whitlam's efforts from the Liberal Opposition party which strongly favoured US bases in the Indian Ocean.[20] In the midst of Conservative opposition becoming critical of India's May 1974 nuclear tests, Canberra's official reaction was relatively mild.

Malcom Fraser of the Liberal-Country coalition, Whitlam's successor, totally reversed Whitlam's Asia-oriented policy, but favoured closer bilateral relations with India. The Fraser government also took the credit for establishing Joint Trade Committee which was an obvious outcome of the first ever bilateral trade agreement concluded in August 1976. But Fraser termed IOZOP concept as "unrealistic" and "a noble ideal". Instead, Fraser viewed the US bases in Diego Garcia, as "essential" and 'relevant' to counter the Soviet naval build up in the region.[21] Canberra also favoured the American naval expansion in the Indian Ocean to safeguard the Australian interests as well as reaffirmed Australia's alliance with US, in view of the latter's significant role in the world affairs for stability and security. Though there was no direct threat to Australia from the Soviet military presence in the Indian Ocean, Canberra largely subscribed to "the concept of balance... at the lowest practicable level" for creating "a climate of restraint" to realise the IOZOP concept.[22] Liberal Party's sworn opposition to IOZOP concept, was evidently sustained even as the Report of Senate Standing Committee on Foreign Affairs and Defence (November 1976) endorsed the IOZOP doctrine.[23]

In his address to Indian Parliament, Fraser, who was the chief guest at the Indian Republic Day Celebrations in January 1979, admitted Australia's perception of Indian Ocean as being distinctly different from India's views. However, Fraser and India's then Prime Minister Morarji Desai exuded confidence that India and Australia together could play an effective role in promoting peace and stability in the region, irrespective of India's position as a proponent of non-aligned movement and Australia's unchequered alliance with the US.[24] Vociferously critical of the Soviet intervention in Afghanistan, Australia assured Pakistan of Australia's economic assistance, obviously because Australia viewed Pakistan as a buffer state in the event of any impending Soviet aggression. During his visit to Delhi in August 1980, Fraser took the issue of super power military presence with Indira Gandhi and later in September, granted the US military facilities on Australian territory to get the Western alliance strengthened against the Soviet naval fleet in the Indian Ocean.[25]

Despite the known differences on this issue, Fraser never did hesitate to discuss the same with Indira Gandhi during his last official visit in August 1981 to New Delhi.[26] At Melbourne, in October 1981, Indira Gandhi called for a total withdrawal of the military bases/troops of the major powers from the Indian Ocean region. She termed the super powers' presence as "an ominous intrusion" into the region and referred to the attempts of outside powers in rearming Pakistan, as "provocative" in nature.[27] From the foregoing account, it is evident that both these two Indian Ocean littoral states had displayed their genuine concern for Indian Ocean security, though each of them was rigidly committed to their respective strategies in ensuring security. It was something like hallucination: India could not expect Indian Ocean to become a zone of peace in the context of the Soviet intervention in Afghanistan.

Australia's 'concept of balance' was reminiscent of competitive regional blocs—NATO versus Warsaw Pact or the military bases of the US in the Philippines and of the USSR in Vietnam. The resolutions adopted at different fora had thus suffered from lack of propriety and commitment on the part of both the nations, particularly when Liberal Country coalition was in power in Australia.

Thus, the new Labor government of Robert James Hawke, much in tune with the established notion, attached prominence to the IOZOP concept. The visit of the Indian Prime Minister Rajiv Gandhi to Australia in October 1986 was regarded by the Australian counterpart Hawke as "an impetus" to get the bilateral relationship revitalised. Hawke further asserted, that both the countries were "concerned to promote peace and security in (our) region".[28] Besides hailing the UN decision of August 1987 for granting India exclusive rights over 52000 sq. km. of area in the Indian Ocean, Australia launched a Centre, exclusively for Indian Regional Studies in Perth, in March, 1988.

Australia, which shifted its "strategic focus from forward defence to self-reliance", found no threat from India to Australia. In fact, Australian Defence Minister, Kim Beazley, justified the Indian naval projection in Bay of Bengal.[29] Later, in February 1989, during his visit to India, Hawke concurred with Rajiv Gandhi on the issue of ensuring stability, peace and cooperation in the Indian Ocean, and declared that both the countries were committed to the IOZOP concept and thereby to the stability and the well being of the Indian Ocean region.[30]

The Rajiv-Hawke rapport based on the personal equation was quite repugnant to the Nehru-Menzies relationship marked by differential temperaments and outlook. Even as the stalemate over NPT persisted, they concurred with each other to the extent of establishing links for mutual benefit. There were series of agreements concluded that facilitated bilateral cooperation in the form of joint ventures. Worth mentioning are the 21 collaborations that came into existence (1988-90), as against 37 similar ventures during the 37 years period (1950-1987). [31] The vital areas of scientific and technical collaborations, valued at several hundreds of millions of Australian dollars, testified to the mutually beneficial relationship. This "personal diplomacy at the prime ministerial level," as Meg Gurry observes, [32] led to the establishment of Australia-India Joint Business Council in late 1986 for harnessing the potentialities of complementary economies and the Joint Ministerial Commission in June 1989, for government-to-government policy discussions.

Regardless of the political instability in India under the National Front government (1989-1991), Canberra had defended India as having been logically entitled to develop its defence forces and sought to strengthen cooperation between the RAN and the Indian navy for protecting the sea lanes. Australia's Minister for Defence Science Gordon Binley in April 1990 extolled the ability of Indian defence forces as significant exclusively to Southeast Asia, but not intended to pose threat to any Australian security interests.[33] In its report of July 1990, the Senate Standing Committee on Foreign Affairs and Trade also found no threat in India's military capabilities to Australia or Southeast Asia.[34] Of much significance was Australia's recognition of India's security concerns and its imperative need for maintaining appropriate military capabilities. For all its better understanding of India's strategic implications, Australia's decision to ship 50 Mirage-III aircraft to Pakistan was contrary to its much professed policy of underscoring South Asia's stability[35]. But this controversy did not deter these littoral states from forging defence cooperation which culminated in the joint naval exercises in Bay of Bengal waters in November 1991, after a gap of 28 years. This new act of naval diplomacy was a compromise to India's non-aligned policy and incidentally served as a major concession to Australia, [36] which was no longer critical of India's naval expansion in view of the rapprochement in the Indo-US relations. India too did not chose to castigate Australia's alliance with the US.

It was at about the same time that India embarked on a new strategy to revamp its relations with its eastern neighbours in the context of the termination of Cold War. The cessation of the Cold War political inhibitions heralded a new era of political bonhomie in the Indo-Australian bilateral relationship. If the Australia-India Council, established in June 1992, was to expand the awareness and understanding between the two countries, Australia's Look West strategy, launched in August 1994 in response to India's Look East Policy of 1992, was intended to become a complementary base for accelerating the economic cooperation. These conscientious efforts, testifying to a singleness of purpose, namely, the sustenance of mutual interests, obviously entailed the compulsions of global economic liberalisation process. The Australian Department of Foreign Affairs & Trade report, *India's Economy at the Midnight Hour* (April 1994), the inauguration of a month-long India-Today 1994 Celebrations in Sydney by the then Indian Vice-President, K.R. Narayanan and the Australia-India New Horizons Campaign, had all testified to Australia's commitment to strengthening bilateral relationship with India. Regardless of the political fluidity in India during 1996-98 under the United Front government, the new government of Liberal-National coalition led by John Howard underscored "the complementarity of the Australian and Indian economies" for realising the "full potential of Australia-India partnership" in 21st Century.

The BJP-Coalition government that succeeded the United Front government equally responded to the sustained efforts of the Howard government at strengthening the bourgeoning the bilateral partnership. Perplexedly enough, the Australian government's reaction to India's nuclear tests of May 1998, was more strident than that of any other country. The official outbursts like "ill-judged step", "flagrant defiance" and "willful disregard" and the punitive measures it advocated stood diametrically opposed to its much expressed-enthusiasm over the steadily growing bilateral relationship. [37] Though Australia, along with other ARF dialogue partners like Canada, Japan and New Zealand, had lobbied for getting India's tests indicted at the ARF meeting, ASEAN member states in a statement, rather preferred to deplore India's tests in strong terms. Curiously enough, the Australian public showed a better grasp of India's nuclear imperatives and critically viewed Canberra's reaction as needless. [38] Thus, having got reconciled to the reality that its vociferous reaction had only drawn a blank, Australia did not like to make the bilateral relationship a hostage to the nuclear issue, lest it should meet with the same fate as the one that resulted from the ideological estrangement caused by the Cold War political equations. Following the lifting of the sanctions by Australia, there began a process of bilateral engagement in the form of high level visits and contacts that expeditiously facilitated the resumption of the normal ties. Australian Foreign Affairs Minister Alexander Downer's initiative for a "strategic dialogue", on the eve of his visit to India in March 2000 that coincided with the visit of the US President Bill Clinton, was based on Australia's recognition of India's importance in the regional and global affairs. At the same time, Downer endorsed India's nuclear deterrence capability on the grounds of perceived threat to its own security. [39] Australia's desire to rediscover a nuclearized India, was once again evident in Howard's "fence mending mission" to India in July 2000, when he exuded confidence in "a new era of political bonhomie and strategic initiative," even as the differences over nuclear issues persisted. [40] The enhanced enthusiasm in engaging India, obviously led to the improved Indo-US relations which made possible for these two Indian Ocean littoral states to concur with the US concept of National Missile Defence. [41] Further, besides giving credence to a common strategic stake in ensuring stability all along the Indian Ocean shipping lanes, they expanded their defence relationship to encompass, among various other issues, the security in the Asia-Pacific region as a whole. [42] Hence it was not at all a matter of surprise that the Australian navy participated in the Indian International Fleet Review in February 2001, another joint naval exercise within a decade since November 1991.

While the US global approach was tuned enough to accommodate the rise of India as a world power, the 9/11 incident served as an incentive to an enhanced solidarity in combating terrorism. India, which had for long confronted the terrorist menace and Australia, which had a perceived threat of terrorism, responded so sharply as to extend support to the American War against terrorism. This incident inspired Australia and India, to concur with each other in their attitude towards the US. It was thus a landmark in the India-Australia bilateral relationship of over 50 years during which, their divergence revolved around the US involvement in the Asia-Pacific region. The Bali incident of October 2002, wherein 88 Australians were among the 202 killed, made Australia vulnerable to the operations of terrorism in its northern neighbourhood of Southeast Asia. India became the first country outside the ASEAN, to cooperate with Australia in the war against terrorism, in the form of an agreement signed during the visit of India's External Affairs Minister, Yaswant Sinha, to Australia in August 2003.[43] India's importance to Australia began to be increasingly realised, as evident from the Australian Prime Minister, John Howard's second visit in March 2006 to India in less than 6 years. If his earlier visit in July 2000 was just four months after the then US President Clinton's visit to India, this visit was close on the heels of the visit of the US President Bush to India, in the first week of March 2006. Howard then observed that the two countries had much in common, the potential of which was being freed from earlier constraints. Though six agreements including an MoU on the framework of cooperation in defence and security related issues were signed by India and Australia during Howard's visit, Howard remained persistently non-committal to the Indian Prime Minister's request to reconsider the ban on the supply of uranium to India.[44] His tough stand was contrary to the spirit of the nuclear deal clinched between India and the US that had brought India into the non-proliferation mainstream and allowed India's civilian nuclear programme for international inspections. Even as India is being recognised not as a nuclear weapon state but as a responsible state, Howard ruled out the question of the supply of uranium to India as the latter was not a party to Non-proliferation Treaty (NPT). Howard at the same time defended his country's sale of uranium to China, on the grounds that the latter had signed the NPT. Howard also categorically asserted that the Indo-US nuclear deal would produce absolutely no impact on Australia's firm decision in this respect. This attitude was not commensurate with India's strong support of Australia's participation in the East Asian Summit in December 2005 vis-à-vis China's opposition. At a later stage, Canberra once again justified its stand on the possibility of signing a nuclear deal with China in April but ruled out uranium sales to India, even while admitting that India's behaviour had been "impeccable as a practitioner of non-proliferation."[45] But the proposed Committee to examine "the form and substance" of the Indo-US accord was of some solace to all those craving for enhanced partnership of India and Australia.

The pattern of alternation between convergences and divergences comes to the fore in the foregoing account of the relations of these two Indian Ocean littoral states, for all their acknowledged commonalties and complementarities. Though this alternation between the two extremes did not lead to any altercation between the two nations at any point of time, it did much to hamper the steady growth of the bilateral relationship very much in evidence in the tardy progress which, one feels like ascribing to the inability of the leaders concerned, to understand each other and to acquire a sound grasp of the situational exigencies so that either of them or both together could rise to the occasion, to act accordingly only to benefit mutually.

End Notes

1. Hugh Finlay, *et al.*, *Australia* (Hawthorn, Victoria: Lonely Planet Publication, 1998).
2. M.V. Macfarlane, "Aboriginal Paleophysiology," in R.L. Kirk and A.G. Thorne, eds., *The Origin of Australians* (Canberra: Australian Institute of Aboriginal Studies, 1976). Also see D. Devahuti, "Prehistoric Links Among Australia, Southeast Asia and India," *The Southeast Asian Review*, Col. 1, No. 1, August 1976, pp. 76-78.
3. *News from Australia*, 7, No. 18, 28 September, 1992, p. 3.
4. Goeffrey Blainey, *The Tyranny of Distance* (Melbourne: 1996), p. 61, quoted by Meg Gurry, "A Tale of Missed Opportunities: Australia's Relations with India since 1947," in Marika Vicziany, ed., *Australia-India Economic Relations: Past, Present and Future*, Indian Ocean Centre for Peace Studies, the University of Western Australia, (Nedlands, W.A.: 1993), pp. 11-12.
5. Quoted in Werner Levi, *Australia's Outlook on Asia* (Chapter IX, Angus & Robertson, Sydney: 1958), p. 112.
6. Senate Standing Committee on Foreign Affairs, Defence and Trade, *Australia-India Relations: Trade and Security*, (Canberra: Australian Government Publishing Service, 1990), p. 10.
7. Gordon Greenwood, *Approaches to Asia: Australian Post-War Policies and Attitudes* (Sydney: McGraw-Hill Book Co., 1974), p. 342.
8. Gordon Greenwood, *Approaches to Asia:*, p. 342.
9. Werner Levi, pp. 111-121.
10. Gordon Greenwood and Norman Harper, eds., *Australia in World Affairs, 1956-1960* (Melbourne: Cheshire, 1963), p. 342.
11. Gordon Greenwood and Norman Harper, eds., *Australia in World Affairs*, pp. 344-45.
12. Meg Gurry, "Leadership and Bilateral Relations: Menzies and Nehru, Australia and India, 1949-1964," *Pacific Affairs*, 65 (4), 1992-93, pp. 510-27.
13. J.D.B. Miller, "The Conditions for Cooperation," (pp. 204-205) and R.G. Neale, "Australia's Changing Relations with India," (p. 84), both in J.D.B. Miller, *India, Japan, Australia: Partners in Asia?* (Canberra: Australian National University Press, 1968).
14. Meg Gurry, "Leadership and Bilateral Relations..., p. 514.
15. *Current Notes on International Affairs*, 33 (10), October 1962, p. 41; 34 (1&2), January-February 1963, pp. 48-50.
16. *Current Notes on International Affairs*, 34 (3), March 1963, p. 22; *Asian Recorder* (*AR*), 9 (17), 23-29 April 1963, p. 5164.
17. *A.R.* 14 (30), 22-28 July, 1968, pp. 8434-37.

18. *A.R.*, 18 (10), 4-10 March, 1972, pp. 10645-46.
19. *A.R.*, 19 (29), 16-22 July 1973, pp. 11492-93; *Indian and Foreign Review* (*I&FR*), 10 (17), 15 June, 1973, pp. 5-6.
20. Australian Opposition leader, Bill Sneedden, in March 1974 criticised the Labour Governments foreign policy as "incoherent, abrasive and inconsistent," *IDSA NR*, April 1974, p. 388 reporting *Patriot*, 13 March, 1974.
21. *Hindustan Times*, 20 December, 1975, *A.R.*, 22 (9), 19-25 February, 1976, p. 13032.
22. *Australian Foreign Affairs Record*, 47 (11), November 1976, pp. 598-600 and 48 (3), March 1977, p. 161.
23. *A.R.*, 23 (6), 29 January-4 February, 1977, p. 161.
24. *Asian Almanac,* 17 (21), 1979, p. 9439-40; *I&FR*, 16 (9), 15 February, 1979, p. 6.
25. *Times of India,* 8 September, 1980; *Mianichi Daily News*, 13 September, 1980.
26. *Times of India,* 21 October, 1981.
27. *Tribune,* 21 October, 1981; *A.R.,* 27 (46), 5-11 November 1981, pp. 16307-310.
28. *AFAR*, 57 (10), October 1986, pp. 901-02.
29. *A.R.*, 33 (41), 8-14 October, 1987, p. 19685, *Australian News*, 3 (16), 19 April, 1988, pp. 3-5.
30. *A.R.* 35 (14), 2-8 April, 1989, pp. 20508-509, Johanna Sutherland, "Australian-Indian Relations: Current Status and Prospects, "*Strategic Analysis*, May 1989, pp. 191-204.
31. *News from Australia* (*NFA*), 5 (17), 1990, p. 1.
32. Meg Gurry, "Leadership and Bilateral Relations…," p. 511.
33. *Australian Foreign Affairs & Trade* (*AFAT*), 61 (4), April 1990, pp, 202-06.
34. Senate Standing Committee on Foreign Affairs, Defence and Trade, *Australia-India Relations: Trade and Security* (Canberra: Australian Govt. Publishing Service: July 1990), pp. 73-92.
35. *Sydney Morning Herald*, 26 April 1990; *NFA*., 5 (13), 14 August, 1990, p. 1 and 5 (20), 28 November, 1990, p. 2.
36. *Hindustan Times*, 8 December, 1991; *Telegraph*, 3 November, 1991.
37. *DFAT*., June 1998, p. 28; *Time*, 13 May 1998; Amit Baruah, "Renewing Ties," *Frontline*, 13 May, 2001, pp. 49-50.
38. *The Hindu*, 30 September, 1998, p. 12.
39. *The Hindu*, 20 March 2000, p. 14; *Times of India*, 7 April 2000; Jenelle Bonnor, *Australia-India Security Relations: Common Interest or Common Disinterest?* Working Paper, No. 67, (New South Wales: Australian Defence Studies Centre, April 2001), p. 14.
40. *The Hindu*, 27 June, 2000, p. 14, 10 July, 2000, p. 13, 11 July, 2000, p. 14, 12 July, 2000, p. 1, 13 July, 2000, p. 14.
41. *The Hindu*, 20 June, 2004, p. 14; 23 June, 2001, p. 12.
42. *The Hindu*, 30 August, 2001, p. 12; 31 August, 2001, p. 114.
43. *The Hindu*, 29 July, 2003.
44. *http://www.mea.gov.in,* 6 March 2006. *Deccan Chronicle*, 7 March 2006. *The Hindu*, 7 March, 2006.
45. *Deccan Chronicle*, 8 March, 2006, *The New Indian Express*, 6 March, 2006, *The Hindu*, 31 March, 2006.

15

Australia-India Relations During the Howard Era

RUPAKJYOTI BORAH

Inspite of sharing several commonalities, India and Australia have not had the best of relations. Both are former British colonies, members of the Commonwealth, successful and functioning democracies, having a common language and sharing a passion for cricket. The relations between the two go back to the late 18th century and early 19th century when coal was shipped from Sydney to Calcutta. During the years after India's independence, Indo-Australian relations failed to pick up. The prime reason was that both of them were in opposite camps—Australia being close to the US while India was a leading member of the Non-Aligned Movement (NAM). Though Australia was geographically almost a part of Asia, it felt that its interests were best served by becoming a British ally and later that of the US.

Australia viewed India as being too difficult and somewhat different from the rest of Asia. For Australians, the image of India was that of a poverty-stricken country and they generally failed to take note of the positive developments in India. There were also worries about communal clashes and internal dissension in India. But the image began to change after the end of the Cold War and the launch of India's economic reforms programme. Australia and India began searching for new identities in the post-Cold War world. They began to shed the baggage of the past. This could only have positive implications for the growth of the bilateral ties.[1] The end of the Cold War forced India's foreign policy mandarins to look anew at the world. In India's case, the collapse of the Soviet Union in 1991 meant the loss of a political, military and economic counterweight to China. The United States emerged as the sole superpower. India's economic crisis of mid-1991, the loss of captive Soviet-bloc markets and the emergence of economic 'tigers' in the East forced India, after decades of looking towards the West, to turn its attention eastwards and announce its desire to 'dance with the tigers in the East'.

At around the same time when India embarked on its economic reforms programme under Prime Minister Narasimha Rao, in Australia Paul Keating succeeded Bob Hawke as Prime Minister in 1991. The relations between the two countries picked up under the Keating administration. A significant development in Indo-Australian naval ties took place in November 1991 when the RAN (Royal Australian Navy) frigate, HMAS Torrens joined three Indian ships in the Bay of Bengal for a four-day joint naval exercise. Australia and India inked a double-taxation agreement in 1991 designed to promote trade and investment between the two countries. In the same year a Joint Working Group on Power was set up and a Special Arrangement on Science and Technology Cooperation was worked out. The year 1992 saw the establishment of the Australia-India Council to encourage the broadening and deepening of Australia-India ties through contacts and exchanges in a wide variety of fields. *India's Economy at the Midnight Hour: Australia's India Strategy*, a report prepared by the East Asia Analytical unit of the Department of Foreign Affairs and Trade, released in 1994 stated that India was changing and Australia's competitors had been quick to realise this. It added that India's growth was likely to be less volatile than China's 'boom-bust' cycles since it had maintained stable and respectable growth rates since independence.[2]

The Labor government was re-elected in March 1993. Paul Keating went on to win a fifth term for Labor at the election held on 13 March 1993, defeating the Liberal-National Coalition led by John Hewson.[3] In August 1994, in a joint statement by the Foreign Minister, Gareth Evans and the Minister for Trade, Bob McMullan, a "Look West" strategy was announced. The "Look West" strategy was unique in that it was for the first time in Australian history that a national strategy had been formulated for the Indian Ocean going beyond security concerns. There was a change in the perception of the Indian Ocean as a moat behind which Australia developed in isolation from its neighbours, to a new realisation of the Indian Ocean being a means of forging closer links with the countries on its shores.[4] On the security front, Australia started to upgrade its almost non-existent security infrastructure on the Western coast. Western Australia tried to project itself as a gateway to Southeast Asia and the Indian Ocean.

There was increased interaction between India and Australia during this period, both at the government and the people-to-people level. The Australia-India Council organised a month-long festival, *India Today 1994*, across various Australian cities between April and May 1994. The festival showcased a wide array of activities like Indian street bazaars, music, dancing, museum displays among others. It also included visits to Australia by distinguished Indian figures including sporting and film personalities and naval ships.

The elections of 2 March 1996 led to the defeat of the Labor party after thirteen years and the Liberal-National coalition swept to power under the leadership of John Howard. There was an apprehension in India that with the new government in power the relations between the two countries would suffer, but it was not to be. The new government carried forward the process of building better and closer links between India and Australia.

The Australia-India *New Horizons* programme was launched in October 1996 in India to promote Australian culture, tourism and business. The programme featured business, public policy, science, technology, educational, cultural and sporting events across six major Indian cities—New Delhi, Mumbai, Kolkata, Bangalore, Chennai and Chandigarh. The campaign included a three-day business forum which began in New Delhi and then moved to Mumbai. This event had its origins in research which pointed out that there was a lack of awareness in major Australian target markets about Australia's capabilities.

India's 'Look-East' policy saw a big improvement in the ties between India and the Southeast Asian countries. India became a full dialogue partner of the ASEAN in the fifth ASEAN summit in Bangkok in December 1995. In July 1996, India became a member of the ARF (ASEAN Regional Forum). The earlier Joint Trade Committees with the ASEAN countries were upgraded as Joint Business Commissions and an India-ASEAN Business Council and ASEAN-India Joint Management Committee were set up. An ASEAN-India fund was created to promote trade, tourism, science and technology and other economic activity.

However a series of events occurred during this period, which gave rise to growing unease in Asia regarding Australia. In early 1997, Pauline Hanson founded the One Nation Party in Australia which attracted support from people who objected to Asian immigration and to special treatment for the Aboriginal people. One-Nation also gained from hostility towards government intervention in the economy, high unemployment, and the established political parties and politicians in general. In 1998, One Nation preferences helped to defeat the Liberal-National Coalition Government in Queensland and in the same year, it secured nearly 1 million votes in a federal election which Prime Minister Howard had called for to get a mandate on the issue of introduction of a goods and service tax (GST) and the complete privatisation of the telecommunications sector.[5]

The growing support base of the One-Nation party attracted widespread media and official attention in Asia. There was a perception in Asia, apparently growing, that Australia was turning into a racist country. The ensuing ruckus did a lot of harm to Australia's image in Asia. However, to the relief of all, Pauline Hanson and her party soon ran out of public support.

During this period, Australia was also trying to build closer ties with the Asia-Pacific region. *In the National Interest*, Australia's Foreign Policy and Trade White Paper of 1997 asserted that "Australia's most important strategic and economic interests lie in a region—the Asia-Pacific—of great cultural and historical diversity. This region covers Southeast Asia, Northeast Asia, the Pacific and the eastern reaches of the Indian Ocean."[6] The White Paper also noted that Australia's economic interests were very closely tied to the Asia-Pacific region. Three out of four of Australia's export dollars were being earned in the APEC markets, which were also the recipient of more than half of Australia's foreign direct investment. This region was very significant for Australia both in terms of security and economic interests. [7]

With regard to India, the White Paper stated:

> India's economy has expanded rapidly during recent years. Domestic economic liberalisation and a much more positive attitude to foreign investment have resulted in a more open economy. Providing these policies are maintained, it is likely that India too will follow an East Asia trajectory. While not in the "tiger" class, growth averaging seven per cent annually in recent years and forecast growth averaging six per cent annum for the next decade will place India among the world's ten largest economics by 2010. With economic growth and closer links with the Asia-Pacific, India will become a more significant influence in regional and global affairs, and a more important trading and investment partner for Australia.[8]

India's Nuclear Test and After

India's ties with Australia suffered a rude jolt when on 11 May 1998 when India tested three nuclear devices in the Pokhran underground testing site in Rajasthan, following it up with two more tests on May 13. The tests evoked widespread condemnation and surprise all across the globe. Australia responded very strongly to these Indian tests. After India's second round of nuclear tests, the Australian government decided to suspend bilateral defence links with India, withdraw its defence adviser from New Delhi, cancel ship and aircraft visits, officer exchanges and other defence-related visits. It also decided to withdraw Australian Defence Force (ADF) personnel undergoing training in India and asked three Indian defence personnel undergoing training during that time in Australia to go back immediately. Canberra also decided to suspend non-humanitarian aid and ministerial and senior official visits.

Australia response to India's nuclear tests in 1998 was in sharp contrast to its response to India's first 'peaceful nuclear explosion' (PNE) in May 1974, which was mild.[9] This mild response in 1974 was guided by its trade interests and nuclear agenda. During that time, the Whitlam government had given up plans to develop nuclear weapons or nuclear power. Australia saw India as a potential customer for enriched Australian uranium.

Australia maintained that its strong stand against India's nuclear tests in 1998 was guided by two main factors. One of them was the strong focus in Australian foreign policy on the prevention of proliferation of nuclear weapons. Public opinion in Australia was very much against nuclear weapons. French nuclear testing in Mururoa Atoll in the South Pacific had led to huge public protests. The present Australian government was in the opposition during that time when it had vehemently criticised the Labor government for its muted response to the French nuclear tests. Therefore, it could not be seen as reacting in a muted manner to India's nuclear tests when it was in power. [10]

India was very upset with Australia's heavy-handed response to India's nuclear tests. The tone of the official Australian condemnation of India's nuclear tests was seen by India as rude, offensive and on occasions abusive. There was a feeling in India that Australia had a poor understanding of India's security needs. There was also anger at Australia's refusal to acknowledge India's legitimate security needs, like the threats emanating from China and Pakistan and Sino-Pakistani military cooperation.[11] India retaliated to the Australian stand by suspending all bilateral military cooperation, disallowing Australian naval ships from visiting Indian ports and territorial waters, and by cancelling all over-flight facilities to Australian military aircraft.

India felt that since Australia was covered by the US nuclear umbrella, it was improper on its part to criticise India. Though Australia was highly critical of France for conducting nuclear tests in the South Pacific, it did not stop exporting uranium to France. The Australian Government was of the view that Australia and others in the region did not want to see France out of the Pacific, and they wanted to work closely with France. According to Australia, under the terms of the NPT, of which it is a signatory, it exports uranium only for peaceful purposes, but this could not be guaranteed. Australia also did not criticise France when the latter resumed nuclear testing in June 1995 after declaring a moratorium in 1992.

The United States had also responded promptly and strongly to the Indian tests. President Clinton while expressing deep disappointment at the nuclear tests, threatened to punish India and asked India's neighbours to refrain from following suit. On 12 May, 1998 President Clinton stated:

> This action by India not only threatens the stability of the region, it directly challenges the firm international consensus to stop the proliferation of weapons of mass destruction. I call on India to announce that it will conduct no further tests, and that it will sign the Comprehensive Test Ban Treaty now and without conditions. I also urge India's neighbours not to follow suit; our laws have very stringent provisions, signed into law by me in 1994, in response to nuclear tests by non-nuclear weapon states. And I intend to implement them fully.[12]

On 13 May, 1998, President Clinton announced the imposition of sanctions against India under Section 102 of the US Arms Export Control Act, also known as the Glenn Amendment. But the Clinton administration was soon pressurised by US business and bank lobbies to enable them to run their activities and operations in India and were joined by the US farm lobby pleading for the protection of their interests.[13] A breakthrough in the strained ties was achieved following the meeting of Jaswant Singh, the Indian Prime Minister's special envoy with the US Deputy Secretary of State Strobe Talbott on 12 June 1998 in Washington.

Revival of Ties

Contrary to the stand taken by the Australian government, many Australian academics and civil society organisations resented Australia's excessively strong criticism of India's nuclear tests. In June 1999, the Senate Foreign Affairs, Defence and Trade References Committee in its report *The 1998 Indian and Pakistani Nuclear Tests*, recommended that the Australian Government re-instate its defence advisers in India and Pakistan and re-establish exchange programmes between Australian Defence Force officers and defence officials from India and Pakistan. It also recommended that the Australian government review its funding to study and research centres focussing on South Asia to develop expertise in this area.[14]

India's Prime Minister Atal Behari Vajpayee paid a visit to Pakistan in February 1999, but in the same year Pakistani troops and militants intruded into the Kargil sector of Jammu and Kashmir. Australia praised India's "admirable restraint" in the subsequent Kargil War, where India successfully evicted all the intruders. This period saw a closer interaction between the United States and India. As part of the Joint Indo-US efforts against terrorism, a Joint Working Group (JWG) to counter terrorism was established in early 2000. T! ; US realised the role India could play in monitoring the sea routes running through the Indian Ocean till the Strait of Malacca, particularly after India escorted its ships passing through the sea lanes of the Indian Ocean till the Strait of Malacca.

In late 1999, the US Congress failed to ratify the CTBT. Suddenly, Australia found itself in an awkward position since it had been very vocal in asking India to sign the CTBT. India's chief negotiator, Arundhati Ghose, declared in the General Assembly that India would never sign the CTBT until the major nuclear powers formulated a time-table for the elimination of their nuclear arsenal.

The slide in the bilateral relations was arrested with the visit of the Australian Deputy Prime Minister Tim Fischer's to India in February 1999. Tim Fischer was the first Australian ministerial visitor after the tests. The Australian Foreign Minister Alexander Downer paid a visit to India in March

2000, around the same time as the US President Bill Clinton. The Australian Prime Minister John Howard embarked on a visit to New Delhi in July 2000, becoming the first Australian Prime Minister to visit India in eleven years. Prime Minister Howard's visit in July 2000 was aimed at adding new vigour and activity into the relation. Prime Minister Howard's visit to India in July 2000 had underlined the transformation in Australian foreign policy in the post-Pokhran II period.

The year 2000 saw a series of high level visits from Australia. These included visits by Shadow Foreign Minister Laurie Brereton and Deputy Premier Hendy Cowan of Western Australia in February 2000, Opposition Leader Kim Beazley in April 2000, Deputy Premier Jim Elder of Queensland in May 2000, Immigration and Multicultural Affairs Minister Philip Ruddock in July 2000, Trade Minister Mark Vaile in October 2000, an Australian Parliamentary delegation led by Andrew Southcott, MP in November 2000. [15]

Both India and Australia realised that the nuclear issue should not hold the entire relationship hostage. The path-breaking visit of the US President Bill Clinton in March 2000 had set the tone for the new American approach towards India. Countries like Japan, Germany, France, Britain and several other countries started adopting a policy of engagement towards India. Australia also did not lag behind.

Though Australia still wanted India to sign the CTBT (Comprehensive Test Ban Treaty), in Canberra there was a realistic appreciation of the extent to which Australia could influence India.[16] During the visit of the Indian External Affairs and Defence Minister, Jaswant Singh to Australia in 2001, there was little doubt that the Indian nuclear tests had been accepted by Australia as *fait accompli*. In a major departure from the Australian position, the issue of India signing the CTBT was not raised during the formal official dialogue. The first official India-Australia Strategic Dialogue was held in New Delhi on 30 August 2001. The talks were "open, constructive and wide-ranging, and demonstrated shared perspectives and common interests on a number of important issues, including in the Asia-Pacific and the Indian Ocean regions"[17]

In the aftermath of the deadly September 11, 2001 attacks on the United States, Australia evoked the ANZUS treaty to come to the aid of America.[18] The terror attacks of 11 September 2001 were a defining moment in United States' ties with India. It shifted the overall dynamics of US foreign policy discourse and provided a springboard for solidarity and understanding between the two countries. It helped to strengthen the notion of a natural alliance between New Delhi and Washington. India's new dalliance with the US helped to further ties with American allies like Australia.

The Bali bomb attack of 12 October 2002 in Indonesia killed 88 Australians.[19] It brought Australia face-to-face with international terrorism and resulted in one of the most profound and far-reaching changes in the

Australian security environment in recent times. India has been facing the problem of terrorism in the border state of Jammu and Kashmir and the North-eastern states for a long time. The 13 December 2001 attack on the Indian Parliament served as a grim reminder of the serious problem of terrorism India was facing. In the light of their shared concerns about global terrorism, India and Australia signed a Memorandum of Understanding on Cooperation in Combating International Terrorism in August 2003. The counter-terrorism protocol reflected the expanding strategic convergence on the bilateral front. The first meeting of the Australia-India Joint Working Group on Counter Terrorism and Immigration was held on 7 March 2003 as an adjunct to the bilateral strategic dialogue.

Areas of Convergence

Australia and India had started coming closer in the post-Cold War era. Both found that they had common interests in Southeast Asia. India's "Look-East" policy had brought it closer to the countries of South-East Asia and East Asia. India's membership of the ASEAN Regional Forum (ARF) in July 1996, the dialogue partnership of the Association of South-East Asian Nations (ASEAN) in December 1995, as well as its membership of the Indian Ocean Rim Association for Regional Cooperation (IOR-ARC) in 1997 together with Australia, brought them even closer.

Australia and India have an important stake in maintaining peace and stability in the Indian Ocean region. This region is home to important sea lines of communication (SLOCs) and maritime choke points. A large volume of international long haul maritime cargo from the Persian Gulf, Africa and Europe passes through the Indian Ocean. India lies approximately half way between the Strait of Hormuz and the Strait of Malacca. This region is very important for Australia given the necessity of maintaining the security of its trade and communication routes through the region. Cooperation between India and Australia is essential for tackling several threats to the safety of the sea lines of communication in the Indian Ocean which include piracy, drug trafficking, gun running, human smuggling, pollution, accidents, mines, closure of choke points, inter-state conflicts and territorial disputes.

Australia and India share a close interest in the stability of Indonesia. Islamic militancy and geographic proximity are at the root of both these countries' interest in Indonesia. India's Andaman and Nicobar group of islands lie close to the restive Indonesian province of Aceh. The southernmost of India's Andaman and Nicobar group of islands is barely 90 nautical miles from Indonesia's Aceh province. India's decision to go ahead with a tri-service Far Eastern Strategic Command at Port Blair in the Andaman and Nicobar Islands gives it tremendous leverage over the sea lanes heading towards the Strait of Malacca, the gateway to Southeast Asia.

There has been a closer interaction between the armed forces of the two countries in the recent past. INS Godavari took part in the Sydney International Fleet Review in 1998. The Royal Australian Navy (RAN) participated in the International Fleet Review at Mumbai in February 2000. An Australian navy frigate, HMAS Adelaide visited India from 9-13 June 2003. The visit coincided with the visit to India by the Maritime Commander of the Royal Australian Navy, Rear Admiral Raydon Grates. His visited was preceded by the successful visit to Australia by the Indian Chief of Naval Staff, Admiral Madhvendra Singh in November 2002. In November 2004, the bilateral defence relations got a major boost with the visit of the Australian Army chief, Lieutenant General Peter Leahy to India. The Royal Australian Navy frigate HMAS Stuart paid a visit to Mumbai in August 2004.

At the 2003 WTO trade talks in Cancun, agricultural and other claims were raised by a new Group of 22 (G 22) led by China and India, which opposed the stand taken by the US and the European Union. Australia saw merit in the G 22's rationale, especially its demands for agricultural liberalization.[20]

The Indian movie industry or Bollywood has played a significant role in promoting greater interaction between the two countries. An increasing number of Bollywood movies are being shot in Australia. Australian locations are in great demand for Bollywood movies. Australia is also providing Indian films with special effects and post-production work.[21] Blockbusters like *Dil Chahta Hai* and *Kaho Na Pyar Hai* have been shot extensively in Australia. Bollywood movies help the Indian Diaspora in identifying themselves with India. Bollywood movies are perhaps "the single strongest agency for the creation of a national mythology of heroism, consumerism, leisure and sociality."[22]

The vibrant Indian community in Australia has helped to promote greater interaction between the two countries. An increasing number of Indian tourists are visiting Australia and vice-versa. There were 26,000 visitors from India in the first four months of 2006, representing an increase of 31 per cent relative to the same period in 2005.[23] Australians and Indians are developing professional and personal interaction in the fields of education, tourism, business, culture, medicine, science, sports, arts, crafts, etc. Australia has, in recent years, emerged as a major destination for Indian students studying abroad. The number of Indian students is increasing at an average annual rate of around 35 per cent since 2003. There are currently around 28,000 Indian students studying in Australia.

Australia has provided aid worth A$ 16 million for the Gangtok and Shillong urban water supply and environmental sanitation schemes. The Gangtok and Shillong schemes have facilitated improved water supply and environmental sanitation services, and developed the capacity of the local governments to implement better water supply and sanitation schemes in

Gangtok and Shillong, which are the capital cities of Sikkim and Meghalaya respectively. In addition, Australia has provided $ 26 million for the Primary Education Enhancement Project (PEEP) which tries to improve school enrolment, attendance, retention and completion rates of children in the age group of 6-11 years. The project places special emphasis on educating girls, children of the urban poor, working children and children with special needs in Bihar, Delhi, Jharkhand and Maharashtra. Australia is also helping India in the realm of hydroelectricity. The Snowy Mountains Engineering Corporation (SMEC) is working on a number of hydroelectric projects in India with special focus on India's Northeastern States. It has undertaken the design work for the Kameng Hydroelectric Project in Arunachal Pradesh which is planned to generate 600 MW of electricity.

In October 2004, Australia and India's two main biotechnology bodies—AusBiotech and the Association of Biotechnology Led Enterprises (ABLE) respectively—formalised institutional linkages through the signing of a MoU. In the arena of sports, there are substantial opportunities for cooperation over the Commonwealth Games, given Melbourne's successful hosting of the Games in 2006. New Delhi would be hosting the new edition of the games in 2010. [24]

In September 2004, the Australian carrier Qantas re-entered the Indian market with the launch of its thrice-weekly non-stop service between Sydney and Mumbai. The tsunami of December 26, 2004 led to a colossal loss of life and property in India in addition to other Southeast countries. Ordinary Australians donated A $ 300m for tsunami relief work to which the government added A $ 1 billion.[25] Australia has also cooperated with India to develop a tsunami early warning system, with a network of national warning centres to be coordinated by UNESCO'S Intergovernmental Oceanographic Commission (IOC).

Both Australia and India are forging closer ties with various Southeast Asian countries. India's 'Look-East' policy led to a big leap forward in the relations between India and ASEAN. The second Indo-ASEAN summit at Bali in Indonesia in October 2003 led to closer ties between the two. Two broad agreements, for comprehensive economic cooperation and for combating terrorism were signed. India also acceded to the ASEAN Treaty of Amity and Cooperation and signed a framework agreement aimed at creating a free trade area in ten years. In 2003, India and Thailand also signed a number of agreements including a landmark free trade agreement. The proposed Free Trade Agreement will lead to a free trade area in goods to begin by the year 2010 and in services and investment by 2006. The Bali meet set its sights on creating a single Southeast Asian market, covering 500 million people with an annual trade of US$720 billion. The level of two-way trade between India and ASEAN is projected to rise to $30 billion by the year 2007. But the larger aim is the building of an ASEAN-India free trade area and developing an

Asian Economic Community by 2020 on the lines of the European Union.[26] India and Singapore signed a Comprehensive Economic Cooperation Agreement in June 2005.

The increasing attention being paid to India was reflected in *Advancing the National Interest*, Australia's Foreign and Trade Policy White Paper of 2003 which noted India's growing weight in international affairs. It stated that India's military capabilities and economy were growing steadily and India's strong economic growth ensured that Australia's exports to India recorded double digit growth annually over the past decade. The White Paper noted that both the countries were committed to developing a more dynamic and forward-looking approach to the bilateral relationship. India's growing strategic influence together with its nuclear capabilities made it necessary for Australia to engage India on strategic matters.[27] The White paper also acknowledged that engagement with Asia was an abiding priority of Australian foreign policy. Asian countries accounted for around 56 per cent ($ 67 billion) of Australia's total merchandise exports in 2002.[28] Australia signed free trade agreements with Singapore in July 2003 and Thailand in July 2004. The inaugural East Asia summit in the Malaysian capital Kuala Lumpur in December 2005 brought India and Australia together along with leaders from 14 other nations including China, South Korea and Japan together with 10 South East Asian countries, and New Zealand.[29] The summit ended with an agreement to hold annual talks on issues such as trade and security.

Australia-India Economic Relations

Along with other areas, Australia-India economic relations have grown steadily in the recent years. Two-way trade in goods totalled $8.2 billion in 2005, with India overtaking Indonesia to become Australia's 12th largest merchandise trading partner. As Australia's 6th largest merchandise export market in 2005, India overtook the UK and Taiwan and has grown faster than any of Australia's other top 30 markets over the past five years. [30]

Australia's investment in India is approximately A$ 2 billion and there are around 512 Australian joint ventures in India. Indian investment in Australia is around A$ 2 billion.[31] This investment covers manufacturing, telecommunications, hotels, minerals processing, food processing, oil and gas and the automotive sector. The construction of the world's largest ammonia plant, located on the Burrup Peninsula in Western Australia's Pilbara region has been completed. Built by the Indian company Burrup Fertilisers Pvt. Ltd. at a cost of A$ 700 million, this plant is expected to produce up to 760,000 tonnes of liquid ammonia per year. [32]

This comes in the wake of investment by Birla and Sterlite in copper resources in Queensland, Western Australia and Tasmania. The top Indian software firms—Tata Consultancy Services, Satyam, Infosys, Pentasoft and

HCL have operations in Australia. There have been many joint ventures between Australian and Indian companies. Sterlite Industries has acquired two copper mines in Tasmania and a copper/gold mine in Queensland. The Aditya Birla Group has acquired copper mines at Nifty (Western Australia) and Mt Gordon (Queensland). Asian Paints acquired Pacific Paints in the State of Queensland.

Areas of Divergences

Australia and India differed over the adoption of the Comprehensive Test Ban Treaty (CTBT) at the Conference on Disarmament in Geneva in August 1996. India was also piqued at Australia's lack of support for India's inclusion in the APEC (Asia Pacific Economic Cooperation). There were also differences between the two over the issue of broadening IOR-ARC's membership.[33] At the ARF meet in Manila in July 1998, Australia supported the US in getting the forum to condemn India. The ASEAN communiqué was subdued reflecting the view of countries like Malaysia, Indonesia and Vietnam who saw India as a bulwark against China.[34] India also felt that Australia did not do enough when Fiji's elected government was overthrown in 2000. Australian forces joined the "coalition of the willing" against Iraq in 2003.[35] India however, inspite of American requests refused to send its troops to Iraq, unless they were under UN supervision.

Improving Indo-US Ties

The development of closer ties between India and the United States has also facilitated the improved ties between India and Australia. During the Cold War, India and the United States had been kept apart by their narrow security interests. But, with the disintegration of the Soviet Union and emergence of the US as the sole superpower, successive Indian governments sought a rapprochement with the US.

The end of the Cold War and the collapse of the Soviet Union accompanied by India's economic reforms initiated a process of gradual shift in the way the two countries perceived each other.[36] During the Gulf War, the Indian Government granted refuelling rights to US military aircraft *en route* to the Middle East. However, India and the US continued to have differences on various issues including the extension of the Non-Proliferation Treaty (NPT) and the Comprehensive Test Ban Treaty (CTBT). India's refusal to sign the CTBT and the nuclear tests of 1998 strained the bilateral ties. However, the dialogue between Jaswant Singh and the US Deputy Secretary of State Strobe Talbott in the aftermath of India's nuclear tests helped to remove the misgivings. Less than two years after India's nuclear tests in May 1998, in March 2000 President Clinton visited India, the first visit by a US president in over 20 years. Since then, India-US relations have developed at an unprecedented pace, especially in the politico-military sphere. The terrorist attack on the Indian Parliament in December 2001 was further evidence that the two countries faced similar threats to their security.

In February 2002, General Richard B. Myers, Chairman of the US Joint Chiefs of Staff visited India as part of the ongoing process to enhance India-US military cooperation. This was the second visit by a Chairman of the Joint Chiefs of Staff within eight months. Paracommandos from the Indian Army and some 200 soldiers of the Special Forces Group and supporting units from the US Pacific Command held joint exercises in India in May 2002. Code-named 'Balance Iroquois' the exercise was backed by elements of the Indian and the US Air Forces.

Indian and American Special Forces paratroopers held joint exercises in Agra in 2002. On the Navy side, the Indian Navy ships Sharda and Sukanya relieved the USS Cowpens to escort ships in the Straits of Malacca and to protect them against terrorist attacks and pirates on the high seas during Operation Enduring Freedom in April 2002. This was followed by several joint search and rescue exercises as well as the *Malabar* exercises in the Arabian Sea, which involved ships and helicopters of both countries intercepting suspicious vessels and completing complicated flying operations. About 2,000 Indian and US Navy personnel took part in *Malabar* 04, a training exercise off the Goa coast of India in October 2004.

In February 2004 for the first time since 1963, eight F-15C aircraft from the 19th Fighter Squadron, Elmendorf Air Force Base, Alaska, set up camp at the Indian Air Force Station, Gwalior, to participate in a dissimilar air combat training (DACT) exercise. The Indian Air Force fielded Jaguars, MiG-21 Bison, Mirage 2000s and SU-30 K aircraft. In another first, India made the largest strategic deployment of its combat aircraft outside its territory when they participated in the multinational Cope Thunder 2004 exercise in Alaska.

The Next Steps in Strategic Partnership initiative, or NSSP—launched in January 2004[37] includes expanded engagement between India and the United States on nuclear regulatory and safety issues and missile defense, ways to enhance cooperation in peaceful uses of space technology, and steps to create the appropriate environment for successful high technology commerce.

Representatives of India and the United States initiated a landmark Open Skies air transport agreement on January 15, 2005. This agreement significantly modernises India-US aviation relations by allowing airlines to make commercial decisions with minimal government intervention. The highpoint of the improved relations between the United States and India came with the visit of the US President George Bush to India in March 2006. The successful Indo-United States agreement on civilian nuclear cooperation was undoubtedly the centrepiece of the visit of President George W. Bush in March 2006.[38] But several other important bilateral agreements and initiatives were also concluded. All these, including the nuclear agreement, essentially flowed from the Joint Statement of 18 July 2005, by President Bush and Prime Minister Manmohan Singh during the latter's visit to the US. Under the nuclear deal, India would separate its civilian and military nuclear facilities and allow the International Atomic Energy Agency (IAEA) to inspect only those facilities which New Delhi has designated to be civilian. Military sites will be off-limits. In exchange, Washington will, after congressional approval, grant India access to civilian nuclear technology and fuel.

Future Prospects

The Indo-Australian bilateral ties got a further boost with the visit of the Australian Prime Minister John Howard to India in March 2006. During the Australian PM's visit, a Trade and Economic Framework (TEF) between the two countries and Memoranda of Understanding (MoUs) on Defence Cooperation, Customs and Biotechnology, a bilateral Air Services Agreement, and Scientific Collaboration Fund were signed. The TEF (Trade and Economic Framework) aims to provide a framework to facilitate future economic development and increase cooperation in such areas as energy and mining, infrastructure development, information and communications technology, services, agriculture, inspection and quarantine and biotechnology. [39]

A central element of India's foreign affairs agenda is 'energy diplomacy', or the need to secure energy supplies to meet India's rapidly growing industrial and consumer demand. Australia is well placed to partner India in this regard, through exports of minerals and fuels and collaboration in areas of joint interest, such as new mining technologies. Australia has vast reserves of uranium, which India is in need of. Australia has agreements for the supply of LNG and uranium to China and similar agreements could also be worked out between India and Australia. During the Australian PM's visit to India, the Indian Prime Minister Manmohan Singh asked John Howard to consider supplying uranium to India. Howard agreed to consider the matter.

Australia has supported India's stand to become a permanent member of the UN Security Council. On its part, India has also begun to realise that it did not pay enough attention to Australia earlier. The increasing attention being paid to India in Australian foreign policy and vice-versa is reflected in the growing number of ministerial visits, bilateral agreements and cooperation in diverse fields. Both the countries have agreed to disagree on certain issues, but keep the momentum going in their bilateral ties. As they say "the journey of a thousand miles begins with a single step".

End Notes

1. Meg Gurry, India: Australia's Neglected Neighbour? in Sandy Gordon and Stephen Henningham (ed.), *India Looks East: An Emerging Power and its Asia-Pacific Neighbours* (Canberra: Australian National University, 1995), p. 245.
2. Department of Foreign Affairs and Trade, *India's Economy at the Midnight Hour: Australia's India Strategy* (Canberra: Australian Government Publishing Service, 1994), p. 4.
3. "History of the Australian Labor party", http://www.alp.org.au/about/history.php
4. Kenneth McPherson, Indian Ocean Regional Dialogues: An Australian Perspective in *India-Australia Public Policy Conference, 1996,* (Perth and New Delhi: Indian Ocean Centre and Centre for Policy Research, 1996), p. 25.
5. Far East and Australasia 2004 (London: Europa Publications, 2003), p. 106.
6. Department of Foreign Affairs and Trade, *In the National Interest, Australia's Foreign and Trade Policy White Paper* (Canberra: Department of Foreign Affairs and Trade, 1997), p. 1.
7. *Ibid*., p. 3.
8. *Ibid*., p. 24.
9. Richard Broinowski, India, China and Australia: The Fractured Triangle, *in South Asia*, Vol. XXIII, Special Issue (2000), p. 145.
10. Jenelle Bonnor, *Australia-India Security Relations: Common Interests or Common Disinterest* (Australian Defence Studies Centre, University of New South Wales, 2001), p. 5.
11. Mohan Malik, Nuclear Proliferation in Asia: The China Factor, in *Australian Journal of International Affairs*, Vol. 53, No. 1, (1999), p. 31.
12. Letter dated 14th May from the Permanent Representative of the United States of America to the Conference on Disarmament transmitting remarks by President Clinton at a Press Conference on 12 May concerning Indian nuclear testing, CD/1505, 14 May, 1998.
13. Chintamani Mahapatra, *Indo-US Relations into the 21st Century* (New Delhi: Knowledge World and IDSA, 1998), pp. 165-66.
14. Senate Foreign Affairs, Defence and Trade References Committee, *The 1998 Indian and Pakistani Nuclear Tests* (Canberra: Parliament of the Commonwealth of Australia, 1999), p. xv.
15. S. Utham Kumar Jamadhagni and C.S. Anuradha, Indo-Australian Strategic Framework: Possibilities for the New Millennium, in *Journal of Indian Ocean Studies*, Vol. 11. No. 1, (April 2003), pp. 29-30.
16. Henry S. Albinski, "Issues in Australian Foreign Policy: January to June 2000", *Australian Journal of Politics and History*, Vol. 46, No. 4, (2000), pp. 554-5.
17. India-Australia Strategic Dialogue, News Release, Australian High Commission, New Delhi, released jointly with the Indian Ministry of External Affairs, 30 August, 2001.
18. Bruce R. Vaughn, Australia's Strategic Identity Post September 11 in Context: Implications for the War Against Terror in Southeast Asia, in *Contemporary Southeast Asia,* Vol. 26, No. 1, (2004) p. 103.
19. Daniel Flitton, Perspectives on Australian Foreign Policy, 2002, in *Australian Journal of International Affairs,* Vol. 57, No. 1, (2003) p. 48.

20. Brendon O'Connor, "Perspectives on Australian Foreign Policy", in *Australian Journal of International Affairs,* Vol. 58, No. 2, (June 2004), p. 212.
21. See "Bollywood in Australia", http://www.idp.com/excellenceaustralia/filmandtv/multicultural/default.asp
22. Arjun Appadurai and Carol A. Breckenridge, "Public Modernity in India'" in C.A. Breckenridge (ed.), *Consuming Modernity. Public Culture in a South Asian World* (Minneapolis: University of Minnesota Press, 1995), p. 8.
23. "Visitor Arrivals Data", Tourism Australia http://www.tourism.australia.com/Research.asp?sub=0318&al=2252
24. "Australia-India sports forum introduced in lead up to Commonwealth Games," Australian High Commission, India, 21 November, 2005, www.ausgovindia.com/ndli/PA_27_2005.html
25. "Has he got the ticker, A Survey of Australia," The *Economist*, May 7, 2005, p. 9.
26. See "India and ASEAN", *The Hindu*, (New Delhi), October 9, 2003.
27. Department of Foreign Affairs and Trade, *Advancing the National Interest* (Canberra: Department of Foreign Affairs and Trade, 2003), pp. 83-4.
28. Department of Foreign Affairs and Trade, *Advancing the National Interest* (Canberra: Department of Foreign Affairs and Trade, 2003), p. 72.
29. Mohan Malik, *"East Asia Summit: More discord than accord"*, http://yaleglobal.yale.edu/display.article?id=6645
30. "Bilateral Economic and Trade Relationship, India Country Brief June 2006," Department of Foreign Affairs and Trade, http://www.dfat.gov.au/geo/india/india-brief.html
31. "India-Australia relations, High Commission of India in Australia," http://www.hcindia-au.org/inausrel.html
32. "World's Biggest Ammonia Plant Opens In Australia's Northwest", http://www.investaustralia.gov.au/index.cfm?id
33. Man Mohini Kaul, Australia-India Relations: Post Pokhran II Phase, *International Studies*, Vol. 37, No. 4 (2000), p. 371.
34. *Times of India* (New Delhi), 28 July, 1998, p. 10.
35. Robert Ayson, A Shift in Focus? Australia and stability in East Asia (Canberra: Australian Strategic Policy Institute, 2005), p. 4.
36. Chintamani Mahapatra, Indo-US relations, in Dipankar Bannerjee (ed.), *Towards an Era of Cooperation, An Indo-Australian dialogue* (New Delhi: IDSA, 1995), p. 209.
37. R. Ramachandran, Changing Equations, *Frontline* (Internet Edition), Vol. 22, Issue 08, April 9-22, 2005 http://www.flonnet.com/fl2208/stories/20050422002601300.htm
38. Amit Baruah, India, U.S. Clinch Deal on Nuclear Deparation, *The Hindu* (New Delhi) March 3, 2006, p. 1.
39. "India Country Brief June 2006," Department of Foreign Affairs and Trade http://www.dfat.gov.au/geo/india/india_brief.html

16

Economic Reforms in India and Australia: Challenges Ahead

JASBIR SINGH

India and Australia have very old relations in respect of trade and economic cooperation. The India-Australia trade goes back to 1791 when a shipment of food supply was sent to Calcutta in British India.[1] This shipment was to provide additional food supply to India. On its return the same ship took textiles, leather wears, tobacco, sugar, rice, candles and soap, etc. After this sail it took about less than 200 years to re-establish the trade links between the two countries in 1990. Some of the commodity exchanges are the same as those that had been traded across the Indian Ocean for centuries. Gold is Australia's largest single export commodity to India, while pearls and gems, jewellery and textiles are amongst India's largest exports to Australia.[2]

Indo-Australian Trade and Economic Relations

Australia's economic reform process pre-dates India's by less than a decade. India, historically protectionist and centrally planned, took up the challenge of economic reform in the early 1990s. The results have been remarkable. Trade between the two countries is flourishing day by day. Export promotion, economic liberalisation and the gradual opening of trade to Australia after 1991 have boosted growth in many sectors. At a time when India began the process of opening of the economy by introducing the trade liberalisation reforms in early 1990s, Australia also established the Australia-India Council (AIC) in an effort to bring the economies and the people of these two countries closer in terms of knowledge, technology and development processes.[3]

When India started its economic reforms, it was Australia's 24th largest trading partner. In 2003, India moved to 15th position and entered Australian top-ten export markets at 9th place. In fact, Australian merchandise exports to India have increased over 400 per cent in the past decade. During the last decade the trade between two countries has increased to 42 per cent between 1998-99 and 2002-03, i.e., from A$ 2.5 billion (1998-99) to A$ 3.55 billion

(2002-03). Bilateral trade has nearly doubled in the past few years.[4] Investment has also accelerated, and Australia is now one of India's top ten investors. India is in the process of becoming one of Australia's most important regional and bilateral partners.[5]

Past Record of Bilateral Relations

Since 1950 efforts have been made to boost Australia's relations with Asia. In January 1950 Colombo Plan was introduced which occupies a prominent place in the history of Australia's relations with Asia.[6] Some 40,000 people from Asia went to study in Australian institutions under the Colombo Plan till 1985. The Colombo Plan provided an important vehicle for Australia to engage with all the countries of South and South-East Asia whether or not they were fellow members of the British Commonwealth.[7] To encourage Australian business to make the most of opportunities arising from the opening up of the Indian economy, the Department of Foreign Affairs in Australia in April-1993 (DFAT, April 1993) released a comprehensive study, *India's Economy at the Midnight Hour: Australia's India Strategy*.[8] The study was optimistic about India's short-to-medium term economic outlook and assessed the Indian market as providing enormous·potential for Australian companies.[9] The release of the Department's India study followed a successful third meeting of the Australia-India Joint Ministerial Commission in Sydney in February 1994.[10] The Department used the joint ministerial commission meeting, which was well attended by Australian private sector representatives, to lobby the Indian Government on key market access and tariff issues, particularly on wool and coal, and to support specific Australian project bids. The meeting was followed by Indian legislative action addressing a number of those issues.[11] Based on an extensive series of interviews, a study *Australia through the Eyes of India* was released by Alexander Downer, MP, Minister for Foreign Affairs on 28 June 1996.[12]

The principal findings of the research are: Australia, for the most part, is perceived to be remote, with a small politically stable population, rich in natural resources, wealthy and economically developed. Australia's focus on Asia is viewed positively, but with disappointment that India has been left out compared with decision makers in East Asia there are relatively fewer Indian decision makers with a comprehensive or even limited knowledge of Australia. In comparison with their counterparts in East Asia, far fewer Indians have studied in Australia or visited for business or tourism. The majority of Indians are unaware of Australia's capacities as a supplier of sophisticated goods and services. It is assumed that Australia has no locally based research and development. Australia ranks well behind several other countries as a potential source of sophisticated goods and services. Laurie Smith and. Priya Ahuja (1996) examined that Australian food exporters are facing many challenges because of turbulence in major regional markets.[13] The study underlines the need for cool-headed assessments of trade opportunities in growing markets such as India. Such an assessment, as set out in it, shows that during the 1990s there has been a broad opening of the Indian economy to foreign investment and significant unilateral tariff reductions. But the agricultural sector has been sheltered from most of the reforms as, to a lesser extent, have some parts of the food-processing sector.

In order to demonstrate Australian Government's serious intention to strengthen her relationship with India, the Australian government, in November 1996, undertook a major promotional campaign called Australia-India *New Horizons*.[14] This campaign was directed squarely at India's decision makers and it features a range of business, science, technology, education, cultural and sporting events in six major Indian cities—New Delhi, Bombay, Calcutta, Bangalore, Madras and Chandigarh. The Government extended core funding of three million dollars to launch the *New Horizons* promotion.[15]

Alexander Downer (2001)[16] highlights how, after a decade of reforms, India's large and diverse economy has become one of the fastest growing emerging market in the world. India is now Australia's twelfth largest export market, up from between twentieth and twenty-fifth a decade ago and Australia's foreign direct investment in India has also increased significantly. While India's medium to long-term growth depends largely on the speed and extent of ongoing reforms, its current growth outlook overshadows that of most other Asian markets, which face slow growth or contraction in the next year or so. Further, developments in several fast growing sectors and states, which provide increasing opportunities for Australian traders and investors, has also been highlighted. In particular, several 'new economy' service sectors like information & technology, telecommunications and finance are growing rapidly, though opportunities also are emerging in 'old economy' sectors like mining and advanced technology manufacturing. Also, a group of four more outward oriented states in the south and west of the country, Gujarat, Karnataka, Maharashtra and Tamil Nadu, where new service industries are concentrated, are performing more strongly than the rest of India and attracting the bulk of new investment.

In 2003, Australian Trade Minister Mark Vaile remarked, "India's ongoing reform process provides opportunities for Australian companies in sectors such as oil, gas & energy development, education, specialist health care services and agriculture." He raised a number of specific issues of concern to Australian exporters. These include lowering India's tariffs on health & medical equipment, coal, wool, wine and other agricultural products. The positive outcome of this interaction was that Nordiko has signed an MoU on environmentally-friendly pest control—the CSIRO strengthened its alliances with India's mining authorities, Victorian Chemicals was able to lobby for a reduction in chemical tariffs, and Clough Offshore has been able to develop some new linkages with the Indian oil & gas market.[16]

In order to establish the institutional linkages, a Memorandum of Understanding (MoU) was signed between Australia and India's two peak biotechnology industry bodies—AusBiotech and the Association of Biotechnology Led Enterprises (ABLE) on 12 October 2004. This has opened up biotechnology partnering and collaborative opportunities between India and Australia.[17] In June 2005, Australian Foreign Minister Alexander Downer visited India with a special focus on the enormous potential of the relationship, which is set to become increasingly important for economic, strategic and people-to-people links for both countries. Both sides expressed satisfaction at the rapid growth in bilateral trade and economic relations in recent years and reiterated their desire to enhance cooperation in this area. Both sides expressed satisfaction at the decision taken during the Joint Ministerial Commission meeting in Australia to commence discussions on the proposed Trade and Economic Frame Agreement (TEF) between India and Australia that have to set up a consultative framework to encourage the growth of trade and economic relations between the two countries. The two sides also agreed to increase interaction in other dimensions of the bilateral relationship, including the areas of energy, science and technology, biotechnology, IT, tourism, education, culture and people-to-people contacts. The contributions of the 200,000 strong Indian communities in Australia and the presence of 21,000 Indian students pursuing higher studies in Australia were acknowledged by both sides as positive factors that were promoting closer bilateral ties.[18] Australian development assistance is playing its part alongside a booming commercially-based education services sector which involves many Australian education institutions—many providing education services in Australia and some setting up off-shore campuses to help service sector in the region.

In order to generate several initiatives designed to deepen the bilateral energy and resources relationship the central element of India's foreign affairs agenda is 'energy diplomacy', or the need to secure energy supplies to meet rapidly growing industrial and consumer demand. Australia is well positioned to partner India in this regard, through exports of minerals and fuels, energy investment opportunities in Australia and collaboration on areas of joint interest, such as new mining technologies. Keeping this in mind, a Joint Working Group (JWG) on Energy and Minerals was established in 1999 and this group last met in Delhi in June 2005. Gary Draffin, CEO, Invest Australia (November 2005), said that it is positive for Australia that major Indian software companies are already well established and expanding their operations here. Also, Australia's position as the most multilingual workforce in the Asia-Pacific region acts as a lure for international companies. In recent years, India has begun to engage in the Asia Pacific region in which Australia has a cultural and geographical affinity. Moreover, Australians share a common language as well as Commonwealth bonds with India.

According to Austrade Research, (October 2004) there are only 1,506 Australian companies exporting to India, which is half of China on 3,101. But the tremendous growth of trade in India means that India will soon join China in increasing market share of world output and in turn, Australian exports. China is Australia's no. 3 trading partner, no. 2 export market and no. 3 source of imports. India is 6th largest merchandise export market and 13th largest trading partner of Australia. The two-way trade in goods in the financial year ending in 2004 between Australia and China was more than four times that between Australia and India. That's not to say Australian trade with India is not increasing dramatically. In the same financial year, Australia's total trade with India grew more than 62 per cent. During the same year India overtook the United Kingdom to become Australia's sixth biggest export market. India may not exceed the growth rates recorded by China in recent years but India is likely to experience higher growth in the next 20 years while China will struggle to maintain its high growth rates.[19]

Benefits to India

Australia is committed to realising the full potential of the Australia-India relationship. To sustain its rapid economic development, India requires world class technologies in areas like telecommunications, electric power generation, infrastructure and resource development, and environmental management. India will also need to strengthen its capacities in services like insurance, banking, education and the full range of professional services. Australia is a leading edge competitor in all of these areas. Already, Australia supplies much of India's cooking coal needs for its steel industry. Australian wool is found in Indian textiles. Australian engineers are helping in highway and port developments. Australian universities and colleges are helping to educate and train Indians. Australian mining skills and technology are being demonstrated at the *Pipawar* coal-mining project. Australia has large foreign banking presence in India; its environmental, telecommunications and medical technology is now widely used in India. Both of these countries are finding markets in each country. India is pressing her case for market access for agro products in Australia while Australia demands further reduction in tariffs on wheat, coal, wool, apples, macadamia nuts, wine and some specialised oils.[20]

The Indian Government has identified Australia as its eighth-largest foreign investor. The investment is now more than A$1 billion, much of it in fast-growing service sectors including ICT, education, health, tourism and leisure, media and finance, as well as mining and in manufacturing. For India, investment in Australia may be quite small but it is growing, with much of it in IT and the energy and minerals sector (including copper mines and an ammonia plant). The two countries share strengths in many fields of research associated with ICT and biotechnology, so it is natural they work together to achieve greater outcome in these areas. India has done an excellent job of fostering ICT companies and has developed a global reputation for excellence, particularly in software engineering. Major investments have been made by a pioneering group of Indian ICT companies in Australia, establishing Global Development Centers, opening the window for other Indian-based companies that recognise Australia's value as a springboard into the Asia Pacific region.[21]

Almost all areas of the Indian economy have been gradually opened to both domestic and foreign private investment: import licensing restrictions on intermediates and capital goods have been virtually eliminated; tariffs have been significantly reduced; full convertibility of foreign-exchange earnings has been established for current account transactions; financial markets have been liberalised to a greater extent; and international standards of regulation have also been introduced in the financial sector. The Indian Government allows 100 per cent foreign investment in many infrastructure sectors, but private ports and aid funding road projects are the most prospective infrastructure sectors for investors and goods and service exporters.[22]

Since the reforms started, four southern and western states, viz., Gujarat, Karnataka, Maharashtra and Tamil Nadu, have achieved significantly stronger real GDP and per capita income growth than other major Indian states. These four high performing states excel because India's economic reforms most benefit industry and services in which they specialise. These states also are more export oriented and in most cases have better infrastructure than other states. Australian companies are becoming increasingly interested in South India, with its high rate of growth and as a large and growing consumer market with high disposable incomes. The Australian Government's export promotion and marketing arm, Austrade, has had an office in Chennai since 1996. This is currently expanding and will include a sharing arrangement with the state of South Australia. Queensland has opened an office in Bangalore and the state of Victoria also plans to do so. Tuticorin and Chennai in South India are the closest Indian ports to Australia and handle most of Australia's exports of pulses, coal and fresh produce. The South has relatively better infrastructure that can assist Australian perishable goods/commodities to penetrate into interior markets. Due to a relatively higher level of industrialisation in the South, there is a growing demand for energy that has been met mainly by coal some of which is imported from Australia. LNG terminals (Liquefied Natural Gas Terminals) are being planned near Chennai and Cochin. General Motors in India is sourcing engines from General Motors Holden in Adelaide. There are more opportunities for Australian auto companies in India than ever in components, technology, tooling and other after-market products. The South India is also headquarters to India's largest retail chains such as Metro Cash and Carry, Dairy Farm International, Food World, Nilgiris, and so on. South India is rightly famous for its software and IT industry. With nearly 25 Indian IT companies in Australia, including, for example, Infosys from Bangalore, Satyam from Hyderabad and Polaris from Chennai, there are opportunities to take up joint development work and for Indian companies to market Australian ICT products in India and third country markets. South India accounted for over a third of the 21000 Indian students who studied in Australia in 2004. In addition there are a number of Australian Universities which are exploring twinning opportunities with Indian Universities as well as establishing a direct marketing presence.[23]

Australia also provides technical assistance to help the Governments of Meghalaya and Sikkim to plan for and deliver improved water and sanitation services, particularly to the poor communities under an agreement signed on 30 October 2003. By improving basic services like water and sanitation, Australia is helping to lay the groundwork for ensuring how the poor can improve their economic prospects and participate more fully in society.

Why Australia be a Partner to India

The visit of Mr. John Howard, in July 2000 heralded a new phase of Australia-India co-operation. This cooperation spans a range of areas. Strategic cooperation was enhanced by the Memorandum of Understanding (MoU) on Cooperation in Combating International Terrorism[24] This MoU was designed to forge closer cooperation between security, intelligence and law enforcement agencies. Australia and India are also currently considering MoUs to facilitate cooperation in other key areas such as defence, immigration, customs and animal quarantine. Efforts to promote bilateral trade have been institutionalised through the establishment of the Joint Ministerial Commission (JMC) and the Joint Business Council (JBC).[25]

With the liberalisation of the Indian economy, there is a growing awareness of imported food products. Many of these products are already being imported from Australia, as it is perceived as a supplier of quality products. Some of the major products/services that have potential demand in India are: Dairy (butter oil, skimmed milk powder and specialty cheese), pulses (mung beans, chickpeas, lentils and field peas), fresh fruits (mainly apples followed by pears, grapes, citrus), raw cotton, abattoir equipment, bulk grain handling and storage services/expertise, processed foods (juices, bakery products, confectionary and cereal snacks), textile materials, textile yarn, pearls, precious and semi-precious stones and jewellery, marine products, floor coverings, footwear, travel goods and handbags, manufactures of base metal, engineering goods/ manufactures, chemicals and related products, and plantation and agricultural products. Also, India's main exports to Australian markets are: pearls—precious and semi-precious stones and gems and jewellery, textiles, marine products, floor coverings, textile yarn, engineering goods and manufactures, chemicals and related products, construction materials, plantation and agricultural products, travel goods and leather and leather manufactures including footwear.[26]

The increasing focus on commerce in Australia's relations with India was reflected in the 1993-94 trade figures. The two-way trade, which stood at less than $100 million in 1982, increased by 3 per cent during 1993-94 to $1.3 billion. Exports decreased by almost 3 per cent to $862 million, reflecting an overall contraction in Indian imports worldwide. Imports increased by 18 per cent to $427 million and in 2004-05 they totalled up to $7.3 billion with India overtaking Indonesia to become Australia's 12th largest merchandise trading partner. Australian merchandise exports to India reached $6 billion in 2004-05, 4.8 per cent of total merchandise exports, the 6th largest merchandise export market in 2004-05, India has overtaken the UK and Taiwan and has grown faster than any of the other top 30 markets over the past five years. Major Australian exports to India (2004) were: non-monetary gold—A$2870 million, coal—A$1190 million, copper ores—A$409 million, wool—A$155 million, other ores—A$46 million. Major Australian imports from India (2004) were: pearls and gems—A$83 million, other textile manufactures—A$54 million, floor coverings—A$40 million, jewellery—A$34 million, crustaceans— A$33 million.[27]

India's bilateral trade with Australia during the past few years is explained as under: Exports during 2000-01 were US$ 405.87 million with a growth of 0.64 per cent; they rose to US$ 584.30 million with a growth of 15.89 per cent in 2003-2004. Imports during 2000-01 were US$ 1062.76 million with a decline of 1.76 per cent they rose to US$ 2649.24 million with a growth of 98.18 per cent in 2003-04. Total trade between both the countries during 2000-01 was US$ 1468.63 million with a decline of 1.11 per cent it rose to US$ 3233.53 million with a growth of 75.64 per cent in 2003-04.[28]

The total value of Australian investments in India during the period between August 1991 and December 2004 was US$146.48 million. The number of Australian joint ventures in India that were approved during the period August 1991 to December 2003 was 491. Of these 312 collaborations were financial and 177 technical. [29]

Australia's trade with India is focused on areas, which have either a traditional or a growing comparative advantage. The trade in cooking coal is a great success. India is Australia's third largest market for this product. The market in thermal coal also offers significant potential, as does the market for LNG exports. The trade relationship is dominated by merchandise trade, although the role of services is growing. Australia exported $852 million worth of services to India in 2004-05, an increase of new prospects continue to emerge in sectors such as ICT, biotechnology, education, tourism, health, film and insurance. Imports of Indian services totalled up $276 million in 2004-05, 20th in the list of service import sources. Australia is India's 8th largest overseas investor, with over $1 billion approved for around 140 joint ventures This investment covers manufacturing, telecommunications, hotels, minerals processing, food processing, oil and gas and the automotive sector. An example is the joint venture announced between Blue Scope Steel and Tata Steel which will take ownership of roll forming and pre-engineered building manufacturing facilities at a cost of A$100 million.[30]

The manufacturing, mining, infrastructure, agriculture, mining and advanced technology are the most prospective areas of common interest of both countries. Key sectors of manufacturing, mining, infrastructure and software now permit 100 per cent FDI, though many sectors still impose foreign ownership limits below 100 per cent. However, with FDI under US$2.5 billion in 2000, India received low per capita FDI inflows by emerging economy standards. Mining reforms were encouraging. India's fiscal regime for mining approached international competitiveness, while oil and gas offered medium term potential. Several progressive states issued more mineral prospecting leases, significantly increasing Australian miners' interest in India. Australian miners investing in India include BHP Billiton and mining juniors Grenfell Resources (base metals) and Mineral Deposits Ltd. (mineral sand mining). While manufacturing sectors are increasingly opening to foreign direct investment; some remaining ownership caps, infrastructure shortages and government regulation have kept foreign investment to modest levels. Nevertheless, several Australian firms have succeeded in the manufacturing sector, usually by bringing high technology processes, skills and products to India. Australian manufactures operating successfully in India include Fosters Group (brewing), Ulco Medical (medical equipment), Clipsal (switches) and Cactus Imaging (high tech billboards).

In recent years, Australia has emerged as a major destination for Indian students studying abroad, who recognise the high quality and cost competitiveness of Australian education services. In 2004, India was the fourth highest source of international students in Australia, with around 21,000 students (a growth of 45 per cent from 2003). Australia is also committed to strengthening links between Australian and Indian educational institutions. This was underlined with the establishment of an education exchange programme and the renewal of a MoU with India on cooperation in science and technology.[31] The science and technology collaboration was consolidated in October 2004 when Australia and India's two peak biotechnology industry bodies—AusBiotech and the Association of Biotechnology Led Enterprises (ABLE) respectively formalised institutional linkages through the signing of a MoU. The progress made through the MoU was reinforced at the AusBiotech National Conference-2004, with the attendance of a significant business delegation from India. Several Australian educational institutions and other companies already involved in these sectors are: Baltec Systems, which has established an Indian office to provide environmental technologies to Indian firms; and the joint venture between Deakin University and the Association of Professional Engineers, Scientists and Managers Australia, to offer advanced degrees in IT in India.

Indian Investment in Australia

Indian investment in Australia is also worth around $1 billion, making Australia the ninth most important destination for Indian foreign direct investment. An example of this investment is the agreement reached between the Western Australian Government and the Oswal group to build the world's largest ammonia plant (valued at $630 million). The key Indian investments in Australia include The Oswal Group and The Aditya Birla Group in the resources sector and Tata Consultancy Services, Birlasoft Australia, Infosys Technologies and Mahindra-British Telecom in the ICT sector.

- The New Delhi-based Oswal Group, one of India's largest companies, is building the world's biggest ammonia plant on the Burrup Peninsula in northern Western Australia. The A$630 million plant is expected to be completed in 2005 and when operational, will produce up to 2200 tonnes of liquid ammonia from natural gas each day over a minimum 25 year period.
- In January 2003, Birla Copper, a unit of the Aditya Birla Group, purchased the Nifty Copper Mine in Western Australia for A$158.8 million—the second largest foreign acquisition by an Indian company. The mine is the third-largest copper resource in Australia and one of the world's top 25 copper deposits. In September 2003, the Aditya Birla Group acquired a second copper mine in Australia — the Mount Gordon Copper Mine in north-west Queensland. These two mines together will cater for more than one third of Birla's copper concentrate requirement for its Dahej smelter in India.
- In the ICT sector, Tata Consultancy Services—India's largest software and Services Company—has developed a new Global Development Centre in Melbourne. The centre currently employs 180 people developing software solutions for some of Australia and New Zealand's largest companies, including NAB, Westpac, ANZ, Fonterra NZ, Hutchison Telecommunications and IBM Australia.
- Birlasoft Australia set up its Australian operations in 2002 and services some of Australia's largest companies such as Coles Myer. It currently employs 190 people in its Melbourne Development Centre, which is more than 12 per cent of its global workforce.
- Infosys Technologies also has a global development centre in Melbourne which employs 550 people. It was one of the first such

centres in the region and is integrated with other Infosys Development Centres located in the US, Europe and India. Australian clients include Suncorp Metway, Vodafone and Telstra.

- Mahindra-British Telecom, an Indian-based telecommunications software and solutions provider, began operations in Australia last year. With 4000 staff, annual global sales of over A$170 million, and customers including AT&T, British Telecom and Ericsson,
- MBT is one of the world's largest providers of technology expertise to the telecommunications industry. MBT's long term strategy is to expand further in Australia as well as the Asia-Pacific region. [32]

Australian Exports to India

Since the early 1990s, Australian exports to India have grown 50 per cent more rapidly than its total exports. Bulk resource and agricultural commodities dominate Australia's exports to India. Successful commodity exporters include BHP Billiton, MIM, AWB Limited (formerly the Australian Wheat Board), Colly Cotton and Scanlan Wools. Service exports like education and tourism also are growing strongly, while IT, environmental, health and media services show promise. Competitively priced higher technology manufactures also are finding markets such as Monash University, RMIT University, Central College (which all enroll large numbers of Indian students), Australian Tourist Commission, Runge Mining (mining software) Australian Hospital Design Group (hospital design, planning and training), Cutting Edge Post (film editing services), Greenspan Technology (environmental instruments) and the International Centre for Application of Solar Energy (alternative energy technologies) and many more.[33]

Wool is Australia's largest agricultural export to India, and the demand for Australian wool has been steadily growing in the Indian market, where wool imports have seen very large growth over the past ten years. India is consistently among the top five markets in the world for Australian wool, with Australian merino wool a key input for India's woollen textiles and garment production. The fact which has been duly recognised by the then Australian High Commissioner to India, Ms Penny Wensley AO, "Australia provides India with approximately 60 per cent of its imported wool and almost all of this wool is used for the manufacture of quality clothing." The India-Australia wool partnership is in the process of creating a valuable 'wool route' enabling both countries to reach third-country markets.[34]

Australian exporters are finding new opportunities as import barriers fall in previously protected markets. Australian firms, which have recently penetrated new Indian markets, include:

- In September 2005, Australian information security specialist company CQR Consulting won a tender for a consulting contract with the Indian branch of a multi-national bank, beating competition from local IT service providers. CQR Consulting will analyse the vulnerability of the bank's online operations.

- In December 2004, Australian engineering company Clough secured a US$215 million contract with India's Oil and Natural Gas to develop a gas field off India's east coast.
- Ausmelt, a designer and supplier of smelting technology, has provided its technology to India's largest copper producer, Birla Copper, as part of the Dahej II expansion project in Gujarat, India. Ausmelt has also been commissioned by Hindustan Zinc Ltd, India's largest producer of lead and zinc, to provide its technology for a new lead smelter as part of the expansion of their facility in Chanderiya, India. The plant is expected to be operational by the end of 2005.
- Berri Ltd, Australia's largest producer of fruit juices, has been exporting packaged juices to India since the late 1990s. Berri now holds a five percent share of the Indian packaged juice market, experiencing a growth of around 30 percent per annum.
- Aushealth, with assistance from Austrade, has been awarded a contract to provide nurse training & other consultancy services to a new hospital being opened in Mumbai.
- Quantum Filtration Medium is a young WA-based company specialising in water treatment. With assistance from Austrade, they have identified direct customers and distributors of water treatment chemicals and secured two trial orders.
- Another infrastructure fund and insurance company AMP's is India's new insurance venture partner.[35]

Conclusion

India's reforms are creating interesting trade and investment opportunities for Australian firms in a range of fast growing 'new economy' sectors and high performing states. Moreover, higher incomes and trade liberalisation are boosting Australian commodity, niche manufactures and services exports to India. Further comprehensive reforms would consolidate growth and expand these opportunities. In the short term, Australian businesses operating in India can expect incremental reforms to continue. As India's reforms deepen, its growth potential is huge. Already Australian businesses are accessing promising trade and investment opportunities and prospects for expanding commercial relations are strong. Both of these countries have to work jointly for the better positioning in the changing economic structure of the region. No doubt, India needs world-class technologies in the field of telecommunications, infrastructural development, power-generation and even in environmental management. In the changing world India also needs to improve her capacity in service sector, viz., banking and insurance, education and other professional services. Australia can, to a great extent, help India in her endeavours in this regard. Australia is supplying cooking coal needs for its steel industry, wool for textile, providing mining skills, engineers working in highway and port development. Australia is also helping India in developing her banking, computers and telecommunication and medical technology. In education sector Australia has also made definite contributions. Not only from Australian but Indian point of view it has been observed that India has also made inroads into the Australian economy by way of trade and investments. The exports in sophisticated products and services, motor vehicles like the Suzuki-Alto and the Maruti Jeep are popular in Australian markets. The other areas of mutual interest are science and technology agreements in waste management, crop viruses and testing pesticide residues in food. Efforts are to be made to change the perceptions of both of these countries regarding their respective economic status and capabilities. Like India, Australia is also a multicultural economy and it is very important that both of these countries should demonstrate the strengths of their economies for mutual benefits.

End Notes

1. In 1791 a British store ship 'Sydney Cove' was sent to Calcutta for food supplies during the famine in Australia.
2. Alexander Downer, Australia can partner India's growth, an interview by Australian Foreign Minister Alexander Downer with *The Hindu* (New Delhi) 6 to 9 June, 2005.
3. Even in the past Australia's contribution to India's economic growth is recognised with the contribution of Late Sir John Crawford in helping India in its Green Revolution.
4. Nick Horden, Australia's India trade set to double, *The Australian Financial Review*, 22 April, 1998.
5. India and Australia have shared a common history, language, common democratic traditions, government structures and common interest in the Indian Ocean. India and Australia are members of commonwealth, founding members of the United Nations and members of Indian Ocean Rim—Association for Regional Cooperation (IOR-ARC), ASEAN Regional Forum (ARF) and also dialogue partners with ASEAN. Further, Indo-Australian relations assume more significance in case of increasing prominence of the Asian-Pacific economic and geo-political relations.
6. In January 1950, an Australian delegation, led by then Minister for External Affairs, Percy Spender took the Australian plans for overseas aid forward to the British Commonwealth Foreign Ministers Meeting in Colombo. The Plan, although then sometimes referred to as the Spender Plan, came to be called the

Colombo Plan. The Colombo Plan began with seven members of the British Commonwealth as members, viz., Australia, Canada, India, New Zealand, Pakistan, Sri Lanka and the United Kingdom.

7. "Australia and the Colombo Plan 1949-1957," Part of the *Documents on Australian Foreign Policy* series published by the Department of Foreign Affairs and Trade, May 2005.
8. *India's Economy at the Midnight Hour: Australia's India Strategy*, Australian DFAT Annual report issued in 1993-94.
9. Working closely with its regional offices and the Australian High Commission in New Delhi, the Department publicised the study widely through a series of seminars conducted in State capitals in Australia and India. Feedback from the Australian private sector and India has been strongly positive.
10. This meeting was organised by DFAT and chaired by the Minister for Trade, Senator McMullan, and the Indian Minister of State for Commerce, Mr. Kamaluddin Ahmed.
11. In accordance with an agreement achieved at the meeting, the Department was to negotiate a bilateral investment promotion and protection agreement. The meeting also agreed to synchronise the next Joint Ministerial Commission (JMC) meeting with the annual meeting of the Australia-India Business Council, and to conduct an intersessional review of the commercial partnership before the next full meeting of the JMC.
12. At the Opening of Indian Textiles Exhibition, Art Gallery of South Australia on 28 June, 1996, Alexander Downer, MP, Minister for Foreign Affairs released the findings of Market Australia's India study: *Australia through the Eyes of India*. This study reveals that while influential Indians see Australia in positive terms as a tolerant multicultural society, for the most part they know very little about contemporary Australia.
13. This study was conducted by Mr. Laurie Smith and Ms. Priya Ahuja (1996) of the Sydney firm, INSTATE Pvt. Ltd. It was co-funded by the Rural Industries Research and Development Corporation's Global Competitiveness Programme. The study examined a range of factors driving change in the processed food market in India and was based on an extensive review of literature and databases in Australia, India and other countries. Fieldwork was conducted in India in January/February 1997. This included data collection, interviews with national and state government agency officials, multinational and domestic companies and peak industry organizations, and visits to a range of retail outlets and distribution/wholesale operations. (e g, machinery, packaging industries). As well, there were interviews with representatives in the food processing sector that had production, financial and/or sales responsibilities; and from the food service sector including the service, distribution and retailing areas.
14. *Australia and India: New Horizons in Our Relations*, by the Hon Alexander Downer, MP, Minister For Foreign Affairs, at the Opening Of Indian Textiles Exhibition, Art Gallery of South Australia, Friday 28 June, 1996.
15. Business forums in New Delhi and Bombay bring together the chief executives of hundreds of leading Australian and Indian businesses, including the ANZ Bank, CRA, Qantas and National Mutual. The forums explore opportunities for collaboration in fields as diverse as mining, information technology,

environmental management and financial services. These will be complemented by a series of business missions drawn from the agribusinesses, mining and tourism industries. An education conference was held in New Delhi to build long-term linkages between two countries in the growing education and training services sector. A coordinated media programme was also held to promote the *New Horizons* message throughout India.

16. Alexander Downer made a major policy statement on Australia's relations with India when he launched a report by the Economic Analytical Unit, Department of Foreign Affairs and Trade, *India: New Economy Old Economy,* in Melbourne on 3 December 2001. The report details case studies of over 30 companies from around Australia, which are trading and investing successfully in many Indian sectors and states. The Australia-India *New Horizons* promotion underlined the importance the Australian Government attaches to the relationship with India, which we will be upgrading across the board. And we will work with India to encourage economic cooperation in the Indian Ocean region.
17. Australian Trade Minister Mark Vaile along with Indian counterpart, Arun Jaitley participated in a two-day Joint Ministerial Commission (JMC) meeting in New Delhi on 20 February 2003. This meeting was also attended by a business delegation comprising representatives from more than 35 Australian companies, who participated in the 14th India-Australia Joint Business Council Meeting.
18. During his visit to India by Mr. John Grace, an AusBiotech Corporate Member, revealed a strong, growing biotechnology industry, which offered significant opportunities for Australian biotechnology companies wishing to form partnerships in India. Mr. Grace's visit was initiated and funded by the Australia-India Council (AIC).
19. Foreign Minister Alexander Downer reiterated Australia's support for India's candidature for the permanent membership of UN Security Council. It was also agreed to organize an exhibition in India on the legendary cricketer, Don Bradman.
20. Tim Harcourt, Celebration of a Trading Nation, *Australian Trade Commission*, Sydney, 26 January 2005.
21. M. Thirwell, *India: the Next Economic Giant* (Sydney: Lowy Institute for International Policy), 13 August 2004.
22. To broaden the relationship between the two countries and for export promotion, by increasing levels of knowledge and understanding between their people the Australia-India Council (AIC) was established in 1992 by the Australian Government. The AIC is serviced by a secretariat located in DFAT, Canberra. The Australian High Commission in New Delhi manages the AIC's activities in India with an in-country manager and support staff. In 1995 the Indian government established a counterpart to the AIC, the India-Australia Council (IAC). The IAC is serviced by a secretariat located in the Confederation of Indian Industry (CII). The AIC and IAC meet periodically to coordinate programmes.
23. Government of India offices and PSUs in Australia include Government of India Tourist Office; State Bank of India (representative office since November 1998 upgraded to branch office in April 2004); New India Assurance Co Ltd (has a presence in Australia since 1955); and Air India (offline station). Engineers India Limited has a presence in Perth. All the major Indian IT companies have a

presence in Australia. These include Infosys; Satyam; TCS; HCL; Polaris Software Lab Ltd; Birlasoft; NIIT; ICICI Infotech; Wipro; Mahindra-British Telecom Ltd; Pentasoft; Kale Consultants Australia P/L; Tata Infotech Limited; and Zensar Technologies. Infosys, Satyam, TCS and Birlasoft have established Software Development Centres in either Sydney or Melbourne. The Taj Group of Hotels has an office in Sydney. Tata Steel has a presence in Brisbane.

24. The Memorandum of Understanding (MoU) on Cooperation in Combating International Terrorism was signed by Australian Foreign Minister Mr. Downer and the then Indian Foreign Minister, Mr. Yashwant Sinha, in 2003.
25. The 8th session of the Indo-Australian Joint Ministerial Commission took place in New Delhi in February 2003. The Joint Ministerial Commission included the Joint Working Group (JWG) on Energy and Minerals; and the Joint Business Group (JBG) on Natural Fibers and Textiles. The last session of the JMC noted that there was significant scope for further expansion in bilateral trade and economic cooperation. The 14th session of the JBC was also simultaneously held with the JMC in New Delhi in February 2003. The delegations to the JBC were coordinated by FICCI from the Indian side and the Australia-India Business Council (AIBC) from the Australian side.
26. Government of India, *The Export Import Databank,* Ministry of Commerce and Industry, 2004.
27. Federation of Indian Chambers of Commerce and Industry, 2004.
28. Government of India, *The Export Import Databank*, Ministry of Commerce and Industry, 2004-05.
29. Government of India, *SIA Newsletter*, Department of Industrial Policy and Promotion, 2004.
30. Federation of Inidan Chambers of Commerce and Industry, 2005.
31. Both were signed during Australian Education Minister Dr. Nelson's visit to India in October 2003. As on 31st March, 2005 there were 2430 students on Australian Development Scholarships studying at Australian universities. Indeed, Australia has become a major supplier of international education. Australia's education services exports grew by 13 per cent in 2003-04 to reach $5.9 billion and are among our fastest growing exports and now our third largest export.
32. *Australia-India Focus*, May-July 2004-Issue 30 and Australia India Business Council's website at www.aibc.org.au/news/htm.
33. Media release from the Australian Department of Foreign Affairs and Trade, 3 December, 2001.
34. *Australia India Focus* 2003; The Australian High Commission and the Woolmark Company celebrated the success of the wool partnership between Australia and India at a fashion evening, Wool 2004, in New Delhi on 8 October, 2003.
35. India responds to sanctions by approving foreign deals, The *Australian Financial Review*, 19 May, 1998.

17

Across the Ocean: Catching the ICT Trail

AMITA SINGH

Continuously expanding applications of information and communication technologies (ICT) are transforming local, national, regional and international economies into network economies, which are the foundations for information societies. They are being built upon expanded and upgraded national telecom networks and the new information infrastructures. The point of entry to participation in these new economies and societies is through local communication networks, which determine the access possibilities and boundaries of opportunity for individuals, organisations and countries. The telecom reform process is directed to creating an environment to foster a massive expansion in the coverage and capabilities of the information infrastructure networks, with national telecom regulators as the key implementers of the policies of reform.

The New Telecom Policy of India was introduced in 1999 after a weak performance of the Telecom Policy of 1994. It struck the core of ICT expansion in its very meaningful set of objectives. The focus of objectives was to increase teledensity and connect rural and remote areas. With 141 million gross subscriber base the telecom service industry in India is growing at the rate of 30 per cent annually and its contribution to the country's Gross Domestic Product (GDP) is one per cent. Telecom Dispute Settlement Appellate Tribunal (TDSAT) Chairman Justice Santosh Hegde informed in a public seminar *(PTI, 26, 2006)* that while India had eight million phones in 1995 its teledensity is a mere 0.8 per cent, the figure rose to 141 million (93 million cellular and 48 million landline) phones and teledensity to 12 per cent last year.[1] The industry is expected to increase its subscriber base to 250 million by the end of 2007.

The two Commonwealth partners were faced with a very similar situation in the early nineties which was to emerge out of the British Colonial frame of telecom policy or the Telegraph Acts in a manner that global integration does not benefit the vendors alone. An introduction of private capital and then opening up to partnerships in service delivery systems suggests that much of the drive was public sector promoted till the beginning of the nineties which witnessed an extremely charged competitive market for telecoms and not taking any initiative would have amounted to a negative impact on the rising market competition through encouragement to unfair means, grey market and obviously hard on the consumers or people. Australia started privatising at almost the same time as India in 1997 and 1999. The Australian Labor Party has always opposed full privatisation and on one occasion at least this had also been opposed by trade unions, Australian Greens and Australian Democrats also. A realistic understanding about the perceived role of ICT can be obtained from the political life of the Labor Party member Lindsay Tanner. In his book he tried to link the use of ICT applications to enhance social justice and economic equality.[2] When he took over the Finance and Consumer Affairs in the subsequent year he looked after communications and community relationships. However, public ownership of Telstra was converted to a majority privately owned in November 2006 with the government share of 51.8 per cent reduced to a mere 17 per cent. Optus is the only other company giving any competition to Telstra. Privatisation in India is more spread out with at least five major companies making the market more competitive and therefore the role of Telecom regulator which is TRAI (Telecom Regulatory Authority of India) assumes a new significance as compared to its Australian counterpart, Australian Competition and Consumer Commission…

The present policy framework of Australian Telecoms was embodied in *The Telecommunications Act 1991*, in which there has been a complex interaction between telecommunications-specific policy and the general framework of National Competition Policy embodied in *The Competition Policy Reform Act 1995* and reflected in the regulatory role of the Australian Competition and Consumer Council (ACCC). The Indian National Telecom Policy of 1994 recognised the need for private investment and the association of the private sector to bridge the resource gap as also to meet the rapidly growing demand for telecommunication services. The policy also recognised that in order to implement the new telecom policy, suitable arrangements would be made to protect and promote the interests of consumers and ensure fair competition. The New Telecom Policy 1999 went further and provided a framework for increased competition.

The purpose of this paper is to argue that the main deficiency in ICT collaboration has been the failure to take adequate account of global shifts, need for value added services and alternative institutional structures designed to exploit economies of scale and scope which could have yielded both a more competitive market structure and services to people. The Australian telecommunications system has undergone radical reform since 1991. Indeed, along with New Zealand, Chile and Guatemala, Australia is viewed as one of the leaders in telecommunications reform.[3] The former public monopoly, comprising Telecom Australia and the Overseas

Telecommunications Corporation (OTC) has been corporatised, taking the name Telstra, and has been only partially privatised. A proposal for full privatisation was put forward in 1998, but abandoned in the face of parliamentary and public opposition. Competition has been fostered through the introduction of a private competitor, Optus in 1991 and the removal of all restrictions on entry in 1997, while Telstra has been subject to special regulation requiring the provision of network access to competitors on favourable terms in markets where it is deemed to be dominant. Australian policy was designed to ensure the survival of at least one competitor for Telstra and to encourage the emergence of as many others as possible. Compared to the reforms undertaken in New Zealand, the existing monopoly carrier was given far less favourable treatment.

India and Australia share trade relations which date back to 1791 when a British store ship 'Sydney Cove' was sent to Calcutta for food supplies during the famine in Australia. A decade later coal and horses were shipped to Calcutta from Newcastle. The coming of globalisation brought innumerable and potentially powerful opportunities for the two across the oceanic landmasses which shared a common administrative history under British. For lack of infrastructure and information sharing the two nations could not tap these opportunities. Also because of the attitude of looking towards USA and a more interactive ethnographic profile of American NRIs, India's initial business opportunities arrived from that country. Of India's software and service exports 68 per cent go to USA.[4] India's offshore ICT services has a share of 25 per cent which is second only to Ireland and according to NASSCOM this market for India will continue to grow to more than $17billion by 2008.[5]

ICT services have played an instrumental role in bringing India out of stagnation and economic depression. TNCs such as American Express, British Airways, GE, Canadian Nortel Networks, US's Texas Instruments, etc. have made the market more competitive. Presently India's domestic market is well developed and ready for a major outflow of FDI since Tata Consultancy, Infosys, Wipro and Satyam computers are at par with foreign rivals.[6] (McKinsey & Co 2003) Indo-Australian collaboration can safely broaden up in ICT services such as customer care, finance, human resources, banking services, billing and payments, administration and content development. Engineering, design, knowledge processing and logistics are further going to generate a major employment market which is slated to show the highest growth in coming times. The prospects of collaboration are bright as the trend of offshoring in India is moving towards higher value added levels for the sustenance of which Australian expertise and experience may be a great support and benefit for both. It may also bring down the cost of offshoring for the home and host country and with proper regulatory mechanism equitable solutions are likely to emerge.

Emerging Trends

During the Ninth Australia-India Joint Ministerial Commission in May 2005 the two countries decided to work on the Trade and Economic Forum to facilitate future development of trade and economy and to boost development in all other areas of mutual interest.

Four trends towards industry wide consolidation through forward and backward mergers need to be noticed which indicate growing prospects for across the ocean collaboration:

- Some foreign affiliates (mainly US and EU) are thinking of selling some of their operations in Australia giving wider space for collaboration to countries like India.
- Fast growing Indian firms see acquisitions-inside and outside India as a way to sustain growth such as TCS, Infosys, Satyam and Wipro.
- Some contract service provider trans-national companies such as IBM and Accenture are acquiring local service providers in the Indian market.
- Increasing consolidation is occurring within India among Indian companies.

Table 1: Growing Indo-Australian Collaboration in Trade and Services

S. No.	*Services/Investments*	*1991-2004*	*In 2004*	*% Increase*
1.	Australian investments in India	Rs. 68437.1crores or A$2138.7 billion	A$ 990.7	2.3 % of the total approved investments in India
2.	No. of Australian Joint ventures in India	512 (332 financial +182 technical)		
3.	Bilateral trade	A$ 4.31 billion	A$ 6.54 billion	52%
4.	Indian imports from Australia	A$ 3.33 billion	A$ 5.42 billion	62.7%
5.	Indian exports to Australia	A$ 977.7 million	A$ 1.12 billion	14.6%

Source: Compiled from the Australian Bureau of Statistics and Invest India Group.

According to the accumulated total of approvals up to August 2004, Australia ranked as the 8th largest source of foreign investments in India. Price Waterhouse Coopers has tremendously undertaken the financial services and control through ICT in both the countries. For the fiscal year July 2003-June 2004 India ranked 7th as Australia's export destination (6th export destination in calendar year 2004) with a share of 4.5 per cent in terms of overall exports. India ranked 26th as Australia's import source with 0.8 per cent market share in Australia's total imports. It ranked 13th as Australia's overall trading partner. Australia's Joint Ministerial Commission and Joint Business Council may act as strong facilitators in the process.

Some Major Shifts in Terms of FDI Investments, Offshoring, Outsourcing and Revitalizing Regulatory Bodies

ICT market is showing a very strong growth in recent years and has brought about substantial returns for Indian investors in Australia. Many Indian companies are investing in Australia. Tata Consultancy Services have already set up a new Global Development Centre in Melbourne. It is expanding to other areas in Australia as well as New Zealand by providing software solutions. Infosys Technologies has already grown in collaboration with Australian companies such as Suncorp Metway, Vodafone and Telstra. Mahindra-British Company which is spreading into the whole of Asia-Pacific region is collaborating with AT&T, British Telecom and Ericsson. Some Australia Companies have signed new strategic relationship with Satyam Computers which is well placed in Melbourne.[7]

Alienation and marginalisation seeps into efforts of reform leading to a completely uneventful and ritualistic policy implementation. The Human Development Report of 2003 admitted that these goals cannot be realised with business as usual approach but the pace of progress must be dramatically accelerated. Significant disparities in the degree of democratic development tarnish the achievement of the millennium development goals (MDG). These are disparities in income, educational attainment, gender and access to resources including training in science, technology, legal frameworks and governance which keep a large majority of people out of the social net. It was also clarified that even though a stronger economic growth was required yet growth alone will not be enough as policies also need to strengthen the links between stronger growth and higher incomes in the poorest households.[8] For achieving this access to education, food, technology and health services becomes a dire requirement of sustaining growth.

Australia is 4th in Human Development Index while India is slowly moving upwards from 127th position yet the relative investments in ICT services show that Australia is rather cautious on investments in this area. Export Oriented FDI projects reveal that though between 2002-2003, Australia's biggest investment has been in IT Services it is a meager 4 per cent share of the total but India on the other hand had 19 per cent share of total investment in IT services. There are reasons to believe that India is fast emerging as an IT destination. Of the more than 300 export oriented ICT projects in developing countries, 37 per cent went to India, 19 per cent to China and 11 per cent to Singapore. Similarly from the 80 per cent FDI in call centres in Asia India bagged 60 projects, China 30 and Malaysia and Singapore 16 each. More than half of these projects came from IT related services. Even in shared service centres more than half of these projects came to India. It is being observed that 50 per cent of Fortune 500 companies have not yet set up any such centres but are likely to do so in near future for which India, China and Philippines are likely to be the most attractive destinations.[9]

What is of particular interest here is that the structure of FDI has shifted towards services which are totally ICT governed. From less than a quarter of the world FDI stock in 1970 it has risen to a little less than half in 1990 and to more than 60 per cent or an estimated $ 4 Trillion in 2002.[10] Therefore services account for 2/3rd of total FDI inflows. It is also seen that the dominance of US firms has now given way to Japan and EU in trade and trade supporting services but the highest concentration of FDI has been in countries such as US and Western Europe where markets attract FDI.

Looking at the composition of services FDI one can notice the shift from trade and finance to ICT enabled corporate services including electricity, water, telecommunications and business where it has risen 14 fold. Even in telecom storage and transport the rise is 16 fold and in business services 9 fold. What is of particular interest for this paper is that FDI inflow is decreasing in developed countries while the outflow is increasing for which India is ranked as the foremost destination for reasons described in the UNDP Report as "Firms are attracted not just by its base of low cost and skilled labour, it also has first mover and agglomeration advantages." The report further states that "the growing technological capabilities of Indian firms and their rising exports, particularly IT services are driving FDI growth." This in turn has been strengthening regulatory systems, reliability of services and consumer protection laws. Thus IT enabled services has opened up doors for partnerships in legal services besides infrastructural issues.

Growing Prospects Towards Value-adding Activities

Value adding activities which have been on the rise between the two countries are a combination of goods and services. There is no universally acceptable definition of services as it may involve tangibles as well as intangibles spread over a large area of activities such as consumer services; producer services, social services and personal services.[11] The World Economic Report 2004 suggests that services include all economic activities included under the "tertiary sector" in UN International Standard Industrial Classification (ISIC) and form the core argument of offshoring business. Offshoring which initially started as rationalisation of customer logistics management has now become 'a cutting edge' of the "global shift" in productive activity.[12] It has been primarily driven by the growing need for a cost-effective arrangement in a competitive business environment yet India and Australia have a fairly open ground to change the rules of offshoring from cost-effective management to learning management between two cultures. An increased research and educational exchanges between the two countries justify the direction which is being taken. A study of sociological, anthropological, political-economy and public administration on one hand and architectural, hospitality management, small entrepreneurial activities, heritage conservation and tourism on the other. The use of ICT in all these activities helps codification, standardisation and digitisation of knowledge which facilitates its relocation with ease and reliability. US has been one of the largest importer of computer and data processing services along with accounting, auditing and book keeping services. Australia has the potential to challenge US existence in the Indian subcontinent and the whole of South Asia due to its proximity to the region. A rapid growth of infrastructure both for global markets and domestic needs in the last decade in India has also been a shot in the arm for regulatory developments in urban services and telecoms. Presently, given the strong democratic dispensation of growth in India, she tops the list of 25 leading destinations for offshoring attractiveness followed by China, Malaysia and Singapore. National Association of Software and Service Companies (NASSCOM) reveal that value of exports of software and other services jumped from less than $0.5 billion to $12 billion since 2000 and its export intensity rose from 58 per cent to 78 per cent.

As trade and services grow with the offshoring of businesses a very high potential for Indo-Australian cooperation unfolds within the field of information technology. At least four bilateral agreements in the last two years point to that:

- Special Agreement on Cooperation in Science and Technology
- MOU concerning Cooperation in the Information Industries
- MOU for cooperation between Karnataka and Queensland
- MOU between NASSCOM and the Australian Information Industry Association (AIIA)

Initiating a New Dialogue in Business Exchange Programme

This however is embedded into an array of emerging concerns. Firstly the impact of ICT collaboration needs to address problems of 'jobless recovery' which USA has been witnessing. The white collar jobs have not increased since 2001 as compared to the average annual gain of 5.5 per cent jobs.[13] (Roach 2004). Yet the UNDP Report states that most of these jobs which are not more than a mere 2.8 per cent only are more due to automation and technical changes such as tellers, answering services, etc., and not due to offshoring specifically. India and Australia can learn from the US experience and can begin early with a more comprehensive platform for innovations simultaneously in other sectors also to absorb displaced labour if any due to ICT dissemination in trade.

Second concern that need to be addressed is the issue of justice and fair-play in offshoring ICT based services so that that the process of offshoring continues to be beneficial to people of both the countries. A fair and sustainable collaboration would mean that substantial gains be shared in the host country itself. A study by Agarwal establishes the fact that US gains twice as much as India from offshoring and a growing concern amongst entrepreneurs in coming times would be to find partners who respect equitable trade sharing.[14] Thus India and Australia are also encountering a new challenge to prepare for adjustments in restructuring international business environment and the new international division of labour specifically in the Asia-Pacific region.

Third, the issue of patenting and programme security be maintained through collaborative institutions on a common platform or most implementation efforts would go waste. An all inclusive exchange programme of commercial and competition law, arbitration and international legal services needs to be invoked. This would mean a renewed need for course restructuring in legal training and law syllabi in Universities of both the countries.

Lastly, is a radical change in mass communication, journalism and media studies activities which would form the life line of ICT collaboration? Most reports and new opportunities from across the world besides efforts that would come through on cultural and anthropological understandings precede any expansion of business. Excellent networking opportunities for Australian and Indian manufacturing firms including the entertainment industry such as film production, editing and animation hold a very wide horizon.

ICT Applications and Grass-root Innovations Towards Participatory Democracy

India and Australia are both active members of the Asia-Pacific Telecommunity and the International Telecommunication Union (ITU). The two countries are seen as leaders in the region and have worked closely together on regional preparation for ITU world conferences on radio frequency spectrum and regulatory matters.

The MoUs with India focus on encouraging cooperation in the field of telecommunications in the following areas:

- Telecommunications services;
- The exchange of information about telecommunications policy, regulation and convergence;

Any development in these areas is likely to bring a qualitative change in governance systems and implementation of government programmes for communities. If applied judiciously it may also bridge the digital divide prevailing in both the countries. Innumerable innovations in grass-root governance are taking place in both India and Australia. These are especially designed to connect remote areas and geographically distanced and socially excluded communities to mainstream governance programmes. One such successful programme called the TIGERS (*Trials of Innovative Government Regional Electronic Services*) delivered a series of new integrated online services in Tasmania. It explored new areas of online service delivery systems and created valuable lessons for governments to follow. Several programmes in India like FRIENDS, GYANDOOT AND E-CHAUPAL have strengthened grass-root democracy by providing reasons for people to participate in governance of the country. These programmes are also instrumental in creating self-help groups and local watch groups which protect environment, aboriginal rights on land and impart entrepreneurial education to less privileged population of remote areas. It has also sparked a new life in pro-poor policies since the centralised systems are splitting now to provide greater space to NGOs and local governance bodies which play a powerful role in widening the horizons of technological transformation.

The completion of the highly successful TIGERS programme in Australia led the Minister for Communications, Information Technology and the Arts, Senator Richard Alston to release two reports (*The TIGERS Report and A Conceptual Analysis of the Performance and Achievements of TIGERS*) which provide detailed conceptualisation and implementation lessons for public policy experts in e-governance programmes in the two countries. The trials have been developed by the Commonwealth's Trials of Innovative Government Electronic Regional Services (TIGERS) Programme, which is developing online services across the three tiers of government. The Tasmanian Premier, Jim Bacon while releasing the reports made an observation that Australia has trained ICT workforce and Tasmania's success in TIGERS programme is attributed to this fact.

However the objectives of signing MoUs by two governments does not specifically mention many concerns of e-governance programmes which, if treated early, may help in replication of these programmes on a larger scale. Due to a lack of the right approach the fear is that ICT collaboration may end up in simply increasing the numbers of BPO (Business Process Outsourcing) Companies rather than a deepening democratic cooperation of participatory institutions of both societies.

Conclusion

India and Australia have a shared history of commonwealth countries and therefore common democratic traditions, legal, financial and administrative structures besides sharing common interests as Indian Ocean littoral States.

Cricket is an abiding passion that has linked people of both these countries. As founder members of the United Nations and members of the Indian Ocean Rim—Association for Regional Cooperation (IOR-ARC), ASEAN Regional Forum (ARF) and dialogue partners with ASEAN the two countries have many forums to work together. With the increasing prominence of the Asia-Pacific region in global geo-politics and economics, Indo-Australian relations assume more significance than ever before. There are concerted efforts on both sides to expand and diversify bilateral relations.

In this context, many high level bilateral visits have been taking place. Visits at Ministerial, Parliamentary and official levels from the Union Government and State Governments are a regular feature in Indo-Australian relations. Various Export Promotion Councils/Chambers of Commerce and Industry have organised these meetings and participated in International fairs held in Australia including the Prime Minister Mr. John Howard's visit to India in July 2000.

ICT Collaboration between the two countries is reaching new peaks as many Indian multinationals like Infosys, Wipro and Tata Consultancy Services are collaborating with Australian Telstra as well as service provider companies. The challenge is to apply technology in such a manner that a sustainable development of both business and society is constructed. This would also initiate a new dialogue in Business Exchange Programmes which in turn would require a reinvention of the dialogue on justice and fair-play to address problems of 'jobless recovery' and the 'digital divide'. Most disciplines may have to update their syllabi to accommodate new challenges in media and mass communication studies. New disciplines would emerge which may need some special treatment for being channels of feeding currents of e-governance.

ICT applications also lead to grassroot innovations towards participatory democracy. Innumerable innovations in grassroot governance are taking place in both India and Australia. These are especially designed to connect remote areas and geographically distanced and socially excluded communities to mainstream governance programmes. There are many experiments from grassroots in both India and Australia such as the TIGERS (*Trials of Innovative Government Regional Electronic Services*) in Tasmania. It explored new areas of online service delivery systems and created valuable lessons for governments to follow. Several programmes in India like FRIENDS, GYANDOOT AND E-CHAUPAL have strengthened grassroot democracy by providing reasons for people to participate in governance of the country. These local experiments also provide the rationale for the growth and advancement of ICT collaboration between the two countries. While there is an increasing need for the replication of good e-governance practices there is also the need for being cautious against ending up this exercise in simply increasing the number of sterile and slipping domains of BPO companies using ICT. Most of the MoUs being signed between the two countries fail to address issues of value-added services in mutual collaborations.

End Notes

1. *PTI*, 26 March, 2006 02:22 Sunday 02.22.:39 am.
2. Tanner Lindsay, *Open Australia* (Sydney Pluto Press, 1996).
3. P. Spiller and C. Cardilli, The Frontier of Telecommunications Deregulation: Small Countries Leading the Pack, *Journal of Economic Perspectives*, Vol. 11, No. 4, (1997) pp. 127-38.
4. K.J. Joseph and Govindan Parayil, India-ASEAN Cooperation in Information and Communication Technologies: Issues and Prospects, *RIS Discussion Paper, No. 70/2004,* Research and Information System for Non-Aligned and Other Developing Countries, New Delhi.
5. UNDP, World Investment Report, *The Shift Towards Services,* (New Delhi: Oxford University Press, 2004).
6. McKinsey & Co, India Information Technology/Business Process Offshoring case summary.
   www.mckinsey.com/knowledge/mgi/newhorizons/reports/IT_BPO.asp (2003)
7. http://www.investaustralia.gov.au
8. UNDP, *Human Development Report 2003* (New Delhi: Oxford University Press, 2004) pp. 1-13.
9. *Ibid.*, No. 5, p. 161.
10. *Ibid.*, p. xx.
11. Harley L. Browning and J. Singelmann (1975), The Emergence of a Service Society: Demographic and Sociological Aspects of Sectoral Transformation of Labour Force in the USA (Springfield, VA: National Technical Information Services, 1975).
12. Peter Dicken, *Global Shift, Transforming the World Economy,* (London: Paul Chapman Publication, 2003).
13. Stephen Roach, The Global Labour Arbitrage, *Global Agenda 2004,* (January 2004), pp. 90-93.
14. Vivek Agarwal and Diana Farrell, Who Wins in Offshoring?, *The McKinsey Quarterly* 2003, pp. 37-43.

18

The Politics of Rising Expectations: Middle Class Experiences of Economic Restructuring in India and Australia

TIMOTHY J. SCRASE AND JOHN ROBINSON

The intensification of globalisation has marked the ascendancy of neo-liberal paradigms in development thinking. Its impact in the Asia-Pacific region, in both developed and developing states, has brought about significant social and cultural change. Over the last decade economically advanced countries such as Australia and developing countries such as India have both vigorously pursued policies of economic liberalisation. The governments of these nations, despite their respectively disparate economic/developmental positions, have mirrored one another in their unswerving faith in liberalisation policies as the solution to the overall improvement of the population's standard of living. As the result, India and Australia, along with others in the Asia Pacific region, have forged ahead with their particular liberal prescriptions for economic reform. While the outcomes from this reform have been as varied as the nations involved, in some significant examples, parallels have emerged, not least of which have been the apparent growth of the, now 'interested', middle class built on the benefits that have been said to have accrued from the liberal structural reforms to the economy.

In light of the above, this paper sets-out to compare and contrast middle class experiences of economic change and restructuring in India and Australia[1]. In the case of the former, research is based on fieldwork in West Bengal with the lower middle classes and which consists of in-depth interviews with both the critics and supporters of privatisation, deregulation and globalisation[2]. This is contrasted with interviews conducted with members of the 'aspirational' class—a cohort of largely middle class, conservative voters in Western Sydney[3]. The Indian research reveals that opinions about the supposed benefits of reforms, and broader societal changes brought about by the globalized media and culture vary according to age and gender. Whereas an optimistic outlook exemplifies the views of young people, the older generations generally defend the state and are suspicious of private capital. While remaining critical of liberalisation, many of our informants nevertheless espouse the government rhetoric of work place restructuring and global competitiveness. On the whole, though, cosmopolitanism and globalism are things they welcome, yet most do not want to lose the secure safety-net provided by the state. In comparison, the research from Australia investigates the propagation of 'mainstream ideals' through the valorisation of particular socio-economic attributes of the so-called 'aspirational class', and the impact this has on the shaping of fiscal policy under the current Howard-led, Liberal coalition government. Rather than addressing the fallout from economic and technological changes from the early 1990s onwards, Howard focused attention on his particular construction of the crisis of disenfranchisement of ordinary Australians (Howard's 'battlers'). This was a crisis to which he could set his *solutions* and thus institute the politics of reassurance of the sovereignty of the mainstream (or, as some have termed it: the 'silent majority'). On the whole, the interviews reveal great support generally for the conservative values and ideologies of the Howard government, yet there remains some hesitancy as to the personal value of fiscal and tax reforms, and ignorance of more general political processes that underlie the reform process. Overall, this paper aims to highlight the complexities and contradictions of the economic reform process, and uncovers the extent to which reforms are essentially an ideological battleground as much as they are about fundamental economic and industrial change.

Conceptual Framework

In the Indian context, according to a number of authors, neo-liberal approaches have become the new orthodoxy in development[4]. The resurrection and hegemony of market driven approaches identify state intervention as inefficient and counterproductive and thereby call for developing countries to privatise state owned enterprises, adopt a range of stabilisation measures to address balance of payment crises, and limit public expenditure. The deleterious effects of these policies on Asia's poor[5] and the positive consequences for the 'new rich'[6] are amply evident. And indeed, in the Australian scenario, the debate over the benefits of the advancing neo-liberal reforms have produced a similarly polarised discussion among the competing analytical positions, although on different contextual ground: while addressing fundamentally similarly framed political and economic issues as India, the debate is occurring on the terrain of a developed economy.[7]

However, beyond these dichotomous analyses, the ways local communities, classes and specific cultural groups confront, challenge or acquiesce to advancing neo-liberal policy platforms in economic and social arenas remains relatively unexplored. In Australia, this analytical vacuum has been apparent in the manner that interpretations have generally been confined to either side of the argument, i.e., one is either in support of, or vehemently against, neo-liberal economic reforms. Likewise, in the Indian scenario, the competing narratives of the supporters of the reforms[8] and their critics[9] overlook experiences of those who don't fit neatly into the extremes of the social spectrum. Thus, it is the intention of this paper to make some contribution in this area.

As the neo-liberal reforms progress, supported as they are by vigorous rhetorical campaigns by business and government, increasing numbers of people find themselves being inexorably drawn towards the seductive discourses of the marketplace, and whether intentionally or not, have begun to replicate the language and/or the practices of neo-liberal 'life'. Thus, in contrast to the mainly strictly polarised accounts of contemporary neo-liberal developments, the research among the respective groups addressed in the two case studies explore the complexities and contradictions of a segment within the middle classes who have become cautiously interested in the proclaimed 'rewards' of the New Economic Policies yet are simultaneously skeptical of whether any personal benefits will accrue. These are people, in both instances, who are confused by old Keynesian/state-interventionist policies and, while hopeful, they nevertheless remain uncertain of the veracity of the claims of neo-liberalism.

Discourses of Global Efficiency and Sound Economic Management: the Dynamics of a *New* Neo-liberal Middle Class Work Culture

In the Indian setting, the question that arose in the interviews was: 'How is it that some workers reproduced ideologies of work efficiency, often in the face of, and in conjunction with, countervailing life-long thinking and practices?' In answering this question we found that the notions of efficiency, privatisation and deregulation (the buzz words of the neo-liberally *inspired* workplace) were rapidly gaining particular currency as the central motifs of the everyday language and practice of workers. This language and related practices were becoming competitive with other 'known' models of operation, and were often indicative of new sets of expectations. Obviously, the discourses, and their 'ways of being', have developed a life of their own such that they have become significantly responsible for developing new understandings of how individuals should govern themselves.

In a theoretical sense, analysts have identified a number of themes of this apparent transformation of consciousness. David Harvey, among others, suggests that the promotion of the work ethic, the nobility of efficiency, productivity, and so on, have been enabled through both persuasive socialisation and coercive maintenance[10]. In this view the State takes a pro-active role in social production. Thus, the inculcation of the population with particular ideologies of the workplace are seen in terms of a power bloc formed between the owners of capital and the political class. The fundamental principle involved in the dissemination of capitalist logic, such as the deployment of ideals of 'efficiency' and 'flexibility', provides the security and maintenance of the economic system. However this was not merely an ideological imposition, but legitimised through the articulation of a common value system, despite it being the values of the dominant classes.[11]

The exemplification of such a hegemonic project involving state activism in the promotion of capitalist relations of production and the construction of the *appropriate* workforce can be found in Stuart Hall's analysis of the Thacherite project[12]. Hall claimed that the Thatcher Government constructed a disciplinary programme to foster capitalist production around ostensibly common objectives, with, in effect, ordinary workers paradoxically consenting to their own exploitation. While profoundly contradictory this governmental programme was nevertheless able to construct "… unity out of difference"[13]. 'Common-sense' was remade, wherein the terminology of the market was 'normalised' and incorporated into a broader package comprising order, family values and respectability—a package that thus formed the everyday conception of what constituted the 'national identity', and as such, the 'proper' moral perspective. This was the development of a "practical material-ideological force" that has a language which maps out social reality clearly and unambiguously[14]. The result: the elevation of a common (or national) wisdom and morality centred on notions of efficiency, flexibility, nationalism and so forth.

According to Branislav Gosovic, a type of global intellectual hegemony (GIH) has become a central characteristic of neo-liberal globalisation of the 1990s.[15] This is perpetuated through the frequent use of particular terminology and clichés that legitimise this paradigm, imbuing it with positive qualities. In the language of GIH, neo-liberal globalisation is presented as new, modern, scientific, results orientated and inevitable. Public institutions are represented negatively as inefficient, in contrast to private institutions[16]. He further adds that individuals, particularly those who are in the service of governments, may have their own reasons for not speaking out against neo-liberalism, including their desire to keep their job and obtain promotions[17]. The eminent French sociologist, Pierre Bourdieu, discusses the insecurities that have become normative under globalisation: growing unemployment and casualisation of the workforce has constrained workers and broken any meaningful resistance[18]. Out of fear, workers strive to become the *most* efficient, flexible and productive worker in an organisation. These forces are universal in their effect and "… the awareness of it never goes away: it is present at every moment in everyone's mind"[19]. People feel that they are replaceable; as a result there is a definite sense that people come to regard work as a privilege, "...a fragile threatened privilege", and most certainly not a right[20].

Another aspect of this phenomenon has been the growing prominence of a political rationality that is geared towards increased personal responsibility. Here, the strategy of replacing old-fashioned regulatory techniques with techniques of self-regulation conceived by Foucaultian scholars[21] may be relevant. Moreover, as Beck suggests, the ideal individual worker will take responsibility for his part in the creation of an efficient and responsible enterprise: any failure is their personal responsibility[22]. The benefit being that individuals can feel a sense of control because they are (ostensibly) "...not passive reflections of circumstances, but active shapers of their own lives"[23].

The Indian Experience: Analysing the Lower Middle Classes

Over the past decade or so much has been said about the growth of the Indian middle class as a consequence of the globalisation of the economy[24]. There is a great deal of interest in the lifestyles and consumption patterns of India's 'new middle class', especially as consumption helps to redefine status for this group[25]. Indian middle-class responses to globalisation of the economy are contradictory, however; while they welcome aspects of cultural globalism embodied in the media, they remain highly critical of the uninterrupted entry of foreign capital[26]. Furthermore, there are problems of combining the lower and upper levels of the middle classes in Asia. For example, policy shifts in development, that openly support structural adjustment, have resulted in the differentiation of the Indian middle classes[27]. Thus, just as it has been noted in research on the middle class and social change in other parts of Asia, these groups should be regarded as class fractions rather than a single unified class[28].

We are therefore concerned with studying a class *fraction*—that is, the lower middle-class. For the purposes of this study, the lower middle class in Bengal have been defined in terms of both a particular economic bracket and a cultural milieu. Their mean household income is just under Rs. 10,000 per month[29]. In cultural terms, this group forms part of the Bengali *bhadralok*; a multivalent term that predominantly means 'respectable people'. The *bhadralok*, over the past two-centuries have been distinguished by their refined behaviour and cultivated taste, but not necessarily substantial wealth and power: a change from their traditional position as a reasonably well-off, educated and cultured status group. The *bhadralok* are now a heterogeneous group and often indigent. They still privilege education for their children and attempt to maintain a veneer of their erstwhile esteemed social status by engaging in writing, music and the arts, but the economic reality of the present has meant that the penchant for cultural pursuit (the traditional status maintainer) is disappearing. Instead, conspicuous consumption has increasingly become an important determinant of status. It is important to note that the downward mobility of the *bhadralok* began several decades ago following the partition of Bengal and is not specifically due to globalisation.

The self-ascription of informants was often couched in terms of being lower middle class. Indeed, their use of the Bengali term *nimno moddhobitto* (lower middle class) suggested the same classification. In a striking contrast to the real poor, other terms used were 'ordinary folk', or 'common folk', or simply, 'those dependent on a salary'. The image of a salary earner is powerful in Bengali culture, which both suggests a distinction from menial wage work as well as earnings from trading. However, it also disguises the real incomes of those civil servants who supplement their total household income by taking bribes. During our fieldwork no one claimed that they were poor, despite their lack of material wealth. On the contrary, there were subtle attempts to distance themselves from the poor.

Our respondents were employed as clerks, lower level professionals and administrators, and in sales and service. However, sociological attempts to operationalise class derived from occupational categories and income only partially explain the position of our informants: as suggested earlier these groups are best understood as class fractions. Suffice to say that neo-Weberian and neo-Marxist accounts shed some light on the social location of a marginal middle class consisting of non-manual wage earners and low-grade technicians. Ultimately however, we do not claim that any of these definitions are completely adequate in analysing class relations in Bengal[30]

Methodology

The narratives of our informants are derived from participant observation and in-depth interviews in Calcutta (now Kolkata) and in Siliguri in North Bengal. This research is ethnographic and qualitative in nature. Despite almost a decade of radical economic reform, there remains little in the way of micro-level sociological research documenting the direct, and indirect, effects of this process of economic reforms for communities and local groups. On the whole, most studies highlight a range of macro political-economic transformations taking place in India[31]. With few exceptions there is a paucity of ethnographic research on the social consequences of changing economic relations[32]. Moreover, it is through the ethnographic method that the respondents' paradoxical views towards liberalization can be revealed.

Fieldwork was conducted over a four-year period (1998-2002) in Calcutta and Siliguri. Using a *snowballing* method, a total 120 people were interviewed (60 per city). Among the respondents there were twenty key informants, most of whom we had known from our earlier research in the late 1980s. Women constituted 48 per cent of our sample, while men, 52 per cent. The overwhelming majority (85%) were employed in the formal or organized sector of the labour force, while 15 per cent were working in the so-called *informal* sector. While most people worked in the public sector, among the formal sector workforce, about a quarter was employed by the private sector, including transnational companies such as Philips. It is important to note however, that none of our respondents had obtained employment in occupations that have consequently emerged from liberalisation. The mean household size was 4.7 persons, with only seven per cent of households having more than seven residents. The types of families were roughly divided between joint and nuclear families.

Findings

Mutually suspicious views existed among public and private sector employees. Public-sector workers equated the private sector with insecurity and exploitation while some within the formal private sector assumed that their counterparts within the public sector lacked work discipline. Such perceptions were rarely grounded in experience or knowledge of the other side. While some private sector respondents' views were largely shaped by media discourses, the public sector workers' critiques were mainly centred on the practices of small firms that lack the protection of government employment. Beyond these extremes were a number of differing positions: the generational divide, public sector workers' own assertions of the need to be more efficient, and the critical consciousness of highly politicised workers. The latter's worldviews were informed by class analysis and subsequently presented a critique of the ethos of market citizenship which asserts that a broader recognition of the disadvantages stemming from privatisation and deregulation—disadvantages not just personal, but also to others. These conflicting sentiments are explored below.

Privatization and Deregulation

An overwhelming majority of respondents disputed privatisation could bring many benefits to people in West Bengal. This related to their attitudes towards the nature of the private sector. A number of people (17%) argued that privatisation would lead to job losses and contribute to growing unemployment. Furthermore, a belief in the advantages of privatisation of state enterprises is largely confined to those in managerial, professional and high-tech positions.

Respondents repeatedly emphasised the safety nets offered in government employment. Not only was private enterprise characterised by insecurity; it was inherently driven by a profit motive. Conversely, government organisations were identified as being more humane. They often compared the callous attitude of the private sector with the compassionate nature of the state. Although it was young people who most readily embraced privatisation and positive views of the private sector, however, when confronted by some of its deleterious effects they became trenchant critics. As a young police woman noted,

> In private organisations you can sack an employee according to the proprietor's whim. It may have nothing to do with the performance of the employee. In government jobs unless you have done anything illegal, you cannot be got rid of like that.
>
> (*Woman Aged 51, Lower Division Clerk, Reserve Bank of India*)

> They overwork you in a private firm according to their whim. In government service you get promoted according to merit. In private enterprise, if they like you, they'll promote you.
>
> (*Male Aged 34, Library Clerk*)

Asserting that IMF clauses on adjustment were farcical, some key informants argued that economic liberalisation was a policy choice engineered entirely by powerful classes and the incumbent government would implement them anyway, in an undemocratic fashion. However, others countered this by pointing out that the Government had excluded citizens from the process and that the reforms had not been implemented according to the original plans. These conflicting perspectives were primarily determined by respondent's respective location in public and private sectors. Those supportive of liberalisation, mainly formal private sector workers, felt that the ethos of hard work and efficiency inherent in the private sector should prevail among government employees. The advocates of liberalist reforms included workers from large private corporations, private school teachers and a handful of highly qualified civil servants—and young people in general. Their opinions were predominantly negative on government employees, particularly their tendencies towards laziness. Typically they were from genteel social backgrounds who had either never worked nor were inclined to public sector employment. Points amply illustrated in excerpts taken from an interview with a tertiary educated single woman in mid-30s.

Tapati[33], a freelance project worker with an average estimated annual income of Rs. 48,000—of which she saves Rs. 4000 per month. The family income is over Rs. 25,000 per month. However, this was not always the case. During her early 20s the family faced disaster, losing the head of the family to untimely death. As the eldest child it was imperative to find employment. As she explained, "…my mother said to me, 'try to find a job—something in the technical area, perhaps. The other children are still studying. You've got to do something'…".

All was not as it seemed amongst the private sector employees: while they dismissed their public sector counterparts for lacking the appropriate resolve, many were well aware of their own exploitative conditions. Some were embittered by the shabby treatment they received from their own firms, and despite their outward praise of their firms, during formal interviews, some spoke confidentially about pending insecurities, particularly in transnational corporations that were experiencing global down-turns. Contradictory attitudes towards the public sector also prevailed among teachers in private schools, who while continually asserting the superiority of their institution over government schools also were anxious to downplay their own job insecurities.

There were, of course, those who were fully supportive of the public sector. They were of the belief that the criticisms that were often levelled by their private sector counterparts were, in the main, unwarranted and erroneous. The following comment from one who had shifted from private sector to public sector challenged the commonly held views:

> ...there is a usual assumption that in the government sector there is no work culture, but if you look around here everyone is deeply involved in their work. You won't even find this kind of commitment within a private firm. No I'll never want privatisation.

As public sector employees they defended their sector's continued existence. And while some respondents acknowledged the deficiencies of their government departments, they were dismissive of the critiques of inefficiency and the absence of work culture. Instead, they asserted that the shortcomings were trivial and we should not obsessively focus on them. More significantly they challenged the bogey of privatisation. One informant surmised, "...If this place is privatised there is no guarantee that it would be more efficient or that people would work more." In general, they were emphatic that government departments should not be judged according to the private sector performances since some key institutions and utilities cannot be privatised.

The failure to attract foreign investment is one of the key arguments used by neo-liberals to promote the need for reform. Indeed, such promotions have led to intense public debates on investment and infrastructure. Our respondents remained unconvinced that transnational corporations will do anything positive concerning investment which will benefit Indians, and were generally suspicious of privatisation and foreign investment. While some respondents' views reflect anti-colonial in attitudes, especially among the older generation, there has been nevertheless a considerable shift in views. Many of the respondents reflected this reality when they argued that though inherently just and rational, bureaucratic procedures of the state might be cumbersome compared with the speed of private enterprise. Even those opposed to privatisation on ideological grounds nevertheless urged government organisations to become more efficient.

Summary of Indian Interview Data

It would be incorrect to assume that our informants espouse the business and government neo-liberal rhetoric because they are deceived by ideology. Clearly they use themes of competition and deregulation in complex ways whereby they neither reject nor accept them. In other words, our respondents do not subscribe to neo-liberal ideologies in a uniform and coherent way. A number of people have internalised the state's rhetoric of global efficiency. The influences of the changing nature of policy orientation in West Bengal are crucial to understanding the responses of people in this study. Whilst remaining critical of liberalisation, many of our informants espouse the government rhetoric of work place restructuring and global competitiveness. The particular world views and lived experiences of the lower middle class show at one level an antipathy toward liberalisation and globalisation and yet, on another, they express a desire for India, and Indians, to move forward and compete in an increasingly globalised, cosmopolitan world. Indeed, as Sridharan has written:

> The post-1991 liberalisation, however, has been sustained, even if the pace of change has been slower than many advocates of reform might have liked. Indeed, unlike many other countries that have undertaken programmes of economic liberalisation, India has introduced reform very gradually. At times the pace of change has been downright glacial, with India's trade and capital regimes remaining among the more restrictive in the world. This can perhaps be explained by, among other factors, the growth of the broadest middle class since the 1980s. This has had the contradictory effect of leading to a support base for liberalisation while at the same the sheer weight of public employees and publicly subsidised agriculturists in this economic category have served to constrain the progress of certain types of economic reforms[34].

Thus, economic liberalisation is by no means an accepted dogma. In various ways there is evidence of fundamental dissatisfaction, frustration and mistrust with the process.

The Australian Scenario: The Advance of Neo-liberalism in Economic Understandings

The evidence indicating the degree of acceptance or otherwise of neo-liberal economic policies by the Australian middle class has been mixed, however, as a host of facts demonstrate, it appears to have nevertheless made successful inroads in shaping generally favourable sentiments among not only the middle class but a significant proportion of the Australian population. That this is indeed the case is demonstrated most effectively in the political arena—where neo-liberal economic reform has been a bi-partisan project for several decades. The political parties capable of forming government in Australia have, over the last twenty-years, fundamentally agreed with the economically liberalist agenda and as such, both major parties have pursued it relentlessly[35]. They have agreed because it is electorally appropriate, and therefore 'safe', for them to do so, especially as it has become the normative, and thus expected, discourse of the electoral marketplace—the *lingua franca* of contemporary political contests.

This bi-partisanship towards the adoption of neoliberal solutions to perceived economic and social ills, and as the means for the establishment of the basis of a multitude of benefits and ongoing prosperity, is significant in itself. The arguments of governments, and therefore the understandings of the electorate, have moved beyond questions concerning whether or not there is a problem with the state's retreat from service provision and nation building, to being concerned with the actual nature and manner of the state's role in facilitating the conditions for economic reform. As Brodie explains, "...state power has been redeployed from social welfare concerns and economic management to the enforcement of the market model in virtually all aspects of life".[36]. And, in most respects, as continuing election results have indicated, the Australian people have taken this on board. That is not to say that there is not a significant body of dissent, simply that the politics of recent years has ensured that dissent in regard to most issues, and particularly in the economic domain, has been segregated, diluted and conflated to an anti-Australian discourse[37].

Some analysts have presented data that has suggested that significant sections of the population, particularly among what he has described as 'middle Australia', are experiencing the 'dark side' of economic reform—where, for example, family life has been placed under increasing strain and difficulty owing to the increased demands of the new economic order[38]. However, there is also evidence to suggest that this indeed may be not as universal as is being suggested. Other research suggests that 'reform fatigue' is perhaps an issue among what may be considered as the traditional middle class constituency: professionals, managers, financial and other technical service workers, and so on, but not among many of the aspiring classes. For instance, Clive Hamilton claims that the lower middle class, or those being addressed by my research, namely the emergent middle classes, or aspiring working class individuals and groups, are seemingly supportive of recent economic developments, to the extent that they want to be included in the economic rewards[39]. That is, they are demanding access to the expanding array of novel consumer goods, upgraded housing, private education and health services, etc, that have long been the prerogative of the traditional middle and upper classes.

In Hamilton's paper, *Over consumption in Australia: the rise of the middle class battler*, he agrees with Pusey's findings which point to growing family strain from increased work hours, growing indebtedness, etc. He nevertheless also found that this was not a disincentive for many, from a number of different socio-economic positions, to pursue the consumerist and upward social and economic mobility goals held out as benefits in the discourses of neo-liberalism as propagated by business organisations and the political parties. The point being, that despite apparent negative effects of pursuing these goals, such as overworking and increased indebtedness, there has been an increasing trend amongst groups of Australians to believe that increased wealth and consumer goods are possible for everyone if they work hard. Which is in itself a significant shift over the last couple of decades in the expectations of many Australians. As Hamilton says,

> Once Australians were known for their willingness to balance work and family life, but the desire for greater consumption, along with labour market reforms, has put an end to that. Although most parents recognise that excessive work harms children, many seem unable to scale down their levels of desire to spend more time at home[40].

And indeed, with Hamilton's analysis in mind, we come to understand the circumstances of the subject group of the research. That is, the so-called 'aspirational class': those from once self-identifying working class backgrounds who, according to media and political reports, have incorporated the discourses of the market to the degree that they find themselves with what Hamilton identifies in his generic description of the attitude of the times, with "...inflated expectations"[41]. Thus, on the face of many indications, these people have abandoned past relationships with Keynesian collectivism as manifest in the strong and involved state, and see their economic and social salvation as existing in the individualist policies of the present political and economic orthodoxy.

The Research Subjects: The Aspirational Class

The point to make at the outset, and it is indeed a most salient factor, is that the subjects of this research, the aspirational class, came to public prominence not by any systematic research or social analysis but instead were the product of the media punditry seeking to explain particular party preferential shifts in critical electorates in increasingly hard fought elections. Thus, it is indeed difficult to be definitive in any authentic sense beyond that which has been propagated in the media as their defining characteristics.

Perhaps, the best way to understand this group is in terms of an *idea*—an idea coined and propagated by the media, and nurtured and employed by parliamentarians as a political mechanism; an idea that was therefore strategically used to illustrate and thus present a particular set of attitudes and political beliefs which, as it happened, was out of the neo-liberal mould. The central theme of the idea that was propagated was of a way of thinking that equates with change: change of mind, of attitude and expectation, and thus, a change of behaviour. And indeed, as the media reported and the politicians endorsed, a central component of this change was identified as a desire amongst this group to adopt the precepts inherent in the discourses of neo-liberalism in their economic and social behaviours, and as such perceive of themselves as an upwardly mobile group of consumers and entrepreneurs. Adding to this sense were the constant interjections in the social discussion of prominent politicians, such as the Prime Minister John Howard, regaling the nation with his belief that we were indeed becoming the "greatest share-owning democracy on the planet."

This group, according to the media and political reports, who had once been regarded (in terms of their familial backgrounds) as working class, and indeed would have once regarded itself as working class, now were looking beyond what this entailed in the past popular imagination. The title of 'working class' allegedly no longer held any material, or indeed romantic allure, for them that perhaps it once would have, but instead it now equated with a stigma: thus it appeared that not being working class anymore was the best way to remove this. This conjunction of media and political constructions is exemplified in Raymond Williams' description of the desire of many in the West in recent decades to shed any tie to a working class past:

> 'Working class' for many people, is simply a memory of poverty, bad housing and exposure, while 'middle class' is a name for money to spend, better housing, and a more furnished and controllable life…the strong sense of 'working' = 'lower' class, with inferiorities and deprivations to which nobody in his senses wants to return'[42].

In a very short time, following their appearance in the media in the late 1990s, the concept of the aspirational class became a widely known component of the political vocabulary employed by political and social commentators. As such, a particularistic detailed profile quickly developed within the media's presentation to denote a supposedly homogenous group with recognisable characteristics and behaviours. Along with the material profile came an address: the outer rapidly expanding suburbs of the major eastern coast cities such as Sydney, Melbourne and Brisbane. However it was the inhabitants of outer suburban Sydney that exemplified this alleged group, principally because this was the site of the electorates that included these fringe suburbs, where significant political shifts to the right were occurring. These once Labor-voting working class electorates were changing orientation to the socially conservative and economically liberal policies of the Liberal National Coalition

Government. The profiles were completed with the identification of the *economies* of their nominated habitats. That is, sites that were experiencing rapid economic growth: in housing estates, service industries (service and technology industries) and industrial development (small manufacturing and warehousing).

The description of the aspirationals have been varied, a product of the sheer number of interpretations. Some such as political scientist Nick Economou (2001) described them as "... upper middle class...[who were] interested in the national debate and...want answers to policy-specific issues"[43]. Whereas others have defined them as 'lower middle class', or indeed, have described them as *hard pressed families* "... living on a financial knife edge as the result of huge mortgages due to Sydney's astronomical land and housing values"[44]. Clearly, many and varied views: a scenario that does little to develop the group beyond the conceptual. However, it is in the analyses offered by politicians that one sees the real essence of the aspirational class as an ideology encapsulated.

Former Labor leader Mark Latham, said by some to be the author of the term 'aspirational class', describes them as shareholders and owners. As he reflected on his former, outer Western Sydney electorate of Werriwa,

The big thing that has changed in the outer suburbs is ownership, small business ownership, share ownership, skills and opportunity. These are working class aspirants who are looking...to better themselves and their families.... I represent an aspirational electorate. An electorate where ownership matters...they're moving into asset accumulation and home ownership.[45]

On the government side of politics, the Liberal Party's local member (Ross Cameron) for the electorate of Parramatta, a middle range Western Sydney electorate, took a remarkable similar view to that of his political opponent in his descriptions of the aspirationals. Following the Conservative Coalition's victory in the 2001 Federal Election he ascribed the win to the local identity with aspirationalism[46]. The media reflected this, as seen comments by a local Parramatta reporter, who stated that:

... I think that the Liberals had a theory that the area was becoming what they call 'aspirational class'. First homebuyers, small business operators who aspire to, I guess, becoming more wealthy. We did speak to some small business operators and one person said, "I aspire to pay my own way and look after myself". And that was very much the mantra that Ross Cameron was reinforcing[47].

The Method

Owing to the diffuse nature (as seen in the array of aspirational interpretations) of the putative subject group, the research clearly had to be confined to themes germane to the media-propagated constructions of the aspirationals. As such, small interview samples (10) within each of the three electorates (Werriwa, Macarthur and Parramatta), with a broader comparative sample taken from the wider Sydney metropolitan area (also 10 respondents) were regarded as appropriate to the task of eliciting a confirmation or otherwise of the attitudes concerning economically liberal policy prescriptions[48]. Thus, each respondent underwent a lengthy 'discussion' of salient contemporary issues, which in turn were analysed in terms of their display of particular thematic strands (such as this theme of the penetration of economic rationalism into their lives). The only variables under consideration for the selection of the interviewees were those of location within the particular electorates and being active economic participants. No specific categories such as gender, age and or ethnic background were established for the analysis.

The questions asked involved issues concerning contemporary developments in economic policy and how these issues were understood. That is: the importance of economics in their lives; what were the key economic questions and how they should best be managed; governmental management of the economy; opinions on economic reforms; globalisation and national economic policy sovereignty; sources of belief in economics, and, hopes and fears (if they existed) about the directions that economic policy was heading.

The Settings

As stated above, the broad setting for the fieldwork among those deemed aspirational took place in their home suburbs in the mid to far west of Sydney: specifically in the electorates of Werriwa, Macarthur and Parramatta. Macarthur was actually described by the Australian Electoral Commission as 'semi-rural', Werriwa as 'outer suburban', while Parramatta was described as 'middle-suburban'. The three electorates have been for many years sites of tight electoral battles which has seen them change party hands on a number of occasions. Although, today two of the electorates are Labor, while only Macarthur is held by the Government (Parramatta having recently changed hands in the 2004 election). However, regardless of their particular party brand, they are all sites that have been identified as aspirational in countless media articles, and attributed, by the media and politicians, with large populations of aspirational voters. It could thus be said that their varied political affiliations are a testament to the earlier point of the lack of any significant ideological differentiation between the major political parties—making elections for these seats a contest of personalities rather than competitive ideological contests. While they were ostensibly diverse, with their differing political party affiliations and the geographical separation of Parramatta from the other two, they nevertheless had the key factor of having been labelled aspirational, and furthermore, they were each sites of vigorous economic development—something that was continuing despite a slowdown in other parts of Sydney.

As such, ideal sites, in terms of alleged transformation of attitude from Keynesianism to Monetarism.

The Findings

The main point to emerge from the study was that while there was no uniformity of view, there nevertheless was a general predisposition towards favouring the possibilities inherent in the neo-liberal discourses. That is, while each respondent offered varying interpretations of the specific questions they remained either generally upbeat, or untroubled, by contemporary economic policies and economic management (as they did or did not understand it). Yet interestingly, in the main, most were unable to offer what would be regarded as a coherent set of understandings of the past and present state of economic reforms—at least, in anything approaching a comprehensive sense. Surprisingly, in terms of the media profile that had been constructed around them as astute observers of the 'economy', they had minimal technical knowledge of the economy's operations; only a partial awareness of the range of reforms that had been undertaken in recent years; and were only marginally interested in the range of extant economic policy matters.[49] What appeared to garner interest were specific issues such as interest rates (the majority were mortgages) and the 'costs' of consumer goods. Thus, economic issues *per se* were predominantly understood in personal terms (or in what might be described as personal cost-benefit-analyses); however, they were all generally in agreement that the economy was being reasonably well managed without really being able to explain the details of how this management was appropriate to the times and the social conditions.

For example: in a typical response, when asked '*whether or not the pace and style of economic reform made them angry, pleased or uninterested*', one respondent said:

> … I have not followed the reform process that closely and therefore I do not know much about it, but from what I am aware of, I do not feel overwhelmed by it (34-year old female public servant)

In another answer to the same question, another said:

> … I am not aware of many of these things as having occurred so it is a bit hard for me to answer that question (32-year old single full time mother of three; recently separated).

In a similar vein, when asked of the '*most pressing reform issues that needed to be addressed by government*'. One respondent, in a somewhat typical fashion, told me that "… Much of it is a bit over my head…it leaves me a bit flat" (40 year female old retail worker). Further, one respondent suggested that reforms: "… we have been told a lot of rubbish about economic reforms", however, he went on to praise the record of economic management of the government, "... I think that Peter Costello has been a good Treasurer and has managed the economy well" (39-year old male self-employed computer technician).

Similar observances on similar questions were found among those from the broader Sydney comparative cohort—surprisingly, from those who may have been considered to have differing opinions, coming as they did from traditional ideologically left-oriented constituencies. One 45 year old male 'consultant' said in answer to the above-mentioned question on '*whether or not economic reforms had pleased, displeased etc*:

> It is hard to say what the years of reforms have actually done, I guess I have been ambivalent...[however, more specifically, he added]...yet, it seems to have served me individually in that I have been able to work outside many of the constraining structures to establish a work style that suits me and allows for diversity and change, to work as an independent-free-flowing consultant.

The above-mentioned *faith* in the current economic policy directions was prevalent among a noticeable majority of the respondents from both the aspirational settings and the broader Sydney metropolitan comparative sample. There were, of course, examples of those who were unhappy with the current economic policy orthodoxy (approximately 20 per cent of all respondents), and there were subjects who were ambivalent about economic issues generally (10 per cent). However, these two groups, like virtually all the rest of the respondents, do not offer an alternative philosophy for governing economic policy matters when presented with the opportunity to do so.

For example: in the sense of the majority of respondents, when asked '*whether or not they believed that the economy served us or that we now served it, and how this should be addressed if it was a problem*', a respondent summarised the general mood and inclination of the respondents (in the way they gave little thought to the broader scenario and focused on personal interpretations), when he said that:

> The economy and the demands of the market certainly have taken on a life of their own, and that is not hard to understand—although I would say that it is not something that I or perhaps anybody else thinks about much. With this in mind, I believe that we should just do what we need to survive, that is, the everyday things we do in the economy. (*45 year old male, self-employed truck driver*)

In a more specific sense the responses generated from the fieldwork interviews amongst those reputed to be aspirationals confirmed the belief that there was certainly an appreciation of the basic themes of neo-liberalism, especially as manifest in the political rhetoric of government—if not any detailed understanding. Most attributed their reasonable (“*although, they could always be better*”) circumstances to the current management that has been very much oriented towards neo-liberalist prescriptions. In fact, most seemed to agree with the proposition that the nation was being ‘soundly’ economically managed. They knew that unemployment was low, inflation was low, and importantly for the majority, interest rates were at an historical low—these were *the* evidence and the substance of sound economic management. Their assessments were personal and extremely pragmatic and as such overrode any consideration of either wider or specific ‘cause and effect’ issues of current economic policy settings. But, they nevertheless expressed their views in the discourse of the market: ‘we need to be more efficient’; ‘we need to work harder’; ‘we need to reduce the influence of trade unions’; ‘implement lower taxes on income’, etc. Sentiments such as these comprised the responses of a clear majority of the interviews. However, when asked about the possible threat posed by significant issues, such as the Current Account Deficit (which is at an historic high), and which could have been construed as ‘bad’ economic management, they either were not aware of it or did not see it in terms of it being a problem for them. It was therefore, an individualistic assessment that was made on one side of the economic policy questions: a scenario that indeed can only be seen as an exemplification of the permeation of neo-liberal inspiration of thoughts, speech and practices of many Australians.

Conclusion

From both the Indian and Australian interviews there was a clear demonstration that things were certainly changing in terms of the increasing influence of neo-liberalist ideologies and prescriptions. It was evident that despite some variations in the data that was specifically context related, the neo-liberal policies was indeed making significant inroads into the thinking, and thus the discourse and practices, of middle class people in both India and Australia.

Expectedly, the Australian data was more uniform, in a comparative sense with that from India, due to two clear factors: population size and its distribution, and the state of economic development. However, these points in themselves perhaps make the finding that there has been a significant penetration of neo-liberalism in both contexts in a somewhat similar scale, all the more convincing. That is, considering India’s massive population imbalance with Australia, and thus with its cultural diversity, the fact that evidence was found there that indicated the presence of neo-liberalist thought in the behaviours and responses of people, albeit in not a uniform and predominant fashion, was powerful in itself. While a large population base might itself suggest that ‘some’ evidence of this presence *would* inevitably be found—simply by sheer statistical probability—that evidence of some change was found and was evident across such a cross-section of the population was strong confirmation that this was more than just a statistical '*possibility*'. In both traditional settings where old practices and emotional attachments remained strong, and in more contemporary scenarios in the public sector, there were *slight cracks* in the facade of long-held views. It was not so much evidence that could be regarded as an epiphany, but evidence that consideration and questioning was occurring. In Australia, with its much smaller population and with a dominant cultural perspective holding sway in the political arena, and thus amongst a significant proportion of the population, the evidence was much more apparent that the cracks had become gaping holes.

Thus, whether in the workplace in West Bengal, or in the investment options and general level of satisfaction with the predominantly neo-liberal economic management of the Australian economy, neo-liberalism has made a significant impact on the lives of citizens. Whether it is an actual change of practices and thinking, or in the beginnings of the process of questioning of older and more traditional modes of operation, such as Keynesian state-interventionist policy prescriptions, changes were afoot, and as such, were being surrounded by an ever growing sense, and indeed repertoire, of expectations— particularly amongst those, who until recently, had very moderate expectations of a vastly different socio-economic environment.

End Notes

1. The Indian section of the paper was prepared by Tim Scrase; the Australian research written by John Robinson. Both authors wrote the concluding sections.
2. Indian field research was jointly carried-out with Dr. Ruchira Ganguly-Scrase (University of Wollongong) and was partially funded by an Australian Research Council small grant; Charles Sturt University; and the University of Wollongong.
3. Australian field research was partially funded by the Faculty of Arts, University of Wollongong.
4. See: John Brohman, Universalism, Eurocentrism, and Ideological bias in Development Studies: From Modernisation to Neo-liberalism, *Third World Quarterly*, Vol. 16, No. 1, 1995, pp. 121-140; Alexandro Portes, Neoliberalism and the Sociology of Development: Emerging Trends and Unanticipated Facts, *Population and Development Review*, Vol. 23, No. 22, 1997, pp. 229-59; Branislav Gosovic (2000), Global Intellectual Hegemony and the International Development Agenda, *International Social Science Journal*, Vol. 52, pp. 447-56.
5. Timothy J. Scrase and T.J.M. Holden Scott Baum, eds., *Globalization, Culture, and Inequality in Asia* (Melbourne: Trans Pacific Press, 2003).
6. Richard Robison and David Goodman, eds., *The New Rich in Asia: Mobile Phones, McDonalds and Middle Class Revolution* (London: Routledge, 1996).
7. As far as this is understood in the terms of the contemporary definitions of 'developed', and 'developing'.

8. J. Bhagavati, *India in Transition: Freeing the Economy* (Oxford: Clarendon Press, 1993); I.J. Ahluwalia and M.D. Little, eds., *India's Economic Reforms and Development: Essays for Manmohan Singh* (New Delhi: Oxford University Press, 1998).
9. Stuart Corbridge and John Harriss, *Reinventing India: Liberalization, Hindu Nationalism and Popular Democracy* (Cambridge: Polity Press, 2000); C.P. Chandrasekhar and Jayati Ghosh, *The Market that Failed: A Decade of Economic Reforms in India* (New Delhi: Left World Books, 2002); Anjan Chakrabarti and Stephen Cullenberg, *Transition and Development in India* (New York: Routledge, 2003).
10. David Harvey, *The Condition of Postmodernity* (Oxford: Blackwell, 1990).
11. Chantal Mouffe, Hegemony and Ideology in Gramsci, in Tony Bennett *et al*. eds., *Culture, Ideology and Social Process: A Reader* (London: The Open University Press, 1981), p. 230.
12. Stuart Hall, *The Hard Road to Renewal: Thatcherism and the Crisis of the Left* (London: Verso, 1988).
13. Hall, Hard Road, p. 166.
14. Hall, Hard Road, p. 143.
15. Branislav Gosovic (2000), "Global Intellectual Hegemony and the International Development Agenda", *International Social Science Journal*, Vol. 52, pp. 447-456.
16. Gosovic, GIH, pp. 450; 453.
17. Gosovic, GIH, p. 452.
18. Pierre Bourdieu, *Acts of Resistance: Against The New Myths of Our Time* (Cambridge Polity Press, 1998).
19. Bourdieu, Acts, p. 82.
20. Bourdieu, Acts, p. 82.
21. Neo-liberalism had led to a model of rational economic action which functions to legitimise and reduce governmental regulation. The government itself becomes a sort of enterprise whose position is to universalise competition and create market shaped systems of action. Neo-liberalism does not locate the rational principle for regulating and diminishing the interference of government in a natural freedom. It instead places it in the context of an artificially arranged liberty that is with the economic rational individual in the form of entrepreneurial and competitive behaviour (See: Thomas Lenke, The Birth Of Bio-Politics: Michel Foucault's Lecture at the *College De France* On Neo Liberal Governmentality, *Economy and Society*, Vol. 30, 2001, pp. 109-207.
22. Ulrich Beck, Living Your Own Life in a Runaway World: Individualisation, Globalisation and Politics, in Will Hutton and Anthony Giddens, eds., *On the Edge: Living with Global Capitalism* (London: Jonathon Cape, 2000), pp. 164-74.
23. Beck, Living Your Own Life, p. 167.
24. Satish Deshpande, After Culture: Renewed Agendas for the Political Economy of India, *Cultural Dynamics*, Vol. 10, No. 2 (July), 1998, pp. 147-169; V.G. Kulkarni, "The Middle Class Bulge, *Far Eastern Economic Review*, Vol. 156, No. 2, 1993, pp. 44-6; Salim Lakha, "The State, Globalization, and the Indian Middle-Class Identity," in Michael Pinches, ed., *Culture and Privilege in Capitalist Asia*, London: Routledge, 1999, pp. 251-274.

25. Arjun Appadurai and Carol Breckenridge, Public Modernity in India, in Arjun Appadurai and Carol Breckenridge, eds., *Consuming Modernity: Public Culture in a South Asian World*, (Minneapolis: University of Minnesota Press, 1995), pp. 1-20; Timothy J. Scrase, Television, the Middle Classes and the Transformation of Cultural Identities in West Bengal, India, *Gazette: The International Journal for Communication Studies*, vol. 64, No. 4, 2002, pp. 323-342; Margit van Wessel, Talking About Consumption: How an Indian Middle Class Dissociates from Middle Class Life, *Cultural Dynamics*, Vol. 16, No. 1, 2004, pp. 93-116.
26. Ruchira Ganguly-Scrase, Paradoxes of Globalization, Liberalization and Gender Equality: The Worldviews of the Lower Middle Classes in West Bengal, *Gender and Society*, Vol. 17, No. 4, 2003, pp. 544-66.
27. Satish Deshpande, After Culture: Renewed Agendas for the Political Economy of India, *Cultural Dynamics*, Vol. 10, No. 2, July 1998, pp. 147-69.
28. Krishna Sen and Maila Stivens, *Gender and Power in Affluent Asia*, (London: Routledge), p. 15.
29. The approximate exchange rate at the time of fieldwork was Indian Rupees (Rs.) 40.00 = US$1.00. Thus, their monthly household income ranges from US$50-200. This concurs with research delineating the 1998-2000 income levels of the middle classes in India reported in E. Sridharan, The Growth and Sectoral Composition of India's Middle Class: Its Impact on the Politics of Economic Liberalization, *India Review*, Vol. 3, No. 4, 2004, pp. 405-428.
30. It has been argued that in West Bengal that "... class stratification is imbedded to a great extent within the hierarchy of castes" (Surajit Sinha and R. Bhattacharya, *Bhadralok* and *Chotolok* in a Rural Area of West Bengal, *Sociological Bulletin*, Vol. 18, 1969, p. 56). More significantly, a complex interlinkage of economic position, status and caste relations and the dynamics of political power shape the formation of social classes in West Bengal.
31. Dipankar Bhattacharya, Political Economy of Reforms, *Economic and Political Weekly*, Vol. XXXIV, No. 23, 1999, pp. 1408-10; R. Nagaraj, What has happened since 1991? Assessment of India's Economic Reforms, *Economic and Political Weekly*, Vol. 32, Nos. 44/45, 1997, pp. 2869-79; Fumiko Oshikawa, *South Asia Under the Economic Reforms* (Osaka: National Museum of Ethnology, 1999); Jorgen Dige Pedersen, Explaining Economic Liberalization in India: State and Society Perspectives, *World Development*, Vol. 28, No. 2, 2000, pp. 265-282. Stuart Corbridge and John Harris, *Reinventing India: Liberalization, Hindu Nationalism and Popular Democracy* (Cambridge: Polity Press, 2000).
32. Lakha, Middle Class Identity; van Wessel, Talking About Consumption.
33. Pseudonyms are used throughout this paper.
34. Sridharan, *The Growth and Sectoral Composition*, pp. 424-25.
35. In fact, the traditional party of labour (the ALP) has perhaps been more vigorous and technocratic in its approach than the traditional party of capital (Liberal party).
36. Cited in Carol Johnson, *Governing Change: From Keating to Howard* (St Lucia: University of Queensland Press, 2000), p. 100.
37. Which in an era of the "War on Terror", immigration problems, etc., has achieved a widespread purchase.

38. Michael Pusey, *The Experience of Middle Australia: The Dark Side of Economic Reform*, (Cambridge: Cambridge University Press, 2003).
39. Clive Hamilton, *Over Consumption in Australia. The Rise of the Middle-class Battler*, (Discussion Paper Number no. 49; Canberra: The Australia Institute, 2002).
40. Hamilton, Over consumption in Australia, p. viii.
41. Hamilton, Over consumption in Australia, p. viii.
42. Raymond Williams *Keywords* (London: Fontana, 1985), p. 60.
43. Nick Economou, *Aston by-election Draws to a Close*, (Transcript of Interview, *7.30 Report 10/7/2001,* Australian Broadcasting Corporation, www.abc.net.au/7.30/; accessed 15/7/05).
44. Mike Head, Australian Election Reveals the Decay of Parliamentary politics, (www.wsws.org/articles/2001/nov2001/aust-n14.shtml; accessed 15/7/05); p. 5.
45. Mark Latham, *Latham Rejoins Labor Front Bench*, (Transcript of Interview, *7.30 Report 23/11/2001,* Australian Broadcasting Corporation, www.abc.net.au/7.30/; accessed 15/7/05).
46. Geraldine Doogue, *Parramatta Election Panel*, (Transcripts of radio programme: *Life Matters 06/11/01*, Radio National, Australian Broadcasting Corporation; www.abc.net.au/rn/lifematters; accessed 28/7/05).
47. Ross Cameron, R. Stewart, J. Smith, and A. Soltau, *Parramatta signals Labor Loss*, (Transcripts of radio programme: *PM, 12/11/01*, Radio National, Australian Broadcasting Corporation; www.abc.net.au/pm; accessed 28/7/05).
48. This 'change of attitude on economic reform' aspect of the study was but one component of a far broader series of research issues aimed at constructing a more generalised worldview: with accompanying issues concerning politics, class, ideology, taxation and fiscal policy, and political philosophy.
49. Indeed, this was the case in the comparative cohort which included areas that had publicly acknowledged traditions of leftist ideological beliefs.

19

Reflections on India-Australia—USA Strategic Triangle

CHINTAMANI MAHAPATRA

The time has come to think the unthinkable. A few years ago, it would have been considered an intellectual madness to speak of a strategic triangle consisting of India, Australia and the United States. In the emerging context of the changing geopolitical transformations, it is perhaps necessary to contemplate upon a strategic triangle of these three countries.

Gone are the days when nation-states around the globe were teaming up with their strategic partners to form military alliances or coming together to avoid participating in the Cold War conflicts. Australia and India belonged to two different groups of nations—the former joined the US-led triangular alliance called ANZUS, a British-led five nations alliance called FPDA (Five Power Defense Arrangement) and the latter provided leadership to large number of Non-Aligned Group of nations. Significantly, the non-aligned India did not have any vital differences with Australia affecting national security. But at the level of Cold War rhetoric the Indian and Australian leadership did not see eye to eye on several international issues. Canberra posed itself as a champion of nuclear non-proliferation and differed with India on this issue. But, if we consider from the hindsight knowledge, Australia did not do anything concrete to harm Indian interests. The Indo-Australian differences over the proliferation issues were confined to political arena and diplomatic moves in international forums. And, in any case, Australia was not alone in its crusade against nuclear proliferation. It largely mirrored non-proliferation concerns of the US and occasionally sounded more serious than Washington on such issues.

The second significant area where Canberra and Washington differed with India was the question of peace and stability in the Indian Ocean region. India championed the cause of a zone of peace in the Indian Ocean and demanded as a very first step removal of big power navies from this region. Australia, on the other hand, welcomed the US presence in the Indian Ocean as a stabilising factor and offered naval facilities to the American navy. Despite these differences, neither Australia nor the US took any major steps that would have hurt Indian interests in the Indian Ocean. Australia as a matter of policy focused more on the eastern front facing the Pacific and, according to Australian analysts, neglected its interests in the Indian Ocean region. The US no doubt established a powerful naval base in Diego Garcia and built a Rapid Reaction Force. But its facilities in the Indian Ocean region were not centred on India. India fell under the jurisdiction of America's Pacific fleet!

It is true that both Australia and the United States had established alliance relationship with India's one of the paramount regional enemies—Pakistan—during the Cold War years. Looking back at those years, one finds that neither Australia nor the United States declared war against India in support of Pakistan at the time of the 1965 or 1971 Indo-Pakistani wars. When Pakistan complained, the US promptly argued that the alliance—Southeast Asia Treaty Organisation (SEATO)—consisting of eight countries, including the US and Australia was a common front against Communist expansionism and nothing else. New Delhi was enraged when the Nixon Administration dispatched the USS fleet Enterprise to the Bay of Bengal in an apparent symbolic warning to India to refrain from attacking West Pakistan. But the fact remains that the US and Australia did precious little to protect East Pakistan, which was almost sure to emerge as an independent country by the time the US battleship reached the Bay of Bengal.

It needs to be appreciated that the Cold War environment was different and it had its own effect on the thinking of scholars and government officials. The suspicious ambiance around the globe generated a tension that prevented optimisation of economic cooperation between countries. Political considerations and strategic imperatives guided economic policies. Despite this phenomenon, India maintained a modicum of economic cooperation and educational exchanges with Australia and the United States. There was no rupture of relationship, although the Cold War climate prevented best possible economic and technological collaborations.

The end of the Cold War, collapse of the Soviet Union, India's emergence as a nuclear weapon power, growing security cooperation between India and the US, India's rise as an economic power house and IT major power, unprecedented increase in the capability of international terrorist organisations marked by the 9/11 incident and the threat of nuclear terrorism have altered the global political landscape, economic scene and security scenario. The emerging scenario appears to have created a near perfect setting for the establishment of a strategic triangle comprising the US, Australia and India.

First of all the Soviet collapse has ended the cold war for all time to come and the cold war equations of the past is no longer going to hunt Indo-US and Indo-Australian ties. It became relatively easy for India to establish better relations with the Americans and the Australians, since those two countries never considered India to be an enemy country. They only grumbled that a non-aligned and democratic country like India preferred to befriend the totalitarian Soviet Communists to establish closer security understanding with the West. This irritation, however, had little logical relevance in view of the fact that the US sought strategic understanding with the largest Communist country in the world, the People's Republic of China. Interestingly, in the post-Cold War era, India, the US and Australia—all three—sought closer economic ties with China. As the US opened a new chapter in its relations with India, Australia did not delay in doing so. The initial excitement was, of course, guided by commercial considerations in the wake of a rising middle class in India and the economic openness adopted by the successive governments in India. Had the Soviet Union remained intact, economic opportunities alone perhaps could not have contributed much to this relationship.

Secondly, India's decision to overtly go nuclear by defying the international efforts to ban nuclear testing did affect India's ties with both the US and Australia. But it was short-lived. The Clinton Administration, which had proposed a policy of "freeze, cap and roll back" to eliminate the nuclear weapons programme in the Indian subcontinent, imposed sanctions on India soon after the Indian nuclear tests of May 1998. Those who complain about the inability of the US to prevent Indian nuclear explosions should realise that the Clinton Administration could do precious little to prevent Pakistan from going nuclear, although it had more leverage over Islamabad than over New Delhi. President Bill Clinton did not waste much time by breast beating. He took the initiative to forge a new kind of cooperative relations with a nuclear India. Even as several rounds of nuclear dialogue continued between high level Indian and American political leadership, President Bill Clinton chose to visit India in March 2000 to craft and implement a new bilateral structure of relationship. Australian Prime Minister followed the footsteps of the US President and decided to put aside Canberra's reservations on nuclear issue by forging a new cooperative relationship with India. Since then both Washington and Canberra have continued to prevent the differences over the nuclear issue from obstructing a new dynamic relations with New Delhi. The official America still clings on to the NPT and the nonproliferation mantra. So does Australia. But the American and Australian leadership have in reality gone ahead with building closer economic as well as security bond with India.

It is all clear that the nuclear irritant will no longer come in the way of establishment of strategic ties between India and the US and India and Australia. The new Indo-US nuclear deal currently in the process of being finalised has the potential to bury the nuclear hatchet that troubled India's bilateral relations with both Australia and the US for decades. It would allow

India to import civilian nuclear technology from the US and other sources and India would no longer be the target of the Nuclear Suppliers' Group, where both the US and Australia are members. It is true that Australia at the moment does not come forward to back the Indo-US nuclear deal. It is partly because a bill to implement this deal is pending in the US Congress and no other step to implement this agreement is possible until the American legislature approves it endorsing amendments to the US Atomic Energy Act. Moreover, Australians dislike to be branded as America's sheriff in this region. By currently distancing itself from toeing the Bush line on this issue, Canberra also seeks to project an independent policy. However, once the US Congress approves the deal, it is very likely that Australia too will be supportive and may agree to sell natural uranium to India. India buying civilian nuclear technology from the US and natural uranium from Australia can bind these three countries in a new strategic rapport that would have a positive fall-out in the entire Indian Ocean region.

Thirdly, Indian Ocean has ceased to be a contentious area, as was the case during the Cold War era. India has conducted a series of naval exercises with the United States in the blue waters of the Indian Ocean. The US naval base in Diego Garcia and the US naval movements in the region are no longer viewed by India as a destabilising phenomenon. Moreover, bidding good-bye to past suspicions over Indian intentions behind its naval expansion, Australia sought to engage India in establishing a new cooperative structure spanning a large number of Indian Ocean littorals. Both the countries became member of a new grouping called Indian Ocean Association for Regional Cooperation (IOARC). Differences between the two countries over details remain. Any new venture of this kind is bound to take time and a trial and error effort. The fact remains that the spirit behind regional cooperation is a positive one. Today, India and Australia and the US all have a convergence of interest in the Indian Ocean region. Preventing piracy, ensuring safety of sea-lanes, maintaining environmental stability and potential of joint efforts to explore and exploit the oceanic resources in the future can contribute towards and facilitate the emergence of triangular security cooperation among India, Australia and the United States.

Fourthly, India is beginning to expand its economic and military presence in the Asia Pacific region. Indian presence in this region was largely unwelcome during Cold War era. Japan and South Korea were alliance partners of the US, China had strategic understanding and ASEAN was by and large pro-US. India's support to Vietnam even after its military intervention in Cambodia was looked with certain amount of condescension by the regional countries. However, by placing a new policy of "Look East" the Indian Government desired to expand its economic engagement with the Asia Pacific countries. The US and Australia have had very close strategic and economic engagement in the Asia Pacific for decades. While the US is a Pacific power and the regional countries welcome the US military presence in this region, Australia over the years has developed larger trade and investment ties with Asia-Pacific countries than with any other part of the world. Today, India, Australia and the US have several common goals and aspirations in the Asia Pacific region. Maintenance of peace and stability, sustaining a stable balance of power, optimising the economic opportunities in this region should bring India, Australia and the US into a common strategic bind. India is relatively a new entrant to the politics of this region in the post-Second World War period, whereas the US and Australia are seasoned participants in the politics, economics and security of this region. India should think in terms of developing closer security and economic understanding with Canberra and Washington to facilitate its own expanding engagement in the Asia Pacific. Some Indians would be averse to even talk of strategic partnership with the US and Australia. But old suspicions and cold war mind-set need to be removed to protect India's growing interest and involvement in the Asia Pacific. Some may even question the credibility of Australia to be part of an Asian balance of power. But such a question would disappear the moment the skeptics would try to understand and recognise the emergence of Australia over the years as a country with a highly sophisticated military machine. A small population with a large territory is highly literate and technologically quite advanced.

Fifthly, the world is increasingly facing security challenges from non-state actors and the security threats traditionally posed by the nation-states are relatively easy to manage through negotiations, arbitration, diplomacy and dialogues. There are ample regional and international organisations to manage and resolve interstate disputes and conflicts. However, mechanisms to tackle the threats generated by the activities of non-state actors are not yet adequate or efficient. The 9/11 incident involving terrorist attacks on the US and a war waged against terrorist networks by the superpower clearly indicate that the world now has to come to terms with the menace of terrorism. This menace cannot be tackled by any single country, even if that country happens to be a superpower. Had there been no 9/11, perhaps India would have had to continue its lone battle against terrorism—a phenomenon that has afflicted India for decades. But now the international community has woken up to the stark reality that states have to combine their efforts and strength to deal with terrorists. There is just the right setting for India to coordinate its anti-terrorist efforts with both the US and Australia. Currently, India is already cooperating with the US in this front and so is the US. Australia is more with the US than with India. There are several problems of definition, priorities and concerns that may create problem for a triangular cooperation in this field. However, these problems should not come in the way for cooperation for long, otherwise the terrorists elements alone will have field day. As South Asian economies liberalise more and more and generate new opportunities for international investors, countries, such as Australia and the US would have to come to terms with South Asian terrorists. Both the countries have shown much determination and substantial cooperation to deal with terrorism in the Middle East and Asia Pacific. India needs to adjust its policies to be more cooperative with Australia and the US in those areas and bargain for a more accommodating and supportive role for Indian efforts against terrorism in South Asia. The difficulties confronting the three countries need to be overcome in individual and regional interests of all these three countries. Future cooperation appears a necessity, since sooner rather than later terrorist groups are likely to become masters in manipulating national differences.

Sixthly, India, Australia and the US are all multicultural democracies. Threats to multicultural societies are increasing day by day in a rapidly globalizing world. Coming together to protect and promote multiculturalism will certainly lead to increasing collaborations and interactions. The threat of communism and the cold war conflicts so preoccupied the countries that even democracies split and failed to make common cause. Today, not communism but non-traditional security threats pose more serious challenges to democracies. One can safely argue that the political cultural and social diversities will compel Canberra and New Delhi and Washington forge common bonds in the near future and the alternative would be unacceptable to all of them.

Last but not the least, the slow but steady growth of the Indian economic liberalisation and an impressive growth rate in recent years has captured the imagination of the American as well as Australian businessmen and investors. There were considerable systemic constraints to India's economic engagement of the US and Australia before 1991. But the end of the Cold War has removed the political barriers and India's economic openness has opened up huge opportunities for Australians and Americans to take advantage of. The US has traditionally been the single largest trading partner of and foreign investor in India. Australian economy is relatively small. But there is ample scope for growth of Indo-Australian economic ties. India offers a huge market for Australia. While Australia has been able to engage China and other Asia Pacific economies in trade and investment, its economic ties with India have not been realised up to the optimum level. The trend has nonetheless been quite encouraging. The strengthening of economic ties among these countries will work as a real cementing factor to the emerging convergence of security and political interests of India, Australia and the United States.

What kind of strategic triangle encompassing India, Australia and the US is likely? At the outset, one can conveniently rule out the possibility of a Cold War-type triangular alliance from rising in the Indian Ocean region. There is no Cold War and thus it is neither desirable nor feasible to imagine a new kind of alliance consisting of these three countries from taking birth. Secondly, this relationship is not even going to be a body that would be expected to be a counterbalance to the rising power of China. The simple reason is based on the fact that the so-called "China threat" debate in many countries in the world has proved to be nothing but a fashionable and enchanting drawing-room discussion. The US leads others in this debate, but no other country has established as extensive and intensive economic networks with China than the US. If there is any one country other than China itself that is responsible for China's unprecedented economic growth, that is the United States. The rest of the countries have been making most of China's economic opening after the US took the lead in constructively engaging China. Now when some analysts in the US begin to articulate the slow emergence of a "China threat", others are not prepared to buy this notion.

China's traditional enemies as well as friends are all seeking to improve their trade and investment relations with China. This list includes both Australia and China. Australians did not have a favourable and positive image of China for decades. They participated in the Korean War and Vietnam War on the side of the United States and viewed China as a threat to Asia-Pacific stability. But the situation is drastically different today. Australians have developed such a positive image of China and that country has set up such an enlarging economic network with China that Canberra can openly differ with the advocates of "China threat"—a phenomenon far from that of the Cold War days. India, unlike Australia, fought a border war with China and continues to have a territorial dispute with China. But even India no longer views China as a threat. The development of nuclear weapons and expansion of the Indian military have inculcated confidence in India that was lost in the 1962 war. But at the same time, the Indian leadership has adopted a pragmatic approach to China by seeking to enhance confidence building through economic engagement, among other things, and waiting for a favourable ambiance to resolve the territorial discord peacefully. Like Australia, even India would refuse point blank to erect any anti-China defense structure. While a section of Americans consider China as the next important challenge to American primacy, they are increasingly aware that even traditional US allies will not agree to anti-China alliance formation. Japan, South Korea, ASEAN, Australia, India all have growing economic and political cooperation with China and none would like to lose it. Thus the strategic triangle consisting of India, the US and Australia is not going to be anti-China in its content and goals.

The strategic triangle then should be aimed at a range of non-military security threats, including terrorism, narcotics trade, small arms proliferation, international crime, piracy, and many others. The second goal should be maintenance of an Asian strategic balance and warding off any threat to such a balance. It is not necessary to identify any country or ideology to form strategic cooperation. As and when a threat arises, a concerted effort should be made to deal with it. A strategic triangle need not always be a negative effort to meet security challenges. It should have a positive dimension. It can enhance the level of friendship and cooperation among the members and provide a safety valve to sort out differences among themselves. Existence of a strategic triangle itself can be a deterrent to future threats from taking shape. In other words, closer military cooperation among Indian, Australian and US and periodic meetings and dialogues will not only be a confidence enhancer but can also work as a bulwark against forces that are yet to incubate and may surface in future in the absence of such an arrangement.

The US will perhaps be more amenable to such an idea of a strategic triangle in the Indian Ocean, whose scope should transcend this particular region and include the larger Middle East and the Pacific. Suspicions and foot-dragging are more likely among Indians and Australians. Australia has an age-old strategic alliance with the US. India is increasingly experiencing strategic convergence with the US. But the strategic cooperation between India and Australia is mostly confined to seminars and dialogues. The idea to shape such a strategic triangle nonetheless is perhaps worth exploring.

20

Combating International Terrorism Post-9/11: Responses of Australia, India and Japan

RAJESH KAPUR

This paper attempts to trace the responses of Australia, India and Japan to international terrorism following the September 11 attacks on the World Trade Centre and the Pentagon. It argues that the resultant, largely unanticipated change in policymaking that has occurred among these countries is actually more robust than many analysts have thus far been prepared to acknowledge.

In the present synchronising world where focus on economy and efforts for prosperity seem to be the guiding principles of the nation states, an enigma always hinders world peace: International Terrorism. No nation or International organisation including the UN has been successful in providing any concrete solution to the problem. A widely accepted definition of International Terrorism is yet to come. The whole human race has suffered from this menace and even now the so-called safe and crime-free countries like Japan, or propagators of liberty and equality like the UK and the USA cannot boast of their immunity from Terrorism. Despite cumulative efforts for combating terrorism, eliminating the threat from the international scenario continues and poses a challenge to be taken seriously as far as security question is concerned. However, it has provided a platform to discuss and deal with the problem at various levels; regional, national and international.

International terrorism is not only confined to killing people but also has become a worldwide network of criminals involved in money laundering, drug and human trafficking, smuggling of arms, technology and goods. All these activities are weakening the nations and strengthening terrorist outfits. Until recently some of these organizations were running parallel governments—the Taliban militia in Afghanistan literally ruled the country.

Australia enjoys the distinction of being a country which has international boundaries merging with that of the continent. Australian differences with Indonesia have taken a back seat, following the Bali bombings and the bombing in front of the Australian Embassy in Jakarta, owing to the fact that more important issues of international terrorism and natural disasters are to be addressed. After this, both nations have come closer than ever before.

Australia is in the due process of combating international terrorism organised as well as signed International counter terrorism conferences and treaties. Being a US ally since World War II, Australia sent military forces to Afghanistan and Iraq. It argued that it was necessary for its security interest and to maintain peace in the world. At the domestic front nineteen security laws were introduced post 9/11. Australia's response to terrorism also paid attention to the relationship between security and human rights. The Australian Government's White Paper in 2004, *Transnational Terrorism: The Threat to Australia*, emphasised new threats and vulnerable security environment facing Australia, particularly from an increase in Islamic fundamentalist terrorism in South East Asia.

The Japanese Comprehensive Security includes free sea routes in the world in general and in the Asia-Pacific, in particular. Since Australia is also threatened by maritime terrorism, such a view was also echoed by the Australian White Paper, which mentions that "transnational terrorists have demonstrated maritime attack capability."[1]

India, Australia and Japan have myriad things in common. Needless to say concern for countering International Terrorism is the foremost one. Other than security issues, bilateral and multilateral trade also impact on policy making. Japan is the largest trading partner of Australia while India is the sixth largest trading partner.

Terrorism is not new to India. It faces state-sponsored terrorism from neighbouring countries. Domestically, several terrorist outfits are operational in many parts of India demanding more autonomy and separate statehood in certain cases. Kashmir has always remained the major bone of contention between India and Pakistan right from Independence. India's multi-cultural, ethnic, lingual, religious identity provides a unity in diversity on one hand and a feeling of alienation to some on the other. India, like Australia and Japan, has many anti-terrorism agencies and strict laws that are updated or changed according to the need of the time. After 9/11, the campaign to combat International Terrorism on the platform provided by US has intensified.

Japan has witnessed ideological and religious terrorism on its soil. In a country where crime rates are considerably low, terrorism no longer exists but imminent threats still loom. Post-9/11, Japan participated in the War on Terror, Reconstruction Assistance to Afghanistan (January 2002) and the Iraq war. The decision of despatching Self Defence Forces (SDF) to Iraq for non-combatant activity made its neighbours suspect Japan of pursuing pre-WWII Militarism. Critics argued this was against Article 9 of the peace constitution. To counter terrorism, Japan passed the Anti-Terrorism Special Measures Law in the Diet during October 2001 followed by many other similar laws.

International terrorism is a serious threat to Asia Pacific and the world at large. Making predictions about the future directions of terrorism is a risky business. For now, the changing perceptions in the International terrorism have forced these countries to accept its multidimensional threat emanating from various directions.

Dimensions of International Terrorism

Terrorists produce, or aim to produce, terror—extreme fear—among their opponents. Although the word "terrorism" is of Latin origin (from *terrere*, to frighten), it found its present place in the modern western vocabularies only in the fourteenth century through the French language. The first English usage was recorded in 1528. The basic mechanism of terror was captured in an ancient Chinese proverb: "kill one, frighten ten thousand."[2]

International terrorism is not a new phenomenon as far as the international community is concerned. It is a war, new in intensity but ancient in nature.[3] The roots of modern international terrorism can be traced back to political developments in the Middle East after the partition of Palestine and the creation of Israel in 1948. The Cold War between the US and the erstwhile USSR led to the world being divided into two hostile camps. Due to the huge expenditure on weapons and security and the memory of WWII still fresh, both superpowers avoided open confrontation. Therefore, they relied on covert warfare and the use of terror to achieve their political ends that resulted in the mushrooming of numerous state-sponsored terrorist groups the world over.

A major problem of any scholar studying international affairs has, been in defining terrorism. There is no precise definition of terrorism or international terrorism that is accepted by the world community. General acceptance of the definition of terrorism is yet to be achieved because of the fact that "[o]ne man's terrorist is another man's freedom fighter".[4] International terrorism is that kind of "[t]errorism conducted with the support of a foreign government or organisation or directed against foreign nationals, institutions, or governments. International terrorism has involved groups seeking to overthrow specific regimes, to rectify national or group grievances, or to undermine international order as an end in itself".[5] International terrorist organisations operate with their widespread global network, which make their operations and attacks easy.

Analysing UN resolutions, passed from time to time provide a means of how the definition of terrorism has evolved over time. In 1972, the UN for the first time realised the threat of international terrorism and decided to adopt resolution for the prevention of international terrorism. Thus, on December 18, 1972, the first ever text of the UN on international terrorism was adopted at the 2114th plenary meeting of the General Assembly.

The subject of the text contained measures to prevent international terrorism which endangered or took innocent human lives or jeopardised fundamental freedoms. It sought to study the underlying causes of those forms of terrorism and act of violence and identified these as lying in the misery, frustration, grievance and despair, which caused some people to sacrifice human lives, including their own, in an attempt to effect radical changes. The inclusion of the right of self-determination was not accepted by colonial powers but many Afro-Asian countries that were reeling under colonial rule were also responsible for the growth of terrorism in international politics. An ad hoc committee to examine the matter was formed. Soviet Russia supported the resolution while US and its allies opposed it. The committee submitted its report without a unanimously accepted definition of international terrorism but it suggested a number of measures for prevention of terrorism and sought cooperation among members.

Finally, in 1987, the Secretary-General convened an international conference to define terrorism and differentiate it from freedom fighting. Taking note of the Secretary-General's report, the UN General Assembly condemned all acts of terrorism, except those fighting for right to self-determination against foreign and racist regimes, as "criminal" wherever and by whomever committed including those which jeopardised friendly relations among states and their security. An overwhelming majority adopted this resolution. Israel and the US, however, voted against this resolution while Honduras abstained. Individual states like Australia, therefore, have been compelled to develop their own definitions for the purposes of enacting legislation to counter the threat.[6]

The UN could define international terrorism by 1987 because of the fact that by this time most of the Afro-Asian colonies were either free or were on the verge of attaining independence. Article 10 of the International Convention against Taking of Hostages made it an extraditable offence.[7]

As is evident from the different attempts to define terrorism, terrorism is the phenomena of creating intimidation among the masses. The most simple definition of international terrorism states that it comprises acts of terrorism that have clear international consequences: incidents in which terrorists go abroad to strike their targets, select victims and target because of their connections to foreign state (diplomats, local executives of officers of foreign corporations), attack airliners in international flights, or force airliners to fly to another country).[8]

Today, terrorists operate mainly on three levels—intra-national, regional and international levels. Terrorism is no longer a largely domestic phenomenon, where a few disgruntled actors espousing leftist or capitalist ambitions committed acts of violence that were primarily aimed at gaining media attention, world publicity and showing the state in a bad light.[9]

A large number of terrorist groups are operating in different parts of the world be they cults like the Aum Shinrikyo or individual nihilists like

Unabomber, or religious fanatics of well-organised terrorist organisation with wide spread network like Al Qaeda. Some people often confuse terrorism to be war for freedom or liberation struggle. But freedom fighters rarely use the means of killing and terrorising ordinary civilians, to achieve their ambitious and dreadful goals. It is often seen that most of the terrorists who claim themselves to be freedom fighters are foreign mercenaries spreading terror for money or for other gains. The Geneva Convention of 12 August 1949, distinguishes a terrorist from a soldier.[10] Later on, the protocols of 1977 were added to Geneva Convention of 1949 through a General Assembly resolution enhancing the sphere of definition of combatant activity but making clear that situations of internal disturbances and tensions such as riots are not armed conflict. Since terrorists do not fulfill the norms of Geneva Convention of 1949 and protocols of 1977 and do not have any obligation as armed forces have, they might not be called as freedom fighters or soldiers.

Terrorism can be classified into several types: state sponsored, ideology-based, against the hegemony of a particular nation, against oppression or exploitation, for gaining power, religious, secessionist (often described as wars for liberation or independence) and so on.

Some states use terrorism as an extension of their foreign policies to achieve some calculated ends. As observed by Clausewitz, "terrorism is politics by other means, distinct from total war."[11] One example of state-sponsored terrorism is terrorism sponsored by the Inter Service Intelligence (ISI) of Pakistan, in India.

Ideology-based terrorist groups are on the decline after the Cold War because most of these groups were based on the Marxist-Leninist ideology—for instance, the Japanese Red Army (JRA). The nature, targets and rhetoric of international terrorism have changed dramatically since the end of the Cold War and the emergence of globalisation.[12] In spite of the fact that the Soviet Union did not support many terrorist groups, Moscow along with several Warsaw Pact countries was a prominent trainer of terrorists.

Religious fanatics of the *Al Qaeda* who are responsible for a number of terrorist attacks throughout the world, and headed by Osama Bin Laden, a Saudi Arabian of Yemeni origin and a multi-millionaire, proclaim themselves as *jihadi* (fighting a religious war). *Harkat-e-Jihad-I-Islami*, the parent organisation of all the groups operating as Islamic crusaders was launched in 1980 with headquarters in Pakistan by bringing together various Afghan dissidents.[13] That was the time when the struggle against the new pro-Soviet dispensation in Kabul was integrated. Later, due to rivalry between leaders a new group emerged as *Harkat-ul-Mujahideen* but again brought together under a new name *Harkat-ul-Ansar* which then reverted to its original name after being banned by the United States government.

A Rand Corporation database of terrorist incidents notes that while there were no groups that could be classified as religious from 1968 to 1980, the first "modern" religious groups appear in 1980 but only two of 64 have been counted. By 1992, this had risen six fold representing a quarter of terrorist organisations that carried out attacks in 1992 (11out of 48). By 1994, a third (16) of 49 identifiable terrorist groups could be classified as religious in character or motivation, and in 1995 they accounted for nearly half (26) out of the 56 known terrorist groups that year. By 1999, at least 64 out of a total of 96 were clearly identifiable as being religiously motivated.[14] Thus, a clear change in the trends of terrorist activities is visible during and since the 1990s.

Although the volume of terrorist incidents world-wide declined in the 1990s according to the statistics of the US Department of State, the proportion of persons killed in terrorist incidents has generally increased. Here, the important thing to be observed is the connections between religion and terrorism which is not new because until the nineteenth century religion provided the only acceptable justifications for terror. However, while religion and terrorism do share a long history, until the 1990s this particular variant had largely been overshadowed by ethnic, nationalist, separatist or ideologically motivated terrorism.

Today, terrorists act on greater scale and variety of motives than in the past. Not only to get publicity or to make their presence felt but also to gain money, power and sometimes territory. Even the sole superpower, the US, is not spared as the terrorist attacks on September 11 2001, on the World Trade Centre (WTC) and the Pentagon show. With the changing patterns of terrorism, the issue of countering terrorism has also come to the centre stage. It is no more a police affair to handle or to check terrorism; now multi-national armies are deployed or brought into action to check terrorism.

By and large, terrorist groups are organised along structured lines in large hierarchical groups, and most of them depend almost entirely on transnational sources for their weapons, funding and even fighters. This is not just an aspect that is seen in a particular part of the globe but holds true for terrorism everywhere whether it may be South Asia, Central Asia, the United States or Europe. For example, all of the groups operating inside India, Afghanistan, China, America, and Central Asia are armed with weapons produced in any other country. Most of these groups have mercenaries within their ranks, and all are funded by transnational operations—money laundering, human trafficking, smuggling and drug trafficking.

Whatever be the nature, purpose, background or ideology of the terrorist groups one commonality shared by all is their reliance on the above-mentioned illegal and criminal sources of funding among which most prominently ranks drugs. For instance, the Colombian Revolutionary Armed Forces (FARC) is by all accounts, the largest single producer of cocaine in the world, although they prefer to leave the distribution to traditional traffickers.[15] The Taliban, when in power in most parts of Afghanistan, were the largest producers of

Heroin. The Liberation Tigers of Tamil Eelam (LTTE), known to be linked to both the Basque separatist ETA and the PKK Kurdistan Workers Party, control a major share of heroin trafficking from South Asia to Western Europe, usually via Thailand. "Thanks to globalisation", observes Michael Radu, "international criminal and terrorist organisations have become intrinsically linked."[16] Besides these sources, money is also collected by acts of kidnappings, hijackings and through the heavy donations given by rich fundamentalists for whom terrorists, especially *jehadis*, are fighting a religious war.

The religious groups and cults have come closest to taking the step towards weapons of mass destruction (WMD). In the past, such acts included attempts to poison the water supplies of major American urban centres, dispersing toxic chemicals through ventilation systems, and recently in Japan, the actual use of chemicals to poison subway train commuters. It appears that the ideology which sustains such religious groups and cults considers the elimination of people who are alien to their belief system as not just pardonable, but desirable. During the "war against terrorism" after the September 11 attacks on the US, it was feared that terrorists might also use biological or chemical weapons in subsequent attacks. Even civilian infrastructure, such as public transportation is now often used to accomplish terrorist goals. Another important means of terrorists is to take innocent people hostages to negotiate with the respective governments of the various countries.

Suicide attacks were, in a sense, actually started by Japanese *kamikaze* pilots during the WWII when they blew up enemy ships. Now, it is the most effective means to spread terror almost throughout the globe. The number of suicide attacks by various terrorist organisations is shown in the following table, for the period 1980 to 2000.[17]

Table 1

Terrorist Organization	*Area of Activity*	*Number of Suicide Attacks*
LTTE	Sri Lanka	168
Hezbollah and Pro-Syrian groups	Lebanon, Kuwait and Argentina	52
The Palestinian Islamic Jihad (PIJ)	Israel	8
Hamas	Israel	22
The Kurdistan Worker Party (PKK)	Turkey	15
Al Qaeda	East Africa	2
Egyptian Islamic Jihad	Croatia	1
Islamic Group (IG)	Pakistan	1
Babbar Khalsa International	India	1
Armed Islamic Group (GIA)	Algeria	1

Terrorists always attack 'soft targets' or places easily vulnerable where fewer efforts are needed to create havoc, panic or intimidation among the masses and simultaneously, maximum attention of the media and the world community is won. In order to popularise the organisation or maximise the impact of the attacks claims, are made by various terrorist organisations for being responsible for the suicide or any general attack. The world of media also plays a major role in bringing demands of terrorists to common household through electronic or print media. Similarly attention of various governments is also drawn by pressurising them by carrying out their attacks mostly on civilian targets and sometimes on military. All the terrorist attacks are widely covered by print media as well as radio and television news channels. It has been said, with some exaggeration and in a lighter vein, that television is so ideally suited to terrorism that the medium would have invented the phenomenon if it had not already existed."[18]

9/11: An Instance of Burgeoning International Terrorism

After understanding the organisation, means, motives, financial sources, support—domestic and international—we move to the most recent and devastating example of the September 11 attack on the US with its far-reaching implications and impact. Terrorists exposed lapses in the US security system and challenged the world's only superpower by using its own airliners. The global impact of the attacks included apparent threat for US and its allies, including Australia, UK and Japan.

What happened on September 11?

Four commercial airline jets on US domestic routes were hijacked, virtually simultaneously, and used in suicide bombings. The targets were the buildings symbolising the US military and economic might. The whole world was shocked after the terrorist attacks on such a devastating scale killing thousands and injuring numerous innocent people belonging to different nationalities.

Early morning on 11September an American Airlines Flight II took off from Boston, bound for Los Angeles, crashed into the north tower of the World Trade Centre in New York. Within minutes, at around 9:03am, United Airlines Flight 175 which took off from Boston and bound for Los Angeles slammed into the south tower of the World Trade Center, Manhattan, New York. The impact of the aircraft and the subsequent fire eventually caused the collapse of both towers at approximately 10:00 am. At around 9:45 am, American Airlines Flight 77, departing to Washington, D.C., blew up with a portion of the Pentagon complex collapsing and going up in flames. Those incidents were followed by the crash of United Airlines Flight 93, on route from New York to San Francisco, into the woods on the outskirts of Pittsburgh at around 10:10 am. The crashes claimed a total of 3,062 lives (as announced by US authorities on 25 February), and left 24 Japanese citizens dead or missing, with 9 bodies confirmed (as of 4 March).[19]

The US's own technology was used against it. It is beyond belief that a few Arabs and Afghans could master such advanced technology and could accomplish such a well-coordinated and high-precision task. They (terrorists) were reasonably educated and technically competent enough to master air flights. They were highly motivated too, and had strong belief in their cause. At the same time, they were fanatics. No organisation took responsibility or claim for the attacks, nevertheless, the US held Osama bin Laden and his terrorist organisation, *Al Qaeda* responsible for the attacks. Several videotapes, recorded telephonic conversations and other documentary proofs were produced by the US intelligence services.

The foreign media interviews in Afghanistan with captured *Al Qaeda* members and other "Arab" volunteers whom Afghans call, "touris Khareji" meaning foreign tourists, reveal that most of them fully expected to kill Americans, came from middle class backgrounds, were relatively better educated and believed the Taliban version of Islam was the ideal form for their own countries. The known backgrounds of the September 11 terrorists suggest that they were not the poor, unfairly treated and marginalised masses of the Islamic world. But most of them were radicalised university graduates who have lost their traditional employment in government-paid universities and other public sector positions and found their carrier aspirations blocked. The same is the situation with young, well-educated, and usually second-generation Muslim immigrants in the West. The problem with them is they never assimilated with the western culture. They rejected the Western, secular, democratic, and individualist environment and joined the terrorist groups not for economic reasons but to fight the increasing interference and threat of western culture. Samuel Huntington's theory of the "Clash of Civilizations" held true to some extent after analysing biographies of such terrorists available on a website.[20]

Further, blaming a particular religion for spreading terrorism cannot be justified. Religion can be seen as both an identity and a faith. Most of the terrorists coincidentally happened to be Muslims and use religion as an identity but not as faith since no religion tells its believers to go against humanity. Though the terrorists claimed they were fighting a religious war or *jihad* in the name of Allah, most Muslim countries criticised the attacks on the US. Osama bin Laden himself was thrown out from Saudi Arabia much before the September 11 attacks. Even in Afghanistan, all Afghans did not agree with him and a civil war continues between the Taliban and the government.

> "Taliban's Islam is an Islam of the fanatical fringe and any violent group is always in need of such a fanatical interpretation of religion

> to bind its followers together," according to Asghar Ali Engineer.[21] Most of the Muslim Ulema and the leaders of Islamic movements condemning the attacks issued statements which say, "We have unequivocally condemned the dastardly terrorist attack on establishments in New York and Washington, whose victims belong to some forty countries and major religions of the world. Islam upholds the sanctity of human life as the Quran declares that killing one innocent human being is like killing the entire human race. The tragedy of September 11 is a crime against humanity and Muslims all over the world mourn all the victims of this aggression as a common loss of America and the whole world."[22]

Scholars the world over condemned the terrorist attacks. A few scholars believe that the attacks are retaliation for the US policy of hegemonising the world: "[t]he impact of the droppings of atomic bombs on two cities were of much greater impact than the September 11 terrorist attacks."[23] However, though what America did in Japan was wrong and a barbaric act against humanity, it was part of a full-fledged war and state policy and the difference between war and terrorism has already been discussed earlier.

American policies in various parts of the world, namely, in Latin America, Vietnam, West-Asia, Central-Asia, Afghanistan and Iraq, where numerous innocent people were killed by the American forces, are attributed as reasons for the September 11 attacks by few scholars. "It is absurd to imagine that the US is putting together an anti-terrorist coalition when it is itself the greatest terrorist and provider of the largest number of non-state terrorists".[24] But, the September 11 attacks have significance because the targets were the two symbolic structures of American global hegemony: one, the financial hub of its industrial empire located in its commercial capital; and the other, the military headquarter of the world's only remaining super power. It is also said that the presidential mansion was also one of the target of the terrorists.

All the terrorist organisations share some common features, the most prominent being a hatred for western democracy and capitalism. This hatred is especially acute towards the US, where it goes far beyond mere traditional ideological differences. The reaction of various established insurgent and terrorist groups to September 11 attacks is significant. The larger or more successful of such groups—the IRA and LTTE—expressed "sympathy" with the victims, while the marginal ones such as the Mexican People's Revolutionary Army (EPR) and the Peruvian Maoists of the Communist Party (the Shining Path) did not.[25]

US President George W. Bush announced the "war against terror" and pledged to bring "criminals to justice or justice to criminals." With its allies, the US opened war with Afghanistan—the shelter of Osama bin Laden under the Taliban regime. Taliban were defeated and a new transition government under the leadership of Hamid Karzai took charge of the country. More than four years have passed but Osama bin Laden and most of the key Al Qaeda operatives who planned and financed the September 11 attacks have not been captured. Osama bin Laden is still the man the United States most wants to find—dead or alive.[26]

However, the activities of *Al Qaeda* are contained by US retaliation and so is the case with its ability to carry out well-coordinated attacks like September 11, because many of the training camps have been eliminated and whole structures have been disrupted. However the possibility of future attacks by terrorists cannot be denied. As many as 5,000 training camps are very much active. The attacks of 11 September 2001, fundamentally changed the understanding of the United States and its allies of the threat posed by terrorism.

Japanese Response

Japan, a key US ally also reacted to the 11 September attacks very promptly, making its intentions clear to the world that terrorism in any form will not be tolerated. Japan has shown its commitment to maintain world peace and has supported the US action against the Afghanistan whether it is Koizumi's 7-point plan announced on September 18, 2001 or the refueling of US warships; Japan joined the "war against terror" wholeheartedly. Interestingly, Japan resolved to pursue rear echelon support during the war.

Japan too had faced the menace of terrorism in the past and the most prominent terrorist groups that operated on its soil and expanded their area of activities to several countries were the Japanese Red Army (JRA)[27] and Aum Shinrikyo.[28]

Motivated by the 1996 seizure of the Japanese ambassador's residence in the Peruvian capital of Lima, Japan reviewed its position on international terrorism and worked to strengthen its crisis management and information gathering systems. It hosted several international counter-terrorism conferences. New laws were passed to counter cult—like organisations. More powers are provided to the SDF to check the menace and also to act more freely.

A great change can be observed in Japan's defence and national policy in the post-September 11 period. A hastily passed law, the anti-terrorism special measures law, was implemented providing the SDF with powers to support non-combat and humanitarian operations, including the transport of weapons and ammunition, to the US-led coalition in the Indian Ocean, and to carry, and if necessary, use weapons. The Japanese Coast Guard was also authorised to fire against suspicious vessels in the Japanese waters, by separate legislation.

In April 2002, the Administration submitted three pieces of legislation to the Diet—Emergency Legislation to Deal With Military Attacks from Abroad, "The Self-Defense Revision Law", and "The Security Council Revision

Law"—which taken together constitute the War Contingency Bills.[29] These laws are destined to transform Japan into a country that participates in war. Since the Constitution lays down the three great basic laws, the renunciation of war, the refusal to take part in combat, and the refusal to bear arms, the three bills are termed necessary by few and unconstitutional by others.

Japan's response this time to the international crisis following the terrorist's attacks was faster than any time before. Though, it learned from its previous experiences when its contribution, especially during the Gulf War, was termed as 'too little and too late' by international community. Japan contributed US$13 billion during the Gulf War. It participated in several peace keeping operations through out the globe, every time it was primarily non-combat in nature and post-conflict role especially those restricted to maintaining peace, reconstruction work and providing relief works to the affected countries, like Cambodia, Mozambique, the Golan Heights, Rwanda and Honduras. It is worth noting here that during the East Timor crisis of 1999-2000, Japanese forces were withheld, as there were chances of getting involved in the conflict.

In the immediate aftermath of the attacks on the WTC and the Pentagon, Japan pledged full support to the US and allies, financially as well as militarily, to some extent. For the first time in the post-Occupation era, Japanese forces never participated, though it provided only rear echelon support of refuelling ships, transferring ammunitions and ration in the war operations.

Japan's foremost concern is to safeguard its overall economic interests. Therefore, Japan continued its relations with Iran—one of the countries termed as being part of the axis of evil by the US president. Japan, on the one hand, is supporting the US "war on terror" while also maintaining amicable relationship with Iran, due to its own vested interest of getting oil from Iran—the biggest provider of oil for Japan's major industries. Eric Heginbotham and Richard J Samuels in their article, "Japan's Dual Hedge," wrote, "Many wondered if Japan might become a US ally more along the lines of the British." The authors further state that, "in the weeks after Koizumi's speech it became clear that the fundamental approach of Japanese foreign policy had not changed". To them, Japan's contribution is much less than that of Italy or Germany; given the fact both the nations have constitutions repudiating war. The reasons given are the pragmatism of the Japanese leaders for whom economic and military security is equally important. They (Japanese) believe in "comprehensive security," which is clearly manifested today in an evolving strategy that can be called "dual hedging."[30]

In addition to all its financial, diplomatic and military contribution Japan decided to play a key role in rebuilding Afghanistan and now in Iraq. There was mild opposition that Japan faced within its boundaries from several intellectuals, for showing an eagerness to assist US in the "war against terror."

Despite this, the Japanese government made its contributions acknowledged by the world community, and with the support of senior politicians like Kiichi Miyazawa, Yasuhiro Nakasone and many others. The foremost reason given in support of Japanese policy of assisting US and its allies was the presence and hence the death of 24 Japanese citizens in the WTC attacks. The protection of the Japanese citizens was of course, a prime concern of the government.[31]

Since 1996, Japan has publicly stated its willingness to host an international conference in Tokyo to contribute to peace and reconstruction in Afghanistan. After the September 11 attacks and the ousting of Taliban regime in Afghanistan, Japan attended the Afghan Reconstruction Steering Group meeting in Brussels on December 20-21, 2001 with the US, the European Union, Japan and Saudi Arabia acting as joint chairs. In response to the Donor Alert issued by the UN Secretary-General an amount totalling US$580 million was provided to support the assistance activities for Afghan refugees undertaken by UN agencies and other international organisations. Japan announced on 4 October 2002 that it was prepared to provide a maximum of US$120 million, or around 20 per cent of the total funding requirements, to meet specific funding requests.[32]

While the debate of constitutional amendment especially of Article 9 is on, Japan has to bear the brunt of the many pro-pacifism groups and critical neighbours. Thus, a more active role of Japan in the international affairs militarily can be expected. Afghan War and then Iraq War provided opportunity to make its presence felt as well as to get the acknowledgement for its contribution from the world community.

Koizumi's overwhelming victory in the 2005 elections can be seen as continuation of the revivalism that also includes tough stand on terrorism and reliance on and support for US policies.

Australian Response

Australia's cordial relations with US have exposed her to the terrorist threat to such an extent that counter terrorism measures have taken over all the attention of the government as well as the people. With the September 11 attacks in the United States and the Bali bombings of 12 October 2002, in which a combined total of 98 Australians were killed, the vulnerability of Australians have also increased. In the past, few Australians had been killed as a result of terrorism. Most of those few were killed overseas and not deliberately targeted as Australians. Two Australians killed by the Irish Republican Army (IRA) in the Netherlands in 1990 were the victims of mistaken identity, the terrorists believing them to be British. In Australia, past acts of terrorism have generally involved attacks against foreign interests—including those of Turkey, Iran, India and Israel. Although Australians were killed in these attacks, Australia was not itself the target. Rather, Australia was the venue for the expression of extremist violence directed at other nations' governments in reaction to events overseas. The bombing of the Hilton Hotel in Sydney on February 13, 1978, in which three Australians died, was targeted at Indian officials attending a Commonwealth Heads of Government Meeting (CHOGM). Australia is now a target of transnational, extremist-Muslim terrorism and Australians are being targeted overseas.[33]

Table 2: Major Attacks Linked to Transnational Extremists—Terrorism since 1992*[34]

Date	*Target*	*Location*	*Fatalities*	*Injured****
29 Dec., 1992	Goldmore Hotel and Gold Coast Hotel	Aden, Yemen	3	6
26 Feb., 1993	World Trade Center	New York, USA	6	1000
13 Nov., 1995	Saudi Arabian National Guard office	Riyadh, Saudi Arabia	7	60
19 Nov., 1995	Egyptian embassy	Islamabad, Pakistan	17	60
7 Aug., 1998	US embassy (coordinated with Dar-es-Salaam attack)	Nairobi, Kenya	291	5000
7 Aug., 1998	US embassy (coordinated with Nairobi attack)	Dar-es-Salaam, Tanzania	10	77
12 Oct., 2000	USS Cole (US Navy warship)	Aden, Yemen	17	39
30 Dec., 2000	Ninoy Aquino International Airport, Blumetritt Light Rail Transit Station, a bus in Cubao, Plaza Ferguson and a petrol station in Makati	Manila, Philippines	22	100+
11 Sep., 2001	World Trade Center (coordinated with other 11 September attacks)	New York, USA	2752 (9)**	2260
11 Sep., 2001	Pentagon (coordinated with other 11 Septem-ber attacks)	Washington DC, USA	189 (1)	80
11 Sep., 2001	Possibly Washington DC (coordinated with other 11 September attacks)	Shanksville, Pennsylvania, US	40	0
11 Apr., 2002	Synagogue	Djerba, Tunisia	16	26

(Contd.)

(*Contd.*)

Date	*Target*	*Location*	*Fatalities*	*Inju-red****
5-08-02	Bus transporting French naval engineers	Karachi, Pakistan	15	25
6 Oct., 2002	MV Limburg (French-owned oil tanker)	Gulf of Aden, Yemen	1	12
12 Oct., 2002	Paddy's Bar and Sari Club (coordinated attacks)	Kuta, Bali, Indonesia	202 (88)**	350
28 Nov., 2002	Kikambala Paradise Hotel	Mombasa, Kenya	15	40
13-5-03	Residential compounds (four coordinated attacks)	Riyadh, S Arabia	34 (1)**	194
16 May, 2003	Restaurant, hotels, Jewish cemetery (five coordinated attacks)	Casablanca, Morocco	43	100
5-08-03	JW Marriott Hotel	Jakarta, Indonesia	12	150
8-11-03	Al-Muhaya housing compound	Riyadh, S Arabia	17	120
15 Nov., 2003	Two synagogues	Istanbul, Turkey	25	300
20 Nov., 2003	British Consulate, HSBC Bank	Istanbul, Turkey	26 (1)**	450
11 Mar., 2004	Railway targets (multiple coordinated attacks)	Madrid, Spain	191	2000
21 Apr., 2004	General Security Service Headquarters	Riyadh, Saudi Arabia	6	145
1 May., 2004	Oil refinery	Yanbu, Saudi Arabia	6 (1)**	25
29-30 May., 2004	Al-Khobar Petroleum Centre, Apicorp complex and the Oasis residential compound	Al-Khobar, S Arabia	22	25

* The data presented focuses on only the major acts of terrorism attributed to the Al Qaeda and its affiliates, and is not a comprehensive list of all attacks. In particular, the table does not include attacks conducted inside Afghanistan and Iraq during the period of the US-led coalition's military activity.

** Australian fatalities are indicated in parentheses.

*** Approximate figures only. Estimates of the number of injured vary with different sources, particularly for large-scale attacks.

Australia is a multi-cultural society with democratic government accommodating people from all walks of life. In the past 25 years, the Australian Muslim community has grown significantly. The 2001 Census counted 281, 578 Muslims living in Australia—an increase of forty per cent since the 1996 Census and an overall rise of ninety-one per cent in the past decade. Some recent estimates suggest Australian Muslims now number between 350,000 and 450,000. Australian Muslims are ethnically diverse. About thirty-five per cent of them were born in Australia. The rest immigrated to Australia from over seventy different countries, including Lebanon, Turkey, Indonesia and Bosnia-Herzegovina. There are over a hundred mosques and at least twenty-one Muslim primary and secondary schools in Australia.[35]

Australia's global interests show the significance and necessity of securing its soil and cititzens from the menace of international terrorism. Australians have a significant presence abroad. Over 3.5 million Australian travel overseas each year—around one million at any one time. Some 720,000 Australians or almost four per cent of the population live overseas. About 120,000 move overseas on a long-term or permanent basis each year.

Australia has an extensive diplomatic network of eighty-six overseas posts as well as other official representations. About 2000 Australian Defence Force personnel are deployed on more than ten operations and training activities around the globe, including in the Middle East, Europe, Africa, South-East Asia and the Pacific. The Australian Federal Police maintains a significant overseas presence, through its International Network and with personnel currently deployed in Cyprus, East Timor and Solomon Islands. Australian non-government organisations also maintain significant overseas representation. A total of 2289 Australians worked overseas through a non-government organisation in 2003.

Australia also has extensive global economic and business interests. Exports account for around twenty per cent of annual gross domestic product. The jobs of one in five Australians now depend directly or indirectly on the export of Australian goods and services. In 2003, Australia's two-way trade in goods and services was valued at A$304 billion, including A$140 billion of Australian exports. In the same year, Australia invested A$152 billion abroad while international investment in Australia totaled over A$233 billion. The Australian dollar is the world's seventh most traded currency.[36]

The IMF estimates that the loss of US output resulting from terrorism-related costs could be as high as 0.75 per cent of Gross Domestic Product, or US$75 billion per year. Any decline in US real GDP compounds and prolongs the adverse impact of economic uncertainty on Asian countries and Australia.[37]

Australian interests can be targeted directly. This was the case in December 2001 when a *Jemaah Islamiyah* plot to bomb the Australian, British and United States diplomatic missions in Singapore was foiled by the Singapore authorities. Similarly, in June 2003 the Thai police uncovered a plan by *Jemaah Islamiyah* to bomb the Australian Embassy in Bangkok together with the embassies of the United States and United Kingdom. Australia has also been named as the primary target for terrorists in Indonesia by an Al Qaeda manual titled *Targeting the cities*.[38] The Australian Attorney General said that, "September 11 changed the international security environment forever. As an ally of the United States, Australia's profile increased significantly. Australia's security environment has altered forever."[39]

It is not surprising that US and Australian responses to terrorism bear similarities. Can-berra's process of adjusting its intelligence to meet the challenges of global terrorism, however, started more than two years before the September 11 attacks, in preparation for the Sydney 2000 Olympic Games. After September 11, the Australian government further strengthened its intelligence capabilities through legislative and funding adjustments. The Australians' way of thinking that their relative isolation distanced them from the immediate threat of large-scale terrorism was shattered by the Bali bombings in 2002, which claimed the lives of 89 Australian citizens.[40]

Immediately after the horrifying events of September 11, Australia offered practical assistance to the United States and military support. In the days immediately after the attack, Australia expressed its resolute support for the US in its determination to bring the perpetrators to justice, as well as expressing concern and sympathy for the victims and their families.

Three days after the attack on the World Trade Centre, the ANZUS treaty was invoked for the first time. The Government took the view, in consultation with the US that Article IV of the ANZUS Treaty applied to the terrorist attacks on the US. This action was taken to underline the gravity of the situation and to demonstrate Australian commitment to working with the US in combating international terrorism.

Three Australians were confirmed dead and a further 69 were missing after the 9/11 attacks. The Australian Prime Minister declared Australia to be at war. Thus, when it was announced that America wanted Australian troops, they were immediately committed.

All the intelligence and law enforcing agencies like—The Australian Security Intelligence Organisation (ASIO), which is the country's oldest existing intelligence organisation, Australian Secret Intelligence Service (ASIS) which is Australia's counterpart to the CIA, the Australian Federal Police, a separate federal law enforcement agency were given special powers. ASIO is not a law enforcement organisation. In addition, Geospatial-Intelligence Agency, Australia's Defence Imagery and Geospatial Organisation (DIGO), responsible for acquiring and interpreting satellite and other imagery, gives Australia an upper hand in collecting information through satellite. Australia has two intelligence assessment agencies. One is the Office of National Assessments (ONA), which is responsible for producing analytical assessments of international developments. In doing so, it draws on secret intelligence collected by other agencies, as well as diplomatic reporting and open source material. The other assessment agency is the Defence Intelligence Organisation (DIO). The DIO's role is to provide intelligence to inform defense and government policy and planning, and to support the planning and conduct of Australian Defence Force operations.[41]

A Joint Counter Terrorism Intelligence Coordination Unit was established in ASIO, with officers from ASIO, ASIS, DIO, DSD, DIGO, and the AFP. The Unit has access to the databases of all relevant agencies, and is designed to ensure the effective sharing and coordination of intelligence information across agencies.

Countless legislative changes were made to strengthen Australia's ability to respond to terrorism. A number of those were of relevance to the collection and use of intelligence.

More powers were given to National Counter Terrorism Committee under National Counter Terrorism Plan. A provision of reviewing NCTP every three years was also introduced. Terrorism and terrorist activities are defined for the legal purpose. Recently an Anti Terrorism Bill has been passed in the parliament where opposition party, despite their differences, have voted with the government in favour of the bill. At the regional level, Australia established a joint operation to curb the terrorist activities. Australia has provided assistance to many other nations in terms of intelligence, military and financial support to counter transnational terrorism. At the international level, Australia's contribution is significant. Australia is a party to 11 of the 12 UN anti-terrorism conventions and the government is considering becoming a party to the remaining one as a matter of priority.[42]

Australia has significantly contributed in the Gulf War II as a major ally of the US though, the government faced opposition at the domestic level. However, the reasons given to participate in the war did not convince many. The US and its allies attacked Iraq on the grounds that terrorists' outfits may get hold of WMD. Critics are of the view that the Iraq War was launched for controlling and gaining more influence in the oil-rich region. Australia and its citizens are facing more threat now than ever before within and outside its boundaries. Its closer connections with US has invited more threats from terrorists which is evident in the recent past be it Bali, Jakarta or Singapore.

With the help of advanced technology and more reliance on human intelligence Australia has avoided or prevented terrorist organisations to harm its interests. The need for laws and physical contribution to the war on terror is well understood but many scholars are of the opinion that all the special powers given to the various agencies pave the way for the gross violation of human rights and personal liberties that are essential for the success of democracies.[43]

Indian Response

Unlike Australia and Japan that have fewer threats from terrorism and better counter terrorism planning and laws, India is the softest target for terrorists because of its huge population and diversity. Even the Parliament and places of worship are no exception. The Charar-i-Sharif and Akshardham attacks proved that the terrorist attacks are driven by motives of getting maximum media coverage and international attention. India condemned the attack on the US in the strongest terms, provided needful and meaningful assistance to the US and allies during the Afghan war.

Indian terrorism, though a perennial problem, could not catch the attention of the world media. It has become the most significant threat to the world. Three wars, over one hundred thousand casualties and wastage of resources and material wealth could not resolve the problem so far. It is a well known fact that Pakistan covertly and overtly sponsors the terrorism in India. It is one of the few nations suffering from all types of terrorism be it ideological, religious, regional, national or international. Internally, India faced secessionist forces demanding separate nations. The demands of *Khalistan* and *Azad* Kashmir proved the most destructive and posed a great challenge to the very existence and the integrity of the country. The *Khalistan* problem is now subsided but the problem of Kashmir still looms over not only India and Pakistan or Indian sub-continent but also over the whole world. It is for this reason that President Clinton once remarked that South Asia is "the most dangerous place on Earth." Many terrorist groups are operational in Kashmir with widespread networks and activities throughout India. Initially, these outfits were confined to Indian Kashmir but gradually international organisations such as the *Harkat-ul-Mujahideen* (HUM), the *Lashkar-e-Toiba* (LET), the *Harkat-ul-Jihad-al-Islami* (HUJI), *Al Badr* and many more started enjoying the loyalty of Indian groups.

An additional consideration when thinking about terrorism in India is its relationship to broader tensions in Indian society. Unlike the predominantly external threat of terrorism in the Australia and Japan, terrorism in India is generally related to separatist movements resulting from the significant ethnic and religious cleavages within Indian society.

Terrorism in India has even claimed the lives of many prominent leaders like Indira and Rajiv Gandhi. In December 1989, daughter of the then Union Home Minister was kidnapped. The Government of India compromised as per the terms of the terrorists. Later on, many such high profile people were either abducted or killed. Domestic terrorism can not be seen separately from international terrorism but India has laws, to tackle terrorism at different levels.[44] For instance, the state of Maharashtra had an Anti-Terrorism Law before the Prevention of the Terrorism Act (POTA) was implemented by Parliament, both of which at times, curbed individual liberties.

Many acts and laws were implemented and then scrapped to check terrorism time and again by the Indian government. It is feared that many a time such laws are misused for settling personal scores or for political vendetta. Indira Gandhi, the then Prime Minister of India, used Maintenance of the Internal Security Act (MISA) 1975 to put all the opposition leaders behind bars. Popular movements were crushed in the name of security. Similarly, the Terrorist and Disruptive Activities Act (TADA) was implemented in 1987.

There have been anti-terrorist laws in India before, each one enacted by the legislature and upheld by the judiciary, albeit with some reluctance and much regret. These laws were always temporary statutes and revoked whenever the situation improved so that these measures did not become a permanent feature of the law of the land. But after a year or two, with fresh spurts of terrorist activities, the statutes have been reintroduced with requisite modifications. TADA had many rigorous provisions, some of which proved to be open to gross abuse in the hands of law enforcement officials. The Supreme Court of India upheld its constitutional validity on the assumption that those entrusted with such draconic statutory powers would act in good faith and for the public good.

The Act gave strong search and seizure powers to the police, who could indict any person on the basis of strong suspicion. Once indicted under TADA, the accused would be tried by a special court according to special procedures. In such trials, well known protections ordinarily available to an accused in a liberal society would be given a go by.

When TADA lapsed, and failed to be extended, there was a vacuum in special anti-terrorist law in India, but there was no improvement in the situation. There were several tragic incidents including the hijacking of Indian Airlines Flight IC-814 and the release of three notorious terrorists by the Government of India to save the lives of innocent civilians and crew. The released terrorists subsequently engaged in activities and made open proclamations of terrorist intent which no government could bear.

In the wake of fresh terrorist activities, the Government of India promulgated an Ordinance, an ad hoc piece of legislation made by the President, when the legislature was not in session. This Ordinance, the Prevention of Terrorism Ordinance (POTO), was drafted along the line of its predecessor, TADA. There was, however, stiff opposition to its enactment as a law.

One of the worst assaults ever on the Parliament was carried out by the terrorists. It was an 'assault' not in the figurative sense, but a real attempt to cause physical harm, with guns and grenades, to the members of Parliament, including the Prime Minister and his cabinet. This sinister attempt failed due to the alertness of security personnel. Unidentified terrorists attacked the Parliament of India on 13 December 2001. All six terrorists dressed in commando fatigues, entered Parliament by car through the VIP gate of the building. The terrorists set off massive blasts and reportedly used AK-47 rifles, RDX and grenades for the attack. One of the terrorists, a human bomb, was reportedly blown to bits when he came under fire from the security personnel. Senior Ministers and over two hundred Members of Parliament were inside the Central Hall of Parliament when the attack took place. Security personnel sealed the entire premises, which saved many lives.

Referring to the incident of 13 December, the Indian Prime Minister said, "It was not an attack only on the building but at the very heart of our governance and symbol of democracy". Terrorists, meanwhile, remain active in and around India, and the potential threat seems alarmingly real. On 22 January, 2002, there was a sudden terrorist attack on the police personnel guarding the American Center in Calcutta in which four people died and some seventeen were injured. It was followed by many similar and devastating attacks in Bangalore, Delhi, Kashmir and in Mumbai which witnessed serial blasts both in 1993 and again in July 2006.

At the international level, India emerged successful in making its voice heard at different multilateral platforms. As a consequence of the September 11 attacks, the western world has learnt a great lesson and particularly US and allies have realised and acknowledged the troubles India has undergone. In the aftermath of September 11, economic sanctions imposed against India and Pakistan for carrying out nuclear tests were lifted by the US and allies. Recently, India and the US signed a nuclear deal for the lifting of US-imposed nuclear technology restraints on India. Attempts are on to create a security arrangement—a possible Asian NATO—comprising the US, India, Japan, Australia and a few more nations.[45] This indicates the clear cut shift in the Indian and US foreign policies since 11 September.

Conclusion

Terrorism is a global menace to which democracies are particularly vulnerable. Concerted global action to counter terrorism and to enact measures, such as sanctions, against countries and governments sponsoring terrorist acts across international borders may well be necessary. There are many commonalities and differences shared by India, Australia and Japan. Overstretched coastal lines, dependence on maritime means of transportation, strategic location, close ties with the US, inter-dependence for the international trade and considerably high number of citizens working abroad and so on, are some of the similarities shared by the three. While Australia and India are multi-cultural, Japan is considered a homogeneous society. The common features shared by them make them more vulnerable to the threat of the international terrorism. Globalisation has globalised terrorism too and therefore, no act of terrorism can be seen in isolation. No nation can claim to be immune of or unaffected by this menace. No country can combat the threat from transnational terrorism on its own. Effective action against terrorism requires a coordinated international response based on close and sustained international cooperation. The need of the hour is to share maximum amount of information, to evolve concrete policies and programmes not only to fight terrorism but also to know the root cause and then, to eliminate the cause through a wider campaign of spreading awareness and education.[46]

All these countries can learn a lot from each others' experiences, and they can share some common platforms to effectively tackle and weed out this menace for ever. If strict measures are not taken in time then all will suffer, as one of the side effects of the system of market economy and globalisation. An effective international system is required, including a reformed United Nations, which can help deliver timely outcomes in the face of these contemporary threats.[47] Complete knowledge of the enemies and their activities can help minimise the losses if not the occurrence of the terrorist attacks. More effective and practical international laws universally accepted and uniformly implemented by all the member nations may be helpful over the longer term.

End Notes

1. *Transnational Terrorism: The Threat to Australia*, White Paper, Government of Australia, 2004, p. 2, www.dfat.gov.au/publications/terrorism, p. 15.
2. *Encyclopedia of World Terrorism*, Vol. 1 (New York: M E Sharpe, Inc., 1997), p. 12.
3. Mahindra S, *Terrorist Games Nations Play* (New Delhi: Lancer Publishers, 1993), p. 15.
4. Harold J Vetter and Gary R Perlstein, *Patterns of Terrorism* (California: Brooks Cole Publishing Company, 1991), p. 3.
5. Ranjit K. Pachnanda, *Terrorist and Response to Terrorist Threat* (New Delhi: UBS Publishers, 2002), p. 4.
6. Australian legislation provides an elaborate definition of terrorism. In Australia, what constitutes an act of terrorism is defined in Commonwealth legislation. The Criminal Code Act 1995 states that a terrorist act means an action or threat of action where the action causes certain defined forms of harm or interference and the action is done or the threat is made with the intention of advancing a political, religious or ideological cause. Further, the Act states that "the action is done or the threat is made with the intention of: (i) coercing, or influencing by intimidation, the government of the Commonwealth or a State, Territory or foreign country, or part of a State, Territory or foreign country; or (ii) intimidating the public or a section of the public;' and where the action (a) causes serious harm that is physical harm to a person; or (b) causes serious damage to property; or (c) causes a person's death; or (d) endangers a person's life, other than the life

of the person taking the action; or (e) creates a serious risk to the health or safety of the public or a section of the public; or (f) seriously interferes with, seriously disrupts, or destroys, an electronic system including, but not limited to: (i) an information system; or (ii) a telecommunications system; or (iii) a financial system; or (iv) a system used for the delivery of essential government services; or (v) a system used for, or by, an essential public utility; or (vi) a system used for, or by, a transport system. The Criminal Code makes it an offence if a person commits a terrorist act, provides or receives training connected with terrorist acts, possesses a thing connected with terrorist acts, collects or makes documents likely to facilitate terrorist acts, or does any act in preparation for or planning of terrorist acts. The penalty for engaging in a terrorist act is life imprisonment. The penalty for other terrorism-related offences outlined above ranges from ten years to life imprisonment." See *Transnational Terrorism: The Threat to Australia*, White Paper, Government of Australia, 2004, p. 2, www.dfat.gov.au/publications/terrorism.

7. *International Convention Against Taking of Hostages*, Adopted by the General Assembly of the United Nations on 17 December 1979, United Nations Treaty Series, Vol. 1316, I-21931. The Convention came into force on 3 June, 1983.
8. David Carlton and Carlo Schaerf, eds., *International Terrorism and World Security*, (London: Croom Helm, 1975), p. 20.
9. Tara Kartha, *Countering Transational Terrorism*, *Strategic Analysis* (New Delhi), Vol. XXIII, No. 1, February 2000, pp. 1831-32.
10. K.R. Singh, International Terrorism as an Instrument of State Policy, *International Studies* (New Delhi), vol. 32, no. 2, 1995, p. 123.
11. *Ibid.*
12. Michael Radu, Terrorism After the Cold War: Trends and Challenges, *Orbis* (Philadelphia), Vol. 46, No. 1, Spring 2002, p. 276.
13. D.R. Goyal, Islamic Terrorism, *World Focus* (New Delhi), Vol. 20, No. 1, January 2000, p. 7.
14. The numbers of active terrorist groups is derived from the RAND Chronology of International Terrorist Incidents. See Bruce Hoffman, *Lessons of 9/11*, Rand Corporation, 2002.
15. Radu, p. 278.
16. *Ibid.*
17. Rohan Gunarathna, Suicide Terrorism: A Global Threat, *Jane's Intelligence Review* (London), Vol. 12, No. 4, April 2000, p. 53.
18. Lawrence Howard, ed., *Terrorism, Roots, Impact, Responses* (New York: Praeger Publishers, 1992), p. 92.
19. *Diplomatic Blue Book*, Ministry of Foreign Affairs, Government of Japan, 2002, p. 11.
20. http://www.azzam.org. Huntington's theory has been challenged and criticised by many scholars. As observed by Edward W. Said, countries like America do not have any particular culture because so many people from all over the world reside there.
21. Asghar Ali Engineer, September 11: Many Messages, *Economic and Political Weekly* (Mumbai), Vol. XXXVI, No. 42, October 20, 2001, pp. 3982-83.
22. *Ibid.*

23. N.D. Jayprakash, Terrorism: Hiroshima to New York, *Economic and Political Weekly*, Vol. XXXVI, No. 42, October 20, 2001, p. 3988.
24. Vaskar Nandy, War Against Terrorism: Perspective on Protest, *Economic and Political Weekly*, Vol. XXXVI, No. 43, October 27, 2001, p. 4061.
25. Radu, p. 278.
26. Mark Hosenball, A War Yet to Be Won, *Newsweek* (New York), Vol. CXXXIX, No. 32, September 9, 2002, p. 20.
27. An international terrorist group formed in 1969 after breaking away from the Japanese Communist League, the Red Army Faction was mainly led by Fusako Shigenobu who was later arrested in November 2000 in Japan. The group was organized to overthrow Japanese Government and monarchy and to help foment world revolution and was mainly active in 1970s. At present, it is based in Syrian-controlled areas of Lebanon.
28. Aum Shinrikyo is a Japanese religious cult obsessed with the apocalypse. This previously obscure group became infamous in 1995 when some of its members released the deadly sarin nerve gas into the Tokyo subway system, killing 13 commuters and injuring nearly 6,000 others.
29. Hisao Maeda, tr. by Adam Lebowitz, *The 2002 Defense Ministry White Paper: Full speed ahead to the national warfare state", rhttp://iticwebarchives.ssrc.org/ZMag/www.zmag.org/content print_article8d6d.html?itemID=3036&sectionID=44*, February 13, 2003.
30. Eric Heginbotham and Richard J Samuels, Japan's Dual Hedge, *Foreign Affairs* (New York), Vol. 18, No. 5, September-October 2002, p. 111.
31. 416 economists of the Japan Society for Political Economy signed the "Appeal from Japanese Scholars of Political Economy to All the People and States of the World-Call for the Rational Actions to Eradicate the Vicious Cycle of Indiscriminate Terrorism and Military Actions," on October 8, 2001. http://www.ne.jp/asahi/homepage/otani/english.htm.
32. *Diplomatic Blue Book 2002*, pp. 20-21.
33. *Transnational Terrorism: The Threat to Australia*, p. 5.
34. *Ibid.*, p. 12.
35. *Ibid.*, p. 21.
36. *Ibid.*, p. 69.
37. *Ibid.*, p. 70.
38. *Ibid.*, p. 71.
39. Australian Attorney General's press release *Counter-Terrorism Measures*, May 14 2002, http://www.ag.gov.au/www/agdHome.nsf/Wed+Pages/305C354AF0D4D4A9CA256BDB000B2AFA?Ope-nDocument.
40. Nicholas Grono, *Strengthening the Global Intelligence Network: Australia's Response to Terrorism*, http://www.cia.gov/csi/kent_csi/pdf/v48i1a03p.pdf.
41. The description of the ASIO's role is taken from the Inspector-General of Intelligence and Security Annual Report 2001-2002, p. 31, as quoted in Grono, *ibid.*
42. *Transnational Terrorism: The Threat to Australia*, p. 82.
43. Simon Bronitt, *Australia's Legal Response to Terrorism: Neither Novel Nor Extraordinary*?, Paper presented at the Castan Centre For Human Rights Law Conference, "Human Rights 2003: The Year in Review," December 4, 2003,

Melbourne, http://www.law.monash.edu.au/castancentre/events/2003/bronitt-paper.pdf.

44. Ved Marwah, India's Internal Security Challenges, IDSA Foundation Day Lecture on November 11, 2003, *Strategic Analysis*, Vol. 27, No. 4, Oct.-Dec. 2003, p. 514.
45. G.V.C. Naidu, US and the Asia Pacific: Future of the Alliance System and Regional Security, *Strategic Analysis*, Vol. 27, No. 4 Oct.-Dec. 2003, p. 528.
46. Aldo Borgu, *Combating Terrorism the Challenge for Policy Making in Australia and the US*, presentation to the 2004 Fulbright Symposium on "Civil-Military Cooperation and the War on Terror," July 5-7, 2004, Brisbane, Australia, www.aspi.org.au/pdf/Fulbright_AB.pdf+Australian+response+to+International +terrorism+after+9/11+pdf&hl=en.
47. Alexander Downer, Securing Australia's Interests—Australian Foreign Policy Priorities, *Australian Journal of International Affairs* (Deakin), Vol. 59, No. 1, March 7-12, 2005, p. 7.

21

India-Australia Strategic Relations in the Post 9/11 World

TEJ PRATAP SINGH

India and Australia have a shared history and language, common democratic traditions, similar legal, financial and government structures and common interests as Indian Ocean littoral States. Cricket is an abiding passion. Both countries are members of the Commonwealth, founder members of the United Nations and members of the Indian Ocean Rim—Association for Regional Cooperation (IOR-ARC), ASEAN Regional Forum (ARF) and dialogue partners with ASEAN. With the increasing prominence of the Asia-Pacific region in global geo-politics and economics, Indo-Australian relations assume much more significance. There are concerted efforts on both sides to expand and diversify bilateral relations.

The present paper aims at analysing the Indo-Australian strategic relationship in the post-9/11 world. The end of cold war and 9/11 event have impacted the entire gamut of international politics and relations. The very nature of threat to national security has changed. Terrorism has emerged as the greatest menace to national security and no nation is safe from it. The nations of the world have been forced to forge strategic partnership to fight the menace of terrorism. In the changed security scenario India and Australia have been compelled to enter into strategic dialogue to protect their polity, economy and society from subversion. However, strategic relation can not be analysed in isolation. Economic, political and socio-cultural aspect, which play vital role in shaping strategic partnership has also been discussed. The paper is mainly focused on the current security challenges that confront both countries and examines at length the efficacy of Indo-Australian strategic convergence.

Historical Perspective

Indo-Australian relations, alternating between extreme hostility and moderate cooperation, have for long been largely influenced by Cold War politics.

Although geographically speaking Australia is part of Asia, both culturally and psychologically it identified itself with Western Europe and America. Dependent entirely on the US for its security Australia remained as an integral part of Western military alliance by becoming a member of Australia-New Zealand-United States (ANZUS) and South East Asia Treaty Organisation (SEATO). Proclaiming a "White Australia" policy since the inception Australia practiced a kind of *apartheid* with regard to immigration. Until five decades ago non-white Afro-Asians were not welcome in Australia. Instead it encouraged largely European immigration. These and related policy pursuits of Australia towards Asia did not go unnoticed. Former prime minister of Malaysia, Mohammed Mahatir advocated the formation of Asia Pacific economic group seeking the exclusion of the US and its clients such as Australia and New Zealand.

In the post-Cold War period, however, there occurred drastic changes in Australia's attitude towards Asia. Not only it gave up its restrictive "white only" immigration policy but more importantly adopted multiculturalism as a new *mantra*. Australia untied itself from Cold-War Western security alliance and identified itself with the security concerns of South East Asia. It declared itself to be an Asian nation and acknowledged that its future lies in Asia. It announced "Look West" policy and tried to mend fences with its immediate South East Asian neighbours.

India on the other hand pursued an independent foreign policy devoid of Cold War bloc politics. However, the demise of Soviet Union and end of Cold War led to major shift in the US policy towards India. In the post-Cold War world, geo-economics dominated geo-strategy and geo-politics. Trade and commerce became important determinants of India's foreign policy. All these factors brought dramatic change in the Australian attitude *vis-à-vis* India paving way for cordial bilateral relation. But just about the time Indo-Australian relations were gaining strength, the momentum received a serious setback in May 1998 following II nuclear detonations of India.

Bilateral political relations were virtually frozen in the wake of India's nuclear tests in May 1998. It may be noted here, even in the height of the Cold War Australia's response to India's first 'peaceful nuclear explosion' (PNE) in May 1974 (Pokhran-I) was mild. In contrast, Australia's reactions to India's nuclear tests of 1998 were very strong and quite critical. Defence ties were cut, the Australian Defence Attaché was withdrawn from New Delhi, besides all aid other than humanitarian aid was suspended.[1] There was, however, no ban on Australian trade and investment in India.

Australia's hostile posturing supplemented by precipitous steps that it took provoked no less strident criticism in India. Public opinion and media reports reacted sharply stating that Australia has already forfeited its international credibility on the issue of nuclear non-proliferation by virtue of its existing ties with the US. For, after all, the Defence Department's *White Paper* of 1994 while espousing the cause of non-proliferation of nuclear weapons, clearly admitted that Australia would "continue to rely on the extended deterrence of the US nuclear capability to deter any nuclear threat or attack on Australia."[2] Australia's special relationship with the US had allowed the nuclear ships of the latter to be stationed in Australian ports, while joint Australian and US defence facilities in North West Cape, Pine Gap and Nurrungar connected Australia to the US nuclear infrastructure through the presence of US C3I facilities.[3] Further, on the nuclear non-proliferation question Australia's stance has always remained equivocal. Not only has Australia viewed critically China's nuclear testing but had also ignored the sub-critical tests by the US and Russia.[4] More than all, Australia had even let the United Kingdom to detonate twelve nuclear weapons on Australian soil during 1952 to 1957.[5] India was of the view that Australia could actively pursue its non-proliferation agenda because it enjoyed the benefits of being under the protective US nuclear umbrella.[6] The one thing Australia did not do was to impose economic sanctions, hence trade between Australia and India continued with Australia having a very large balance of trade surplus with India. This trade surplus had to be maintained in the interest of Australia.[7] It was argued that Australia critical stance was largely on account of its desire to please Washington.

Strategic Convergence

Generally speaking, foreign policies are shaped from interest perceptions, which revolve around three basic objectives of maintaining political sovereignty, territorial integrity and security and economic advancement. Relations between Australia and India have been governed by the respective global and regional perspectives of the two countries.[8] India and Australia have several commonalties. Both are members of the Commonwealth, have similar political structure, fusion of federal system with the parliamentary democracy, similar laws and judicial system and English language. Their interests converge in South East Asia. Both are in favour of stable, strong, secular and democratic South East Asia. Both are apprehensive of growing Chinese presence in the Asia Pacific region. India and Australia can collaborate with each other for the stability of South East Asia and Asia-Pacific.

Both India and Australia as members of IOR-ARC can have mutually beneficial relation in the Indian Ocean region and can collaborate with each other for peace, security and prosperity of the region. Indian Ocean is vital for both the nations because almost all their trade passes through Indian Ocean. Protection of sea-lanes passing through Indian Ocean is essential for the economic survival of both. No woder, Australia, India and South Africa—the three most important nations of the Indian Ocean region—are cooperating with each other for the peace, stability and prosperity of the region through IOR-ARC.

In the post-9/11 world, terrorism has emerged as the most serious threat to world peace, stability and security. India is victim of the scourge of terrorism. In the post-9/11 world the world has taken note of the threat posed by the terrorism to India. Here again Indian interests converge with Australia. South East Asia particularly Indonesia has been plagued by sporadic incidence of terrorism. The improvement in Indo-US relation has brought Australia closer to India. Now with the US blessings both the nations are cooperating in the field of defence. Their military cooperation is deepening and strengthening in the post-9/11 period.

India is pursuing "Look East" policy and Australia is pursuing "Look West" policy. Both these policies inevitably merge with each other. Geo-strategic compulsions have forced these countries to come together. Geo-economics has further deepened their relations. India needs technology and investment and Australia needs market. Both can help each other in the field of trade and commerce. Both are exporters of primary products and so both have common interest in WTO. Indo-Australian trade has recorded rapid growth in the 21st century. Now India ranks among the top 10 trading partners of Australia. There still exists vast scope for growth in Indo-Australian trade.

Traditionally, Australia's foreign policy focus has been on East Asia, a region stretching from Japan at one end and Thailand at the other. India has been relegated into a separate 'box' and relations with it treated as such. Some very obvious facts have been consistently overlooked by Australian policy makers. Not only is India the largest power in the ocean named after it, it also has the largest navy and coastguard of any littoral state between the two most important commercial straits in the world—Hormuz and Malacca. In addition, not only are the Straits of Malacca and the Strait of Lombok acknowledged to be two of the most crucial strategic straits in the world, more than half the world's maritime trade passes through them. Finally, a sizeable proportion of Australia's maritime trade towards the West passes through the Strait of Lombok and then through Malacca.[9]

The first Indo-Australian strategic dialogue was held on 30 August 2001. The dialogue focused on issues concerning economic security, energy security and security of the Asia-Pacific region. India and Australia were declared to be 'factors for stability' in the Asia-Pacific region. Strategically, India has been only recently recognised as an important player in regional affairs. India's growing role in the wider Asia Pacific strategic system will have more influence on Australia's security. "India is increasingly important to the wider regional strategic balance. This has not only increased Australia's interest in building contact on security issues with India; it has also made India more interested in Australia's distinctive approach and outlook on regional security affairs. The

Government hopes that early progress can be made in setting up the kind of dialogue that will allow us to explore and better understand one another's perspectives."[10]

Meanwhile, Track II dialogues with a similar agenda—the Australia-India Security Roundtable—are held periodically, supported by the Australia-India Council which is funded by the Australian government, and involving distinguished analysts from both countries. During the Labor government of Prime Minister Paul Keating (1991-96), multiculturalism became the new *mantra* by which Australian acceptance by Asian countries became easier and this engagement with Asia led to the announcement of the "Look West" policy.[11]

More than a thousand miles from its mainland, India has a naval, air and coastguard presence in the Andaman and Nicobar group of islands, the south most of which is barely 90 nautical miles from the Indonesian province of Aceh. Of the 600-island cluster, over 300 are inhabited and are suspected of being used as transit points by gun runners, smugglers and poachers. The region is also notorious for acts of piracy. Recognising this, India has been coordinating its efforts to combat these threats not only with countries in the region but with countries as far away as Japan.

In August 2001, India decided to set up its first tri-services command, the Far Eastern Strategic Command based at Port Blair in the Andamans. Military command post at Port Blair is strategically placed at the head of the Straits of Malacca. India's reason for this new post is to counter the increasing Chinese influence in South East Asia, but the decision brings Indian defence forces much closer to Australia.[12] India is planning to have a full strength army and an air base in the Andamans. This will give India not only strategic depth but also the potential to protect maritime traffic bound for Australia and the South China Sea. This combined with rapid developments in Indo-US strategic relations and the US' declared policy of ensuring international security in cooperation with allies and friends provides Australia with fertile opportunities to enhance security cooperation with India.

Instead of the traditional East Asia perspective, Australian emphasis, however, should change to an Asia-Pacific one. Given the nature of subjects covered in the strategic dialogue, it appears that a tentative start has been made. Greater naval cooperation with India would be a good starting point and a case could be made for the establishment of an Australian coastguard to become part of a network of regional coastguards policing non-military threats. Greater recognition should be given to the fact that the threats in the region are largely non-military-piracy, drugs, arms and people smuggling, etc., threats which India and Australia share in common.[13]

Indo-Australian relationship has been one which both of them have taken a little too much for granted. And the time has certainly arrived to inject some new vigour and energy into the relationship. They are very different but they also have many things in common. People to people links between societies are always important. Recently Australia passed the United Kingdom to be second only to the United States as a country in which Indian students of all kinds chose to study. There are between 100,000 and 150,000 Australians of Indian heritage.[14]

India and Australia have not always looked at foreign policy issues from the same perspective. They have had their differences in the past and it is pointless to pretend otherwise, admitted Australian Prime Minister John Howard. However, even at a time of difficulty and stress in the relationship, there has been a common thread of respect and understanding.[15]

Australia's Security Interests and Objectives

Australian High Commissioner to India, Penny Wensley while addressing the Indian National Defence College on 13 August 2002, identified five strategic objectives. Australia's most important long-term strategic objective is to ensure the defence of Australia and its direct approaches. A second objective is to foster the security of Australia's immediate neighbourhood. A third is to work with others to promote stability and cooperation in Southeast Asia. A fourth is to contribute in appropriate ways to maintaining strategic stability in the Asia-Pacific region. Australia wants to avoid the emergence of a security environment dominated by any powers whose strategic interests might be inimical to Australia's and to avoid destabilising competition between the region's major powers. And a fifth objective is to contribute to the efforts of the international community, especially the United Nations, to uphold global security.[16]

Australia has strong, abiding and inter-related economic and security interests in Asia. Australia places a very high priority on its continued and expanded engagement with Asia, and the relationship with India is high on that agenda. Australia also has a strong stake in the stability of the South Pacific region. Australia's security focus continues to be the Asia-Pacific region, where Australian interests are most directly engaged. Australia conducts regular bilateral and multilateral security dialogues with regional countries and major powers. These are important elements in Australia's security strategy, and provide an opportunity to share views on global and regional security issues, promote transparency and underline Australia's commitment to working cooperatively on security. A feature of these dialogues is that they involve both foreign affairs and defence officials. Australia's network of such dialogues, almost held annually, is now comprehensive, and includes the United States, Japan, the ROK, China, Indonesia, Thailand, Vietnam and the Philippines. Australia has expanded this web by holding bilateral security dialogues with three new and very important partners, India, the EU and NATO.

Australia continues to view the ARF as valuable in promoting stable relationships between the major powers, and as a useful complement to the bilateral alliances and dialogues which are at the heart of the region's security architecture. The ARF would benefit from developing further its preventive diplomacy agenda, and the role of defence representatives. It is also important that the ARF responds appropriately and vigorously to the challenge of terrorism. In the Indian Ocean region, Australia values the work of the IOR-ARC. It is a useful body for guiding trade facilitation and development in the region, especially through the exchange of information to members' business communities. In this sense, although it is not security architecture *per se*, it holds scope to contribute more over time to the region's prosperity, interconnectedness and stability.

Bilateral and regional cooperation in the Asia-Pacific and beyond has begun to intensify, however, continued effort, commitment and vigilance by all regional states is required if the region's relative peace and prosperity is to endure. A variety of fundamental security challenges remain, in the region and globally, including terrorism and a host of other trans-boundary problems, as well as unresolved territorial disputes, ethnic divisions and separatism, and the proliferation of weapons of mass destruction.

Terrorism

The increasing threat of international terrorism and the growing need for regional security cannot be ignored post-Bali and post-9/11 terrorist attacks. The two major trends in the rapidly developing Australia-India relationship are convergence of interests and the diversity of interactions.[17] Australia is committed to international action against terrorism. Following 9/11, Australia for the first time invoked its ANZUS security alliance with the United States, and has subsequently contributed substantially to coalition anti-terrorist military operations. Within Australia, in the aftermath of 9/11, there have been significant counter-terrorism initiatives, increasing the capacity of government agencies to prevent terrorism, improvements to the relevant legislative frameworks, and tightening of aviation security. Progress has been made towards integrating State and Federal authorities in a national framework for dealing with transnational crime and terrorism.

Beyond the national framework Australia is also playing its part through diplomatic channels to strengthen the architecture of international cooperation to defeat permanently and comprehensively terrorism. Australia is party to eleven important international legal instruments of international anti-terrorism cooperation; including the Convention for the Suppression of the Financing of Terrorism, and the Convention for the Suppression of Terrorist Bombings. A number of terrorist groups that have been active on Indian territory or in countries neighbouring India have been proscribed in Australia.

Australia like India has played a leading role at the UN in efforts to finalise the proposed Comprehensive Convention against Terrorism. Australia's contribution has been especially strong on the most contentious issue of achieving an agreed definition of terrorism. Australia has also been active in developing ways in which the Asia-Pacific's multilateral security body, the ASEAN Regional Forum, can play a substantial part in combating terrorism. The ARF has shown constructive focus in addressing the terrorism challenge. Strong cooperation between regional governments is critical in combating terrorism, especially in the exchange of information and intelligence to identify terrorist threats at the earliest possible stage.

Beyond terrorism, the illegal small arms trade and illegal immigration, the list of trans-boundary challenges confronting Australia and the region is a long one. It includes organised crime, the drug trade, piracy, money laundering, cyber attack, the impacts of environmental degradation, pandemics, problems of governance and lawlessness, and problems arising from development difficulties and economic disparities. Many of these issues are interconnected and have security implications.

Australia-India Relationship: Cooperation and Dialogue

There are long-standing bonds between the two countries: their nature as multicultural societies with democratic systems of government: the legacy of their shared Commonwealth background and in the military field, too, there are old and meaningful ties, including shared experience in two world wars. Despite all of this, there was a time when both the countries paid insufficient attention to the bilateral relationship. The Cold War played its part in that. But today the tempo of Australia-India relations is quickening because of mutuality of interests, and because both governments have come to recognise these realities. The trade and business relationship has reached an all-time high and is in excellent shape. While bilateral trade is balanced in Australia's favour, its expansion has been in both directions. Along with exports, Australian investment is playing a key role in Indian economic growth. Socio-economic and political bonds are given further depth and meaning by private sector and people-to-people programmes and contacts.

In this comprehensive relationship of building upon mutual interest, in a world of change and many security challenges, the strategic element has not been overlooked. Descriptions of Australia and India as Indian Ocean neighbours are more than just symbolic when one sees the sheer proximity of the Andaman Islands to Australia's Christmas Island. But increasingly it is the shifting global and geopolitical realities which point toward convergence of interests and the logic of engagement. Australia recognises India as a major power. India's significance stems not just from its size and geographic position, but from its economic modernisation, its military capabilities, and its evolving diplomatic engagement with a range of powers.

As a country's energy needs and global economic engagement rise, so does the importance of secure sea lanes, especially given transnational threats like terrorism and piracy. Australia is aware of the possibility that its role as a major supplier of LNG in the Asia-Pacific may one day extend to India. Maritime security focus of India is expected to grow in future. Australia and India will have converging and complementary interests in the India Ocean. The experts in the second-track Australia-India security roundtable recommended "closer bilateral defence and military cooperation more appropriate to the level of shared interests, including moving beyond training exchanges to exploring working directly together at a military level".[18] Penny Wensley observed that "there is a set of serious strategic concerns which the two countries share. These strategic concerns are to reduce or avoid large-scale interstate tensions in the Asia-Pacific and Indian Ocean regions, particularly emphasis on countering terrorism and other transnational threats to their democratic societies and growing economies. These are some of the issues on which Indo-Australian interests are converging."[19]

The most promising trend on the bilateral front between India and Australia is the growing strategic cooperation. India and Australia have a rich diversity of experiences in peacekeeping operations, rescue and rehabilitation tasks and fighting sea piracies. Stability and reconstruction of a war and terrorism-torn Afghanistan is another concern. A robust and harmonious Asia-Pacific community would not be a distant dream once India and Australia take a proactive approach in their bilateral relationship. The democratic values and the secular culture of India and Australia would help in dealing with issues of human security, free and unfettered world trade, political stability devoid of violence and terrorism, and above all, tolerance of ethnic, religious and other differences.[20]

End Notes

1. Richard Broinowski, India, China and Australia: The Fractured Triangle, *South Asia,* Vol. 23, Special Issue (2000), p. 145.
2. *Defending Australia,* Defence White Paper 1994, p. 96.
3. Joseph A, Camilleri, *ANZUS: Australia's Predicament in the Nuclear Age* (Melbourne 1987) pp. 94-95.
4. Michael Hillman, The Grand Old Duke of York: Indo-Australian Relations Post-Test, *South Asia*, Vol. 23, Special Issue (2000), pp. 153-54.
5. Richard Broinowski, No. 1, p. 146.
6. K. Subrahmanyam, Australian N-Stand, *Economic Times* (New Delhi), 27 June, 1995.

7. Marika Vicziany, Australia-India Security Dialogues: Academic Leadership in the Diplomatic Vacuum, *South Asia*, Vol. 23, Special Issue (2000), p. 161.
8. Shanta Nedungadi Verma, India and Australia towards Forging a Dynamic Relationship, in D. Gopal ed., *Australia in the Emerging Global Order,* (New Delhi: Shipra, 2003) p. 256.
9. Ravi Tomar, Australia-India Relations: Strategic Convergence?, http://www.aph.gov.au/library/pubs/rn/index.htm
10. White Paper on Defence Policy, 2000, cited by S. Utham Kumar Jamadhagni and C.S. Anuradha, Indo-Australian Strategic Framework: Possibilities for the New Millennium, *Journal of Indian Ocean Studies,* Vol. 11, No. 1, April 2003, p. 31-32.
11. L.J. Perry, The Irrelevance of being Asian, *Asian Studies Review,* Vol. 18, No. 2, pp. 113-18.
12. *Ibid.*, No. 9, p. 164.
13. *Ibid.,* No. 12.
14. Prime Minister John Howard Address to the India-Australia Council & The Confederation of Indian Industry New Delhi, 11July 2000, http://www.pm.gov.au/news/speeches/index.cfm
15. *Ibid.*
16. Penny Wensley, High Commissioner of Australia to India, http://www.ausgovindia.com/speeches/index.htm
17. Penny Wensley, High Commissioner of Australia to India, http://www.ignou.ac.in/news1.htm
18. *Ibid.,* http://www.ausgovindia.com/speeches/index.htm
19. Ibid, http://www.ausgovindia.com/speeches/index.htm
20. http://www.ignou.ac.in/news1.htm

22

Energy Security and the Indian Ocean Region: Constructing an Indian Ocean Energy Community

DENNIS RUMLEY & SANJAY CHATURVEDI

Energy is a key element of national economic development and is therefore an essential component of national security.[1] Given the 'underdeveloped' nature of most Indian Ocean states, then this truism has especially significant regional as well as global implications. Discussions over whether 2004-05 indeed represented the third major global 'oil shock' since the second world war, among other things, have focussed renewed attention on questions of energy security. In any event, to a significant degree, the price of energy is associated with supplier stability.[2] Furthermore, from a global perspective, significant investments in the energy sector over the next three decades will be necessary in order to meet growing demand and to avoid a major global economic crisis.[3]

Partly as a result of natural endowment coupled with underdevelopment, while some Indian Ocean states are energy-deficient, several others possess important energy surpluses. In an era of depleting global energy reserves in a context of rapidly increasing demand, the locations of such energy surpluses have become sites for competition between the energy-deficient North and the development-deficient South. This evolving process has a number of other fundamental security implications, not the least of which is the emergence of an international resources diplomacy overlain with the construction of a traditional military security rationale for the 'defence of energy' as part of a new global geopolitics of energy agenda. This, in turn, is likely to result in the reconfiguration of some geopolitical alignments that are significantly different from and may be in conflict with those associated with remnant Cold War and other 'traditional' security arrangements, since access to energy supplies and markets will continue to be one of the principal driving forces in national strategies and international relations.[4] Indeed, the very idea of an "axis of oil" as the basis of a potential "new partnership" between Russia and the United States is indicative of the power of energy security in facilitating geopolitical change.[5]

In the future, the Indian Ocean Region will become increasingly important to any discussion of energy security, not only because of the critical importance of regional states as energy suppliers, but also because of the essential role of the Ocean as an energy route. The central argument of this paper is that in order to maximise regional energy security, regional states should give serious consideration, not only to policies of energy diversification towards renewable sources, but more particularly to cooperative policies which are aimed at the creation of an Indian Ocean Energy Community (IOEC). Failure in this regard, we shall argue, will facilitate the neo-liberal, neo-conservative agenda of securitising the energy flows.

The Energy Security Concept

The case has been well put against the "traditionalists" who want to restrict discussions of security solely to politico-military issues, compared to the "wideners" who want to extend the concept to include economic, social and environmental aspects of security.[6] The present attempt unequivocally belongs to the latter orientation because energy is becoming increasingly securitised. However, since the energy security concept itself is contested, some writers discuss it only in the context of problems associated with "security of supply".[7] We take a different approach to what we understand to be a multidimensional energy security concept.

Bracken (2000) has argued that one of the critical factors in the creation of a 21st century geopolitical paradigm is the redrawing of the world energy map as many Asian states seek to industrialise.[8] Increasing competition for energy supplies and for the control over energy route ways increases the probability of inter-state conflict. In the Indian Ocean Region, while some regional states are 'energy-dependent'—for example, India (coal) and Singapore (oil)—on the other hand, several Indian Ocean states are net energy exporters and, on a global scale, the region contains some very significant 'resource holders'. Apart from the Gulf states for oil and natural gas, these include India, Australia and South Africa for coal, and Australia and South Africa for uranium. However, in terms of the significance of energy in their overall trade profile, five regional states—Australia, Iran, UAE, Indonesia and Oman—could be regarded as "energy-niche economies".

It is clear that Indian Ocean regional governments will increasingly develop a range of policies to monitor and enhance national energy security.[9] Furthermore, in general, from the viewpoint of supply, energy security policy tools will include prevention, deterrence, containment and crisis management.[10] However, the concrete application of energy security thinking in the Indian Ocean Region exemplifies a spectrum of policy responses associated with energy transportation questions, issues associated with trends in energy consumption and problems of maritime boundary delimitation, among others.

Since the world's energy supply is likely to remain a prime target for terrorists, maintaining the security of energy route ways is an essential cooperative element in any energy security strategy.[11] Furthermore, in the context of energy scarcity, energy supply locations are likely to become zones of conflict especially where land or sea boundaries are not clearly delimited, irrespective of any idealist views concerning potential cooperation.

Stakeholders in Indian Ocean Energy Security

Apart from regional energy holders, such as those in the Persian Gulf, the principal stakeholders in Indian Ocean energy security are those developing states in Asia, especially China and India, which possess a rapidly increasing demand for energy, and those energy-deficient states of the North (Europe, Japan and the United States). 'Protecting' the stake is critical to the economic security of these states. In this regard, it has been suggested that one of the several explanatory reasons for the more than 725 US military bases around the world is to afford protection for American dependence on imported oil supplies.[12] However, achieving energy security through the use of military force, as in the case of protecting access to oil in the 1991 Gulf War, should be seen as only one of many potential management strategies.

It has been argued that, in the long-term, the domestic application of non-military strategies, such as energy efficiency policies and the use of alternative energy sources, will guarantee energy security.[13] On the other hand, the geopolitics of energy security for Indian Ocean energy stakeholders must also involve different forms of regional cooperation with neighbouring states as well as a variety of aspects of a resources diplomacy strategy both with near neighbours and especially with distant suppliers. In short, maximising energy security necessarily implies the application of a combination of both a domestic and an international management agenda. This paper deals briefly with three of the Indian Ocean's most important Asian stakeholders—India, Japan and China, respectively.

India

The issues surrounding India's search for energy security are located in an environment characterised by a complex interaction between geopolitics and geoeconomics. With an expected GDP growth of eight per cent at the end of the Tenth Plan, energy demand is expected to grow at a rate of five per cent. Current per capita commercial primary energy consumption in India is 350 kg OE. If India's energy consumption grows to the level of the developed countries, which is about 10 times more than India's, the life of its meagre proven commercial energy reserves will be just three years for oil and five years for gas. Uranium reserves will last for six years and coal reserves will have a life span of 15 years. Thus, energy has become a strategic resource for the country.[14] The geoeconomics of energy security is obliging India to geopolitically reorient itself in terms of its immediate neighbourhood and beyond. Given India's economic growth rate, and since the industrial sector is the largest consumer of energy, the fact that India will be among the top four global energy consumers by the end of the first half of this century requires the development of an appropriate energy security policy. This is especially important since current proven energy reserves will be insufficient to meet the projected demand.

Current policy not only involves accessing new energy supplies and the construction of a South Asian regional energy grid, but also incorporates a resources diplomacy strategy by which Indian public sector companies are encouraged to acquire stakes in foreign oilfields. However, two of the more complex geoeconomic and geopolitical options involve gas pipeline proposals from Iran and from Bangladesh. Clearly, the long-mooted 'peace pipeline' from Iran through Pakistan to India has the potential to contribute to regional peace and stability and the Bangladesh-India proposal also demonstrates the complex interaction between geoeconomics and geopolitics. Regional cooperation on both options not only would help to maximise India's energy security, but would transform present hostile borders into transborder zones of cooperation. To achieve this, however, requires breaking through the "prison of old cartography and territoriality".

Japan

Currently Japan is the most energy insecure state on earth and thus maximising Japanese energy security remains a significant global issue given the importance of its economy. Due to its paucity of energy resources and the regional competition for energy supplies in Northeast Asia, Japan has been pushed towards a greater dependence on untapped energy reserves in the developing world, towards a greater reliance on nuclear energy and towards a much greater investment in alternative energy sources and energy technology.

Energy dependence has meant that Japanese policy-makers have been especially concerned with issues associated with "supply risk" and thus nuclear power is regarded as an attractive long-term option because it can be seen as a "semi-domestic energy source". It is also argued that the use of nuclear energy is one means of mitigating climate change. Japanese resources diplomacy with important Indian Ocean Region energy suppliers is another important policy element. In addition, like other extra-regional stakeholders, maintaining the security of Indian Ocean energy route ways is critical. Notwithstanding regional energy competition, Japan has been exploring energy linkages with Russia, especially in terms of possible oil and gas pipelines. Furthermore, greater regional cooperation, especially with South Korea, is a prospect for the future. However, perhaps the most geopolitically sensitive alternative energy security issue has been Japan's involvement in the International Thermonuclear Experimental Reactor (ITER) proposal, which, if it had been located in Japan, would have generated large quantities of cheap power but would have also turned it into a virtual thermonuclear superpower.

China

China is already the world's biggest consumer of coal and is second in oil and electricity, but its share per head of oil and gas has only just reached about 10 per cent of the world's average level.[15] In the next two decades, China's already considerable demand for energy will dramatically increase along with its dependence on energy imports resulting in increased regional and global energy resources competition. However, as has been pointed out, China's energy deficit cannot be considered simply in the same terms as that of Japan, for example, since it is not import-dependent in the same sense.[16] Rather, China's energy deficit is extremely complex and much more nuanced and structural and arises primarily as a result of a flawed national energy policy. Consequently, China represents a case of the simultaneous co-existence of an energy surplus and energy deficit.

One of the outcomes associated with this situation is that China has been taking a renewed interest in Indian Ocean energy holders and in the maintenance of secure energy supply lines. These developments, in turn, have become a cause for concern among some regional states. From a Chinese perspective, though, increasing its engagement with energy-rich Indian Ocean states should be viewed as no more than an extension of its new resources diplomacy strategy that began to emerge from the early 1990s. However, Chinese Indian Ocean engagement must be considered on the basis of a needs-based as well as an ambition-based rationale. On the one hand, in the short-term, China's increasing global economic interdependence implies the adoption of a cooperative security strategy. On the other hand, appropriate management of resources competition is essential to avoid potential energy conflicts in the future.[17]

Approaches to Energy Insecurity

Notwithstanding the appropriate management of competition for energy resources and the emergence of cooperative approaches, the combination of increasing global energy demand, growing energy shortages and proliferating energy ownership contests may well be contributing to an "emerging landscape of conflict", one of the ultimate potential outcomes of which is an 'energy war'. For the most part, however, states of the Indian Ocean Region and elsewhere are more likely to pursue negotiated rather than conflictual outcomes to the challenges of energy insecurity.[18] There exist at least three clusters of policy approaches to this issue that can be identified—a demand strategy, a supply strategy and a cooperative strategy. The essential goal of the demand strategy is to implement a range of conservation policies and practices designed to reduce demand and thus enhance environmental security. One of the additional outcomes of this strategy is that it will reduce the relative cost of energy per unit of output, and, to a degree, this has already been happening with oil—that is, since the first oil shock in 1973, the world now uses about 40 per cent less oil for each unit of output.[19]

A supply strategy, though equally multifaceted, is fundamentally concerned with the 'domestication' of energy supplies. This involves locating new domestic supplies of energy, using alternative energy sources, reducing imports of energy and/or finding alternative more secure routes for energy transportation. Using alternative domestic energy sources in this strategy will likely have a contradictory impact on environmental security. On the one hand, it will accelerate interest in the use of renewable clean energy sources. On the other hand, however, such a strategy will almost inevitably lead to a regional increase in the use of nuclear energy and thus an increase in the demand for uranium from relatively stable and secure Indian Ocean states such as Australia and South Africa.

A third policy approach to the problem of energy insecurity represents the opposite of energy conflict and involves a range of strategies including bilateral energy cooperation, regional cooperation and the development of a regional energy security community with its own well-developed and secure linkages. Among other things, such secure linkages may well emerge out of an increase in regional "pipeline diplomacy", since pipeline sabotage is potentially a significant security problem in the Indian Ocean Region.[20]

According to R.K. Pachauri (2005), the director of Tata Energy Research Institute (TERI), New Delhi, "energy security and, therefore, the prospects of stable and healthy economic growth would depend on timely initiatives involving not only energy supply sectors but major energy-consuming sectors too."[21] The following observations by him, in our view, have relevance not only for India but for the entire Indian Ocean Region (IOR). It could be highly misleading to assume, argues Pachauri, "that securing the oil supply for a particular country's growing demand would be adequate in itself to ensure energy security. An enlightened energy policy demands that in addition to an assurance of steady economic growth and the ability to withstand future oil price shocks, the very structure of a country's economy should also match the assurance of sustainable and manageable supply options".[22]

In the light of issues raised above, a question that needs to be addressed with a sense of urgency is this: to what an extent are the actual practices in the IOR dictated and driven by the principles of energy security from below? And to what an extent are such principles institutionalised? A critical assessment of the 'usual' functioning of the transport sector in most of the countries of the Indian Ocean region revels that, with a shift in the share of both passenger and freight transport away from rail to the oil-intensive road transport, it is becoming increasingly oil-intensive.

In short, the Indian Ocean region not only needs an efficient energy supply industry, diverse sources of energy ranging from oil to solar and wind, but more importantly an economic structure which uses energy efficiently. The transport sector, the commercial complexes and residential buildings under construction could easily lock the region into an energy intensive pattern that undermines energy security.

Environmental Security and Energy Security

To a significant degree, 'traditional' Cold War concepts of energy security still dominate the foreign policies of many states. However, other factors have become increasingly important in the 21st century, especially the impacts of globalisation, the privileged status given to the market and the continued emergence of 'non-traditional' security considerations associated with regionalism and with environmental and human security. It is evident, for example, that, in the Indian Ocean Region, there is a controversial relationship between energy resources and standards of living and human development for those states that are supply holders. In addition, central to any consideration of the relationship between environmental security and energy security is the question of 'energy sustainability', the key elements of which that have to be reconciled include sufficient growth in energy supply to meet need, energy efficiency and conservation, public health concerns and the protection of the biosphere and the prevention of more localised types of pollution.[23]

The debate over climate change is central to energy sustainability concerns and the relationship between carbon dioxide emissions and climate change is much more than a function of cost. However, in the United States, for example, energy is very cheap because its price does not reflect any environmental costs and their implications for human health.[24] To a significant degree, this issue lies close to the heart of what might be called an 'energy-environmental security dilemma'. On the one hand, taking a purely market view from the perspective of hydrocarbons, only a price shock is likely to encourage an increase in environmental security. On the other hand, such a price shock may also contribute to the adoption of alternatives which could turn out to be more environmentally insecure. The first option could mean the adoption of alternative clean renewables. The second option could mean an increase in nuclear energy with all of its attendant potentially problematical environmental consequences.

As is well known, combating human-induced climate change requires states to reduce the carbon intensity of their economies, and it has been argued that, by 2025, G8 members should generate at least 25 per cent of all of their electricity from renewable sources.[25] However, to some commentators, climate change is happening so rapidly that a 2025 deadline will be too late to avoid its most serious implications, and that, in fact, the only major solution to solving global warming is for the rapid expansion of nuclear power.[26] This argument is especially relevant for the ten states possessing the world's largest absolute volumes of carbon dioxide emissions—USA, China, Russia, Japan, India, Germany, Canada, South Korea, Italy and France. In 2004, of these states, only China, India and South Korea were projected to have significant increases in nuclear power over the next two decades, while, by 2025, both Germany and Italy were projected to have no nuclear power.[27] However, the 2004-5 'oil shock' has prompted the United States to seemingly reassess its position on nuclear energy, and, in a speech in April 2005, the US President declared that, "a secure energy future for America must include more nuclear power".[28]

Apart from the current small amounts of nuclear power generated by India and South Africa, one possible regional scenario from this perspective of climate change is that other Indian Ocean states will also seriously consider the development of nuclear power programmes. Iran has already indicated its intention in this regard. Furthermore, Indonesia, even though in favour of increased regional cooperation in the field of renewable energy, continues to debate the development of nuclear power, an option which it shelved in 1997. As it stands, the current plan is for Indonesia to begin the construction of its first nuclear power station in 2010, with a view to commencing nuclear power production in 2016.[29]

Looking ahead, then, the question is not whether the Indian Ocean Region shall remain central to the emerging global geopolitics of energy resource competition. What remains unclear, however, is whether or not the problematic of who gets, what, when, where and how, in the context of energy security, will be addressed through diplomacy and dialogue by various stake-holders in the Indian Ocean energy security context. After all, it is difficult to overlook the fact that, "the strategic military posturing of the US in the Arabian Peninsula, the maritime deployment of the US-led Multinational Force enforcing UN sanctions on Iraq, as well as the military occupation of Iraq and the deployment in Central Asia give to the geopolitics of oil in this region a strong military tone".[30]

Securitisation of Energy Flows: Maps of Neo-liberal Geopolitics

Energy security, unlike other aspects of non-traditional security, has always been intimately related to military security.[31] More often than not, it is the hegemonic consumer-states that have sought to maintain an uninterrupted supply of energy at an affordable price, through the threat and/or actual use of military power. It is equally useful to be reminded of the fact that, "after 'black gold' was discovered in Persia in 1908, this resource drastically exacerbated the stakes in the struggle over the spoils of the Ottoman empire and the Western security imperatives to prevent the (re)emergence of a powerful regional rival".[32] With the energy-military security nexus peaking and asserting itself nearly globally, the prospects of a serious conflict in the Indian Ocean Region between the imperatives of energy-social security broadly defined, and the quick-fix strategy of 'securitising' energy flows practiced by the hegemonic power(s) can not be dismissed that easily. Those who choose to address the individual and societal dimensions of energy security have been widely criticised on several grounds, especially after the painful events of 9/11 and its aftermath. It is argued, for example, that shifting the focus away from states and military threats to human-social security is desirable only when threats such as the Iraqi weapons of destruction programme ceases to exist.[33] We are further cautioned that, so long as rogue states, weapons of mass destruction and terrorism prevail, such threats to world order will continue to cancel out other loftier ideas.

Partha Chatterjee (2004) has argued that, at a time when international interventions of various kinds on the lesser powers are both common and legitimate, it could well be that we are more likely to witness rivalry and conflict in the international system. One significant site of potential conflict between the dollar and the euro economic regions is already visible.[34] A second site of potential conflict is over the control of strategic resources such as oil. A third may be emerging over the spectacular rise of China and its economy that could soon make it a potential global rival of Western powers. According to Chatterjee more or less similar kinds of competitive metropolitan interests were at play at the time of imperial annexations and conflicts in the 19th century.

Are we seeing a similar attempt now to stake out territories of exclusive control and spheres of influence? Is this the hidden significance of the differences among the major powers over the Anglo-American occupation of Iraq? Can this be the reason why the US political establishment has veered from the multilateral, globalising, neo-liberalism of the Clinton period to the unilateral, ultra-nationalist, neo-conservatism of the Bush regime?[35]

Questions raised by Chatterjee acquire greater salience and significance when placed in the context of the growing militarisation of Indian Ocean space and the 'great base race' in the Indian Ocean littoral.[36] According to Berlin, a number of factors and forces are at work in what he describes as 'enlarged global subsystem' linking states in an interactive strategic space, that in recent history were relatively separate from one another: "...some regional powers now are gaining the wealth, power and confidence to concern themselves with their external security. To this extent, the new bases reflect these states' perceived need either to erect defences against one another or, in some cases, against potential intervention or 'meddling' in the region by external powers".[37]

The Indian Ocean in the Geopolitical Vision of the United States

There is a growing body of evidence to suggest that a significant shift in American geopolitical thinking on the Heartland-Rimland equation is already under way.[38] In October 1999, the Department of Defense decided to reassign senior command authority over American forces in Central Asia from the Pacific Command to the Central Command. Throughout the Cold War, for example, Central Asia had been perceived as a peripheral concern, firmly entrenched within the Soviet sphere of influence, and situated on a remote edge of the Pacific Command's main areas of responsibility—China, Japan, and the Korean Peninsula.

Central Asia

However, this is no longer the case. The growing importance of landlocked Central Asia and its resource endowment in mainstream U.S. geopolitical thinking has an important bearing on the larger geopolitical setting of the Indian Ocean Region.[39] The region, which stretches from the Ural Mountains to China's western border, with vast reserves of oil and natural gas lying in and around the Caspian Sea, is being increasingly perceived as an object of the so-called 'New Great Game'. Since the U.S. forces in the Persian Gulf region fall within the jurisdiction of the Central Command, the assumption of control by the latter over Central Asia implies that a new strategic map of the 'vital interests of the US and its allies is more or less in place'. To quote Michael Klare (2001):

> Behind this shift in strategic geography is a new emphasis on the protection of supplies of vital resources, especially oil and natural gas. Whereas Cold War-era divisions were created and alliances formed along ideological lines, economic competition now drives international relations—and competition over access to these vital economic assets has intensified accordingly. Because an interruption in the supply of natural resources would portend severe economic consequences, the major importing countries now consider the protection of this flow a significant national concern. In addition, with global energy consumption rising by an estimated two percent annually, competition for access to large energy reserves will only grow more intense in the years to come.[40]

Accordingly, security establishments have started paying much greater attention to problems arising from intensified competition over access to critical materials—especially those such as oil that often lie in contested or politically unstable areas. As the National Security Council observed in the White House's 1999 annual report on U.S. security policy, 'the United States will continue to have a vital interest in ensuring access to foreign oil supplies'.[41] Therefore, the report concluded, "we must continue to be mindful of the need for regional stability and security in key producing areas to ensure our access to, and the free flow of, these resources".[42] More recently, it has been argued by the Shadow Defense Secretary of the United Kingdom, that, "it would be a positive development to consider establishing an Energy Security Directorate within the Ministry of Defense, which could work with the producing and transit countries to improve cooperative mechanisms should supplies be threatened".[43] No sub-region of the Indian Ocean looms as large in these geopolitical calculations as the 'Middle East' does, which has also been referred to as the 'Eurasian Energy Heartland'.[44]

The Greater Middle East

More recently, a new term, the "Greater Middle East" has entered the realm of competing geopolitical imaginations of new Heartlands of the 21st century.[45] The Greater Middle East, occupying a 'pivotal' position at the juncture of Europe, Africa and Asia, is described as the 'sum' of the core Middle East, North Africa, the African Horn, South Asia and ex-Soviet Central Asia. It is said to be occupying,

> ...a crucial position with respect to some of the major issue areas of the cotemporary era. Those issue areas are energy sources and availability; the proliferation of weapons of mass destruction (WMD) and their delivery systems; and the dangerous pairings involving Israel and the Arabs, Iran and Iraq, and India and Pakistan. Surely, this region in its aggregate has come to be viewed by the contending and aspiring world powers—the United States, Russia, a united Europe, China—as a strategic prize, maybe the strategic prize.[46]
>
> (*Emphasis given*)

What David Harvey (2003) has described as The New Imperialism is now unabashedly articulating itself through global market dynamics of neo-liberal capitalism as well as neo-conservative ideologies and norms.[47] According to Harvey, rather than focusing solely on Iraq, we should consider the "geopolitical condition and significance of the Middle East as a whole in relation to global capitalism".[48] He also emphasises the need to approach the oil question from a broader perspective and in terms of the following proposition: "whoever controls the Middle East controls the global oil spigot and whoever controls the global oil spigot can control the global economy, at least in the near future".[49] The geoeconomic script written by neoconservative intellectuals and institutions of statecraft incorporates in fact a kind of neo-liberal geopolitics in which the arguments for intervention are made in the name of connecting disconnected parts of the globalised world system.[50] Military interventions, however, as Harvey points out,

> ...are the tip of the imperialist iceberg. Hegemonic state power is typically deployed to ensure and promote those external and international institutional arrangements through which the asymmetries of exchange relations can so work as to benefit the hegemonic power. It is through such means that tribute is in effect extracted from the rest of the world. Free trade and open capital markets have become primary means through to advantage the monopoly powers based in the advanced capitalist countries that already dominate trade, production, services and finance within the capitalist world. The primary vehicle for accumulation by dispossession, therefore, has been the forcing open of markets throughout the world by institutional pressures exercised through the IMF and the WTO, backed by the power of the United States (and to a lesser extent Europe) to deny access to its own vast market to those countries that refuse to dismantle their protections.[51]

The Non-Integrating Gap

One of the better-known protagonists of neo-liberal geopolitics is the US Department of Defense assistant, Thomas Barnett; the author of a widely cited Esquire magazine article on 'The Pentagon's New Map' and the architect of so-called war-map games.[52] The 'compelling' geopolitical script that he has created and delivered to several thousand high-level U.S. government officials was expanded and published as The Pentagon's New Map: War and Peace in the Twenty First Century (2004) and quickly became a *New York Times* bestseller.

In Barnett's geopolitical imagination, the USA has now assumed the role and responsibility of the global 'systems manager' who, on a daily basis, has to apply the new global security maxim that 'disconnection defines danger'. According to him, America stands at historic moment characterised by not only extraordinary threats but also the promise that globalisation may be expanded from a closed club of prosperous countries to a planet-wide reality. He is not only convinced that such a future is worth creating, he believes that U.S. 'security exports' can actually make it happen.

The Pentagon's 'New' map is being drawn around much of the world's mid-section, encircling the regions from where threats to national and global security are likely to emanate, namely the Non-Integrating Gap. The Gap stretches from the Andean states of Latin America and the Caribbean Basin to sub-Saharan Africa, the Middle East and Central Asia, and much of

Southeast Asia. In Barnett's view, the Gap is 'dangerous' because it is disconnected from the institutions and infrastructure of economic globalisation. He is of the view, therefore, that the Gap needs to be integrated into globalisation's Functioning Core in order to prevent further terrorist attacks like 9/11. This alone, he proclaims, could bring about durable and just peace.

Since disconnectedness is now said to be 'the clear and present danger', the US and its allies must ensure that the Gap keeps shrinking at all costs. Furthermore, Barnett argues, the U.S. military is now due for a strategic shift. Rather than getting embroiled in wars against great powers, the US should follow an entirely different strategy that anticipates a series of long-term 'aggressive' engagements in the Gap, for the sake of a future worth creating. Involving major changes in every aspect of military organisation, foreign policy, and national strategy, the implications of Barnett's new grand strategy are rather profound and far reaching.

What Barnett has laid out is a pseudo-scientific rationale for a 'new' security strategy that the neo-conservative intellectuals and institutions of statecraft in the United States have wanted to pursue since the end of the Cold War, and even more desperately since 9/11. There are some remarkable similarities between Thomas Barnett and his *The Pentagon's New Map* and George Kennan and his famous *X Article*. Whereas the latter revealed the grand strategy of Soviet containment in the aftermath of World War II, the former attempts to provide an equally grand strategy of connecting the places and peoples that remain disconnected to the agenda of US-dictated corporate globalisation in the aftermath of the Cold War. As succinctly put by Susan Roberts, Anna Secor and Matthew Sparke:

> In the neo-liberal approach, the geopolitics of inter-imperial rivalry, the Monroe doctrine, and the ideas about hemispheric control...are eclipsed by a new global vision of almost infinite openness and interdependency. In contrast also to the Cold War era, danger is no longer imagined as something that should be contained at a disconnected distance. Now, by way of a complete counterpoint, danger is itself being defined as disconnection from the global system.[53]

Iraqi Oil

One good example of how complex issues related to energy security from below in the Indian Ocean region are being implicated in the broader and deeper context of neo-liberal geopolitics, is the manner in which control of the Iraqi oil sector is furnishing the Bush administration with the opportunity of testing a 'freedom oil' policy. As Philippe Le Billon and Fouad El Khatib put it so forcefully:

> Narratives around freedom versus evil have been extensively used by the Bush administration in its discursive construction of terrorism and the justification of the 'war on terror'. The same need to contrast the 'Saddam era' from the (US) 'liberation era' entails that oil come to play a different role for the population than is associated in the 'oil curse' narrative commonly used to portray the previous Iraqi regime (and most of those in the region). In other words, oil needs to bring 'freedom' rather than 'evil' in Iraq and the broader region. Such discursive construction entails a number of policies, whereby the US would take an active role in creating and sustaining a political and institutional environment, as well as investment and infrastructure, in which oil and oil revenues consolidate a stable democratic regime and lessen regional tension—thereby also resolving some of these conflicts and dilemmas between energy and broader foreign policy goals.[54]

The aggressive engagement in Iraq is further justified in terms of self-proclaimed 'moral exceptionalism'[55], ruthlessly pursued 'manifest destiny' and zealously guarded experience of the moral geography of the 'frontier'. The 'democratic' disciplining of 'failing'/'fading' states of Afghanistan and Iraq through the exercise of military power by the one and only superpower suggests at the same time performance of power relations generally understood as 'dominance'. As argued by David Campbell, "with...the globalisation of contingency, the erasure of the markers of certainty, and the rarefaction of political discourse, reproducing the identity of "the United States" and containing challenges to it are likely to acquire new discourses of danger...In this context, there is no shortage on the horizons of world politics of potential candidates for new discourses of danger (such as AIDS, "terrorism", and the general sign of anarchy and uncertainty."[56]

In the light of above mentioned factors and forces, various attempts at building regional and sub-regional partnerships/alliances, as building blocks for an Indian Ocean Energy Community, discussed in this paper, are, therefore, likely to be undermined by 'coercive Western Energy Security Strategies' and the North-South dimensions of resource conflicts.[57] Equally important in this regard is the reality of growing militarisation of the Indian Ocean by the major regional and global powers.

Military Geographies, Militarised Spaces and the 'security' of Sea Lanes of Communication in the Indian Ocean Region

Rachel Wood in her seminal work on Military Geographies talks about generally ignored, 'military space'.[58] She draws our attention not only to the expanding military control of domestic spaces around the world by the state-security establishments/industries but also to the foreign military control of sovereign territory. According to Wood, "we can not be ignorant of militarism and military activities in shaping the geographies of the contemporary world...Militarism and military activities shape the earth...".[59] The manner in which military and militarised geographies are shaping the world ocean space, especially the Indian Ocean, today demands and deserves critical attention.

Few would deny that the vulnerability of these vital sea lanes of communication to maritime terrorism, piracy, drug trafficking, gun running, ecological degradation and so on in the context of peaceful uses of the straits and safe regulation of global trade, including the energy sector. However, as argued and illustrated at length by Robert Beckman (2002), the problem of piracy and armed robbery against ships in South East Asia defies simply and straightforward answers.[60] One good sign, however, is that there is a growing realisation in favour of enhanced regional and sub-regional cooperation. According to Beckman, the governments in the region should cooperate with the International Maritime Bureau (IMB) Reporting Centre in Kuala Lumpur, which should serve as the nodal reporting centre for all incidents of piracy and maritime robbery in the region.[61] Cooperation between the IMO/national governments and the shipping community is equally vital, which could also result in the setting up of a broad-based expert group for the purposes of reviewing legal issues (including domestic legislation) that arise from enhanced cooperation at bilateral and regional levels to prevent and suppress piracy.

Energy flows through the Indian Ocean space pass through vital sea lanes of communication, especially the Straits of Hormuz and Malacca. For example, it is well known that the Straits of Malacca are transited by over 72 per cent east-bound loaded tankers on a global basis from the Indian Ocean to the Pacific Ocean, thus making it one of the busiest and longest waterways in the world. The Straits are approximately 800 kilometres in length and varies in width from 300 kilometres in the North to about 18 kilometres at the southern extremity. The greater part of the navigational channels goes through the territorial seas of Indonesia and Malaysia.

The United States has acted to protect the freedom of navigation in the Straits of Hormuz for several decades. More recently, especially after 9/11, the Straits of Malacca too have been relocated on the geostrategic map of US vital interests. One major event that has acted as a major catalyst in this regard happened on December 9, 2002. On that day, in the Arabian Sea, the Spanish Navy stopped the So San, a North Korean-registered vessel that had switched flags on the high seas. Within no time, American Naval officers joined their Spanish counterparts and uncovered 15 Scud missiles buried beneath a consignment of cement. The incident drew the attention of the Bush Administration as well as a fretful post-9/11 news media. The Spanish and

American officials did, however, reluctantly acknowledge that, while they may have boarded the ship legally, they lacked any basis to seize its cargo. The So San was subsequently released and allowed to sail on to port in Yemen. The incident made U.S. security officials argue that the So San's cargo represented only a tip of a global iceberg in weapons proliferation and that international law appeared to let the bulk of such cargoes pass with impunity. With 80 per cent of world trade by mass (about 5.6 billion tons) borne by ocean-going cargo ships, the threat became obvious. President Bush is said to have proclaimed: "The next 9/11 could happen at sea".[62]

The United States has subsequently implemented its "Proliferation Security Initiative" (PSI), calling upon "like-minded states" to join the programme of ship-boarding and information sharing, with the aim of combating the proliferation of nuclear weapons among so-called "rogue states." The PSI was announced on May 31, 2003 by President Bush as a counter-proliferation programme geared to the suppression of the traffic in unconventional weapons (often called "weapons of mass destruction" or "WMDs"). In September 2003, the states then participating in PSI meetings (the United States, Australia, France, Germany, Italy, Japan, the Netherlands, Poland, Portugal, Spain, and the United Kingdom) set out "Interdiction Principles for the Proliferation Security Initiative" (PSI Principles). The key objective of the PSI Principles was to ensure more coordination in impeding and stopping ocean shipments of WMDs, delivery systems, and related materials "to and from states and non-state actors of proliferation concern." The PSI Principles included a system of interdicting suspect vessels in any part of the world ocean.

Neoconservative cartographic anxieties of the Bush administration, underlying the literal text of the PSI, have been interrogated at some length by Timothy Perry.[63] His argument is that the manner in which the United States might be forced by such anxieties in the Bush administration to utilise the PSI in practice will not only blur jurisdictional boundaries between the ocean zones, but seriously undermine the customary international law of the sea. Whereas Stuart Elden has shown how, against the backdrop of war on terror, the two predominant meanings of 'territorial sovereignty' (namely occupying territory by force and that states are sovereign within their respective geopolitical realms and territorial borders) are now increasingly in tension.[64] It is in this context that we need to locate Malaysia's growing concern about the possibility of the PSI, wittingly or unwittingly, in undermining its sovereign rights over territorial waters.

Concluding Observations

For those who believe in the idea of an Indian Ocean energy community, it is important to emphasise that the Indian Ocean is a 'Third World' Ocean. The region is home to a vast majority of the poorest of the poor. For the marginalised and deprived, the priority is the satisfaction of such basic human needs as jobs, food, health services, education, housing, clean water and sanitation. Energy plays a central role in ensuring the delivery of most of these services. The proposed Indian Ocean energy community has its work cut out for it with hundreds of millions lacking access to electricity, and an equally large number of people still relying on traditional biomass fuels.

The local practices throughout the Indian Ocean Region, in contrast to the 'global truths' constructed by the neo-liberals as well as neo-conservatives, suggest beyond doubt that deprivation in energy has enormous impacts on the lives of poor people; in other words on the human security of Indian Ocean peoples. As aptly argued by Kanti Bajpai, "the point of human security studies…is to describe a map of violence that goes well beyond the map created by the neo-realist/statist view of security. Evidence suggests that the map is much larger than the map of inter-state violence. With all its imperfections, a human security audit, done systematically and rigorously, will map a massive area of human experience that is presently unmapped (or mapped in bits and pieces). Its promise is not to get every contour absolutely right; it is rather, to start to fill it, however incompletely, what is presently a very blurry picture—a picture of a turbulent and complex world system, composed of a ramifying set of actors and linkages, as well as an emergent world society increasingly latticed by globalised norms and institutions".[65]

The energy sector will continue to play a central role in the social and economic development of the Indian Ocean Region. It is self-defeating in both the short and long run to deny the vital links that exist between the energy sector and poverty reduction—through income, health, education, gender, and the environment. The energy securitisation paradigm is ideologically blind to the complexity involved in energy security. There is also a wilful denial of the fact that energy sector has to work closely with other sectors in order to tackle energy deprivation. Easier said than done, eradicating energy deprivation calls for tough public policy choices that include, but do not exhaust, delicate balancing of diverse interests and sustained commitment. It needs to be emphasised that energy communities can not be imposed from above but need to be created through co-operative practices from below.

Do we see any signs of an Indian Ocean energy security community as yet or it is more or less a wishful thinking? Even if the ground realities are yet to be touched and transformed in a meaningful manner by the widened understanding of energy security, the paradigm of energy-human security it seems has captured the imaginations of several policy-makers in the Indian Ocean Region, and hopefully, even beyond. In his most recent book, Zbigniew Brzezinski has made a forceful argument in favour of the USA offering 'global leadership' rather than asserting 'global domination' on what he would still perceive as the Eurasian chessboard.[66] According to him, "together, the United States and the European Union represent the core of global political stability and economic wealth".[67] The proverbial billion-dollar question facing the United States today, according to Brzezinski, is this: How to strike a balance between sovereign hegemony and an emerging global community, and how to resolve the dangerous contradiction between the values of democracy and the imperatives of global power".[68] This, according to him, "…remains America's dilemma in the age of globalization".

The above-mentioned work by Brzezinski appears to suggest that while the dominant security paradigm within the United States is one of 'keeping the violent peace', there is the dawning of a recognition that this might turn out to be increasingly difficult, not the least as trends in asymmetric warfare make it exceptionally difficult to maintain control by conventional means. It has also been argued by some analysts that, "the United States cannot and should not resist the end of the American era. To do so would only risk alienating and provoking conflict with a rising Europe and an ascendant Asia…If armed with the right politics and the right policies, the United States may well be able to manage peacefully the transition from unipolarity to multipolarity, thereby ensuring that the stability and prosperity attained under its watch will extend well beyond its primacy".[69]

While such alternative thinking might at present be limited to just a few far-sighted individuals in the military, academic and policy communities, there is potential for this to develop into a substantial intellectual movement that assists in effecting a paradigm shift. Such a paradigm shift is needed both among and within nation-states globally, and not simply among Indian Ocean states, despite the obvious appeal of both neo-liberal geopolitics and realism. Realism is "easy to grasp because it portrays the world in clear friend-or-foe terms".[70] Whereas, on the other hand, the appeal of neoliberal geopolitics lies in its reductionism. Both are hopelessly incapable, however, of ensuring energy security to peoples at large.

The Indian Ocean's energy issues, we have argued, are complex as well as diverse in nature. Even though the state and the non-state stakeholders in Indian Ocean energy security issues may have competing interests, some analysts are of the view that, "with the market playing an increasingly important role in energy security, economic geopolitics suggests that the costs of rivalry over strategic energy resources and supply are vastly outweighed by the benefits of cooperation…in fact, cooperation in energy security issues could pave the way for overall regional security co-operation".[71] At the heart of an enlightened politics of energy security should lie a relentless questioning of the claim put forward by a neoliberal geopolitics that peace and prosperity can only truly prevail in areas where the one and only superpower and its allies have established military bases to aid and assist corporate globalization.

End Notes

1. R.C. Keith, ed., *Energy, Security and Economic Development in East Asia* (New York: St Martin's Press 1986).
2. D. Yergin, *The Prize: The Epic Quest for Oil, Money and Power*, (New York: Simon and Schuster, 1992).
3. International Energy Agency, *World Energy Outlook*, (Paris: OECD/IEA, 2002)
4. See Yergin No. 2 and Clingendael International Energy Programme (CIEP) (*Study of Energy Supply Security and Geopolitics, Final Report*, (The Hague, 2004).
5. D.G. Victor and N.M. Victor, Axis of oil? *Foreign Affairs*, Vol. 82, No. 2, 2003, pp. 47-61.
6. M. Alagappa, "Rethinking Security: A Critical Review and Appraisal of the Debate', in M. Alagappa, (ed.), *Asian Security Practice: Material and Ideational Influences* (Palo Alto, Stanford University Press, 1998), pp. 27-64. Also see B. Buzan, O. Wæver, and J. de Wilde, *Security: A New Framework for Analysis* (Boulder: Lynne Rienner. 1998).
7. *CIEP*, No. 4, pp. 43-4.
8. P. Bracken, *Fire in the East: The Rise of Asian Military Power and the Second Nuclear Age* (New York: Perennial, 2000).
9. Australian Government, *Securing Australia's Energy Future* (Canberra: Department of the Prime Minister and Cabinet, 2004).
10. *CIEP*, No. 4, p. 26.
11. G. Luft, and A. Korin, Terrorism Goes to Sea, *Foreign Affairs*, Vol. 83, No. 6, 2004, pp. 61-71.
12. C. Johnson, *The Sorrows of Empire: Militarism, Secrecy, and the End of the Republic* (New York: Henry Holt, 2004).
13. Alagappa, No. 6, p. 686.
14. S.K. Sharma, Energy: Take a Holistic Approach, *The Tribune* (Special Supplement on India: The Tasks Ahead) Chandigarh, India. 24th of September, 2006).
15. R. Callick, Massive Room for Growth in China's Share of Oil and Gas, *The Australian*, 10 May, 2006.
16. D. Rumley, and S. Chaturvedi, eds., *Energy Security and the Indian Ocean Region* (New Delhi: South Asian Publishers, 2005), pp. 166-88. See also D. Rumley and S. Chaturvedi, eds., *Geopolitical Orientations, Regionalism and Security in the Indian Ocean* (New Delhi: South Asian Publishers, 2004).
17. *Ibid.*
18. Michael Klare, *Resource Wars: The New Landscape of Global Conflict* (New York: Holt, 2002), p. 23.
19. H. McRae, It shouldn't happen now, but there's nothing like the black stuff for leaving us in the mire, *The Independent on Sunday*, 20 June, 2004, p. 14.
20. G. Luft, Pipeline sabotage is terrorist's weapon of choice, *Energy Security*, 28 March, 2005, Institute for the Analysis of Global Security.
21. R.K. Pachauri, The Black Gold's Curse: Despite Several Myths, Energy Security has become new Global Concern, *Outlook*, New Delhi, 2 May, 2005.
22. *Ibid.*

23. G.H. Brundtland, *Our Common Future*, Australian Edition (Melbourne: OUP, 1990), p. 213.
24. P. Hawken, *The Ecology of Commerce: A Declaration of Sustainability* (New York: HarperCollins, 1993), p. 76.
25. International Climate Change Taskforce (ICCT), *Meeting the Climate Challenge* (London: The Institute for Public Policy Research, 2005).
26. M. McCarthy, "Only Nuclear Power can Now Halt Global Warming", *The Independent*, 24 May, 2004).
27. United States Energy Information Administration, International Energy Outlook 2004, p. 170.
28. CNN, Bush urges more refineries, nuclear plants, CNN.com, 27 April, 2005.
29. Agence France-Presse, Indonesia Agonises on Nuclear Switch, *The West Australian*, 20 April, 2005, p. 28.
30. Billon, P.L., The Geopolitics of Resource Wars, *Geopolitics*, Vol. 9, No. 1, 2004, p. 4.
31. G. Dietl, New Threats to Oil and Gas in West Asia: Issue in India's Security, *Strategic Analysis*, Vol. 28, No. 3, 2004, pp. 373-89.
32. P.L. Billon and F.E. Khatib, From Free Oil to 'Freedom Oil': Terrorism, War and US Geopolitics in the Persian Gulf, *Geopolitics*, Vol. 9, No. 1, 2004, pp. 109.
33. P. Bilgin, Individual and Societal Dimensions of Security, *International Studies Review*, Vol. 5, 2003, pp. 203-22.
34. Partha Chatterjee, Empire After Globalization, *Economic and Political Weekly*, 2004, (Internet edition).
35. *Ibid.*
36. D. Berlin, The 'Great Base Race' in the Indian Ocean Littoral: Conflict Prevention or Stimulation, *Contemporary South Asia*, Vol. 13, No. 3, 2004, pp. 239-55.
37. *Ibid.*
38. Klare, No. 18.
39. S. Mahalingam, Energy and Security in a Changing World, *Strategic Analysis*, Vol. 28, No. 2, 2004, pp. 249-71.
40. Klare, No. 18.
41. S. Peters, Coercive Western Energy Security Strategies: 'Resource Wars' as a New Threat to Global Security, *Geopolitics*, Vol. 9, No. 1, 2004, pp. 195-196.
42. *Ibid.*
43. See L. Fox, How to Stop Terrorists Turning Off Our Lights, *The Sunday Telegraph*, 21 May, 2006, pp. 22.
44. K.R. Singh, Geo-strategy of Commercial Energy, *International Studies*, Vol. 39, No. 3, 2002, p. 288.
45. Robert Harkavy, Strategic Geography and the Greater Middle East, *Naval War College Review*, LIV, No. 4, Autumn 2001.
46. *Ibid.*
47. David Harvey, *The New Imperialism* (Oxford: Oxford University Press, 2003).
48. *Ibid.*, p. 19.
49. *Ibid.*
50. S. Dalby, Calling 911: Geopolitics, Security and America's New War, *Geopolitics*, Vol. 8, No. 3, 2003, pp. 61-86.

51. Harvey, No. 47, p. 181.
52. Thomas P.M. Barnett, *The Pentagon's New Map: War and Peace in the Twenty-First Century* (New York: Putnam's, 2004). Also see T.P.R. Barnett, The Pentagon's New Map, *Esquire*, March, 2003. http://www.nwc.navy.mil/newrulessets/The PentagonsNewMap.htn
53. Susan Roberts, Anna Secor, and Matthew Sparke, Neoliberal Geopolitics, *Antipode*, Vol. 35, No. 5, 2003, pp. 888-89.
54. P.L. Billon and F.E. Khatib, No. 32, pp. 127-28.
55. J. Agnew, An Excess of National Exceptionalism: Towards a New Political Geography of American Foreign Policy, *Political Geography Quarterly*, Vol. 2, No. 22, 1983, pp. 152-66.
56. David Campbell, *Writing Security: United States Foreign Policy and the Politics of Identity* (Minneapolis: University of Minnesota Press, 1998), pp. 170-71.
57. Peters, No. 41.
58. Rachel Wood, *Military Geographies* (Malden: Blackwell, 2004)
59. *Ibid.*, p. 159.
60. Robert Beckman, Combating Piracy and Armed Robbery Against Ships in South East Asia: The Way Forward, *Ocean Development and International Law*, Vol. 33, 2002, pp. 317-41.
61. *Ibid.*
62. J.S. Burnett, The Next 9/11 Could Happen at Sea", *New York Times*, 22 February, 2005 at A 17.
63. Timothy C. Perry, "Blurring the Ocean Zones: The Effect of the Proliferation Security Initiative on the Customary International Law of the Sea, *Ocean Development and International Law*, Vol. 37, No. 1, 2006, pp. 33-53.
64. Stuart Elden, Territorial Integrity and the War on Terror, *Environment and Planning*, 2005, A, 37, pp. 2083-2104.
65. Kanti Bajpai, Beyond Comprehensive Security: Human Security in *Comprehensive Security: Perspectives from India's Regions. Seminar Proceedings* (New Delhi: Policy Research Group, 2002), pp. 214-25.
66. Zbigniew Brzezinski, *The Choice: Global Domination or Global Leadership* (New York: Basic Books, 2004).
67. *Ibid.*, p. 89.
68. *Ibid.*, 138.
69. C.A. Kupchan, *The End of the American Era: U.S. Foreign Policy and the Geopolitics of the Twenty-First Century* (New York: Vinatage Books, 2002), p. 247.
70. *Ibid.*, p. 234.
71. S.R. Dadwal, *Rethinking Energy Security in India* (New Delhi: Knowledge World, 2002), p. 83.

23

Energy Resource Management: Experience and Prospects of Australia and India

NABEEL AJMAL MANCHERI

Energy plays an important role in economic and social development of any country. People like to discuss whether the world is running out of oil and gas, and the big oil companies round the world have now joined in with warnings about energy shortages and the need to retool our economies on a more energy-efficient basis. Sufficient supply of energy is essential for the proper working of the economy. Further; due to the ubiquitous role of this commodity energy policy cannot be defined without taking into account the interrelations between the energy sphere and the economy sphere as a whole. Energy resources themselves are not the problem. The problem is the management of the world's vast energy resources, and all the complex political and economic decisions and choices and events that surround that management task. Indeed the energy strategies of Australia and India reflect their unique political decision making systems and their pervasive role in the world energy market.

India is a large and growing energy consumer, with a global impact on energy security and the environment. India is becoming increasingly important in the world energy scene. Its population passed one billion in 2000, and is growing substantially faster than that of China. India remains the first in the world in terms of annual increase in population, currently about 16 million. Measured using purchasing power parities, India is already the world's fifth largest economy, and expected to be one of the fastest growing countries over the next two decades. In 1999, India imported about two-thirds of its crude oil requirements and has also become a net importer of coal, it's most important energy carrier. As the economy grows the fossil fuel import dependency will rise, augmented by large imports of natural gas to fuel the expected increase in the demand for this fuel. The increased import dependency will make the Indian economy more vulnerable to price fluctuations or supply disruptions. India already suffers from serious local air pollution and growing energy demand, to a large extent based on coal, poses an important challenge for the health of millions of people. India has also become an important influence on the global environment with its share of global CO_2 emissions expected to increase as its economy grows.

India's demand for commercial energy is expected by 2020 to increase by more than 2.5 times from today's level.[1] Underpinning this trend will be the ongoing growth in population, as well as the number of people living in urban areas, aspiration towards higher living standards with reliable energy services provided to a higher share of the population, growth in industrial production and growth in the demand for motorized transport of goods and people. For India to tackle the economic and environmental challenge of its demand growth it is important to have a good understanding of how these and other factors have shaped and will shape energy use in the various sectors of the economy.

Australia is a major energy producer and exporter. At current depletion rates, the country has 820 years of brown coal, 290 years of hard coal, 270 years of uranium, 36 years of natural gas and 13 years of oil. About half of Australia's energy production is exported. Australia is the world's largest coal exporter and coal is Australia's largest export industry, accounting for 1 per cent of GDP and 10 per cent of total exports. Australia ranks third in liquefied natural gas (LNG) exports to Asia.

The Australian energy sector and energy policy are heavily influenced by the country's natural circumstances and general market approach to economic issues. Australia is the world's sixth-largest country; roughly 80 per cent larger in land mass than the EU-25 countries together. With a population of 20 million people, it has the lowest population density in the OECD. The country is rich in mineral resources, including coal, oil and natural gas. As an island nation, it has no land boundaries and is a substantial distance from most of its major trading partners. From 1993 through 2003, Australian gross domestic product grew at an average annual rate of 3.9 per cent while unemployment fell to a 27-year low in November 2004 with a rate of 5.2 per cent. The generally light-handed government approach to the economy is reflected in the energy sector. Energy policy is also influenced by Australia's federal structure with six states and two territories. Like all IEA countries, Australia strives to achieve the three E's of energy policy: Economic efficiency, Energy security and Environmental sustainability. The federal government's June 2004 energy White Paper explains the strategy to meet these objectives and is a commendable document developed in a transparent manner that gives predictability to all stakeholders. Regarding economic efficiency, Australia fares well. It has some of the lowest prices in the IEA for electricity, coal and gas. For example, industrial electricity prices are 38 per cent below the IEA average and household prices are 31 per cent below the average. There is a great deal of choice at the retail level, allowing many customers to select their preferred supplier. In addition, Australia successfully exploits its domestic fuel resources in the international market. The coal, oil and gas industries employ 120,000 people and provide more than AUD 24 billion annually in export revenue, equal to about one-fifth of the country's total export revenue.[2]

Australian energy security is sound. Security is enhanced substantially by the endowment of domestic fuels (albeit with declining oil production), extensive energy delivery infrastructure and good access to world markets. In 2003, net oil import dependence reached 14 per cent and government forecasts project this figure will rise to 37 per cent in 2010 and 46 per cent by 2020. However, the fluid market in crudes and products means this should not pose an undue threat. Significant indigenous coal and natural gas resources also play an important part in enhancing Australia's energy security.

Economics of Energy in India and Australia

Energy is one of the most important inputs for development and economists usually consider energy as a fourth factor of production. Unfortunately, either India or Australia has not been focused on energy policy in an integrated sense. All—both public and private—associated with energy sector are yet to work within a common framework for optimum utilisation of energy resources for the overall growth and development of the economy.

India's economic growth peaked only recently, after decades of gradual growth, unlike the decreasing trend observed in China and the slow de-coupling of energy and economic growth observed in OECD countries like Australia. GDP growth in India averaged 4.8 per cent annually from 1971 to 1990. It accelerated in 1993, and averaged 7 per cent per year in the 1993-1997 period, followed by a slight slowdown in 1998 and 1999. However, high population growth has dampened per capita income. Although it is the world's fifth-largest economy, India is below the top 100 countries in terms of per capita GDP, substantially lower than the developing-world average.[3] Table 1 illustrates how India ranked in 1997 in terms of its shares of GDP, population, Total Primary Energy Supply (TPES) and CO_2 emissions. The same shares are also shown for 2020, based on the IEA *World Energy Outlook* 2002 reference case. For commercial energy, India ranked seventh in the world in 1997, with 3.1 per cent of world demand, up from around 1.3 per cent in 1971. India is one of the world largest consumers of combustible renewable and waste (CRW), constituting nearly one-fifth the world's total use of these fuels. When these fuels are included, India's current share of world primary energy use rises to nearly 5 per cent. With its size, fast growth in energy demand and the significance of coal in its fuel mix, India has also become an important contributor to global GHG emissions. Despite its extremely low per capita CO_2 emissions. India contributed 4 per cent of the total world CO_2 emissions in 1997, about the same as Germany.[4]

Table 1: India in the Global Context (Share and Rank in the World)

	1997		*2020*	*Increments*
	Share Per cent	*Rank*	*Share Per cent*	*Share Per cent*
GDP in PPP terms	4.0	5th	5.9	7.6
Population	16.6	2nd	17	18.3
TPES (excl. CRW)	3.1	7th	5.3	9.1
Coal	6.8	3rd	10	16.7
Oil	2.6	11th	4.6	8.1
Final electricity demand	3.0	8th	5.3	8.3
CRW	18.2	2nd	16.2	9.6
TPES (incl. CRW)	4.8	5th	6.3	11.9
CO_2 emissions	3.9	6th	6.2	10.1

Source: IEA-WEO-200.

Note: CRW = Combustible Renewables and Waste. Due to its non-commercial nature and questions related to reliability of data, CRW is given separately.

The International Energy Agency (IEA) estimates that India would require $665 billion as investments in the power sector during the period 2001-2030. The government has urgently to create conditions by which this level of investment materialises not only from government allocations and internal resource generation, but increasingly from private sector investments. The provision of free power to any group of consumers cannot inspire any investor to sink his resources to provide inputs for a sick industry.

Australia has exhibited robust economic growth over the last decade, most recently with a 3.7 per cent increase in real gross domestic product (GDP) in 2003 and moving in and around 3.0 per cent in the following years. As a result, Australia is one of the world's fastest growing industrialised countries. Such growth has occurred in spite of weak export demand and a strong Australian dollar that has depressed exports, as well as severe droughts during 2002 and 2003. Australia's access to abundant energy resources contributes greatly to living standards and the health of this nation's economy. Australia's energy resources provide consumers with low-cost energy, underpinning the competitiveness of other Australian industries.

The energy sector is an essential component of the Australian economy. Expenditure on energy in Australia in 2002-03 was about $50 billion. Energy exports of coal, natural gas, oil, petroleum products and uranium amounted to $24.2 billion.[5] The resources sector (petroleum and minerals industries) in Australia makes a significant economic and social contribution to the Australian economy. The resources sector is the nation's largest single export sector. Over 80 per cent of its output is exported, accounting for around 36 per cent of Australia's total goods and services exports. In 2003-04, the minerals and petroleum industries produced 6.4 per cent of Australia's GDP of A$784 billion and earned 48 per cent of Australia's merchandise exports. Australia is the world's largest exporter of coal, accounting for about one-third of the world trade. In 2003-04, Australia produced around 66 per cent of its liquid petroleum needs and all of its gas needs. The market value of crude oil and gas production in 2002-03 was around A$18 billion, with exports valued at around A$9.9 billion. Energy resources make a significant contribution to government revenue, both nationally and at state level. Australia collects around $13 billion annually from fuel excise, that is, around 7 per cent of total revenue. Secondary taxation of energy resources will raise another $2.1 billion for the Australian Government (Australian Government Budget 2004-05) in 2003-04 and a further $1.5 billion for state and territory governments (State and Northern Territory Budgets 2002-03 and 2003-04)

The ability of Australia's minerals and energy sector to sustain its growth and expand its contribution to national economic performance in the medium and longer terms depends critically on the amount of investment in minerals exploration. Most of the strong growth in the minerals and energy sector of recent years is underpinned by minerals exploration expenditure of the past decade. In 2003-04, total Australian minerals and petroleum exploration expenditure was virtually steady at A$1.73 billion. This follows a rise of 13 per cent in 2002-03, among the major commodity categories, petroleum expenditure fell in 2003-04.

Supply of Primary Sources of Commercial Energy in India and Australia

Traditionally, a large part of the total energy supply in India is drawn from non-commercial energy sources such as fuel wood, cow dung, and charcoal and crop residues. It was estimated that over 60 per cent of the India house holds depend upon these traditional sources of energy. Out of the total rural energy consumption, about 65 per cent is met through fuel wood. However, over the years, there has been a significant change in the pattern of supply of energy in the country. The share of commercial fuels in the total energy supply in India has risen from 41 per cent in 1970-71 to approximately 70 in 2003-04. In 1999, India's total primary energy supply was 480Mtoe (million tonne oil equivalent) of which combustible, renewables and waste (CRW) accounted for approximately 198 Mtoe or 41.2 per cent. Including CRW coal is the most important energy sources, with a share of 33 per cent followed oil and petroleum products with share of 20 per cent and more than half of the crude oil and petroleum product supply is imported. Indigenous energy sources account for 80 per cent of India's energy supply, of which about half is CRW.

India is relatively well endowed with both exhaustible and renewable energy resources. Coal, oil, and natural gas are the three primary commercial sources of energy. Over the years, there has been a significant change in the pattern of supply and consumption of energy. The share of commercial fuels in the total energy supply in India has risen from 41 per cent in 1970-71 to approximately 70 per cent in 2003-04, despite the dominance of the traditional fuels in the energy sector in India. The total domestic primary commercial energy supply in India has risen from 147.05 MTOE (million tonnes of oil equivalent) in 1970/71 to 248 MTOE in 2003. Table 2 gives the break up of primary energy supply for various fuels from 1970 onwards.

Table 2: Production of Primary Energy Sources of Conventional Energy in India

Source	*1970/71*	*1980/81*	*1990/91*	*2001/02*	*2002/03*
Coal and lignite (MT)	76.34	119.02	228.13	352.60	367.29
Crude oil (MT)	6.82	10.51	33.02	32.03	33.04
Natural gas (BCM)	1.45	2.36	18.00	29.71	31.40
Nuclear power (BkWh)	2.42	3.00	6.14	19.48	19.39
Hydro power (BkWh)	25.25	46.54	71.66	73.70	64.10
Wind power (BkWh)			0.03	1.97	2.1

MT—Million tonnes;
BCM—billion cubic meter
BkWh—Billion Kilowatt hour
Source: MoC (2004a) and CEA (2003).

Australia is the world's fourth largest producer and the largest exporter of coal (IEA 2003). Australia has significant reserves of natural gas and supplies about 8 per cent of the world's liquefied natural gas (LNG) trade. Reserves of liquid petroleum are less abundant but still significant, particularly in view of how lightly Australia has been explored. Australia's reasonably assured resources of uranium at less than US$40 per kilogram make up 40 per cent of world resources.

Australia has extensive renewable energy resources, some of which are currently used to varying degrees such as hydro, wind and solar, and some of which are yet to be used such as waves and hot dry rocks. Australia has world-class access to wind and solar energy. Fossil fuels are Australia's major energy sources: oil, black coal, natural gas and brown coal provide 35, 28, 19 and 13 per cent respectively of primary energy needs.

Renewable sources currently supply 5 per cent. Natural gas and renewables use for electricity will grow significantly. While the use of wind and solar energy is expected to grow significantly over the next 20 years, it will do so from a very small base. Coal and oil will continue to be by far the most important primary energy sources. Uranium is not used as an energy source in Australia but is exported under stringent safeguard arrangements to ensure it is used for exclusively peaceful purposes and is fully accounted for throughout the nuclear fuel cycle. Potentially, liquid fuels could be produced from Australia's gas, coal or shale oil resources and biomass sources.

Australia's large land area has considerable wind and solar resources, and its geology and geography provide excellent potential for power from waves and underground heat sources. Large-scale hydropower potential has been largely exploited, while some potential for smaller-scale hydro remains. Australia's biomass resources are significant but present ecosystem management challenges. Although the use of renewable energy in Australia is relatively modest, the country has a successful renewable support scheme and some of the lowest prices for renewables in the IEA. Renewable energy development are influenced by the predominance of accessible, well-located, inexpensive fossil fuels and an approach to climate change that is based on securing least-cost abatement opportunities. Nevertheless, government activity supporting renewable energy has risen in recent years. The Mandatory Renewable Energy Target (MRET) system mandates that electricity retailers and wholesale buyers acquire renewables certificates equal to a certain percentage of their electricity sales; likely to be around 3.5 per cent in 2010. MRET has resulted in substantial new capacity in a wide range of different technologies, particularly wind, solar and hydro. Costs for the certificates are below what other IEA countries are paying as part of renewables "premium" over conventional fuels. While the government has chosen not to expand the MRET target at this time, additional policies could be considered to support the further development of the country's world class renewable energy resources and technologies. In addition, the benefits of renewables use in areas that may be profitable in an Australian context, such as off-grid power and summer electricity peaks, should be further explored. The Solar Cities initiative is likely to advance this possibility.

Electricity plays a pivotal role in Australia and is important for international competitiveness, industrial employment and economic development. It also has a great consequence on the environment as 50 per cent of Australian energy-based GHGs come from power generation. Australia was one of the pioneers in energy sector microeconomic reform and should be commended for its vision and implementation of a liberalised market. The country now has one of the most transparent and competitive electricity markets in the world and could serve as a model for other countries. Electricity prices are low by international standards on both retail and wholesale levels with some of the lowest electricity prices in the IEA and the world. Although electricity security is sound, it will continue to be monitored as in all IEA countries.

Coal plays a major role in providing Australia with low energy prices and sound energy security. In 2003, it accounted for 43 per cent of TPES and 77 per cent of all electricity generation. The most pressing short-term concern for the industry is a constrained export infrastructure in these times of high prices and demand; however, several major expansions are planned. While infrastructure expansion is largely the responsibility of industry, the federal government can nevertheless work with the states to help in a number of important ways, including the review of Environmental Impact Statements (EIS) in a timely manner, providing leasing for rail tracks, making any state-owned land available for appropriate development and facilitating a dialogue with the governments of purchasing countries to co-ordinate their off take with the domestic supply chain. In large part because of coal's high carbon content, Australia's GHG emissions intensity is one of the highest in the world. Electricity from coal-fired plants has more than twice the CO_2 emissions per unit than electricity from gas-fired combined-cycle plants. A number of collaborative efforts between private and government stakeholders have formed to develop technologies that can curb coal emissions.

The Australian natural gas sector has experienced major reforms and structural change since the mid-1990s with the separation of formerly integrated companies and the introduction of third party access (TPA) to transmission and distribution pipelines. There has been significant investment for expansion and integration of the gas transmission network, which has enhanced competition and security of supply. In 2003, natural gas accounted for 20 per cent of primary supply although its production and use are expected to expand dramatically with a 184 per cent growth in production between 2003 and 2020 and a 97 per cent growth in domestic use. Most of the gas reserves are located in the north-west of the country, far from demand centres and are most likely to be exploited as liquefied natural gas (LNG) projects. Although competition in the global LNG market is fierce, Australia offers several advantages compared with other LNG suppliers, mainly political and economic stability and proximity to Asian demand centres.

Oil accounts for about one-third of Australian primary energy supply. The country has substantial domestic production, which has stayed at a relatively constant level since 1990. The government, through the Australian Bureau of Agricultural and Resource Economics, projects that domestic oil production will remain flat in the coming years and that increasing oil demand will cause import reliance to rise, reaching 37 per cent in 2010 and 46 per cent in 2020. More conservative forecasts from Geo-science Australia predict a steady downturn in Australian oil production over the next two decades as existing fields mature and new discoveries are limited. Given the liquidity of global and regional crude and products markets, this does not necessarily pose a security of supply problem. The government is interested in keeping Australia an attractive investment destination for oil exploration and production. It considers the country's oil resources to be under-explored and would like to see greater activity to exploit domestic oil. The efforts being made to encourage more activity such as a tax uplift and government geo-science pre-competitive surveys appear to be sound, particularly given that these actions are targeted on the so-called "frontier areas" which remain largely unexplored.

While Australia does not generate electricity from nuclear power, it does have substantial uranium reserves and is a major global uranium exporter. In 2002, total Australian economically demonstrated uranium resources were estimated at 702, 000 tonnes, with the majority of the resources located in South Australia, the Northern Territory and Western Australia. Continuing stable uranium exports from Australia contribute to global security of supply.

Aggregate and Sectoral Energy Demand and Intensity

India urgently needs modern energy to support its large, expanding population and grooving economy. The country has vast coal reserves which may have supplied a major share of its primary energy supply. Coal also contributes decisively to India's energy security, since the country has limited oil and natural gas production. The International Energy Agency, for instance, has projected that in the year 2030 India would be consuming over 5 million barrels of oil a day. This growth in demand is predicated on a massive increase in passenger vehicle ownership and use in the country, with the total number reaching almost 200 million vehicles by 2020. This scenario is clearly not acceptable, because such a projection carries with it a grave danger to the energy security of the country not only for the terminal period of 2030, but much earlier.

One such factor is changes in economic structure. These changes can have an impact on the energy per GDP ratio since GDP represents economic activities that require energy services in varying degrees. For example, generating one unit of GDP from producing electronics requires much less energy than if the same unit of GDP is generated from producing steel. Thus, a shift away from heavy industries (e.g. steel) to less energy-intensive production (e.g. electronics) could drive down a country's energy demand, all else being equal. This shift towards a less energy-intensive structure has injected a downward force on the energy per GDP ratio in a majority of IEA countries since the 1970s. Today demand for commercial energy has soared with population and economic growth and with rapid urbanisation. Power generation rose from 4.1TWH in 1947 to 442 TWH in 1998. But per capita electricity consumption is still one of the lowest world wide—416KWH in 1998 compared with 15.6 KWH in 19950.

The Indian economy underwent significant changes between 1971 and 1990 with the industry and service sectors expanding while agriculture lost ground (Table 3). The structural change towards more industrial production may offer some explanation to the increasing energy per GDP ratio, as the energy intensity (energy per value added) in this sector is much higher than for agriculture. In fact, in 1990 generating one rupee in the industry sector required on average about 20 times the amount of commercial energy as if the same rupee had been generated within the agriculture sector. The shift from agriculture to services has less impact on energy per GDP, as the intensities in these two sectors are more comparable.

Table 3 also indicates that increasing intensity in the industry sector between 1971 and 1990 may have boosted energy per GDP. Whether this growth is resulting from structural changes within the industrial sector itself, due to a higher share of energy intensive raw materials in the production mix, or from deteriorating energy efficiency is difficult to say without more disaggregated data than what is included in Table 4. In addition, it can be expected that substitution of non-commercial fuel by commercial fuels has pushed up the industrial energy intensity to some degree. This can probably explain the large increase in agriculture intensity over the same period.

Table 3: Economic Structure, Energy Shares and Intensities

Sectors	*1971*			*1990*			*1997*		
	GDP Share in per cent	*Energy Share* in per cent*	*Intensity***	*GDP share in per cent*	*Energy Share* in per cent*	*Intensity****	*GDP share* in per cent*	*Energy Share** in per cent*	*Intensity****
Industry	14	45	115	19	54	144	20	51	125
Agriculture	40	2	1.6	28	4	7.3	23	5	11.1
Services	16	3	6.2	19	1	3.3	20	1	3.6
Transport		30	10.8		23	11.6		25	12.3
Residential		15	7.6		14	10.5		14	10.8
*Sum*****	70	94		65	97		64	97	

* Shares for sectoral energy use in total final consumption of commercial fuels based on IEA statistics.

** Intensity is for industry, agriculture and services are calculated as commercial energy use divided by value added in the sector (toe/million 1980/81Rs). Intensity for transport is simply transport energy use divided by *total* GDP and for residential intensity is energy use per unit of personal expenditures. Both measured in toe/million 1980/81Rs. The values of the intensities in these two sectors are therefore not comparable with those of the other three. See also below.

*** The sum of energy shares does not add up to 100 per cent since there is some energy consumed that is defined as non-energy use. The GDP shares do not add up to 100 per cent due to value added generated outside the sectors included here.

Between 1990 and 1997 the share of industry in total GDP increased one percentage point, inducing a moderate upward force on the energy per GDP ratio. However, during the same period industrial energy intensity fell significantly, offering at least partly an explanation to the reversal of the trend in energy per GDP. In this period, agriculture continued its diminishing share of economic activity, although the sector still plays an important role as a main income source in rural areas, which contain three-quarters of the population and two-thirds of the labour force.

The energy shares for residential and transport is also shown in Table 3. Energy demand for transport was growing slower than in industry and other sectors before 1990 but accelerated in the 1990s as the fastest growing sector. Transport also accounted for more than half of incremental oil demand between 1971 and 1997. The energy intensity for transport in Table 4 is calculated from dividing transport energy use by total GDP as there is no good measure of economic activity in this sector that covers all travel and hauling activities within the broad transport sector. The residential sector's share of total commercial energy demand has been relatively stable since 1971. The intensity for residential is calculated as commercial energy per unit of private consumption expenditure and reflects how commercial energy has evolved with private income. However, neither of the intensities for the two sectors is good measures of how the efficiency of energy use is developing. To provide more insights of how energy use and efficiency are developing in these two sectors, as well as for capturing the development within important industrial branches, more detailed information than presented in Table 3 is clearly needed.

Economic Structure, Energy Shares and Intensities of Australia

Petroleum products are an important part of energy consumption in Australia. Petroleum products are responsible for 52 per cent of final energy consumed in Australia. More importantly, liquid petroleum products fuel very nearly 100 per cent of the transport market. Of these fuels, 95 per cent are produced by Australia's 8 major refineries: Around 95 per cent of the petroleum products consumed in Australia are produced by the local refineries and these refineries are reliant mainly on imported crude oils with just under 20 per cent sourced from the Middle East, 40 per cent from Asia and 40 per cent from Australia's own production. Consequently, Australian transport fuel consumers are exposed to international disruptions to crude oil because 60 per cent of refinery input is sourced from overseas.

Australia is a net importer of liquid hydrocarbons (including crude oil, LPG and other refined and semi-refined petroleum products). In 2004-05, Australia exported around 778 petajoules of liquid fuels (excluding LNG but including international bunkers) and imported around 1451 petajoules. Exports of liquid fuels fell in 2004-05, while imports rose. The increase in net imports corresponded with a decrease in domestic oil production, which offset a moderate increase in domestic refinery output.[6]

Australian electricity production is estimated to have risen by around 8.5 per cent during 2000-01 and 2004-05. However, production of hydroelectricity fell by around 6 per cent in this period as the water flow available to hydro power generators, particularly in New South Wales, Victoria and Tasmania, was severely affected by continued dry conditions.[7]

Australian Electricity demand has expanded strongly in the last 20 years by more than 4 per cent per year, and has doubled over the last two decades. Electricity generation is a major primary energy user, equal to around 40 per cent of total primary energy. Coal, which produced 78 per cent of electricity in 2000-01, will remain the main energy source for electricity generation despite substantial growth in natural gas and renewables. Australia's domestic reserves of oil are less abundant, but are nonetheless significant and play a useful role in meeting demand for transport fuels. In value terms, Australia produces enough oil to meet around 80 to 85 per cent of its domestic fuel needs. This is in stark contrast with most other developed economies which rely very heavily (and often exclusively) on imported oil.

Table 4: Sectoral Final Consumption of Energy in 1973 and 2003, Australia

In Mtoe	*1973*	*2003*
Industry	16 mtoe	23 mtoe
Transport	14 mtoe	29 mtoe
Other Sectors*	9 mtoe	17 mtoe

* Includes residential, commercial, and public services, agriculture and non-specified.

Source: www.iea.org/statist.

Over the past thirty years, energy consumption in Australia has more than doubled from around 2700 petajoules to more than 5500 petajoules a year. The average annual rate of growth in consumption has fallen from a peak of 5.8 per cent in 1988-89 to 1.9 per cent in 2004-05. The growth in total consumption was higher in transport sector compared to industry and other sectors; it doubled from 14Mtoe to 29Mtoe between 1973 and 2003. Energy demand in the transport sector has been more volatile than usual in the past few years, mainly as a result of high oil prices and changes in international tourism. Energy consumption in the aviation transport industry fell in both 2001-02 and 2002-03, before rising slightly in 2003-04 and more strongly in 2004-05. Total energy consumption in the manufacturing sector rose by 1.6 per cent in 2004-05 (ABARE, Energy update 2006, p. 3).

Until the early 1990s total energy consumption tended to grow at a rate that closely matched the rate of growth in gross domestic product. Since then, energy consumption has tended to grow more slowly than gross domestic product. This decline in the 'energy intensity' of the Australian economy can be attributed to two main factors—greater energy efficiency through technological improvements and fuel switching, and the rapid growth of less energy intensive sectors, such as services, relative to the more moderate growth of more energy intensive sectors such as manufacturing and mining. Australian energy intensity is quite high with primary energy per unit of gross domestic product (GDP) 35 per cent above the IEA average. This is largely due to the country's vast spaces, large reserves of low-cost black and brown coal, predominance of energy-intensive industries and low energy prices. Traditionally, energy policy has focused on the supply side but greater attention is now being paid to the benefits of demand restraint. The June 2004 energy White Paper states that energy efficiency can increase both GDP and employment. The National Framework for Energy Efficiency (NFEE) has been established and the Productivity Commission (PC) will complete a year-long inquiry into the benefits of energy efficiency in August 2005. The Australian energy sector stands to benefit from greater government efforts to improve energy efficiency throughout the economy.

Energy Objectives of India and Australia

Since India and Australia are dissimilar in their resource endowments and needs both countries have different strategies for the development and management of energy sector.

India primarily concentrates on the following objectives:

Provide clean and affordable energy to all; to meet the energy needs of all segments of India's population in the most efficient and cost-effective manner promoting rapid economic growth while ensuring long-term sustainability; promote the design and establishment of decentralised energy service providers; design a basket of differentiated services available at differential prices to empower poorer customers to make a choice; ensure security of energy supply; map all energy resources and develop a databank of technology choices, efficiencies and costs to facilitate evaluation of trade-offs between alternative energy paths; facilitate investments in energy systems and efficiency improvements with the help of the private sector; encourage commercially-driven goal-oriented private and decentralized R&D (research and development) efforts; channel public R&D funds towards reducing cost of energy delivery to the poor; prepare energy plans to meet unforeseen emergency situations.

Improve the efficiency of the energy system; open up energy markets to allow a larger number of players'—public and private—in all market segments;

adequately empower independent regulatory authorities; adopt uniform pricing principles, internalising environmental costs, across all energy sub-sectors for meaningful competition and efficient resource allocation; de-link the social function of subsidy provision from energy pricing decisions; institutionalize preparation of information systems, and communication and education programmes for promoting energy efficiency; reduce the adverse environmental impacts of energy use; accelerate the development and market adoption of environmentally friendly technologies; and strategically exploit opportunities arising out of international agreements such as climate change and the WTO (World Trade Organization) to meet energy goals.

The Australian Government's approach in developing the nation's energy resources is guided by the following broad principles: Private decision makers should be allowed to manage risk in a regulatory framework that is predictable, transparent, equitable and timely: Energy resource developments should be required to comply with standards of environmental performance which are commensurate with those imposed on other sectors of the economy. Commercial decisions should determine the nature and timing of energy resource developments, with government interventions being transparent and allowing commercial interests to seek least-cost solutions to government objectives (e.g. environment, safety or good resource management objectives). Government objectives should generally be driven by sector-wide policy mechanisms rather than impose inconsistent requirements on individual projects/private investor. Significant investment is required to maintain and enhance the economic benefits available from the development of the country's abundant energy resources. The competition for this investment from other countries rich in energy resources is intense. To improve Australia's investment competitiveness, the Australian Government will build upon existing, sound energy resource development policies by seeking to maintain Australia's world-leading position as a low-risk investment destination by implementing a strategy to improve land access approval processes ensuring that proponents of new energy projects take a responsible approach to addressing their greenhouse gas emissions, and those greenhouse requirements for new energy projects are commensurate with those requirements imposed on other sectors of the Australian economy.

Australia's energy efficiency performance has not been as strong as of other nations. Improving this performance is a high priority for government. Australia has a high degree of in-built energy security flowing from its extensive energy resource endowment, existing infrastructure and access to imported fuels. Ensuring adequate investment in energy infrastructure will be critical to maintaining Australia's future energy security. Energy security policies also need to be mindful of the need to maintain competitive energy prices as very high levels of security impose high costs. Government policy in the energy sector must simultaneously deliver prosperity, security and sustainability.

Potential Areas for Collaboration

Stable Prices, Revenue Growth

1. Create a deep, liquid and transparent Asia-Pacific energy market

Capacity Creation and Physical Supply

1. Co-invest in building emergency response mechanisms, e.g., strategic reserves, cross-border inventories
2. Coordinate efforts to ensure physical security of key logistical choke points
3. Cooperate in projects that increase LNG supply from Middle East, West Africa, Central Asia
4. Create a pan-Asia-Pacific gas grid

Making the Partnerships Endure

1. Share information on supply, demand, inventory positions.
2. Pursue multilateral projects to strengthen cooperation, e.g., joint research on energy technologies, standardised product specifications
3. Strengthen National Oil Companies/National Coal Companies through corporatisation and regional cooperation.

Conclusion

This paper has touched several aspects of energy scenario particularly existing demand energy supply and economic growth in Australia and India. It is found that though the production of indigenous sources of primary commercial energy has been increasing since the last three decades they have fallen well short of the energy requirement of India. This widening gap between domestic supply of and demand for energy has increased the dependence on external markets to ease supply constraints.

In the case of Australia the energy security is sound. Security is enhanced substantially by the endowment of domestic fuels, extensive energy delivery infrastructure and good access to world markets. The two extreme cases of India and Australia provide a good opportunity to both countries in the field of energy cooperation. Indian companies can take part in the energy investment activities in Australia. Further, India would also like to avail the facilities of technology regarding the energy Research and Development in the near future from Australia.

End Notes

1. IEA, *World Energy Outlook*, (November 2000).

2. On average in 2004, one Australian dollar (AUD) =USD 0.734.As of 6 June 2005, AUD 1 =USD 0.765.
3. World Bank, *India Country Brief* <http://www.worldbank.org/html/extdr/regions/htm>
4. IEA, No. 1.
5. Australian Economic Outlook: A Near and Medium Perspective. http://www.abareeconomics.com/publications, June 2006. p. 2.
6. *Ibid.*, p. 2.
7. *Ibid.*

24

Australia and India: Indian Ocean Security

VANLALTLUANGI ARUNA RUTH

The Indian Ocean is the third largest of the five oceans in the world and covers twenty per cent of the water expanse lapping the shores of three continents. The southern Asia, the Arabian Peninsula, Africa, the Malay Peninsula, the Sunda Islands, Australia and Antarctica surround it. It also represents Europe and America by way of colonies or ownership of islands.

The Indian Ocean provides in abundance living and non-living resource and renewable and non-polluting sources of energy. The natural resources found in the Indian Ocean are oil, gas, fish, shrimp, sand and gravel aggregates, placer deposits, and polymetallic nodules. Its fish are of great and growing importance to the bordering countries for domestic consumption and export. Fishing fleets from Russia, Japan, South Korea, and Taiwan exploit the Indian Ocean, mainly for shrimp and tuna. Large reserves of hydrocarbons are being tapped in the offshore areas of Saudi Arabia, Iran, India, and Western Australia. The Indian Ocean provides major Sea Lines of Communication (SLOCs) connecting the West Asia, Africa, and East Asia with Europe and the Americas. It carries heavy traffic of petroleum and petroleum products from Persian Gulf and Indonesia, which is critical for all countries but specially for growing world economies like India, China, Australia and Japan.

Several factors have led to the escalation of tensions in the Indian Ocean region. These include wars in Afghanistan and Iraq, rapidly growing military presence, the Pakistani and Iranian nuclear proliferation, ethnic tensions, religious fundamentalism, political instability in the states and terrorism. Drugs and arms smuggling that support the terrorist activities are rampant in the Indian Ocean region. The Indian Ocean has a very unstable geopolitics from its history and through out the Cold War. The external powers had used the region as a ground for proxy wars and used it for their ideological dominance. Efforts have been made to enhance regional security through economic cooperation. While the military alliances have failed the economic forums have been successful till date.

Australia and India are two of the three politically stable democracies in Indian Ocean (the third being South Africa), which have stake and common interest in the stability of region. Both the countries stand for democracy and their cooperation in jointly preserving the peace and prosperity of the Indian Ocean region is critical to the stability and security in Indian Ocean. Both the nations have wide ranging multilateral and bilateral agreements with various nations, which also become their areas of influence. Australia has taken initiative to be the founder member of the Indian Ocean Rim Association for Regional Cooperation (IOR-ARC). Both the nations can use their influence to bring in peace in the region. Hence, there is convergence of interests and roles in the security and prosperity of Indian Ocean, which need to be studied and analysed in reference to both nations.

The aim of this paper is to study the convergence of Australia and India over Indian Ocean Security. The Indian Ocean links East Asia to West Asia and Europe, carries energy and about forty percent of world trade. This has brought the interest of India and Australia to a common platform along with other countries of the region.

Factors Contributing to the Importance of Indian Ocean

The Indian Ocean is a very important area of concern and it is therefore necessary to understand the factor that contributes to the importance of Indian Ocean. The criticality of the region is seeking the attention of the countries that are interested in the security of the Indian Ocean.

Geographical

There are 28 countries in the rim representing Africa, Asia, and Australian continents and from Europe by way of colonies or ownership of islands. The region also compromises of the insular States and landlocked countries, whose interest depends on the Indian Ocean either directly or indirectly.

Historical

The Indian Ocean (IO) region is the birthplace of the maritime civilisation. It provided a highway linking a variety of people, culture and economies. The civilisations in Egypt, Arabia, Mesopotamia, the Persian highlands, the Indian subcontinent and insular South East Asia had access to the Ocean and developed their maritime trading links. Through—out history, the lands of Indian Ocean have been influenced by external regional civilisations in the Mediterranean and East Asia by the Persian, Greeks, Romans and Arabs. Even the Dutch, French, Portuguese and the English had dominated the Asian and East Asian regions *via* IO waters. The trade was started intensely by the imperialist. IO water provided a medium for movement of commodities, men and material from one corner to the other of the world.

Geopolitics of the Region

The countries constituting Indian Ocean Region represent about a third of the world's population and one fourth of the landmass of the whole world. Though high levels of poverty characterise most of the region, it has 40 per cent of the world's oil and gas reserves. It is the locus of important international sea lines of communication (SLOCs). The region has the largest populations of the major religions of the world namely Islam, Hinduism and Buddhism. In the rim, India and Pakistan, the world's two newest nuclear weapons states have added the nuclear dimension. Close on the heels in nuclear weapons pursuit is Iran, which most observers believe has a robust programme to acquire nuclear weapons. The region has become a breeding place for international terrorism with Pakistan and Afghanistan becoming focal points. Golden triangle and Golden crescent are two areas that are famous for narcotics and terrorism. Along with India some of the littoral states appear to be on a path of sustained economic progress. The Indian Ocean region suffers from a high level of international and internal conflicts and is a key venue for international piracy.

In the 1970s, the Indian Oceans region's northern rim was known as the 'arc of crisis'.[1] At least half of the world's significant armed conflicts have been fought in or between the littorals and hinterland states of Indian Ocean. The region has been an arena of increased diplomatic and military activity on the part of a variety of littoral states as well as external powers in last few years. The process of decolonisation since the fifties and sixties around Indian Ocean Rim has had consequential effect in this region. Independence was given to colonies in rapid succession. New states were formed having differing political, economic, military, social viability. Though some countries have developed into stable nations, there are countries that are still unstable. There is political instability in Afghanistan, Pakistan, Iraq, Myanmar, Thailand, Indonesia, Cambodia, Somalia, Mozambique, and Zimbabwe. Almost all the countries in the Indian Ocean have the experience of inner conflicts and separatist movements. Separatist movements in countries like Sri Lanka, Indonesia, and some of the African countries have had strong repercussions on the stability in the region as these have resulted in intervention by external powers. Afghanistan and Iraq have experienced wars with external powers. The instability prevailing in many countries of Indian Ocean region is a cause of concern as it leads to vacuum of power, which leads to threat of undemocratic elements taking over power in the nation. Countries like Pakistan, Bangladesh and Myanmar have been unable to set up a stable regime and have been struggling along since independence. As a result of inner instability in the region, there are states, which are vulnerable to external intervention. Indonesian intervention in East Timor in 1975 is an example. Militia forces with external support from Indonesia caused disturbances impacting the surrounding nations. The military coups in Indonesian and Thailand, Pakistan and Myanmar were threats to the peaceful democratic surrounding. In recent times, China is seeking a seaport in Pakistan and a naval base in Myanmar. The presence of China in these countries will lead to prolonging the existing forms of military dictatorships in these countries.

Indian Ocean has always been under the influence of external intervention. In the present scenario there have been efforts to keep out the intervention of external powers in the Indian Ocean and enhance the regional cooperation and forces to keep up with the security of the region. The United States unquestionably has been the most dominant player in the Indian Ocean. Although there has been a realisation to enhance regional cooperation, there are countries that depend on the US presence in the region for their security. Inspite of the inconveniences to many countries, there have been efforts by such countries to develop closer ties with the United States. However, the most concerning role of the external intervention in the region has been that of China. Some countries and observers have seen Chinese growth in the region as clandestine strategic competition with US.

Rapid growth in regional wealth and integration is conventionally seen as a facilitator for enhanced regional security.[2] There have been significant contributions made and realised by the governments to make the security of the region work together to generate wealth and to lift the economic and social indicators of the peoples. In this regard, there has been an emerging process in the regional cooperation in the Indian Ocean. The Indian Ocean Rim Association for Regional Cooperation (IOR-ARC) is one such association forged under initiative from Australia. Though it is not a trade bloc, its twelve members including India and Australia are focussing on trade liberalisation, facilitation and promotion for the member countries. ASEAN Regional Forum has had a successful long run till date. This can be compared to other unsuccessful alliances or forums, which were organised only for security purpose. Vinod Grover, Secretary West of the Indian Ministry of External Affairs, in his keynote address to International Forum on the Indian Ocean Initiative (IFIOR) said: "It is best to work together on something that unites us rather than on that which separates us. It is our firm belief that economic cooperation and the resultant growth and development of our Indian Ocean World will itself have a beneficent leavening influence on the political and security climate of the region." Thus in the Indian Ocean Region, economic growth is an important instrument in defusing the potential regional conflicts. It would make it easier to deal with security issues in the Indian Ocean if economic growth of the region is considered simultaneously, as it will be in the interest for all nations.

Sea Lanes of Communication (SLOCs)

Sea lines of communication form the lifeline of the countries as they carry the bulk oil from the Persian Gulf. Keeping the SLOCs clear and secure is a critical concern for each state. Countries like Japan, India, China, South Korea, etc., heavily rely on the oil supply through these sea-lanes. China was one of the sixth largest exporters of oil, but since 1994, it has been a net importer of oil. In order to ensure its energy flow, China has expanded its navy to the Indian Ocean with its base in Pakistan. Since most of the global trade including that in the Indian Ocean region is sea-borne, in strategic sense the control of any of the choke points militarily can cause major tension in the region and seriously interfere with the interest of other countries. The major chokepoints are the Strait of Malacca in the east and Gulf of Aden and Suez Canal in the west. There are a number of other narrow choke points like Straits of Hormuz, Lombuk and the Sunda Strait, which are also sensitive. Any disruption will have consequences on the energy flow, which could be unfavourable to the dependent countries. The strategic importance of Indian Ocean Sea-lanes was recognised by the British and they set their suzerainty through the naval bases to ensure their control. After they withdrew, the Americans entered and made their presence in the Indian Ocean with their bases in the Gulf and at Diego Garcia. The risk involved in the sea borne transportation of oil is a deep security concern for many nations, involving serious political conflicts. The oil producing nations are controlling and managing the international oil market. Possibilities of oil being suspended by oil exporting countries through a collective political intervention or any geopolitical incident could temporarily halt oil production or close shipping routes. Security and access to SLOCs is of increasing importance, as these sea lines are the maritime highways for vast trade flows critical to the rapidly growing prosperity not only of the Indian Ocean region, but also for the entire Asia-Pacific. It therefore becomes very vital for countries in the Indian Ocean to cooperate among themselves, to keep the shipping route safe and always open as their economic lifeline depends on these routes.

The critical economic importance of the SLOCs in the region suggests that neither the ASEAN nations nor other major Indian Ocean regional powers have any interest in posing military threats to regional SLOCs. However, the threat scenarios should be analysed. One such threat is that of disruption of SLOCs by conflicts involving actions by China to enforce claims on Taiwan or the Spartly islands, or to oil fields disputed with Vietnam. A Chinese Foreign Ministry statement in April 1995 denied any threat to freedom of navigation, stating: "While safeguarding its sovereignty over the Nansha (Spartly) Islands and its maritime rights and interests, China will fulfil its duty of guaranteeing freedom of navigation for foreign ships and air routes through and over the international passage of the South China Sea according to international law."[3] However, the PRC missile firings to areas off Taiwan's seaports in early 1996 again heightened concern. Conflict potential in the Taiwan Strait and the Spartly remains a real concern.

Crime at Sea

Crime at sea is one of the major threats commonly faced in Indian Ocean. The crimes include piracy, maritime terrorism, drug trafficking, gun running, human smuggling and pollution.

More than eighty percent of the world's opium is produced in this region. The Golden Crescent countries in the South West Asia, consisting of mainly Afghanistan, Iran and Pakistan and in the Southeast Asia, the Golden Triangle consisting of Myanmar, Laos and Thailand are the major producers of opium. Large amount of drug trafficking takes place through sea. Drugs generate vast amounts of money that has been sustaining the growth of terrorist activities in the region and around the world. Maritime drug trafficking generates vast amounts of money for international organised crime syndicates and terrorist organisations. Laundered through the international financial system, this money provides a huge source of virtually untraceable funds. These monetary assets can then be used to bribe government officials, bypass established financial controls, and fund additional illegal activities, including arms trafficking, migrant smuggling, and terrorist operations.

Between 1 and 30 April 2005, there have been 37 cases of piracy and maritime armed crime incidents reported.[4] Piracy and incidents of maritime crime tend to be concentrated in areas of heavy commercial maritime activity, especially where there is significant political and economic instability, or in regions with little or no maritime law enforcement capacity.

These activities further ensure a steady supply of weapons and cash for criminal and terrorist activities as well as the means for the separatist underground movements. Crime at sea, therefore, is one of the major concerns in Indian Ocean waters.

Terrorism

The world entered a new era of international terrorism and uncertain after 11 September 2001 attack. But the Indian Ocean Region was not new to this kind of threat, as it has been witnessing these threats for decades. The terrorist activities have been a cause of instability and potential threat to all the countries in the region as almost all the states are vulnerable to it. Terrorism is the major impediment to poverty alleviation, social development and in general, the well being of many nations in the modern world. The epicentre of Islamic fundamentalist and extremist terrorism is located in Pakistan and Afghanistan, along with the Persian Gulf countries. These terrorist activities are extended all over the region. Indonesia's management of internal security matters continues to bear on regional security. There have been threats from the fundamentalist, who oppose the values of democracy, to form Taliban style nation in the East Asia region.[5] The militia forces from Indonesian and East Timor are the immediate threats to the security of Australia in the region. Almost all countries, either directly or indirectly, are being used by networks of terrorists. Pakistan has become a breeding ground for international terrorism. Apart from its involvement in Kashmir and Afghanistan, the role of the Pakistani fundamentalist activists in other countries including those in Central Asia is well known. There are three main Islamic fundamentalist groups namely *Lashkar-e-Toiba* (LeT), *Jaish-e-Mohammad* (JeM) and *Hizb-ul-Mujahiddeen* (HuM)—all of them are headquartered in Pakistan. These groups with their bases in Pakistan are major terrorist threats to India. Although insurgent groups in Southeast Asia's terrorist brotherhood do not share the same goals, they cooperate across national boundaries for logistics, training, weapons and safe havens. For example, *Jemaah Islamiyah* (JI) and the Free Aceh Movement (GAM) have trained with the Moro Islamic Liberation Front (MILF) in camps in the southern Philippines; GAM smuggles weapons with the Thai terrorist group Pattani United Liberation Organization (PULO), and many terrorists use regional connections to move from country to country. LTTE which is one of the major terrorist outfits contributing to instability in South Asia is also responsible for gun running, narcotics smuggling and helping other clandestine armed groups operating in the South Asian region. LTTE has been active in Thailand for two decades and has used Thailand, both to acquire weapons, training of cadres and using it as transit country for weapons smuggling.

The Sri Lankan civil war is one of the war-torn area in the Indian Ocean region. The island nation has great importance, it is critical to the sea-lines of communication and much of the trade and naval activity in the Indian Ocean take place here. Trincomalee has the capacity to serve as a major naval base, and an extra regional naval force could well dominate the sea routes in the area and disrupt shipping. Due to its geography it has a primary role in security. The heightened conflict with the LTTE in the recent months has been a cause of concern on the security of the region and on the safety of SLOCs.

The links between terrorism and drugs have made the situation in Asia more volatile. The phenomenon of weapons proliferation linked with growing narcotics trafficking, money laundering, and war patronage has been a big challenge in the region. The world opium productions are located in this region and so are the terrorist bases. These ongoing practices are the factors that aggravate the instability of the region.

Acts of maritime terrorism in the Indian Ocean region include attack by the Tamil Tigers against merchant shipping. The suicide bomb attack on the USS *Cole* in Yemen in 2000 and the attack on the French tanker 'Limburg' off the coast of Yemen in early October 2002 are attributed to *Al Qaeda*.[6]. Over eighty per cent of the terrorist organisations with a capability for maritime terrorism operate in the areas and seas to the West of India. Over ninety per cent of successful maritime terrorist strikes have taken place in these areas.[7] These terrorist organisation threatens the stability and thus it is required that there is one-minded resolution in the states of the Indian Ocean countries to combat the threat of terrorism in a more integrated and fierce manner.

Nuclear and Weapons of Mass Destruction (WMD) Threats

Nuclear and WMD proliferation is yet another sensitive issue in Indian Ocean region itself. Pakistan is identified as the epicentre of nuclear proliferation[8]. Proliferation of nuclear weapons or WMD will increase the possibility of nuclear war. Such WMDs de-stabilise international or regional relations and may be used to infringe upon the national sovereignty of individual nation-states. Their falling in the hands of terrorists cannot be ruled out. The exposure of key Pakistani figure Abdul Qadeer Khan as being the kingpin of the nuclear black market has been shocking. He had been operating for so many years leading to proliferation of the nuclear technologies to nations like Iran, Libya and North Korea. Having benefited from funds contributed by Libya, Iran and Saudi Arabia for its clandestine military nuclear projects, Pakistan also has been the epicentre of state-sponsored nuclear proliferation since the late 1980s.[9] Lately focus is on Iran to discourage it from enriching its nuclear fuels, and is being persuaded by all the countries and UN to reconsider its nuclear initiative. North Korea, which had been cooperating, with Pakistan for weapons technology has been diplomatically dealt with to cap its nuclear policy after years of uncertainty. Though India has not signed the NPT but it has made commitment that she would not make the first move in using the nuclear weapon or engage in the proliferation of the technology.[10] The threat of nuclear weapons or any WMD falling in the hands of terrorists is real.

Presence and Interests of Non-regional Countries in the Indian Ocean

The Indian Ocean was the main route to colonisation in the Asian countries and its sea-lanes were important for the transport of goods and material. Geo-strategic and economic importance of Indian Ocean increased with the discovery of minerals, oil and natural gas. The importance of uninterrupted flow of oil from gulf led to countries seeking the protection of sea-lanes from the very beginning. The naval domination enabled the British to mobilise vast colonial resources from IO hinterland during both world wars. The strategic importance was recognised by the British and they set their suzerainty through the naval bases to ensure control. In the quest for presence in the Indian Ocean there has been presence of naval powers for their security and interest. Even though the British withdrew, the Americans entered and made their presence in the IO with their bases in the Gulf and at Diego Garcia. The erstwhile superpowers, USSR and USA had permanent presence in the IO, but with the disintegration of USSR, USA is the sole super power maintaining its base in Diego Garcia. Different non-regional countries have stakes in the ocean waters.

United States of America

The US presence has been the most dominating factor in the Indian Ocean in spite of its being an extra-regional power. The US interest has been to ensure the flow of oil from the oil producing countries in the West Asia, which has two-thirds of the world's proven oil reserves.[11] The Diego Garcia island in the Indian Ocean is located perfectly from a strategic point of view. The Fifth Fleet in the Persian Gulf had been established in 1996 for permanent deployment in the Indian Ocean to bolster the US Middle East Force. The massive Fifth Fleet, which in size and capability is equivalent to the Sixth and Seventh Fleet together, watches over the oil fields of Arabia. The Fifth Fleet warships executed the US missile strikes during the war in Afghanistan.[12] The US has been seeking eastern Sri Lanka's Trincomalee port, which is one of the world's biggest natural deep-sea harbours for staging point for its naval assets stationed in and around its Diego Garcia base. The US has the capability to project military power and a well-defined strategy to pursue its policy of pre-eminence in the region. It has demonstrated the will to reinforce America's long-term military commitment to the region.[13]

US views India as an important expanding economy and recognises India's stable democracy and its effort in maintaining the balance of power in the region. India has signed a 10-year defence agreement with the United States on 29 June 2005. The US has been looking forward to India to serve as a bulwark against China as it has become more active in the Indian Ocean. Also, there are some areas where the US navy cannot operate, such as the Malacca Straits, where India's presence might be seen as less threatening than that of the US.[14] The United States is Australia's most important economic partner and closest security ally. The US is Australia's second largest merchandise export market and also the most important services market. It is also the Australia's largest import source for both merchandise and services. Australia has long been a close friend and security ally of the United States. The historical and cultural bonds, shared common values underline the enduring strength of their defence and security alliance. In the Indian Ocean, Australia depends on the US for its security of Sea-Lanes. Both Australia and India have friendly ties with US in relation to Indian Ocean.

China

China's is an emerging power. China's growing power is not a matter of mere economic bulk. China's interest in the Indian Ocean has been growing and has been a challenge to the regional powers in the Ocean. China securing naval bases in Pakistan and in Myanmar shows its growing interest in the Indian Ocean. To counter balance the China's setting its naval establishment in Pakistan and Myanmar, India has started a naval project (Seabird) in Karwar seaport on Arabian Sea in Karnataka[15]. Ensuring continuous supply of energy has come to be the most important pre-requisite for China's presence in Indian Ocean. Despite being the world's sixth largest oil producer, China has been a net importer of oil since 1994. The Gwadar port will enable China to monitor its energy shipments from the Persian Gulf through which eighty percent of the world's energy exports flows. As of today, eighty five per cent of China's trade is sea-based. Also, with its twenty six shipyards, China has emerged the fourth largest shipbuilder. Thus for both reasons, China needs assured access and control over its adjacent oceans.[16] There has been a considerable increase in China's dependence of seafood too. Besides its control over the South China Sea, it wants to obtain strategic advantage of an extended operational reach into the Indian Ocean and the Pacific. This will enable China to exercise control over sea-lanes of Japan and South Korea, who also are heavily dependent on imported energy and food.

Even though India has had a history of territorial disputes and a war with China, there has been considerable stable growth of economic relations with China. India and China have agreed to work together in energy security and at the multilateral level at the WTO to support an open, fair, equitable and transparent rule-based multilateral trade system.[17] India and China also have started a defense strategic partnership on 11 April 2005. China accords Australia an important place in its regional agenda. Like Japan, China also relies on imported raw materials, especially energy. Australia is seen as a source of secure energy. China definitely is seen challenging Australia's role in the region due to its expansion in the region, economic relations with Papua New Guinea and open negotiations with the Irian Jaya independence movement. China has been trying to expand its influence in the Indian Ocean. China's expansion of interest in the Indian Ocean has been causing concern to the regional powers as well as US, who has been till now a dominant and unquestioned power in the region.

Japan

Japan is an Asian and Pacific power. It is one of the world's largest economic powers. Even though much Japan's interaction lies in the Pacific, its interest in the Indian Ocean is also of primary importance as Japan's energy supply flows through the Indian Ocean. Japan emerges as a major player in securing the maritime safety as its interest lay in ensuring the safe passage of its energy supplies en route from the Middle East. Japan imported 87.1 per cent of its crude oil from the Middle East and 6.4 per cent from Asia and South East Asia. Since the vast bulk of these supplies travel by ship, Japan is almost totally dependent on safe passage through the Indian Ocean to meet national energy requirements particularly crude oil.[18] Japan has been relying on the US security umbrella for Indian Ocean sea-lane defence. Japan's willingness to play a greater role in the western Pacific Ocean has had direct consequences for the sea-lane defence in the Indian Ocean as it has enabled the US navy to deploy it fleet. This move has been beneficial to both Japan and the US for their safety of sea-lanes in Indian Ocean. Japan's defence and military capability is strictly limited by country's constitution. Thus, there is a restriction for Japan to contribute to the regional and international security.[19] But Japan being a stable democratic country is a key element in the stability of the oceanic region. Japan has been Australia's largest export market. Australia and Japan both strategically depend on the US for security in the Indian Ocean though they are not tied together in direct security links. Both the countries relationship has been based on the confluence of strategic, political and economic interest and bilateral relation that have grown in the last fifty years.[20]

India and Japan have traditionally had cordial relation from the very beginning and have had cultural exchanges since 1956. Japan has been the second largest destination of Indian exports and has been providing assistance to India.[21] Japan has proposed a military exchange programme to India in which it can use Japanese naval and coastguard bases for joint exercises. This has enhanced the bilateral relations with India.

Commonality in security interest of Japan, Australia and India has been displayed by their efforts avoid destabilising rivalry between the major regional powers in the Indian Ocean, preventing the emergence of regional hegemony, preventing the proliferation of weapon of mass destruction and helping the littoral states in strengthening their security.

South Korea

Though not a regional country, it uses India Ocean region and the sea routes heavily as it is one of the world's largest economies. The Republic of Korea (South Korea) is the world's fifth largest oil importer energy market, and the second largest importer of Liquefied Natural Gas (LNG). It imports all of its crude oil from the Persian Gulf region, with Saudi Arabia supplying about one-third of the country's import requirements in 2004. South Korea also relies on imported liquefied natural gas (LNG) from Qatar, Indonesia, Malaysia, and Oman, with a smaller volume coming from Brunei, all being Indian Ocean countries. Its imports of coal come mainly from Australia and

China, with the United States also among the suppliers. It cooperates and depends on the US for its security and interests.

France

France has its military base in Djibouti Reunion and Mayotte where several thousands of soldiers from several European states are stationed.

Russia

The erstwhile USSR had its permanent presence in the Indian Ocean to maintain its steady supply of oil and maintaining the balance of power in the region with US. Russian presence in the ocean has been to exploit resources such as fish, tuna and shrimp. Russia has been playing a positive role in the region for the balance of power, to counter terrorism and proliferation of nuclear weapon. It has been trying to dissuade Iran's nuclear development and achieve Iranian compromise on it by the sale of air defence missiles to Iran. India has welcomed Russian interest in projecting its naval power in the Indian Ocean and held naval exercises with the Russians near Indian shores recently. India's growing naval ambitions represent an expanding area of interest for Russian manufacturers. Russia is of greater importance for India as a major source of military hardware, which India requires for her drive for a blue water navy.

Australia and Russia enjoy positive bilateral relations. There has been an increase in bilateral cooperation in a number of important international and multilateral areas, including non-proliferation issues and regional security. One of the developments that has most helped to broaden the bilateral relationship has been the establishment of regular political-military talks.

Israel

Israel's contact has been absent from the Asian countries but Israel has been in close participation in the political process in the Middle East. Its Indian Ocean interest is bound by the Middle East countries, which are its immediate neighbours and have been in constant conflict with Israel. Israel has shown its interest with the Indian Ocean countries especially in the area of terrorism. Its cooperation with India has been of vital importance India and Israel are sharing a common democratic community and have been struggling through the wars of terrorism in their respective surroundings. The alliance between India and Israel—one an open member of the international nuclear club and the other a secret member—is based predominantly on military and intelligence cooperation. Israel has become the second-largest supplier of arms for India, next only to Russia. Israel has provided India with sea-to-sea missile radar and other similar systems, border monitoring equipment, and night vision devices. Israel responded quickly to India's desperate requests for arms, despite pressures from various quarters not to supply ammunition to a party engaged in war. Israeli intelligence agencies have been intensifying their relations with India security apparatus and are now understood to be heavily involved in helping New Delhi combat Islamic militants in the disputed province of Kashmir.[22]

Israel and Australia share a very sound diplomatic relationship with each other. Viewing each other as stable democracies and sharing sound fundamental views they have been strong supporters of each other. Israel has been importing vast amounts of coal from Australia. Israel exports to Australia constitute agro-technology, machinery and electronics. Australia has been in support of Israel for long and has sided with it in all the wars.

Regional Trade and Security Alliances

Indian Ocean Region has seen many alliances from within the region and from outside the region for trade and security. The history of Indian Ocean region since the Cold War days has been characterised by the dominance and expansion of the super power. During the Cold War, the UN declaration 'Indian Ocean Zone of Peace' was the product of the geo-political environment of its time and it addressed the superpower rivalry. It exclusively dealt with the conventional security issues and threats and the approach was institutionally aligned and rigid. The issues could not be resolved because of the absence of a consensual, non-confrontational process.[23] Therefore, there was no way of forcing countries to comply with the resolutions or initiative that did not meet their own agendas first. Over the years, the UN Adhoc Committee on the Indian Ocean has not been able to reach agreement on the manner of implementation of the 1971 Declaration of the Indian Ocean as a Zone of Peace, though the validity of the objectives and the vision of the Declaration remained unchanged. The IOZP mechanism to address the security issues does not have any relevance in today's changed environment. Similarly, the second track initiative of International Forum on the Indian Ocean Initiative in Perth in June 1995 was also not much acceptable. The conference included a security work group session that led to acrimonious exchange with key players. Unlike the past alliances which dealt with wide ranging issues encompassing politics, security and economics there seems to be an awareness and acceptance that in the present post cold war era, the formation of economic alliances is crucial for the sustained economic growth which in turn is essential for the retention of policy autonomy and the maintenance of overall national and regional security. Regional alliances now focus primarily on economic-related issues. [24]

Many organisations in the Indian Ocean region are working together in order to enhance the trade and security system. These organisations are of importance as the regional stability depends much on their cooperation.

Organisations like the South Asian Association for Regional Cooperation (SAARC), Association of Southeast Asian Nations (ASEAN), Indian Ocean Rim Association of Regional Cooperation (IOR-ARC). ASEAN Regional Forum (ARF), M7 group Mauritius Seven group (M7). The new cooperation that has been forming as the East Asian summit, which constitutes ASEA countries including Japan, China, South Korea, India, Australia and New Zealand. Asia-Pacific Economic Cooperation (APEC) was established growing interdependence among Asia-Pacific economies. With energy supply moving to pacific countries APEC has interest in maintaining security dimension in the region as well. These economic alliances have integrated the countries together and enabled them to arrive at the common purpose of development. This common strategic perspective has given security priorities among these member states. Realising the need for cooperation in the common interest, the Indian Ocean Commission also is focussing on the Economic cooperation.[25] Thus, there is a concentrated effort on avoiding and managing conflict among themselves in order to achieve their areas of interest.

Australia and India

Till recent times Australia and India relationship has been characterised by divergences. India's size and strategic situation along with its economic growth has now become a priority to Australia. With India "look east" policy and Australia "look west" policy at the same time, there has been initiatives by both the countries in order to build-up on the convergences. The trade and security has been an area of cooperation. The Indian Ocean security also draws attention of both the countries as the security and stability of the Indian Ocean region is of primary concern for both the countries.

India and Australia have the Indian Ocean as a common geographical and economic denominator. This common strategic relation has prospects for both the countries to have warmer relations. The economic and security importance of the IO has been realised by both the countries as both have their trade and energy supply passing through this Ocean. India depends on the imported oil that passes through this water. Australia is a leading exporter of natural gas resource and depends heavily on the Indian Ocean. More than three fourths of Australian export and over two-third of its import are located within the region[26], which passes though the IO waters. Hence, the need to maintain secure sea-lanes is paramount to both the countries. The economic growth and living standard of the Australian population depends on exports, with one in every five jobs accounted for by exports.[27] Thus, any disruption in the trade would result into adverse effect on Australian economy. Crimes at sea and the maritime terrorism are also the major threats faced by both the nations. Thus Australia and India are very much interested to see the security of all Indian Ocean sea-lanes and chokepoints from all the sides.

With both the nations experiencing terrorism and extremist fundamentalism in their respective neighbourhood, they are in a position to understand each other's security concerns in the regions. Both have committed themselves to war against terrorism and have a common outlook to regional and global threats. Both the countries are aware of the terrorist links in the Indian Ocean and the combination of narcotics and arms smuggling. Recently there have been raids related to an investigation of a group suspected of providing assistance and finance to LTTE terrorist outfit in Australia. The premises raided were believed to be a front office that apparently served as the headquarters for the LTTE's operations in Australia.[28] Both the countries are aware of their responsibilities by not allowing their lands to become safe haven for the terrorists and preventing any support for them from their soil. Both the countries have common agenda to ward off the terrorist activities and cooperate with each other in intelligence and combating skill.

China's growing power has been causing unrest not only to India but also equally to Australia. Both the nations are seeing the pace of growth of China influence and are aware of threats of instability and imbalance in the region. Australia has also been concerned about China's role in Papua New Guinea and opened negotiations with the Irian Jaya independence movement in Indonesia. The expansionist policy of China has made not only both the countries but also other regional countries to re-look their defence perspective.

India's security is very much linked to the dynamics related to its regional strategic and security environment. India's location in the Indian Ocean region is next to the epicentre of terrorism— Pakistan, which not only has been sponsoring state terrorism but also has been a source of nuclear proliferation. India has been struggling with insurgency in the Kashmir region. It has already fought three wars with Pakistan. China is yet another crucial threat for India as it has been expanding its military forces and naval presence in the Indian Ocean on both the sides of India by setting up naval bases at Gwadar in Pakistan and the naval port in Myanmar. Sri Lanka down south has been engaged for decades in ethnic violence and has been a security challenge for India. India has lost its Prime Minister Rajiv Gandhi at the hands of the LTTE militants of Sri Lanka. The surrounding countries of Pakistan, Afghanistan Myanmar, Bangladesh, and Nepal are countries that are unstable and have been a challenge to India with insurgency and refugee problem. Afghanistan has a history of turmoil and war and is recovering after US war on Taliban. India itself has been coping up with ethnic tension internally and with secessionist movements and militancy in the northeast and other parts of the country.

Australia's strategic and security environment has changed in recent years. China's growing power has been a challenge to many countries as well as to Australia posing a threat to regional instability. The military conflict between north and South Korea is also an area of concern for Australia. Australia environment has changed since 9/11 terrorist attack and the Bali bombing in Indonesia. Next-door, Indonesian, Malaysia, Thailand and Philippines have been engaged in extremist Islamic fundamentalism. *Jemaah Islamiyah* has been found to have links with *Al Qaeda.* Its efforts at establishing an Islamic regime is a threat to the democratic values of Australia.

India's economic liberalisation, its vast market and its outward looking orientation has attracted Australia's attention. Both Australia and India as members of Commonwealth countries have much in common—not only do they share democratic values, they have similar legal, financial and governmental structure and have common interest in the Indian Ocean littoral states.

Both being emerging middle powers in the region have been playing a major role in order to secure stability in the Indian Ocean region. Their concern of trade and energy supply emanates from the ocean lanes making their cooperation imminent in the oceanic security. Their security concerns are very similar in their respective regions and have made both the nations to stand together in the global fight against terrorism regionally and globally. The cooperation between Australia and India would contribute to the peace keeping and help in the balancing of power in the Ocean along with the regional powers.

Following the 11 September, 2001 attack, the International Maritime Organisation (IMO) has given high priority to prevent and suppress terrorist attacks against ships and improve security aboard and ashore with the introduction of a proposed International Ship and Port Facility Security Code (ISPS Code)[29]. This code includes requirement of ship and port facilities such as provision of security plan and officers, onboard equipment and arrangement for monitoring and controlling access. This provides a scope for India and Australia to cooperate in the Indian Ocean at a regional level, for stability and security in the IO from the maritime terrorist threats. There are possibilities of cooperation and liaison on Strategic Counter-Terrorism, which would require an intelligence collection, analysis and assessment capability for maritime security. Navies have to play a more important role in securing its sea-lanes and security of maritime. Amongst the twelve indigenous navies of the region possessing major surface and sub-surface combatants, India continues to remain the largest navy, followed by Pakistan, Australia, Indonesia, Iran, and Thailand.[30] The Royal Australian Navy and Indian Navy can, on these premises, have possibilities to have joint patrolling in the Indian Ocean along with the collaboration of the regional naval forces.

Emerging Role of Australia and India in Indian Ocean

By virtue of its geographical position, India has a natural interest in maintaining the Indian Ocean as a region free from military rivalries. India is a player in supporting all naval missions, including escorting and responding to regional crises. The dynamics of the region need the balance of power. Australia too has been concerned with the expansion of China. Though Australia is a naval power in the Pacific Ocean but in the Indian Ocean its alignment has been under the security ambit of US. Australia along with the regional navies and as well as the South African navy has a potential role to play to bring about a balance of power in the Indian Ocean. The need to maintain peace and to keep off threats of expansion in the Indian Ocean is very important, as the control over the sea is the first step to control of the land. This suggestion does not reflect a military alliance but is motivated by the idea that despite the diversity, measures should be pursued collectively which will enhance the security of the region as a whole.

Conclusion

Amidst multiplicity of interests in Indian Ocean, there is convergence of outlook and interest of Australia and India. It is recommended that confidence-building measures along the lines of convergent issues be taken to build up the relationships and atmosphere for more active role by the Australia and India. The role of Australia and India as leading nations in the region is important for international security and needs to be strengthened. To begin with, political declarations are important but in the long run, these are not enough. Means of communication and dialogue have to be established in order to substantiate the political declarations. This implies a degree of transparency. Cooperation specific issues in region such as maritime security, sharing of intelligence, joint actions against terrorism, proactive role in flushing out the terrorist bases in the region are potential areas for consideration.

Both Australia and India as stable democracies are part of several regional alliances and forums where they have strong standing and influence as individual nations. Both can influence such regional alliances or forums to have a broader consensus on the stability and security in the Indian Ocean region. Intra regional consensus between various regional forums and associations will go a long way in achieving the aim of Indian Ocean security where the large movements like UN declaration on Indian Ocean Zone of Peace have failed.

End Notes

1. Speech by Senator Ian Campbell to Open the Bilateral Seminar, www.dfat.gov.au, 10 November, 2005,
2. Speech by Senator Ian Campbell to Open the Bilateral Seminar, www.dfat.gov.au, 10 November, 2005,

3. *Beijing Review*, Beijing, 14 May, 1995, pp. 22.
4. International Terrorism and Organised Crime Group (ITOCG) Maritime, www.rncom.mod.uk/maritime, 10 November, 2005.
5. Speech by Foreign Minister Alexander Downer, www.foreignminister.gov.au, 17 November 2005, www.foreignminister.gov.au
6. Sam Bateman, Comprehensive Maritime security in the Indian Ocean Region. In D. Gopal and D. Rumley, ed., India *and Australia issues: Issues and Opportunity*. (AuthorsPress, New Delhi, 2004).
7. Strategic counter-terrorism, http://www.saag.org/, 10 November, 2005.
8. Paper presented at the second Indo-Japanese Dialogue on Cooperation in Maritime affairs in New Delhi April 5-7, 2004
9. Paper No. 904, 11 November 2005, www.saag.org/papers,
10. Issue No 25, *Annual Report 2003-04*, India Defence, www.satribune.com, 11November, 2005.
11. *International Socialist Review* Issue 15, (December 2000-January 2001) Retrieved on November 15 from www.isreview.org
12. Ramtanu Maitra, All at sea in the Indian Ocean, *A times on line*, Issue, 22 January 2004, www.atimes.com, 15 November, 2005
13. Ramtanu Maitra, All at sea in the Indian Ocean, *atimes on line*, Issue, 22 January, 2004, www.atimes.com, 15 November, 2005
14. Adam Wolfe, Yeygeny Bendersky and Federico Bordonardo, India, China, the U.S. and the Balance of Power in the Indian Ocean, http://www.zmag.org, 12 November, 2005.
15. Rajat Pandith Karwar naval base project back on track, http://www.defenceindia.com
16. Swaran Singh, China's Indian Ocean Policy: Compulsions vs. Ambitions, http://www.stratmag.com, 02 November, 2005.
17. Indo-China Trade Relations, *Economy Watch*, www.economywatch.com/world_economy/china, 12 November, 2005
18. Figurers from Japan Almanac 2000, http://mit.edu/mit-japan, 12 November 2005.
19. Asia Security Challenges, No. 1839, 04 April, 2005, www.heritage.org, 16 November, 2005.
20. H. S Prabhakar, Japan-Australia Relations, In D. Gopal and D. Rumley, ed., *Australia In The Global Emerging Order (*Shipra Press, New Delhi, 2002*)*
21. The History of Japanese-Indian Exchange, www.mofa.go.jp/region, 22 October, 2005.
22. Sharon is coming to India dated, May 27, 2003, retrieved on November 18 from www.fpif.org.
23. P.J. Botha, The Management Of Security. Published in Monograph No. 9, Diplomat and Defenders, February 1997
24. Ad Hoc Committee on Indian Ocean. 451st meeting (PM), Press release, GA/IO/4, 26/07/2005, www.onlinedemocracy.ca, 12 November, 2005.
25. The Future of the Indian Ocean Commission, www.ecdpm.org, 20 November, 2005
26. Abdul Nafey, Australia security: A Paradigm shift?, In D. Gopal and D. Rumley, ed., *India and Australia issues: Issues and Opportunities.* (AuthorPress, New Delhi, 2005)

27. Sam Bateman, Comprehensive Maritime security in the Indian Ocean Region. In D. Gopal and D. Rumley, ed., India *and Australia: Issues and Opportunity*. (Authors Press, New Delhi, 2004).
28. Friday, November 25, 2005, The *Hindu,* p. 1.
29. The International Ship and Port Facility Security Code (ISPS Code) is a comprehensive set of measures to enhance the security of ships and port facilities, developed in response to the perceived threats to ships and port facilities in the wake of the 9/11 attacks in the United States. http://www.imo.org/home.asp
30. Trends in Naval Power in South Asia and the Indian Ocean, *SAPRA Bulletin Article*, www.subcontinent.com, 05 November, 2005.

25

Non-Traditional Challenges to Indian Ocean Security: Prospects for India-Australia Co-operation

S. UTHAM KUMAR JAMADHAGNI AND S.I. HUMAYUN

India's "look East" and Australia's "look West" policies converge on the East Asian region geographically and the Asia-Pacific region strategically[1]. With cultural underpinnings of yore, economic imperative of accessing new markets and strengthening old ones, regional maritime issues and the common desire of building a safer world, Australia and India have struck common ground. The common strategic need for maintaining secure sea-lanes for facilitating the smooth transport of oil and other commodities; dealing with issues of maritime security like smuggling of small arms, drug trafficking and illegal migration; restricting influence of extra-regional powers in the Indian Ocean Region; and equipping to face new challenges to regional security such as the threat of religious fundamentalism spilling on to the dangerous contours of terrorism, impel a greater interaction between these two countries. This article seeks to emphasise that while a beginning has been made by the recent mutual high-level exchanges, more fillip is necessary. It is time Australia and India deepened and widened the scope and potential of this relationship.

Earth is an ocean planet. As one of the septet that makes this water mass, Indian Ocean is of special relevance. Named after India and bordering all of its 7000 km shoreline, Indian Ocean assumes increased importance to us. Being the only all-time navigable ocean (while the others are covered with ice in many regions), Indian Ocean gains added fillip. The Indian Ocean Region possesses a wealth of resources, both living in the form of abundant marine life and non-living in the form of mineral and ore deposits and fossil fuel. The disruption of energy flows in particular is a considerable security concern for littoral states, as most of their energy lifelines are sea-based. Since energy is critical in influencing the geo-political strategies of a nation, any turbulence in the supply has serious security concerns. Strategically too Indian Ocean has remained the mainstay of Indian naval ambitions. In fact, the publication of India's new *Maritime Doctrine* is quite explicit on the central status of the Indian Ocean in Indian strategic thought and on India's determination to constitute the most important influence in the region as a whole[2].

India as a growing economy has quadrupling oil needs and depends heavily on imports oil. With a population that would be the highest in the world in the next few decades India's energy needs are ever increasing. India is currently the world's seventh largest oil consumer and is expected to become the fifth largest by 2020. The third largest consumer of petroleum products soon, India's energy security is of paramount importance.

Since a major portion of this is to be fulfilled by imports and other means of transport like the pipelines over land or under the sea are still on the drawing boards, ships through "vulnerable sea lanes" will be the major routes[3]. The Persian Gulf has emerged as one of the main suppliers of energy fuel. Thus the safety of SLOCs is a prime strategic and economic requirement. Australia's sea-lanes on the other hand are its economic lifelines. With almost all of its trade plying through the seas and facing some unique challenges, Indian Ocean is vital to Australia. The shipping routes are marked with the archipelagic choke points that dot its northern waters. Interestingly, by the Sandison theory, ships bound for Australia and New Zealand can be spotted at a distance away.[4]

Being home to many choke points such as the straits of Hormuz, Straits of Malacca, Lombok and the Sunda Straits, these waters carry one fourth of the world's entire marine cargo and almost two thirds of oil shipments. Any disruption in traffic flow through these points can have disastrous consequences[5]. The choke point of Malacca faces the twin problem of piracy the incidence of which is one of the highest in the world here. Maritime interests in and around the busy ports of this region are extremely vulnerable as they might be regarded as high value targets of any future attack. Analysts of the region fear that there is even the probability of an oil tanker being sunk in the Malacca straits. This is truly a transnational issue and requires regional cooperation.

Terrorism both land-based and maritime is rampant in South East Asia as well as in the Indian neighbourhood. With similar situation confronting India and Australia and an interlaying region of interest in East Asia, the two have hit common ground. The commonalities of possessing similar geo-strategic locations—as important states in the Indian Ocean regions; the British colonial experience, English serving as *Lingua Franca*, common structures like the Parliament and Constitution can only help enhance the relations. There is reason for optimism about the prospect for warmer relations in the future due to the following factors. India and Australia have the Indian Ocean as a common geographical and economic denominator. Being the lone perennial warm water ocean, the Indian Ocean moves half of the world's marine trade through its waters. With an energy dependent economy India has to depend on imported oil that plies through these waters. An island country and as a leading exporter of natural resources, Australia depends heavily on the Indian Ocean. Hence the need to maintain secure sea-lanes is paramount to both countries.

The inter-lying region of South East Asia evinces significant interest in both countries. India once ruled these countries and its cultural influence continues to this day.[6] Australia as the regional 'big-brother' and a major trading partner has huge stakes in the region. While India has recently reverted focus on the region, it is yet to build on its past relations, Australia has exhibited active involvement in the political, security and economic issues of the South East Asian region. With increasing trade relations with the countries of the East, India has higher stakes in the region in the years to come. Trade volumes with the ASEAN countries have more than doubled in a decade. From a mere US$ 1484 million in 1993 Indian market has emerged as one of the largest importers of South East Asian goods. The value has increased five fold[7]. The recently concluded Free Trade Agreements with countries like Thailand and Singapore are set to contribute to this trend. Expanding markets and larger import flows imply not only economic prosperity but also vulnerability at sea. The incidence of piracy, armed robbery and maritime terrorism are on the rise and has placed a premium on the complexity of sea-lane defence.

The recent concern regarding terrorist attacks and the Australian conception that the focus on the Asia-Pacific in both economic and strategic terms, on the part of Australia and the possibility of use of Australia as an informed interlocutor for the South East Asian region and as an ally of the United States, veers India and Australia closer. In setting up an anti-terrorist squad, in monitoring the political events of South East Asia and in aiming to realise a region of relative peace and security both countries have a lot at stake.

After the emergence of the concept of 'Comprehensive Security', the non-traditional security issues gained more importance than the traditional military concerns. The non-traditional aspect has the potential of crossing all barriers of this globe. Economy plays a vital role in this age of globalisation. Sea routes are more important for the economic growth of a region. Hence, the security of these waters becomes more important because of their vulnerabilities. Despite maritime bonding with all its 36 Littoral States, the Indian Ocean region has unfortunately not seen the emergence of a vibrant trans-oceanic community.

Maritime Security is multi-dimensional and multifaceted and involves military and non-military issues. Other than naval threats and challenges (military security issues), arms trafficking, vulnerability of sea-lanes of communications (SLOCs), narcoterrorism, as well as piracy (hard non-military security issues) along with illegal fishing and illegal migration.

Maritime Terrorism

The event of 9/11 marked a watershed in the international security environment. Non-state actors and non-state identities have assumed more importance. In the wake of the tragic events of 9/11 in USA, the International Maritime Organisation (IMO) called for a review of measures to combat violence and crime at sea. A resolution calling for the review of existing international legal and technical measures and procedures to prevent acts of terrorism that threaten the security of ships at sea and ports was also adopted[8]. The fight against this old and persistent issue has received a boost with the backing of the International community, particularly the USA.

While the search for terrorists and their personification in *Al-Qaida* continues on land, at sea the international community is hunting for Bin laden's terror ships, termed the 'Phantom fleet'. The main idea is to prevent Osama Bin Laden and *Al-Qaida* operatives from escaping via the sea or terrorising the maritime arena. Most of the Indian Ocean Region littoral states have been infected by religious fundamentalism/terrorism. South East Asian states like Indonesia, Malaysia and Philippines are home to a considerable number of groups, which have similar ideologies like *Al-Qaida*. These countries also have contact points between offshoots of *Al-Qaida and* terrorist groups in South East Asia in various places. As terrorism displayed a tendency to globalise, South East Asia has turned into a stage for global war against terrorism. The Bali bombing, which is blamed on *Jemaah Islamiah* (JI), a terrorist group based in Indonesia, marks the onset of a spiral of violence. Groups like Indonesia based *Gerakan Aceh Merdeka* (GAM), Malaysian-based *Kumpulan Mujahideen Malaysian* (KMM), Philippine-based *Moro Islamic Liberation Front* (MILF) and *Abu Sayyaf* Group (ASG) have the ability to manoeuvre at sea. The tanker *Penrider*, which was attacked in the straits of Malacca in August 2003, is suspected of being intercepted by GAM [9]. The MILF is connected with JI and *Al-Qaida* and even before the war on terrorism in Afghanistan, more than 1000 Muslim rebels were thought to be already *Al-Qaida* trained[10]. Presence of all these groups in straits of Malacca, which has been considered as a 'Lifeline of Indian Ocean" is under threat. Attacks in the region will certainly cause problem for both India and Australia.

India has had successes against the menace of piracy. A Japanese ship *Alondra Rainbow* with a 7000 tonne aluminium ingot cargo set sail from the port of Kuala Tanjong in Indonesia to Japanese port of Miike. Fire armed and masked pirates attacked the ship and let the crew blind folded and adrift. On receiving a warning from the Piracy Reporting Centre at Kuala Lumpur and assessing rightly that the captured ship would cross the Indian Ocean, the Indian Coast guard stepped up vigil. The ship was then reported to be seen at 66 miles southwest off Cape Comorin, India's southern tip. The ICGS Tarabai located the ship on 14 November 1999. The colour, name were changed to

Mega Rama and after repeated warnings the ship radioed that it was destined for Port Fujira and could not stop. ICGS Veera and Annie Besant—two coast guard surface ships and the navy's warship INS Prahar, joined the rescue effort and succeeded in apprehending the ship[11]. The ship was then towed to Mumbai where judicial proceedings were undertaken. The incident is often sighted as exhibition of India's commitment and ability to curb piracy in the region. Indian experience with *Alandra Rainbow* incident which was caught by combined efforts of Indian Coast Guard/Navy operation in the Arabian Sea which brought a major recognition to the Indian maritime agencies.

Emergence of sea Tigers in Palk Bay is another credible fighting force in India's maritime neighbourhood that has to be taken for consideration. Sri Lankan Foreign intelligence agencies estimates the strength of the sea tigers at 2000 to 3000 cadres with latest equipments acquired from several countries in Asia and Europe to enhance their fighting capabilities[12]. In addition to its maritime capacity there are two worrying factors. First is their ability and willingness to place boats and other equipment at the disposal of terrorist organisations of other countries. In 1995 for example the LTTE helped an Islamic insurgent group (the Abu Sayyaf or the Moro Islamic Liberation Front of the Philippines) by carrying a consignment of arms and ammunition donated by the *Harkat-ul-Mujahideen* (HUM—then known as *Harkat-ul-Ansar*), from Pakistan to the southern Philippines.

Second, in addition to its fleet of merchant vessels, the LTTE has a naval wing capable of conventional as well as unconventional military action on the sea. The Sethusamudram Ship Canal Project touted as a boon to Indian maritime interests could also be a source of concern from the LTTE point of view. Whether this path breaking developmental project ushers in prosperity to this impoverished region; pares down national transit time or checks the movement of the LTTE can only be felt in the future. Viewing all the above-mentioned facts India's future policy toward counter maritime terrorism should be a cooperative one. Though Australia is not directly threatened by the maritime terrorism, it has faced few situations, which made her to think over it. The attacks of 9/11 and Bali underlined the need of fresh perception towards the terrorism. Incidents like *USS Cole* and *MV Limburg* in the past triggered the possibilities and dangers of the present trends in maritime terrorism. Australia's geography, which is very near to South East Asia, which is considered as a hub of terrorists, has also made her to prepare to counter. With all their advanced technologies and their experiences India and Australia should act together to face this devil.

Piracy at Sea

Piracy at sea is considered as an international crime. Pirates have always been romanticised by writers and filmmakers something akin to a maritime Robin

Hood. The modern piracy employs violence to target ships' crews, passengers and ship owners for commercial and instant political gains. Major regions of sea piracy include the South China Sea, Indonesian and Philippine waters. The 2004 Annual Piracy Report published by the International Maritime Bureau (IMB) was released in Feb 2005, highlighted the inability of maritime nations who are unable to control sea piracy in their waters particularly Indonesia (93 piratical attacks). There were a total of 325 piracy attacks on shipping in 2004. In the South Asian context, Bangladesh topped the list with 17 attacks, Indian ports witnessed 15 attacks and reportedly there were no piracy related incidents in waters of Sri Lanka, Pakistan and Maldives. Overall in 2004, the Indian Subcontinent witnessed 32 attacks as against 82 incidents reported in 2003[13]. This is an appreciable development in countering piracy.

Drugs and Arms Trafficking

Drug and arms trafficking go hand in hand and is prevalent throughout the world. Closer home Australia's porous border in the northern territory makes it a target for drug smuggling. Also, Marshal islands are particularly vulnerable to drug smuggling because they are dispersed over an area encompassing two million square miles of ocean. International drug trafficking syndicate therefore view the region as a key transhipment point for drug headed for richer nationals. In Philippines, Chinese organised crime groups are joining with their Philippine counter parts to import metamphetamine hydrochloride (known as *Shabu*) into the Philippines[14]. Asia has two of the largest opiate producing countries in the world—Myanmar (Golden Triangle) and Afghanistan (Golden Crescent), which lie in close proximity to India. India with its vast coastline offers ideal locations for landing and transhipment of drug. Though not of alarming proportions, India is seen as a conduit due to its geographic locations. Although there have been some recent instances of drug apprehensions at airports, no major seizures have been effected in the recent past. Infiltration of drugs into a state will strike at the root of society, damage, the basic unit, namely the human being, and cause social instability. Another factor, which will cause social instability and contributes both to international crime and terrorism, is small arms trafficking. A study conducted by the Council on Security Cooperation in the Asia-Pacific Centre (CSCAP) among other things noted that small arms are weapons of choice for most trans-national criminal activity and that there is often a strong linkage between weak states and proliferation of small arms. The increase in small arms trafficking shows the emergence of irregular armed conflicts on a large scale[15]. According to CSCAP, South and South East Asia are particularly vulnerable to the scourge of small arms trafficking due to various factors. Added to the unresolved conflicts in Asia including those over land and sea borders, as well as those that are more ethnic or religious, fuel the need for small arms. With land borders becoming progressively tamper proof, the sea route becomes much easier and extensively used. Presence of many terrorist groups, mostly religious extremists in nature in South East Asian countries are greater threat to the Indian Ocean SLOCs. This has to be properly addressed by both India and Australia.

Conclusion

Futuristic estimates on oil dependence, prospecting newer export markets, deepening understanding and influence of the interlaying Asian landmass, and the need to build a peaceful and secure Asia-Pacific region and in turn ensuring a safer global environment have forced India and Australia to extend a firmer handshake. This could lay the foundation for a more meaningful closer strategic and political cooperation. The relations could now take off in a big way as security, economy and the sheer need for diversification of foci on the foreign policy front have brought both India and Australia closer than ever before.

Political, ethnic and social problems like the rise of fissiparous tendencies in the name of race, religion, language or political belief; the advent of Islamic fundamentalism, use of violence and terror and general political instability log the region. Being strong naval powers of this region, India and Australia with their long coastlines and vast untapped marine reserves, studying potential conflict zones, processes and structures for cooperation and consultation are imminent to their very survival and rise to pre-eminence.

Identifying areas of mutual interest and concern in the realms of economy (like the issue of globalisation and its effect on nations), global security (like the importance of the Indian Ocean region, the scepter of terrorism, its causes and related concerns especially unique to this part of the world), and diplomacy (as in the need for bilateral understanding of foreign policy directions), will broaden the scope of the relationship. Strategic interests and similar geo political conditions could only facilitate such eventuality. How these factors are best utilised will determine the future strategic ties of two of the most important players in the Asia pacific region.

End Notes

1. S. Utham Kumar Jamadhagni and C.S. Anuradha, Indo-Australian Strategic Framework: Possibilities for the New Millennium, *Journal of Indian Ocean Studies*, Vol. 11, No. 1, April 2003, p. 24.
2. http://www.arabnews.com/?page=4&section=0&article=83442&d=8&m=6&y=2006
3. Admiral Mehta, Sureesh, Address at the Seminar on 'India's Oceanic Neighbours: Emerging Strategic Issues and Concerns' (Chennai: SIOS and University of Madras, February 24, 2006).

4. This theory was defined by J.M. Sandison in his article in *Pacific Defence Reporter*, April 1986, p. 4.
5. Ghosh, P.K. 'Maritime Security Challenges in South Asia and the Indian Ocean: Response Strategies' *Maritime Security in Asia Conference* (Honolulu, Hawaii: Center for Strategic and International Studies—American-Pacific Sealanes Security Institute, January 18-20, 2004) p. 1. http://community.middlebury.edu/~scs/docs/ghosh,%20maritime%20security%20challenges%20in%20SAsia%20&%20Indian%20Ocean.pdf
6. The South Indian kings conquered parts of South East Asia and the influence is pronounced in the cultural realm to this day (as evident from the Indonesian traditional theatre form called *Gamelan* where the epic Ramayana is performed. See Peter Stack's East meets East in a Hindu Epic, *San Francisco Chronicle*, March 30, 1997), and also by the political and economic clout of the ethnic population settled there.
7. *ASEAN Statistical Yearbook*, 2005 Chapter V, Merchandise Trade pp. 70-71 http://www.aseansec.org/SYB2005/Chapter-5.pdf
8. Imo 2004: Focus On Maritime Security, A Message From The Secretary-General Of The International Maritime Organization, Efthimios Mitropoulos http://www.imo.org/includes/blastDataOnly.asp/data_id%3D9885/Englishmessage.pdf
9. "More regional cooperation needed to combat piracy", Radio Singapore International, 13 August, 2003.
10. Barry Desker and Kumar Ramakrishna. Formulating an indirect strategy in Southeast Asia, *The Washington Quarterly*, Spring 2002.
11. For a detailed description of the entire episode refer to the Indian Coast Guard website http://indiancoastguard.nic.in
12. Suryanarayan, V., Sea Tigers and Indian Security, *Journal of Indian Ocean Studies*, Vol. 12, No. 3, December 2004, p. 407.
13. IMB Piracy Report 2004.
14. Conference report, *Transnational Security threats in Asia*, http://www.apcss.org/Publications/Transnational%20Report%20version%2020%20Dec%202000.html
15. See *'Maritime Security measures take shape at IMO'* http//www.imo.org/newsroom/mainframe.asp?topic_id=583&doc_id=2435

26

India and Australia in United Nations Peacekeeping Operations: Convergence and Divergences

YESHI CHOEDON

India and Australia have the distinction of being for long the contributors to UN peacekeeping operations. In fact, both countries were actively involved in the UN peace efforts in the formative years when the United Nations evolved the tradition of sending peace missions and commissions to deal with crisis situations. In the UN Charter's scheme of things, they were not expected to play prominent role in the maintenance of international peace and security as both of them are 'middle powers'. However, due to deadlock that ensued in the Security Council as a consequence of the Cold War, the middle power countries like India and Australia got the opportunity to make substantial contribution both in the conceptualisation and operationalisation of the peacekeeping system.

This paper attempts to present a comparative perspective of attitude, policies and role of India and Australia towards the UN peacekeeping operations. It attempts to analyse not only the actual participation but also the rationale of their involvement in the various operations. The paper highlights the area of convergences and divergences of the two countries on issues relating to UN peacekeeping operations. It concludes with the emphasis on the need for a joint initiative by India and Australia along with other like-minded countries to reclaim the preeminent position of United Nations in matters concerning to peace and security.

India's Participation during the Cold War

Apart from the idealistic reasons of India's support to the United Nations, there are many features of commonalties between its main foreign policy objectives and that of the UN Charter.[1] It tried to achieve a beneficial blend of national and larger interests. India was not enthusiastic about strengthening of the United Nations militarily. It held the view that peace should not be secured by a constant preparation for war. Instead of viewing the United Nations as instrument of coercion, India was in favour of viewing it as an instrument of persuasion where tool of moderation and mediation could play major role in sorting out the differences and conflicts among the comity of nations. These ideas were put into practice at the formative stage of the United Nations when the UN Security Council was unable to take decision on the conflict-situations due deadlock between the two Super Powers. Instead of watching the deterioration of situations helplessly, the United Nations developed the practice of sending UN observers and commissions to oversee the compliance of cease-fire resolutions. It was a means of asserting moral authority of the United Nations. India was a participant in some of these commissions and observer groups. From these practices gradually evolved the concept of peacekeeping.[2]

The Korean crisis presented to India both a challenge and opportunity to put into the practice its idea of managing the conflict by non-military means and its nonaligned foreign policy. India was firmly against participation in the UN military action, being particularly critical of what it perceived as the partisan involvement of the United States. Despite its strong objections, India did send humanitarian aid to Korea, comprising a field ambulance unit and a small contingent of officers and other troops. Throughout the period of UN action in Korea, India made persistent diplomatic endeavours to have the military campaign terminated as soon as possible and to initiate the process of a peaceful political solution.[3] India also played active part in repatriation efforts. Its role in Korea crisis served to raised the profile of India at the United Nations and can therefore be regarded as instrumental in establishing the precedents for its active participation in the subsequent UN operations as a peacekeeper.

The first major peacekeeping operation was the United Nations Emergency Force (UNEF) which was entrusted with the task of supervising the withdrawal of invading forces from Egyptian territory and the subsequent monitoring of armistice lines. India was actively involved in the consultations associated with both the conceptualisation and concretisation of the UNEF-I during the month of November 1956.[4] It made liberal contribution to UNEF both in terms of men and material. But what distinguished India from other states which had made similar contributions was that, more than any other contributor, India did what it did with full appreciation of the fact that UNEF symbolised an idea—the idea that there was an alternative to reliance upon military strength.

Two years later, the United Nations succeeded in preventing the Lebanese crisis from developing into a major threat to world peace. On receiving complaint from the Lebanese government against the intervention of the United

Arab Republic, a UN Observation Group (UNOGIL) was dispatched. India actively supported the establishment of the UNOGIL in order to forestall the possibility of Great Power involvement in an area of conflict and to bring it under the UN umbrella before the rival Powers of two blocs arrived there.[5] India tried its best to see that the UNOGIL retained its non-military character and its Small-Power composition.

The United Nations Operation on the Congo (ONUC) was undertaken in response to a request by the Congolese Government for military assistance to safeguard the integrity of the infant republic against secessionist forces and foreign intervention. India played a particularly pivotal role in ONUC. The ONUC, functioning on the pattern of the UNEF, proved ineffective to deal with the fast-deteriorating situation in the Congo. The secessionist groups grew in strength and number. The Government of the Congo became a subject of dispute between two rival factions. In this kind of threatening situation, India was substantially involved in the conversion of the ONUC from a non-military to a military force. The Government of India agreed to contribute and committed itself heavily to the ONUC, both militarily and financially. As a matter of fact, the Indian battalion constituted the largest single unit under the UN Command. India lost a total of 36 troops in the Congo, with a further 124 wounded—its first major causalities in a UN operation. It also contributed substantial financial aid and humanitarian assistance to ONUC, despite considerable domestic opposition.[6]

Thus, India's active participation in the formative stage of UN Peacekeeping Operations indicates that it was the foremost among those who tried to prevent the United Nations from being paralysed as a result of the Cold War. India insisted that military strength should not be considered as the sole component of the capability of the United Nations. India made substantial contribution in conceptualisation of this innovative approach to peace and also in developing the basic guiding principles that served in good trait in the subsequent UN Peacekeeping Operations. "India's credentials as a nonaligned country acceptable to all parties concerned were impeccable and the skill and maturity of Indian diplomacy was well recognised. Consequently, India has been in demand as an honest-broker".[7]

Subsequently, however, India played low-key participation in the peacekeeping operations such as UN Force in Cyprus (UNFICYP), which commenced in 1964, UN Temporary Executive Authority (UNTEA) in West Irain. During the period 1964-1987, the United Nations had launched a total of six peacekeeping operations. India in its capacity as the non-permanent member in the Security Council co-sponsored the proposals for setting up in 1973-1974 two operations, UNEF II and the UNDOF, both in Middle East. And yet the Indian troops did not participate in any one of them. The reasons for the lack of enthusiasm and participation of India in these later peacekeeping operations could be traced to, among other things, its preoccupation with own security on its border with China and Pakistan and also due to the heavy financial burden resulting from the ONUC and UNEF operations. It could also be attributed to the lack of dynamic leadership with international stature after the death of Jawaharlal Nehru.[8]

Participation in the Post-Cold War

The post-Cold War period witnessed new threats and challenges to international security. The world is faced with enormous upsurge in ethnic, religious and other local conflicts, which have serious humanitarian implications and consequences for international peace and security. Indeed the end of Cold War found the United Nations in greater demand than ever before and the UN peacekeeping operations are now involved on an unprecedented scale in conflicts around the globe. The nature of these peacekeeping operations has changed significantly over the years. Instead of dealing with conflicts between states, as the Charter envisaged, the United Nations has been involved in operations designed to restore peace and stability within individual states.[9] In other words, the United Nations has been dealing with situations essentially within domestic jurisdiction of states. This practice in effect amounts to a creative interpretation of the Charter. Most of these operations are carried out on the basis of humanitarian intervention.

India did not shirk its responsibility in these challenging situations. It has been once again deeply involved in most of the second generations of peacekeeping operations. Although India has strong reservation about the humanitarian intervention, it actively participated in these operations to make difference in the process. Over the years, India has provided around 75,000 troops and police forces to around 38 United Nations peacekeeping operations. Indian troops have taken part in some of the most difficult and risky operations and have often suffered casualties. Thus, India did not lag behind in playing its due role in the post-cold war era. (See Annexure-I: List of peace missions in which India participated).

Among the post-Cold war UN peacekeeping operations, Somalia is considered one of the most difficult and challenging operations. Indian naval ships and personnel were involved in patrolling duties off the Somali coast, in humanitarian assistance on shore, and also transportation of men and materials for the United Nations. The United Nations Operation in Somalia (UNOSOM II), which was authorised to establish in December 1992, was mandated to carry out peace enforcement action under chapter VII. The Indian contingent successfully combined the conflicting roles of coercive disarmament of various warring clans and humanitarian relief to the civilian population. Although large areas were under its operation, there were minimum civilian causalities. In spite of suffering causalities, the Indian contingent exercised utmost restraint in firing in self-defence. The Indian soldiers in Somalia demonstrated how the soldiers could shoulder the responsibilities of peace building activities to win the hearts and minds of the people in the conflict zone. The Indian contingent dug a large number of wells, constructed schools and mosques, and ran mobile dispensaries and relief camps, which provided vetenary care, and medical and humanitarian relief to large number of Somalis and their livestock.[10]

The Indian contingent received much acclaim and recognition for their work in Somalia. Some Somali leaders praised the humanitarian and friendly approach adopted by Indian troops. General Mohammed Liqliquato, a respected neutral Somali leader commented, "The Indians took pains to understand our culture and tradition. And coming from a developing country, they also empathised with our problems. They are the most effective among the UN troops".[11]

General Mohammed Morgan, a powerful faction leader narrated that in March 1994, when an Irish convoy being escorted by the Indian troops was ambushed near Baidao, Indian troops immediately turned on them, destroying three vehicles, killing nine militia and capturing a dozen others. They then called in the clan leaders to explain what had happened and to resolve the issue before it escalated.[12] This way of handling the issues had earned the respect and confidence of the locals.

The ethnic bloodshed and breakup of the former Republic of Yugoslavia can be regarded as perhaps the worst tragedy of the European continent since the Second World War. The Indian representative at the United Nations expressed its concern of the deteriorating situation in Yugoslavia and indicated that India favoured a restructured federation. In February 1992 the Security Council endorsed the dispatch of a UN Protection Force (UNPROFOR). This force consisted of a contingent from 30 countries and General Satish Nambiar of India was appointed as the first Head of the Mission and Force Commander. He was the only Indian representative in the UN force in Yugoslavia and this force remained predominantly European in character.[13] General Satish Nambiar resigned in 1993 because his impartiality and efficiency did not suit the politics of certain European countries which persuaded the UN Secretary General to dilute his command by foisting political advisers from pliable countries on him. He resigned though he still had long tenure to complete.[14]

Another notable UN peacekeeping operation of special interest to the study of Indian participation is that of United Nations Assistance Mission in Sierra Leone (UNAMSIL). Initially, India provided a medical unit and civilian personnel to the UN Mission. When the UN mission was upgraded in 1999, India provided two infantry battalion groups, a quick reaction company, a field engineering company, a level III medical facility, a Special Forces company, an artillery and transport and attack helicopters. Indian Maj. General

V.K. Jetley was the first UN Force Commander in Sierra Leone. India was one of the few who willingly contributed the personnel for this operation. The other contributions came from the African region which was already on the ground such as from Nigeria, Ghana, Guinea and Kenya. The Indian contingent was one of the largest contingents in the operation. The deputies as well as the political advisers of Major General Jetley were from Nigeria, who found his impartiality and his frankness unacceptable and unpalatable. They consistently tried to subvert his command and his operational plans. The UN Secretary General himself was opaquely critical of General Jetley in the beginning. The discipline, cohesion and efficiency of the UN peacekeeping force continued to be disrupted by the political motivation of the West African states involved in Sierra Leone and equally importantly by the attraction of the large depository of diamonds in that country. Military commanders of African countries and political figures involved with the peacekeeping operations, according to General Jetley, were getting directly involved in diamond trade and diamond smuggling. He brought all this to the notice of the concerned authority at the UN headquarters. Some of the governments of the African states build up pressure on the United Nations and Jetley was asked to come on leave to defuse the tension. Once he reached India, the UN secretariat conveyed a message to the Government of India that they do not want him back as commander of the peacekeeping force. The government of India took the decision to withdraw the entire Indian contingent from Sierra Leone.[15] This incident highlights the drawbacks of taking the forces to the UN peacekeeping operations from the countries of the region as such operations become subject to the political and other motivations, which affect the integrity and credibility of peacekeeping operations.

Apart from the army, India has sent police force and other civilians to participate in the second generation of peacekeeping operations. Recently India committed to contribute troops to UN peacekeeping operation in Sudan. The UN Security Council voted in March 2005 to send a total of 10,000 troops to southern Sudan to support implementation of the peace accord between the Government and the Sudan People's Liberation Movement after two decades of civil war. They are also expected to perform certain other functions relating to humanitarian assistance and protection and promotion of human rights. India has contributed 1,033 troops, 21 police and 22 military observers to the operation till date.[16]

Rationale for India's Participation

India's participation in the peacekeeping operations demonstrated India's commitment to the objectives set out in the UN Charter. It is often claimed from the idealist perspective that India has risked the lives of its soldiers in peacekeeping efforts of the United Nations, not for any strategic gain, but in the service of an ideal. It has participated in UN Peacekeeping out of an obligation to protect the international peace and to preserve international norms and values. From the realist perspective it is obvious that a state's activities bound to be related to protecting and promoting national interests.[17] In that respect, India's participation in UN peacekeeping operations serves some of its own national interests.

India's commitment to the maintenance of international peace has been acknowledged over the years by the successive Secretaries General and the officials of the UN Secretariat. Further, the effectiveness of such participation and contribution to UN peacekeeping efforts has drawn respect and praise from fellow peacekeepers of other countries that have served jointly with India commanders, observers and contingents in various parts of the worlds.[18] Therefore, in terms of projecting a positive image of India as a nation and of its military as a highly professional and well-trained force, much has already been achieved. This has contributed to India's national interests of building a good image at the global level.

The Indian participation in the UN peacekeeping operations also served its geo-strategic interests.[19] This is most notable in the case of various East and Southeast Asian missions in Korea, Indo-China, Indonesia (West Irain) and Cambodia, which were all perceived in India to be vital to its conception of both regional stability and international order. India has major stake in the peace and stability in the Middle East not only because of the geo-strategic reason but also because of the traditional relationship with this region. India has participated in several missions in the region (Egypt, Iran-Iraq, Kuwait, Yemen and Lebanon). The free flow of energy (oil and gas) supplies and the openness of international waterways (the Suez Canal, the Persian Gulf) are other important factors which led India to participate actively in the UN operations. Because of its geographical location and social and economic connection, Somalia can also be regarded as of geo-strategic importance to India.

India's participation in Congo, Angola, Mozambique, Rwanda, Liberia, Sierra Leone and Sudan operations can be explained as an expression of its solidarity with non-aligned countries. India has often taken strong anti-colonial stance, as in the Congo and Indonesia, where it regarded the conflict as one of aggression primarily perpetrated by a colonial power, such as Belgium or the Netherlands. India still perceives most of the recent African wars as the continuing legacy of the colonial era[20].

India's participation in the UN peacekeeping operations in Central America and former Yugoslavia, does not appear to link directly with India's national interest. They can be seen as an attempt to project India as important player in the international stage. This kind of projection and image building is essential as India's contribution to UN peacekeeping operations is presented as one of the major bases of its claim to a permanent membership of the Security Council.

India also possesses the fourth largest army in the world and one of the most professionally trained troops. They have been put to use in many types of activities within the country. It is thus well suited to serve in a wide variety of conflict situations in the world. In turn, these operations provide Indian troops with valuable experience and also earned substantial amount of revenue from such missions. The United Nations reimburses about $1,000 per month, per personnel.[21] In fact, opinion is fast gathering that one of the major reasons underlying the increase in the participation of the developing countries in the peacekeeping operations is the substantial reimbursement they get from the United Nations.

It also appears that regional rivalry plays a part in India's active participation in the UN peacekeeping operations. The fellow South Asian nations such as Pakistan, Bangladesh and Nepal have begun to make sizeable contributions in terms of manpower to UN peacekeeping activities in the post cold war period. There is clearly an element of sub-continental competition about such deployments. Above all, one of the main reasons for India's participation in UN peacekeeping operations is that it is one of the few currently available ways to be a player in world affairs and to affect international outcomes in demonstrative ways.[22]

Australia's Participation during the Cold War

Australia, under the Labor government took active part in the conferences in the 1940s leading to formation of the United Nations. With the 'enthusiasm of an idealist and the satisfaction of a creator', the Australian government saw the United Nations as a means of reducing international tensions and an opportunity for Middle and Small Powers to influence the Major Powers.[23] Just like other Middle Powers, Australia too was in favour of restricting the use of veto power by the Great powers and also tried to play its role in the void created by the deadlock between the two Super Powers. When the United Nations was not in the position to take action in the crises, Australia along with other Middle Powers like India participated in the peace missions and commissions established by the United Nations, which, as mentioned earlier, turned out to be the forerunners of peacekeeping operation.

Unlike India, Australia participated in the bloc politics and joined the military alliance of Western bloc during the Cold War period. The right-wing Liberal government that took office in December 1949 was particularly concerned with what it saw as a rising tide of communism throughout the world and Asia in particular. The Korean War, to which Australia promptly dispatched military, naval, and air forces in 1950 to fight under the UN flag, confirmed this threat perception. The ANZUS treaty signed by Australia, New Zealand, and the United States in 1951 provided much-needed assurance that a 'great and powerful friend' would underwrite Australian defense. The balance of power rather than collective security under the United Nations had come to dominate Australian thinking on peace and security matters. Thus, Australian government did not look to the United Nations for security. It sought an insurance policy to ward of a threat to its territorial integrity by allying with the Western bloc led by the United States.[24]

In fact it was so paranoid with the Asian nationalism and communism that Australia was among the most rigid opponent of the decolonisation of European empires in Asian region.[25] Australia fought against communism alongside the United States not only in Korea (1950-53) but also in Vietnam (1962-72), and alongside Britain in Malaya (1950-60) and Borneo (1963-66). Because of its above involvement it was left with few resources with which to support UN peacekeeping operations even if Australia had wished to contribute more.[26]

Australia contemplated participation in the UNEF-I in 1956. However, Australian Prime Minister's support for the use of force by Britain in the Suez crisis led Egypt to object any Australian presence in UNEF.[27] By way of compensation, perhaps, a small number of Australian military observers were sent to the UN Truce Supervision Organization (UNTSO) from 1956 onwards, which was originally established in 1948 to maintain peace between Israel and Arab neighbours. Australian involvement with UNTSO began with four military observers and later on increased its observers and it is continuing to participate till date. Australians also participated in UN Military Observer Group in India and Pakistan (UNMOGIP) from 1950 when General R.H. Nimmo was appointed Chief Military Observer in UNMOGIP. It continued to participate in it up to 1985. It withdrew its participation since 1985 when the government of the day considered that Australia was over-committed to the United Nations.[28] The only other commitments before 1970s were medical unit for UN Temporary Executive Authority (UNTEA) in West New Guinea in 1962 and a police contribution to UN Force in Cyprus (UNFICYP) from 1964. The Australian contribution to UNFICYP commenced with 40 policemen in May 1964 and later increased their contribution and it is continuing its participation till date.

The years from 1972, when Australia withdrew its troops from Vietnam and when voters in Australia elected Labor Party to power after being in opposition 23 years, one witnessed great willingness of Australia to take part in the peacekeeping operations. The new government offered 500 personnel to UNEF II in the Middle East in 1973 and 200 infantry to UNICPY in 1974. However, the United Nations rejected both the proposals. Australia began contributing forces to UNEF II in July 1976 and continued with its contribution up to 1979.[29]

When UN Iran-Iraq Military Observer Group (UNIIMOG) was established in August 1988, fifteen-man contingent from August participated in it. All the Australians served on the Iranian side of the cease-fire line because Iraq objected to Australian presence in its held territory. This was due to the fact that an Australian government scientist, Dr. Peter Dunn, was a member of the UN team that had proved Iraqi use of chemical weapons. Australia participated in the mission till the end of the operation, i.e., 1990.

Participation in the Post Cold War

As Australia faces less threat to its security in the changed international scenario of the Post Cold War period, it found useful to get its military engaged in the UN peacekeeping activities to demonstrate the value of the military to its community. Further, it could not afford to remain unaffected by the global trend of more active involvement with the UN peacekeeping operations whose demand has been increased in many folds. Thus, in 1989-90 Australia made its largest contribution up to that time (304 personnel) to UN Transitional Assistance Group (UNTAG) in Namibia. It was essentially a traditional peacekeeping operation under Chapter VI of the UN Charter. It had the task of supervising the electoral arrangements to affect transfer of power from South Africa to independent Namibian government. Australian involvement was related to the stance the Labor government had taken in southern African issues, including opposition to the apartheid regime in South Africa. The success of this operation reinforced Australia's readiness to undertake more peacekeeping tasks.[30]

One of the most significant involvements in peacekeeping activities in its own region was in the case of Cambodia. Australia was keenly concerned about the crisis as it considered it as the single greatest source of instability in its region and it fed tension and hostility between the countries in the region. Given the active involvement of its Foreign Minister, Gareth Evans, in the diplomacy leading to Paris agreement of 1991, it was incumbent upon Australia to make a significant contribution to the UN peacekeeping operations established subsequently.[31] In March 1992 UN Transitional Authority in Cambodia (UNTAC) was established to supervise the cease-fire and general election in Cambodia. UNTAC's military component consisted of 16,000 personnel from 32 countries. Australia contributed 500 personnel and air transport at a later stage. The Force Commander of this highly demanding and complex operation was Australia's Lieutenant General J.M. Sanderson. Australia played leading role in developing cooperative regional approach to the UN operation. This had benefited not only to the effectiveness of the UN operation but also to strengthen regional relations.[32] In fact through its proposal of security dialogue in the region and its policy of 'comprehensive engagement', Australia was looking for a new multilateral partnership and potential political leadership for Australia in the region. The Cambodia crisis provided forum for practicing these policy objectives.[33]

The Australian government was also ready to participate more substantially in peacekeeping further afield. It has made contribution to UN Mission for the Referendum in Western Sahara (MINURSO) since 1991, UN Operation in Somalia (UNOSOM-I and II) in 1992, and UN Assistance Mission to Rwanda (UNAMIR) in 1994. It also participated in the US—led Unified Task force (UNITAF) in Somalia from 1992 to 1993 upon the request from United States. Apart from the humanitarian concern, alliance consideration played a major role in participation in this operation. Initially, it deliberately did not participate in the UN operation in the former Yugoslavia as it was of the opinion that the European powers should take the leading role. Australia's Colonel J.B. Wilson along with three other Australian officers was among the 50 UNTSO observers temporarily re-deployed to UN Protection Force (UNPROFOR) in former Yugoslavia.

Australia's commitment declined to low level from 1995 once more after Cambodian operation completed and its forces returned from Somalia and Rwanda. This posture is similar to that of the United States and other western countries whose participation has declined as well. However, development of crisis in East Timor in its neighbourhood made it to preside over the one of the biggest peacekeeping operations. It participated in the intervention in East Timor in September 1999 under International Force East Timor (INTERFET), followed by a leading role in the military component of UN Transitional Administration in East Timor (UNTAET) between 2000 and 2002. The Australian contribution to UN Mission in East Timor (UNAMET) was substantial and it included of civilian police (among them the UNAMET police commander) and the resources of the Electoral Commission, which assembled the electoral roll and completed the ballot, and contributed supplies and logistics.[34] Australia had also consistently contributed the large number of troops to nation-building activities of the United Nations Mission of Support in East Timor (UNMISET) which was in operation from May 2002 to June 2005. Australia also remains one of the largest bilateral donors in Timor Leste, having provided $400 million in assistance since 1999.[35] It also contributed its personnel to UN Office in Timor Leste (UNOTIL), which has established on 20 May 2005. On the whole, East Timor has been the single most important involvement by Australia in UN peacekeeping in the post-cold war era. Without Australia taking the leading role, it is unlikely that international intervention would have occurred.

Overall, Australian participation in the UN peacekeeping operations is determined, among others, by the regional developments affecting Australia, the position adopted by the United States, and the role played by the United Nations in the crises. It has participated in around 27 UN peacekeeping operations (See Anexure-II). Australia is among the top twelve contributors to the UN Budget, and is among the handful of those making payments in full and in time.

Rationale of Australia's Participation

Australia's participation in the UN peacekeeping operations has been strongly influenced by the realist perspective. During the Cold War, Peacekeeping was, for most of the time, a minor activity for Australia as its primary concern was of its place in the Western bloc. Its commitments to UN peacekeeping operations had to be seen within the context of relations with the United States or in some cases with Britain. It was also motivated by its desire to play, role in international relations as, Middle Power and to maintain good relations with the rest of the world. In some cases, like that of the Suez crisis, Australia's offer of troops for peacekeeping operations has been rejected by the countries in the conflict due to its closeness to its western allies. This kind of constrains on its participation was removed with the end of the Cold War and thereafter Australia could make larger and more independent contribution to the UN peacekeeping activities.

One of the most important motivations to participate in the peacekeeping operations has been to promote its national security. With the end of Cold War and the United States calling its allies to manage their own security, Australia tended to look to the United Nations for the security apart from its effort to establish more understanding relations with its Southeast Asian neighbours. Its efforts are directed towards maintaining security and stability of its region. Its major participation in the UN peacekeeping operations has strong regional focus. It has been more predisposed to contribute to peacekeeping operations in Southeast Asia and the Pacific Islands than in regions farther field.[36] That is the reason of its strong involvement in both diplomatic activities designed to promote settlement, like in the case of Cambodia and East Timor, and in ensuing peacekeeping operations.

Through the peacekeeping operations Australia attempted to develop cooperative relationship with its neighbouring states in resolving regional crisis. It tends to perceive UN peacekeeping operations as a means to promote stability in Australia's neighbourhood, which in turn contributes to its regional interests and also contributes directly or indirectly to its national security. For example, Australia's involvement in East Timor is not only for the benefit of the East Timorese to build their emerging nation but also in the interests of stability and security of the region.[37] In the case of East Timor, not only of regional security but also its own economic interest is also involved. It is interested in the gas and oil in this region and signed the Timor Gap Treaty with Indonesia in December 1989 and it was replaced by Timor Sea Treaty on 30 May 2002, after independence of East Timor.[38] Further, increased dialogue with regional neighbours, including reciprocal training of UN peacekeepers and exchanges in strategic issues, hoped to create an environment for discussing possible regional responses to conflict in the future.[39] Thus the principal focus of its involvement in UN peacekeeping operations has been the defense of Australia and its efforts to promote the security of its immediate region.

By contrast, Australia has shown far less interest in peacekeeping in Latin America and Europe. For example, the numbers of Australian peacekeepers involved in the former Yugoslavia was far less than that of New Zealand. Its engagement in UN peacekeeping operations in Africa continent reflects both its humanitarian concerns and readiness to serve alongside the United States. For Australia, making a commitment to peacekeeping operations in certain circumstances could be a means for strengthening the alliance with the United States. It could also strengthen Australia's bargaining position in the event of Australia requiring support from the US. For example, with the US request for assistance and its positive response in Somalia, Australia believed that it was important to reinforce old ties with the US during the uncertainties of the post cold war era. Even its participation in operations like Afghanistan, Former Yugoslavia, has been influence by its alliance relationship with the United States.[40]

Moral consideration of the need to contribute to the resolution of major international humanitarian crises is also another motivating factor of its involvement in UN peacekeeping operations. There was a moral imperative to assist the UN-sanctioned operations like in Somalia, Rwanda and Sudan. Like other peoples, Australians were deeply moved by the haunting television images of famine and death in those countries.[41] Thus, humanitarian requirements demanded Australia's participation in UN peacekeeping operations far from home. Similarly, unimaginable internal genocidal horror in Cambodia and suffering caused to ordinary people in East Timor are the other factors which prompted Australia to get involved in UN peace keeping operations. These humanitarian involvements enable it to project itself as "responsible international player" or "good international citizen".

Its participation in some of the peacekeeping operations can be rationalised as its commitment to contribute to the capacity of the international community to deal with major crisis. It has participated in the UN peacekeeping operations, like in the Middle East, as it is interested in developing and strengthening the UN's role in preventing and containing conflict throughout the world.[42] Thus, its involvement in peacekeeping operations served not only its national interests narrowly defined, but also contributed to the goal of a just world and promotion of international cooperation. Peacekeeping seemed an ideal issue for implementing some of the goals of good international citizenship. Another rationale of its involvement in the operations is to improve Australia's international standing both within its region and further afield, which in turn helps it to expand its influence and role in international relations.[43]

The operational and training advantages for the Australian Defence Force (ADF) can be a factor in consideration of its participation in UN peacekeeping operations.[44] For example the Somalia situation seemed almost an ideal testing ground for a part of Australia's Operational Deployment Force. Similarly, its commitment to other peacekeeping operations has also provided an extended opportunity to test the ADF's command and control, logistics support and movement systems at all level.[45]

Convergences and Divergences

There are more areas of divergences than convergences between the two countries in the issues relating to UN peacekeeping operations. One striking area of convergence is that both of them are Middle Powers and the Cold War gave them the opportunity to play important role in the maintenance of international peace and security through the system of UN peacekeeping operations. Both of them displayed their commitment to strengthen the United Nations and made their contribution through their active participation in its peace activities. Both of them are interested in projecting the image of responsible Powers or 'good international citizen' through their deeds. At the same time, they consciously promoted their strategic, security, regional and economic interests while participating in the UN peacekeeping operations. Because of their long experience in the UN peacekeeping efforts, they realise the need of special training of their personnel as peace keepers and set up Peacekeeping Centres in early 1990s. The Centres train not only their own personnel but also of other countries as well.

Another major area of convergence is the need to consult the troop contributing countries (TCCs). The troop contributors are key players who know the situation on the ground better than most, who are in daily touch with developments and who can advise on the basis of practical experience on what needs to be done. But the Security Council rarely consulted them and their advice was rarely taken seriously. India and Australia along with other like-minded countries, tried to ensure that troop contributors are allowed to sit on the deliberations that precede setting up a mission, or reviewing its conduct, applying mid-course corrections, and so on. These decisions affect the performance and even lives of the troops. Both India and Australia continue to demand a more extensive policy input by those TCC. The Council held its first private meeting with the TCC on the UN Mission in Sierra Leone (UNAMSIL) in early October 2000, when faced with a crisis on the withdrawal of India and Jordan, the two leading contributors to UNAMSIL. Since then both India and Australia have been involved in the mechanism for strengthening cooperation among the Security Council, the troop-contributing countries and the Secretariat.[46]

Another area of convergence is the need of a strong financial basis for peacekeeping operations. The financial constraint has been a major stumbling block in the effectiveness of peacekeeping operations since the very beginning itself. The financial crisis of the peacekeeping operations has become more acute in the post Cold-War period as they were given expansive tasks to perform without sufficient financial backing and some of the developed countries refused to pay their assessed contribution. In the process, the troop contributing countries suffer from delay in reimbursement of huge amounts and created a tremendous strain on them.[47] The Indian representative was of the opinion that "If peacekeeping was considered a priority for the Organisation and its members, its financing must be addressed in a more concerted, serious and purposeful manner."[48] The Australian representative said, "Ultimately, it is our responsibility, as Member States, to support a stronger and more effective United Nations peacekeeping capacity. This includes placing the financing of peacekeeping on a surer footing and paying our assessed contribution in full and on time."[49]

In the area of divergence, their difference in attitude toward handling the international crises militarily has overarching influence. India's strong inclination to tone down military aspects of the United Nations was perhaps initially related to its own national tradition and national strength. It held the view that peace should not be secured by a constant preparation for war. Instead of viewing the United Nations as instrument of coercion, India was in favour of viewing it as instrument of persuasion where tool of moderation and mediation could play major role in sorting out the differences and conflict among the comity of nations. This also influenced it to adopt nonaligned foreign policy instead of joining military alliance of the two blocs. Commensurate to this policy India played pioneering role in conceptualisation and operationalisation of the UN peacekeeping operations. Even in the post Cold-War period, India was against the authorization of 'use of force' in the UN peacekeeping operations, and also the prevailing doctrine of 'humanitarian intervention'.[50]

On the other hand, Australia participated in the bloc politics and joined the military alliance of the Western bloc during Cold War period. It not only participated on the side of the United States in the Korean War but also signed military alliance treaty with New Zealand, and the United States in 1951. This treaty provided much-needed assurance that a 'great and powerful friend' would underwrite Australian defense. The balance of power rather than collective security under the United Nations had come to dominate Australian thinking on peace and security. Even in the post Cold War period, Australia joined US initiated military action such as Gulf War-I and War against Taliban and it is a strong supporter of US led war against terrorism. It has no inhibition in participation in 'use of force' in UN operations. So the military element in its foreign policy is consistently strong.

There is also divergence in their motivation to participate in UN peacekeeping operations. India's main rationale for participation in the peacekeeping operations has been the consideration of its geostrategic interests and expression of its solidarity with non-aligned countries in their hour of difficulties. This is most notable in the case of various East and Southeast Asian UN missions in Korea, Indo-China, Indonesia (West Irain) and Cambodia, which were all perceived in India to be vital to its conception of both regional stability and international order. India has major stake in the peace and stability in the Middle East not only because of the geo-strategic reason but also because of the traditional relationship with this region. India has participated in several missions in the region. India's participation in Congo, Angola, Mozambique, Rwanda, Liberia and Sierra Leone operations can be explained as an expression of its solidarity with non-aligned countries. India has often taken strong anti-colonial stance, as in the Congo and Indonesia, when it regarded the conflict as one of aggression primarily perpetrated by a colonial power, such as Belgium or the Netherlands. India still perceives most of the recent African wars as the continuing legacy of the colonial era[51].

Australia's participation in the UN peacekeeping operations has been strongly focussed on national and regional security. It is more predisposed to contribute to peacekeeping operations in Southeast Asia and the Pacific Islands than in regions farther field. That is the reason of its strong involvement in both diplomatic activities designed to promote settlement, like in the case of Cambodia and East Timor, and in ensuing peacekeeping operations. Through peacekeeping operations its tries to develop cooperative relationship with its neighbouring states in solving regional crisis. Thus the principal focus of its involvement in UN peacekeeping operations has been the defense of Australia and its efforts to promote the security of its immediate region. In some cases making a commitment to peacekeeping operations could be a means for strengthening the alliance with the United States. It could also strengthen Australia's bargaining position in the event of Australia requiring support from the US.

Their stand is also diverse on the issue of sub-contracting peacekeeping operations to the regional organisations. The Indian representative stated in the Security Council that "Neighbours and regional Powers were excluded because, by definition, they could not be disinterested. The United Nations understood, quite rightly, that successful peacekeeping could be carried out only by countries that were neutral and had no interests of their own to pursue".[52] The former Indian Prime Minister, Narasimha Rao was reported to have said that "international peacekeeping forces should be selected from regions and areas far removed from where they are to be sent for undertaking credible operations."[53] This could certainly be regarded as a vindication of Indian participation in Central American peacekeeping operations as well as in Africa. The Indian representatives have been warning that the Security Council could use the "regionalisation as a device to shirk the exerçise of its global responsibility for peace and security."[54]

Australia is in favour of regional cooperation and regional responses to the crisis in its region. Thus it seems to have no inhibition in sub-contracting peacekeeping tasks to the regional organisations. Through peacekeeping operations, like in Cambodia and East Timor, Australia has tried to develop cooperative relationship with its neighbouring States in solving regional crisis. Further, increased dialogue with regional neighbours, including reciprocal training of UN peacekeepers and exchanges in strategic issues, hoped to create an environment for discussing possible regional responses to regional conflict in the future.[55]

Another divergence between the two countries is in relation to the issue of stand-by forces for UN peacekeeping activities. The United Nations faces a major problem in finding troops for an operation and deploys them on time. It is necessary to have ready availability of troops with appropriate equipment. The UN Secretariat ascertained the willingness of member countries to earmark forces within the country as stand-by for the UN peacekeeping operations. In this connection the Government of India has assured the UN Headquarters in September 1994 of its readiness to earmark about a brigade group as stand-by for UN peacekeeping operations when required.[56] The dispatch of force, or part of it, when requested by the United Nations, would be a political decision. India tends to adopt a more critical and reflective stance, judging each new operation on its relative merits and demerits. For instance, India studiously avoided any military involvement in the UN Transitional Administration in East Timor (UNTAET), as it neither wished to upset good relations with Indonesia nor stoke the fires of separatism at home.

Australia felt that it is not necessary to earmark forces for UN activities as its prevailing defence structure and training is good enough for any eventuality and therefore declined to have stand-by force. In spite of its enhanced profile, however, peacekeeping continued to be seen as a 'supplementary activity' which should not determine Australia's defence force structure. The document on *Peacekeeping Policy* stated that "our principal focus remains...the defence of Australia and promotion of our interests within our neighbourhood. These priorities will in turn determine the priorities for our force structure, and the training and readiness of the ADF (Australian Defence force)". Nor was it considered appropriate to "maintain units on standby specifically for peacekeeping operations" or "signify units as being available for peacekeeping".[57] Senator Gareth Evans has expressed an interest in earmarking forces for UN service but he did not press for it. In 1990 Australia provided the United Nations with wide-ranging list of capabilities that could be most usefully contributed for peacekeeping tasks. It is not intended that all or even many of these elements be deployed concurrently, but it is a good guide to the type of contribution the ADF is best placed to make.[58]

India is also not in favour of submitting its peacekeeping forces under the jurisdiction of the International Criminal Court. India is of the opinion that its peacekeepers are answerable for their behaviour to authorities within the established institutions, not to institutions whose jurisdiction India does not recognise. India believes that the UN Security Council's decision to submit the UN peacekeepers to the International Criminal Court (ICC) will have broad ramifications for the peacekeeping operations as well as for troop-contributing countries.[59] On the other hand, Australia supported the ICC as "powerful instrument for bringing to justice perpetrators of crimes against humanitarian personnel, as well, obviously, as perpetrators of other war crimes and crimes against humanity."[60] It urged all the States to begin their domestic processes for ratification of the ICC Statue.

Although both the countries are the longest contributors to the UN peacekeeping operations, Indian contribution is much more substantial than that of the Australian. Even in the Post Cold-war period, India has been invariably among the top five contributors in the world. Whereas Australian ranking among the contributors has been declining from 2003 onwards, dropping from tens to sixties (See Annexure-III).

Despite the insubstantial participation, Australia got much more 'actual recognition' than India in terms of position in the UN establishment, specifically in the UN Department of Peacekeeping Operations (UNDPKO). This Department is the nerve centre of planning, preparation, conduct and direction of all the UN filed operations. Geographically, the UNDPKO can be said to be quite representative but in terms of equity, the appointment pattern seems to be rather one sided. The Western and industrialised States, including Australia, occupy majority of the professional posts. The presentation of India was 5, whereas that of Australia was 8. It is indicative of the fact that most of the people planning and managing the peacekeeping operations are having less of field experience. This has make the Indian representative ask "Why should those who risk the lives of their soldiers have to perennially satisfy themselves with secondary positions while those who do not, walk away with the honours?."[61]

Conclusion

India and Australia have played active role in the UN peacekeeping activities since its inception. Their personnel have participated in the full gamut of UN peacekeeping operations from military observation to counter-insurgency operations, from humanitarian tasks such as relief, medical assistance and rehabilitation, to support for electoral processes, maintaining law and order; and other peace building activities. While Army has provided by far the greatest numbers, air force and navy personnel and also other civilians from both countries have participated as well. India's policy of nonalignment facilitated it to take active part in the UN peacekeeping operations, especially during the Cold War period.

Australia's participation in the UN peacekeeping operations was less substantial than that of India due to, among other things, its involvement in wars along its western allies. The highlight of Australia's participation in the UN peacekeeping operations during the Cold War is that despite Australia being the part of Western bloc, its was able to assert the role of Middle Power and manage to exert a degree of independence. In the post-Cold War era, both the countries actively participated in the second generation of the peacekeeping operations. However, India invariably remained among the top five contributors, whereas Australia had been among the top ten up to 2002 and started sliding down in 2003 and at present it is holding sixty fourth rank as contributor. Paradoxically, despite its insubstantial participation, Australia got much more 'actual recognition' than India in terms of position in the UN establishment, specifically in the UN Department of Peacekeeping Operation (UNDPKO).

It is obvious from the above analysis that there are major areas of divergences between the two countries on UN peacekeeping operations. It can be regarded as reflection of differences in their wider foreign policy orientation. In term of withdrawal of the peacekeepers in the midst of operations, its active endorsement of humanitarian intervention, decreasing in its participation in the operations since 1995 are some of the similarity of its position with that of the western countries. There are various nuances in their motivation in getting involved in the UN peacekeeping operations but both of them have strong urge to strengthen the United Nations and contribute to the maintenance of international peace and security. Building their image as responsible power and increasing their influence in international relations are the other major motivating factors of their involvement in the UN peace efforts. As the Middle and emerging Powers of the world, they have special responsibility to restore United Nations to its preeminent position of managing crises among the comity of nations. Therefore, it is imperative to narrow down their differences and develop more cooperative relations to play their role effectively in the challenging times of the twenty first century, which is frequently refer to as Century of Asia.

End Notes

1. Francis Parakatil, *India and United Nations Peacekeeping Operations* (Delhi, 1975), pp. 7-32.
2. Swadesh Rana, India, the United Nations, and World Peace, in Rajan, M.S., ed., *India's Foreign Relations* (Bombay, 1976), pp. 255-307.
3. Swadesh Rana, ibid, pp. 265-66; Parakatil, No. 1, p. 60.
4. C.S.R. Murthy, India and UN Peacekeeping Operations: Issues in Policy and

Participation, (unpublished paper) presented at National Seminar on 'India, UN and the Emerging World Order' held at Jawaharlal Nehru University, New Delhi, on 17-19, October 1995, pp. 12-13; Ramakrishna Reddy, *India's Policy in the United Nations* (New Jersey, 1968), pp. 94-96; see also Inder Jit Rikhye, United Nations Peace-Keeping Operations and India, in Grover, Verinder, ed., *International Relations and foreign Policy of India Vol. 10* (New Delhi, 1992), pp. 81-84.

5. Swadesh Rana, No. 2, p. 271; Rikhye, ibid, pp. 84-87.
6. Alan Bullion, "India and UN Peacekeeping ", in Edward Moxon-Brown, ed., *A Future for Peacekeeping?* (New York, 1998), p. 62; Reddy, n. 4, pp. 97-100; Parakatil, n.1, pp. 125-126.
7. S.N. Misra, *India: The Cold War Years* (New Delhi, 1994), p. 204.
8. Parakatil, n. 1, pp. 138-139.
9. Eva Bertram, "Reinventing Government: The Promise and the Perils of United Nations Peace Building", *The Journal of Conflict Resolution,* Vol. 39, No. 3, September 1995, pp. 387-417.
10. *The Indian Army: United Nations Peacekeeping Operations* (New Delhi, 1997), pp. 76-90.
11. Bullion, No. 6, p. 66.
12. *Ibid.*
13. *The Indian Army*, No. 10, pp. 61.
14. J.N. Dixit, The UN must rise above regional politics in its peacekeeping: Pulling out of skullduggery, *Telegraph* (Calcutta), 15 October 2000.
15. *Ibid.*; see also Alan James Bullion, India, David Sorenson and Pia Christina Wood, ed., The Politics of Peacekeeping in the Post-Cold War Era (London, 2005), pp. 201-202.
16. *The Hindu,* (Delhi), September 6, 2005; see also http://www.un.org/Depts/dpko/dpko/dnote.htm
17. Luara Neack, UN Peace-keeping: In the Interest of Community or Self?, *Journal of Peace Research*, Vol. 32, No. 2, 1995, pp. 181-95; see also Davis B. Borrow, and Mark A. Boyer, Maintaining System Stability: Contributions to Peacekeeping Operations, *The Journal of Conflict Resolution*, Vol. 41, No. 6, December 1997, pp. 725-29.
18. Satish Nambiar, India's role in United Nations Peacekeeping, in Mody and Mehrish ed., *India's Role in the United Nations* (New Delhi, 1995), p. 12.
19. Ibid.; see also Bullion, India, No. 15, p. 198.
20. Nambiar, No. 18, p. 12-14; see also Bullion, No. 15, p. 199.
21. Borrow and Boyer, No. 17, p. 727.
22. *Ibid*, p. 729.
23. Hugh Smith, Australia, in Sorenson, David S., and Wood, Pia Christina, ed., No. 15, p. 9; Chintamani Mahapatra, "Australia, United States and the Asian Security", Gopal, D., ed., *Australia in the Emerging Global Order: Evolving Australia-Indian Relations* (Delhi, 2002), p. 85.
24. Mahapatra, Chintamani, *ibid.*
25. David Lowe, Australia at the United Nations in the 1950s: The Paradox of Empire,

Australian Journal of International Affairs, Vol. 51, No. 2, July 1997, p. 171.

26. Mahapatra, Chintamani, n. 23, p. 88.
27. Smith, No. 23, p. 10.
28. Neil James, A Brief History of Australian Participation in Multinational Peacekeeping, Hugh Smith, ed., *Peacekeeping: Challenges for the Future* (Canberra, 1993), p. 198.
29. *Ibid.*, p. 203.
30. Smith, No. 23, p. 11.
31. Gareth Evans, The Comprehensive Political Settlement to the Cambodia Conflict: An Exercise in Cooperating for Peace, Hugh, Smith, ed., *International Peacekeeping: Building on the Cambodia Experience* (Canberra, 1994), pp. 1-13.
32. Robert Ray, International Peacekeeping: Australian and Regional Perspectives, Hugh, ibid, pp. 99-103.
33. C.S.R. Murthy, Australia and the United Nations in a Changing World, Gopal, D. ed., No. 23, p. 274.
34. Katsumi Ishizuka, Australia's Policy Towards East Timor, *The Round Table*, Vol. 93, No. 374, April 2004, p. 282; see also James, Cotton, "'Peacekeeping' in East Timor: An Australian Policy Departure", *Australian Journal of International Affairs*, vol. 53, No. 3, November 1999, pp. 237-246.
35. Statement by Ambassador Peter Tesch at the UN Security Council on May 16, 2005 see http://www.australainUN.org
36. Derek McDougall, Australia's Peacekeeping Role in the Post-Cold War Era, *Contemporary Southeast Asia*, Vol. 24, No. 3, p. 595.
37. UN Document, A/55/PV.20, 18 September 2000, p. 28.
38. Ishizukz, No. 34, pp. 277-283.
39. Robert Ray, Peacekeeping and Peacemaking-The Challenge for the Future, Smith, ed., No. 28, p. 170.
40. Richard Woolcott, Foreign Policy priorities for the Howard Government's Fourth Term: Australia, Asia and America in the Post-11th September World, *Australian Journal of International Affairs*, Vol. 59, No. 2, June 2005, pp. 141-152; see also Amin Saikal, Afghanistan, Terrorism, and American and Australian Responses, *Australian Journal of International Affairs*, Vol. 56, No. 1, January 2002, pp. 23-30.
41. Robert G. Patman, Disarming Somalia: The Contrasting Fortunes of United States and Australian Peacekeepers During United Nations Intervention, 1992-1993, *African Affairs*, vol. 96, No. 385, October 1997, p. 520.
42. Ray, No. 32, p. 102.
43. McDougall, n. 36, p. 594.
44. Wilson, Lessons From UN Operation in Yugoslavia, in Smith, Hugh, ed., n. 28, p. 118-119.
45. Graeme Cheeseman, Structuring the Australian Defence Force for United Nations Operations: Change and Resistance, Tom Woodhouse, and Robert Bruce, ed., *Peacekeeping and Peacemaking: Towards Effective Intervention in Post-Cold War Conflicts* (London, 1998), pp. 243-44.

46. UN Document, A/C.4/56/SR.21, 23 December 2002, p. 12; see also S/PV.4257, 16 January 2001, pp. 15-16.
47. UN Document, A/C.4/57/SR.14, November 26, 2002, p. 9.
48. UN Document, A/C.5/54/SR.65, July 11, 2000, p. 13.
49. UN Document, A/55/PV.20, 18 September 2000, p. 28.
50. For example see the Indian representative's speech at the United Nations A/c-4/55/SR.21, 16 March 2001, pp. 5-6; see also S/PV.4223, 15 November 2000, p. 23.
51. Nambiar, No. 18, p. 12-14; see also Bullion, "India", Sorenson and Wood ed., No. 15, p. 199.
52. UN Document, S/PV/4223, 15 November 2000, p. 23.
53. Hindustan times, New Delhi, 12 August 1994.
54. UN Document, S/PV.4970, 17 May, 2004, 14.
55. Ray, Robert, No. 39, p. 170.
56. H.K. Srivastava, Indian Defence and Peacekeeping: Are the Two Competitive or Supplementary?, *India Defence Review*, New Delhi, vol. 9, No. 4, October-December, 1994, p. 58.
57. Cheeseman, No. 45, p. 233.
58. Ray, No. 32, p. 174-75.
59. UN Document, S/PV.4568, 10 July, 2002, p. 14.
60. UN Document, A/PV.4100, 9 February, 2000, p. 7.
61. Statement by Mr. V.K. Number, Permanent Representative at the Special Committee on Peacekeeping Operations on March 4, 2003, see http//www/un.int/india/ind691.pdf

Annexure I

List of Peacekeeping Operations in Which India Participated

- UN Emergency Force-I-Gaza Strip/Egypt & Israel; (UNEF-I Nov 56 to JUN. 67)
- UN Observation Group in Lebanon (UNOGIL-JUN 58 to Dec 58)
- UN Operations in Congo (ONUC-Jul 60 to JUN 64)
- UN Security Force in West New Guinea (West Iran) (UNSF-Oct 62 to Apr 63)
- UN Yemen Observation Mission (UNYOM-Jul 63 to Sep 64)
- UN Peacekeeping Force in Cyprus (UNFICYP-Jan 64 to Dec 76)
- UN Secretary General's Representative in Dominic Republic (DOMREP-May 65 to Oct 66)
- UN Iran-Iraq Military Observer Group (UNIIMOG-Aug 88 to Feb 91)
- UN Transition Assistance Group in Namibia (UNTAG-May 89 to May 91)

- Organisation De Nations UNies AU Central America/Nicaragua (ONUCA-Nov 89 to Jan 92)
- UN Observer Mission in El Salvador (ONUSAL-Jul 91 To Apr 95)
- UN Iraq-Kuwait Observer Mission (UNIKOM-Apr 91-Till Date)
- UN Advance Mission in Cambodia (UNAMIC-Oct 91 to Mar 92)
- UN Transitional Authority in Cambodia (UNTAC-Feb 92 to Sep 93)
- UN Military Liaison Team in Cambodia (UNMLT-Sep 93 to May 94)
- UN Protection Force in Former Yugoslavia (UNPROFOR-Mar 92 to Mar 93)
- UN Operations in Mozambique (ONUMOZ-Dec 92 to Oct 94)
- UN Operations in Somalia-II (UNOSOM-II Mar 93 to Dec 94)
- UN Observer Mission in Liberia (UNOMIL-Sep 93 to Sep 97)
- UN Assistance Mission for Rwanda (UNAMIR-Oct 93 to Mar 96)
- UN Advance Mission in Cambodia (UNAMIC-Oct 91 to Mar 92)
- UN Transitional Authority in Cambodia (UNTAC-Feb 92 to Sep 93)
- UN Military Liaison Team in Cambodia (UNMLT-Sep 93 to May 94)
- UN Mission In Bosnia & Herzegovina (UNMIBH-Dec 95 to Till Date)
- UN Observer Mission In Sierra Leone (UNOMSIL-Jul 98 to Oct 99)
- UN Assistance Mission in Sierra Leone (UNAMSIL-Nov 99 to Feb 01)
- UN Angola Verification Mission-I (UNAVEM-I June 89-May 91)
- UN Angola Verification Mission-II (UNAVEM-II-May 91-Feb 95)
- UN Angola Verification Mission-III (UNAVEM-III Feb 95 to Jun 97)
- UN Observer Mission in Angola (UNOMA-Jul 97 to Jul 99)
- UN Interim Force in Lebanon (UNIFIL-Nov 98 to Till Date)
- UN Mission in Congo (MONUC—Nov 1999 till date)
- UN Mission in Ethiopia and Eritrea (UNMEE—Mar 2001 till date)
- UN Mission in Angola (UNMA-Jul 2002-till date)
- UN Operation in Burundi (ONUB—June 2004 till date)
- UN Operation in Cote d'Ivoire (ONUCI-April 2004 till date
- UN Intrim Administration in Kosovo (UNMIK—10 June 1999 till date)
- UN Mission in Sudan (UMMIS-March 2005 till date)

Source: http://www.indianarmy.nic.in/arunpk.htm also http://www.un.org/Depts/dpko/dpko/dnote.htm

Annexure-II

Table of Australia's Participation in Peacekeeping Operations

Name of Operation	*Dates of Operation*	*Total Number of Australians Involved**	*Role of Australians*
UN Truce Supervision Organisation [Israel and neighbours] (UNTSO)	1948-present	13	military observers (Australians deployed 1950-1985)
UN Military Observer Group in India and Pakistan (UNMOGIP)	1949-present	18	military observers and air transport (Austra-lians deployed 1950-1985)
UN Yemen Observation Mission (UNYOM)	1963-1964	2	military observers (Australians deployed June-November 1963)
UN Force in Cyprus (UNFICYP)	1964-present	50 (currently 15 Federal Police)	maintenance of law and order
UN India-Pakistan Observation Mission (UNIPOM)	1965-1966	4	military observers
UN Emergency Force II [Sinai] (UNEF-II)	1973-1979	50	air (helicopter) support
UN Disengagement Observer Force [Syria] (UNDOF)	1974-present	a few (curren-tly nil)	military observers de-tached from UNTSO
UN Interim Force in Lebanon (UNIFIL)	1978-present	a few (currently nil)	military observers de-tached from UNTSO
UN Iran-Iraq Military Observer Group (UNIIMOG)	1988-1990	15	military observers (Australians deplo-yed 1988-1990)
UN Transition Assistance Group [Namibia] (UNTAG)	1989-1990	338	engineering support, supervision of elections
UN Advance Mission in Cambodia (Absorbed by UNTAC in March 1992) (UNAMIC)	1991-1992	65	communications

(*Contd.*)

(*Contd.*)

Name of Operation	*Dates of Operation*	*Total Number of Australians Involved**	*Role of Australians*
UN Mission for the Referendum in Western Sahara (MINURSO)	1991-present	45	communications, medical (Australians deployed 1991-1994)
UN Transitional Authority in Cambodia (UNTAC)	1992-1993	564	Force Commander, communications, transport, assisting the election, maintai-ning law and order, helicopters
First UN Operation in Somalia (UNOSOM-I)	1992-1993	30	movement control and other support
Unified Task Force in Somalia (UNITAF)	1992-1993	937; one RAN ship	protecting delivery of humanitarian aid
UN Protection Force in Croatia, Bosnia-Her-zegovina and Mace-donia (UNPROFOR)	1992-1995	a few	military observers and liaison (Australians deployed 1992-1993)
UN Operation in Mo-zambique (ONUMOZ)	1992-1995	20	police, mine clea-rance (Australians deployed 1994)
Second UN Operation in Somalia (UNOSPM-II)	1993-1995	30	movement control and other support
UN Assistance Mission in Rwanda (UNAMIR)	1993-1996	308	medical personnel, infantry protection, support troops (Australians deployed 1994-1996)
UN Verification Mission in Guatemala (MINUGUA)	1997	1	observer
UN Assistance Mission to East Timor (UNAMET)	1999	50	police monitors, election support, military liaison
UN Transitional Ad-ministration in East Timor (UNTAET)	1999-		
May 2002	2,000	assist in ad-ministration of independence from Indone-sia, protect te-rritory border	

(*Contd.*)

(Contd.)

Name of Operation	Dates of Operation	Total Number of Australians Involved*	Role of Australians
UN Mission of Support In East Timor (UNIMSET)	20 May 2002- 20 May 2005		
UN Mission in Ethiopia And Eritrea (UNMEE)	July 2000- Present		
UN Assistance Mission in Afghanistan (UNAMA)	March 2002- Present		
UN Mission in the Sudan (UNMIS)	March 2005- Present		
UN Office in Timor Leste (UNTOIL)	20 May 2005— Present		

Source: http://www.dva.gov.au/commem/commac/studies/anzacsk/res1.htm also http://www.un.org/Depts/dpko/dpko/dnote.htm

Annexure-III

Table of Ranking and Percentage of Contribution to the UN Peacekeeping Operations Since 2000

Date/Year	*India*	*Australia*	*India's Total Contribution*	*Australia's Total Contribution*	*UN's Total Peacekeeprs*	*Total Numbers of Contributing Countries*
31December, 2000	Rank: 3 Percent:7.24	Rank: 6 Percent:4.31	2,738	1,629	37,803	89
30 June, 2001	Rank: 3 Percent:6.31	Rank: 8 Percent:3.63	2,791	1,606	44,223	89
31December, 2001	Rank: 4 Percent:6.12	Rank: 9 Percent: 3.25	2,883	1,529	47,108	87
30 June, 2002	Rank: 4 Percent:6.67	Rank: 10 Percent:2,80	3,022	1,270	45,333	88
31December, 2002	Rank: 4 Percent: 6.93	Rank: 10 Percent:2.37	2,746	940	39,652	89
30 June, 2003	Rank: 2 Percent:7.48	Rank: 12 Percent: 2.46	2,719	893	36,369	89
31December, 2003	Rank: 4 Percent:6.29	Rank: 28 Percent: 0.78	2,882	357	45,815	94

(*Contd.*)

(*Contd.*)

Date/Year	*India*	*Australia*	*India's Total Contribution*	*Australia's Total Contribution*	*UN's Total Peacekeeprs*	*Total Numbers of Contributing Countries*
30June 2004	Rank: 5 Percent:5.20	Rank: 46 Percent:0.27	2,928	151	56,261	97
31December 2004	Rank: 3 Percent:6.04	Rank: 47 Percent:0.22	3,912	140	64,720	102
30 June 2005	Rank: 3 Percent:9.23	Rank: 65 Percent:0.06	6,176	41	66,936	105
31 December 2005	Rank: 3 Percent:10.47	Rank: 64 Percent:0.07	7,284	50	68,838	108

Source: http://www.un.org/Depts/dpko/dpko/dnote.htm

Annexure-IV

Geographic Distribution of Professional Posts in DPKO (as of 29 February 2000)

Americas and Caribbean	*Europe*	*Africa*	*Asia, Pacific and Middle East*
US (29)	France (8)	Ghana (3)	Australia (8)
Canada (9)	Italy (7)	Zimbabwe (3)	Japan (6)
Brazil (3)	UK (7)	Algeria (2)	India (5)
Argentina (2)	Germany (6)	Kenya (2)	South Korea (5)
Trinidad & Tobago (1)	Sweden (6)	Rwanda (2)	Nepal (3)
	Russia (5)	S. Africa (2)	New Zealand (3)
Jamaica (1)	Norway (5)	S. Leone (1)	Thailand (3)
Benin (1)	Ireland (4)	Senegal (1)	China (2)
Dominican Republic (1)	Denmark (3)	Tanzania (1)	Bangladesh (2)
	Poland (2)	Zaire (1)	Malaysia (2)
Uruguay (1)	Romania (2)	Zambia (1)	Philippines (2)
St. Vincent (1)	Finland (2)	Swaziland (1)	Sri Lanka (2)
	Portugal (1)	Cameroon (1)	Pakistan (1)
	Armenia (1)	Guyana (1)	Indonesia (1)
	Belgium (1)	Ethiopia (1)	Fiji (1)
	BiH (1)	Eritrea (1)	Mongolia (1)
	Bulgaria (1)	Guinea Bissau (1)	
	Hungary (1)	Sudan (1)	
	Netherlands (1)	Tunisia (1)	
	Slovakia (1)	Turkey (1)	
	Spain (1)	Lesotho (1)	
	Yugoslavia (1)		

Source: UN Department of Peacekeeping Operations.

Index

Contributors

Amita Singh is Professor, Centre for the Study of Law and Governance, Jawaharlal Nehru University, New Delhi.

Auriol Weigold is in the Division of Communication and Education, University of Canberra, Australia.

Chintamani Mahapatra is Associate Professor at the School of International Studies, Jawaharlal Nehru University, New Delhi. He was a Commonwealth Scholar at the University of London.

D. Gopal is Australian Studies Programme Coordinator and Professor of Political Science, School of Social Sciences, IGNOU.

David Walker is Professor of Australian Studies, Deakin University, Melbourne, Australia.

Dennis Rumley is Associate Professor, School of Social Studies and Cultural Studies, University of Western Australia. He has been Professor of Australian Studies at the University of Tokyo.

Greg Battye is Head of the School of Creative Communication, University of Canberra. He holds a Doctor of Creative Arts degree from Wollongong University.

Jasbir Singh is Associate Professor in Economics at the Department of Economics, University of Jammu (J&K).

John Robinson is a Ph.D candidate in Sociology, Faculty of Arts, University of Wollongong, Australia.

Nabeel Ajmal Mancheri is Research Scholar, Centre for East Asian studies, School of International Studies, Jawaharlal Nehru University, New Delhi

Peter Gale is a Senior Lecturer in Australian Studies and Research Degree Coordinator in the Unaipon School, Division of Arts, Education and Social Sciences at the University of South Australia.

Peter Putnis is Professor of Communication Studies at the University of Canberra, Australia.

Priti Singh is Assistant Professor, Centre for US, Canadian and Latin American Studies, School of International Studies, Jawaharlal Nehru University, New Delhi.

Rajesh Kapoor is Research Scholar, School of International Studies, Jawaharlal Nehru University, New Delhi.

Roberta Julian is Director, Tasmanian Institute of Law Enforcement Studies, University of Tasmania, Australia

Ruchira Ganguly-Scrase is Senior Lecturer, School of Social Sciences, Media and Communication, University of Wollongong, Australia

Rupakjyoti Borah is Research Scholar, School of International Studies, Jawaharlal Nehru University, New Delhi.

S. Uttam Kumar Jamadhagni is Lecturer, Department of Defence and Strategic Studies, University of Madras, Chennai.

S.I. Humayun is Project Associate, Department of Defence and Strategic Studies, University of Madras, Chennai.

Sailaja Gullapalli is Research Associate, Gandhi Smriti and Darshan Samiti, New Delhi

Sanjay Chaturvedi is Reader in Political Science, Coordinator, Centre for Geo-Politics, Department of Political Science, Panjab University, Chandigarh.

Susan Cowan is at the School of Language, Literature and Communication, UNSW at ADFA Canberra, ACT 2600.

Swaraj Basu is Professor of History, School of Social Sciences, Indira Gandhi National Open University, New Delhi.

Tej Pratap Singh is Reader in Political Science, Banaras Hindu University, Varanasi

Timothy J. Scrase is Deputy Director, Centre for Asia Pacific Social Transformation Studies (CAPSTRANS) and Senior Lecturer in Sociology, University of Wollongong, Australia.

Vanlaltluangi Aruna Ruth is Research Scholar, School of International Studies, Jawaharlal Nehru University, New Delhi.

Varalaxmi Naik is Research Scholar, Centre for East Asian Studies, School of International Studies, Jawaharlal Nehru University, New Delhi.

Y. Yagama Reddy is Director, Centre for Southeast Asian and Pacific Studies, Venkateshwara University, Tirupati.

Yeshi Choedon is Associate Professor in International Organisation at the School of International Studies, Jawaharlal Nehru University, New Delhi.